# A DAY AT

A GUIDE TO BRITAIN'S MAJOR RACECOURSES

# THE RACES

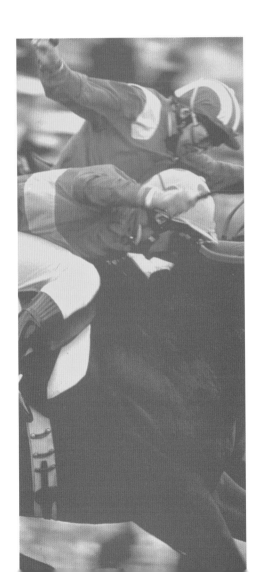

**AA A Day at the Races**

Produced by AA Publishing

| | |
|---|---|
| Written and edited by: | Penny Hicks |
| Additional research by: | Dominic Goldberg |
| Special feature and course descriptions by: | John Francome |
| Design by: | Design Directions Ltd, Twyford, Berks |
| Illustrations: | KAG Design Ltd |

Advertisements:

Head of Advertisement Sales: Christopher Heard tel: 0256 20123 ext 21544

Advertisement Production:     Karen Weeks tel: 0256 20123 ext 21545

Printed and bound
in Great Britain by:     William Clowes Ltd, Beccles and London

The contents of this publication are believed correct at the time of printing. Nevertheless the Publisher cannot be held responsible for any errors or omissions or for changes in the details given in this guide or for the consequences of any reliance on the information provided in the same. Although every effort has been made to ensure accuracy we always welcome any information from readers to assist in such efforts and to keep the book up to date.

A CIP catalogue record of this book is available from the British Library.

Published by AA Publishing which is a trading name of Automobile Association Developments Limited whose registered office is Norfolk House, Priestley Road, Basingstoke, Hampshire RG24 9NY, Registered number 1878835

ISBN 0  7495 0749 7

## Acknowledgments

The AA would like to thank the following for their help and co-operation in compliling this guide:

The British Horseracing Board, 42 Portman Square, London W1H 0EN Telephone: 071 396 0011

The Racecourse Association Limited, Winkfield Road, Ascot, Berkshire SL5 7HX Telephone: Ascot (0344) 25912

The Jockey Club, Newmarket

The Irish Tourist Board, 150 New Bond Street, London W1Y 0AQ Telephone: 071 493 3201

The Managers/Clerk of Courses of all the featured racecourses in Britain and Ireland

The Automobile Association also wishes to thank the following libraries for their assistance in the preparation of this book

ALLSPORT UK Ltd, Cover and title page Royal Ascot 1992 (Chris Cole)

SPORTING PICTURES (UK) LTD, 3 Tic Tac Man, 4 York Race Course, 5 Bookmakers, Cheltenham, 6 Cheltenham Races, 7 Looking through binoculars, 10 York Race Course, 11 York Race Course, 12 Tote, 13 Cheltenham, 14 Bookie.

# Contents

# About the Book

*In this guide we aim to provide essential information for those who have never been to the races as well as offering a useful reference to lifelong devotees of horse racing. All the course information has been supplied by the racecourses themselves; the directory of where to stay and where to eat comes from the AA's database of inspected establishments.*

United Kingdom national area codes are due to change by 16 April 1995. The digit 1 should be dialled after the first 0 of area codes.

However, five UK cities will have completely new area codes and one digit added to subscriber numbers:

Leeds (0532) XXXXXX becomes (0113) 2XX XXXX
Sheffield (0742) XXXXXX becomes (0114) 2XX XXXX
Nottingham (0602) XXXXXX becomes (0115) 9XX XXXX
Leicester (0533) XXXXXX becomes (0116) 2XX XXXX
Bristol (0272) XXXXX becomes (0117) 9XX XXXX

## ON THE COURSE

### Admission prices

With only one or two exceptions, the prices we have quoted are those which were charged during 1993. The courses do, of course, reserve the right to make any changes they feel necessary.

As in all things, you get what you pay for and the more expensive enclosures will provide the best facilities and sometimes the best view.

### Dress

Along with the best facilities and view, the most expensive enclosures will also expect the best-dressed racegoers. This is not to say that you need a Royal Ascot outfit (unless, of course, that is where you are going), but men will usually need a collar and tie or a polo-neck; jeans and T-shirts are rarely

allowed and some will not allow open-necked or short-sleeved shirts. Ascot is, in fact, a good example – their 'no jeans' rule in the Members and Tattersalls enclosures is rigorously enforced by bowler hatted gatemen.

### Drinks

Some courses do not allow racegoers to take alcohol into the course with them and many have rules preventing you from wandering around the enclosures with a drink in your hand. To avoid embarrassment, check on arrival just what the rules are and stick to them.

### Fixtures

The calendars of events published for each course cover the period from publication in April 1994 until the end of the year. The details were believed to be correct at the time of publication, but some fixtures were still to be confirmed and others will be subject to unavoidable last minute changes as circumstances change.

The same applies to the times of first races where they have been quoted. We strongly recommend that you check beforehand to avoid disappointment – a contact address and telephone number has been given for each course, or contact the Racecourse Association, Winkfield Road, Ascot, Berkshire SL5 7HX, ☎ Ascot (0344) 25912.

6

## WHERE TO STAY AND WHERE TO EAT

All of the accommodation and restaurants listed in this guide has been drawn from the AA's database of inspected establishments and includes hotels, restaurants, guesthouses, farmhouses, pubs and campsites. The general rule in selecting them for inclusion in this guide has been that they are within about a ten-mile radius of the racecourse to which we have attached them. Where we were unable to include a satisfactory number of places to stay using this rule, we did venture a little further afield, but they are rarely more than twenty miles away. More comprehensive information on the establishments listed, together with details of all the above kinds of accommodation throughout Britain and Ireland, can be found in the following AA annual guides:

| | |
|---|---|
| **AA Hotels and Restaurants in Britain and Ireland** | **£12.99** |
| **AA-inspected Bed and Breakfast in Britain and Ireland** | **£7.99** |
| **AA Camping and Caravanning in Britain and Ireland** | **£7.99** |
| **Britain's Best Pubs** | **£9.99** |

## AA CLASSIFICATIONS

Various classifications of accommodation and restaurants have been used. Firstly the AA's famous star ratings, which are subject to a rigorous and complicated system of inspection points and quality ratings. However, a simplified explanation of what they mean follows – remember that stars are for facilities; percentages, red stars and rosettes are for quality.

## HOTEL CLASSIFICATIONS

★ Hotels generally of a small scale with good, but often simple furnishings, facilities and food. This category sometimes includes private hotels where requirements for public access and full lunch service may be relaxed. Not all bedrooms will necessarily have en suite facilities. These hotels are often managed by the proprietor and there may well be a more personal atmosphere than in larger establishments.

★★ Small to medium sized hotels offering more in the way of facilities such as telephones and televisions in bedrooms. Like one star hotels, this category can also include private hotels. At least half the bedrooms will have full en suite facilities. These can be proprietor managed or group owned.

★★★ Medium sized hotels offering more spacious accommodation and a greater range of facilities and services. Generally these will include a full reception service as well as more formal restaurant and bar arrangements. You can expect all rooms to provide en suite facilities, most of which will include a bath. Though often individually owned, this category encompasses a greater number of company owned properties.

★★★★ Generally large hotels with spacious accommodation including availability of private suites. This category of hotel normally provides a full range of formal hotel services including room service, reception and porterage and may well offer more than one dining operation. En suite facilities in all rooms should include both bath and shower. High standards of comfort and food are expected at this level.

★★★★★ Large luxury hotels offering the highest international standards of accommodation, facilities, services and cuisine.

(RED) Where you see this beside the star rating, it means that the hotel has been awarded Red Stars for outstanding levels of hospitality, service, food and comfort. There are only 96 Red Star hotels in the whole of Britain and Ireland.

You will notice that some of the hotels listed do not have a star rating beside them. These are lodges, which cannot be compared to traditional hotels. They offer reasonably priced accommodation catering for overnight stops and offering good, functional bedrooms with private facilities. They are usually situated adjacent to a motorway or roadside restaurant and have no food facilities of their own.

## PERCENTAGES

Percentage ratings have been given to each of the hotels to represent the difference in quality between hotels within a particular star rating, reflecting the inspectors' experiences at the time of inspection:

**50% - 59%** A sound hotel which meets all the minimum standards for AA star rating and which overall provides modest but acceptable levels of accommodation, facilities and service.

**60% – 69%** A particularly sound hotel which exceeds the minimum requirements for its star rating by offering higher standards in certain areas of its operation.

**70% – 79%** Overall a very good hotel which can be strongly recommended for providing a high level of service, food and accommodation often with excellent standards in certain area of its operation

NB Red star hotels do not have percentage ratings because the award of red stars deems it unnecessary.

## ROSETTES

These denote the quality of the food served at AA-inspected hotels and restaurants:

❀ Enjoyable food, carefully prepared, that reflects a high level of culinary skill

❀❀ A high standard of food that demonstrates a serious, dedicated approach to cooking

❀❀❀ Very fine food prepared with considerable flair, imagination and originality

❀❀❀❀ Excellent standards of cuisine, service and wine, consistently achieved

❀❀❀❀❀ Outstanding cuisine, service and wine that reaches the highest international standards

## CAMPSITE PENNANT RATINGS

Pennant ratings provide an objective guide to the basic range of facilities and equipment available on a site.

► **Site licence**

Site density not more than 30 per acre of land suitable for camping

At least 6 pitches allocated to touring units and at least 10% of site capacity for tourers if there are more than 60 pitches

Separate flush toilets with 2 washbasins and 2 WCs (ladies), 2 washbasins, 1 WC and 1 urinal (men) for 30 pitches

tap water supply of good quality and quantity

Waste water disposal facilities within reasonable walking distance of any touring pitch

adequate arrangements for collection, storage and disposal of refuse, clearly indicated

fire precautions that meet local authority regulations

well-drained ground and provision of some level ground suitable for tents and motor caravans

entrance and access roads of adequate width and surface

### ►► all one-pennant facilities, plus:

at least 15% of pitches allocated to tourers

separate washrooms with hot and cold water direct to each basin

point for disposal of chemical toilet contents with adjacent flushing and rinsing facilities (unless not allowed by local authority)

externally lit sanitary facilities

warden available at certain times of the day

### ►►► all the aforementioned, plus:

one shower or bath with hot and cold water for each sex per 40 pitches

deep sinks for washing clothes, and spin dryers

electric shaver points, mirrors and sockets for hairdryers in washrooms

all-night lighting of sanitary facilities or push-button time switches

daily shopping facilities for basic foods on site or within reasonable walking distance

adequate roads to perimeter and services

warden in attendance during day; contact number for night-time emergencies

### ►►►► all the aforementioned, plus:

at least 25% of pitches allocated for tourers

2 washbasins per sex for 25 pitches, 1 shower per sex for 30 pitches

all night permanent lighting of toilet blocks

washing up facilities with hot and cold water

signed reception office

signposted late arrivals enclosure, appropriately sited

well signed and properly maintained first aid room with washbasin

properly equipped site shop offering good selection of food, household and domestic products and camping/caravanning spares

access routes to essential facilities lit after dark

childrens playground, fenced or in safe area. Area for ball games away from pitches and tents

some site landscaping

hard standings for touring van wheel runs and hook-ups

provision of fast food take away or a means of quickly heating ready-prepared frozen meals (eg a microwave)

public telephone on site

### ►►►►► These sites are now designated as Holiday Centres because of the range of leisure facilities they offer on site:

a comprehensive range of services and equipment

at least 50% of pitches allocated to tourers

24-hour supervision by warden on site

automated laundry with at least two of the following permanently installed: washing machines, tumble dryers, irons and ironing boards

2 washbasins per sex for 20 pitches, 1 shower per sex for 30 pitches

heated washrooms if site open between October and Easter

range of facilities for indoor and outdoor recreation for adults

indoor recreational facilities for children separate from those provided for adults

cafe or restaurant

visitors' car park

You may notice that some sites do not have a pennant rating at all. These are known as 'Venture' sites and they cater for self-contained campers and caravanners who take everything with them, including a toilet, and are literally just looking for a pitch, a water supply and chemical disposal point.

CREDIT CARDS
1 Access/Eurocard/Mastercard
2 American Express
3 Barclaycard/Visa
4 Carte Blanche
5 Diners

9

# Picking a Winner

*Some expert advice from
John Francome*

*There are 59 racecourses in Great Britain
that offer a variety of racing unequalled
anywhere else in the world, so that when
it comes to planning a day out, the British
racegoer is almost spoilt for choice. From
the pomp and ceremony of Royal Ascot
in mid-June, to the damp and drizzle of
a National Hunt fixture in winter, there
is something different to be found and
enjoyed wherever you go. Not only does
the atmosphere vary greatly between
courses, but also their configuration and
characteristics.*

Unlike America where all the tracks have flat contours, and the horses only ever race in an anti-clockwise direction, British courses differ immensely. Fontwell Park in Sussex, for example, is a tight figure-of-eight jumping course set on the side of a fairly steep hill, and has a small country town feel to it, whereas Newcastle is a large, fairly level galloping track, catering for both flat and jump racing. Although the Tyneside course attracts large numbers of enthusiastic racegoers, it has a much more 'open' feel to it.

Wherever you decide to go for your day out, remember that almost without exception, racecourses are quite a few degrees cooler than anywhere else, so if the weather is moderate, be prepared and dress accordingly. Whilst on the subject of what to wear, unless you are attending a meeting where morning dress is to be worn, the general rule is that you should be smart but comfortable. Unlike many other areas of society, dress and behaviour standards on the racecourse have been maintained, so that if you do not conform you will feel out of place.

A day spent at the races will be made much more interesting if you try your hand at finding the winners. Whether, having selected a horse, you decide to actually put money on it is your choice, but provided you allot yourself a certain amount which you are prepared to lose (and don't exceed it), little harm will be done, and much fun can be had.

It is quite possible to back the occasional winner because it reminds you of your mother-in-law, or because the colours are similar to one of your favourite sweaters, but if you use this method you can be sure of ending up with an empty wallet after a very short time. There isn't any easy way to make money from betting, but there are a few elementary rules that will stop you losing too much.

From the millions of punters who bet regularly, there are less than a dozen who make their living from it, and they are all devoted to the form book, and are very good judges of a horse in the flesh. The form book is a weekly publication which records details of every race run, including distance, going (ground conditions), jockeys who ride each horse, and weight carried, etc, as well as the time in which the race was won. It also gives an abbreviated account of how each horse ran, and position throughout the race, together with its finishing place. As with humans, some are best at shorter distances on soft ground, while others may excel with a test of stamina on a firmer surface. Whatever their preference, the most accurate way of assessing a horse's ability is by the time it takes to cover a certain distance, having taken into consideration such variables as weight carried, ground conditions and course gradient.

Using this method as his basis, a mathematician named Phil Bull set up Timeform in 1948, and it has been successfully selecting winners ever since. If you are just an occasional punter or first time racegoer, it is a waste of money going to the expense of buying a form book, when a Timeform Racecard can be bought at every race meeting for as little as £3. This card will assess the chance of each horse in every race, giving it a rating, together with a short summary of racing characteristics, which will include any peculiarities such as 'the horse normally sweats profusely before a race'.

The coverage given to racing in our national daily press is excellent, but having saved on the expense of a form book, it is worthwhile to buy one of the two daily sports papers – the *Sporting Life* and the *Racing Post*, as they not only give a very good race analysis but also carry a reasonable amount of form and endless amounts of useful information to help in the quest for winners. For certain race meetings, the *Sporting Life* prints the colours of each horse alongside its name, which is of considerable assistance when trying to pinpoint the runners throughout the race.

The art of race-reading is one of the most difficult in the industry, and is one which takes years to master. If you can manage to take proper account of how two horses are running in the same race after your first couple of attempts, then you are doing well.

Binoculars can be hired at every racecourse for very little money. The professionals recommend 8 x 40 magnification for all courses except those such as Aintree where the runners race a long way from the stands, when they use 10 x 50.

### USING YOUR JUDGEMENT

Having mentioned how invaluable is the form book when evaluating a race, remember that it is definitely not infallible, otherwise we would all be millionaires. What it cannot do is tell you how a horse is feeling, either physically or mentally, and this is where you as the punter may use your own judgement. Racehorses in general hold many of the same characteristics as their human counterparts. Physically the sprinters which run between five and seven furlongs, are nearly all heavily muscled with large hindquarters, built for speed, while the narrow, wiry types are the distance runners of one and a half miles or more.

The shape of middle-distance horses falls somewhere between the two. Standing alongside the paddock, scrutinising each horse and assessing their physical differences can give you endless pleasure. It can also be very rewarding, particularly at the start of any season, when some horses will be a lot fitter than others, or when the race is for horses making their racecourse debut and there is no form to go on.

Apart from its overall shape and look of fitness, the horse you choose should also look well in itself, with bright eyes and healthy looking coat with a good shine to it. It should also be relaxed yet aware. Horses that get over-excited before a race tend to use up too much nervous energy, which can affect their performance. Always use your eyes in conjunction with your Timeform card when assessing runners, as sometimes there will be an exception to the rule. Timeform will usually note whether or not to ignore the fact that a particular horse looks thoroughly poor in its condition, or is on its toes in the paddock, because it does not affect its racing performance.

Having watched the horses in the paddock and made your short-list, it often pays to move yourself into a position where you have a good view of the runners as they canter to post, so that you can see how they move. It isn't always possible to learn much from watching the sprinters, because many look as if their legs are tied together until they get their joints properly warmed up, but for the remainder you should be looking for a very easy-actioned horse whose feet barely seem to rise above the level of the grass if the ground is good or firmer. When conditions are soft, or testing, look for a horse with a rounded knee action. Horses with big feet are less likely to get stuck in the mud, so be on the look out for this in the paddock.

In mid-summer remember that smaller animals cope with heat more easily because the surface area of skin does not increase proportionally with mass.

### Placing your bet

So there you are; you've picked your horse, you've watched it move to post, and now you want to back it. The choice is between the Tote and Bookmaker. The Tote is a pool bet system where a certain percentage of stakes is refunded to winners, so that before the race you only have an approximation of the odds likely to be returned if you win. The Tote also offers a number of excellent bets that can pay out at very rewarding odds if successful, such as a 'dual forecast' where you have to pick the first two horses home (in any order), or a 'tri-cast' which includes finding the first three. Believe me, just finding the winner is hard enough!

The Tote 'Jackpot' carries a significant first prize with it, and is won by selecting the winners of the first six races. The Tote Placepot is won by finding a horse to be placed in the first six races. Both bets are entered by filling in a card prior to the start of the first race.

Walking up and down the lines of bookmakers looking for the best price you can find your horse at is one of the major attractions of British racing, and is considerably more fun than queuing for a ticket at a Tote office window. Odds between different bookmakers can vary quite significantly. The bookmakers who are pitched furthest from the grandstand are inclined to offer slightly bigger odds in order to attract custom. Unless a horse you fancy is at a very big price, I do not recommend betting each way, as it is expensive if you don't collect. Far better to have £2 to win on two horses in the same race than have £2 each way on one.

### THE RACE IS ON

Once the bet is struck and you have received your ticket, find yourself a good place in the stands and watch closely how your horse runs, so that even if it doesn't win, you will have learned something about it. If it is doing all of its best work at the end of the race then it will probably be suited to a longer race, or a more demanding course, or maybe it is hampered at a crucial stage of the race and is genuinely unlucky.

Whatever happens, try to come away knowing a little more about the horse in general, but above all, make sure you enjoy yourself.
It's only a game!

# Racing in Ireland

No one is quite sure when Ireland's love affair with the horse and horse racing began, but it has certainly become an integral part of the national heritage. Its epicentre is The Curragh (whose gaelic interpretation is 'horse place') in County Kildare, with records of racing going back to the reign of the Celtic kings. At present there are nearly 1300 horses in training on the plains of the Curragh and its racecourse hosts no less than five Classics.

There are 25 courses in Ireland which offer varying degrees of facilities and racing, but one thing that is guaranteed at all of them is a tremendous atmosphere - few know how to enjoy themselves like the Irish, and the warmth of their welcome to visitors is renowned. Meetings are informal and children are always welcome. Five of the major Irish courses are featured in the guide, beginning on page 215, with a complete list of the rest on page 229.

**Further information is available from:**

**The Irish Tourist Board**
150 New Bond Street, London W1Y 0AQ
☎ 071-493 3201

or

**The Racing Board**
Leopardstown Racecourse, Foxrock, Dublin 18
☎ 01 351 965 or 01 289 2888

These two Boards have jointly produced a brochure on Horse Racing in Ireland, which gives details of inclusive holiday packages by air and sea and includes many Classics and Festival meetings.

## FESTIVAL MEETINGS IN IRELAND

Festival meetings are a great attraction, many of them having related activities to carry the festivities on beyond the gates of the racecourse. The Tralee Festival in August offers two evening meetings and four afternoons of racing during the same week that the town is alive with processions, music, theatre and the famous Rose of Tralee contest. Listowel's six-day September festival is part of the Harvest Festival of Ireland - a week-long carnival of fun through the streets - and Galway's Autumn Festival coincides with the opening of the oyster season and its associated celebrations.

Fairyhouse Easter Festival - *April*

Punchestown Spring Festival - *April*

Killarney Spring Festival - *May*

Bellewstown Summer Festival - *July*

Killarney Festival - *July*

Galway Summer Festival - *July*

Tramore Festival - *August*

The Rose of Tralee Festival - *September*

Galway Autumn Festival - *September*

Listowel Festival - *September*

Christmas Festival at Leopardstown - *December*

Christmas Festival at Limerick - *December*

## HOW TO GET THERE

**By air:** Flights are available from most major British airports to Belfast, Dublin, Cork, Shannon, Knock and Carrickfinn (Co Donegal), with internal flights from Dublin to Kerry, Galway and Sligo. A wide range of promotional fares are generally available.

**By sea:** Car and passenger ferry services operate on the following routes:

Holyhead -  Dun Laoghaire (Stena Sealink)

Holyhead -  Dublin ( B & I)

Holyhead -  Dublin (Sea Cat)

Fishguard -  Rosslare (Stena Sealink)

Pembroke -  Rosslare (B & I)

Swansea -  Cork (Swansea Cork Ferries)

Cairnryan -  Larne (P & O European Ferries)

Stranraer -  Larne (Stena Sealink)

Stranraer -  Belfast (Sea Cat Scotland)

Douglas -  Dublin (Isle of Man Steam Packet Company)

### TELEPHONING IRELAND
The international dialling code from Britain to the Republic of Ireland is 010 353. The initial 0 of the area code is not needed when dialling from outside the Republic.

# Aintree

*Aintree plays host to the most famous race in the world - the Grand National. This amazing spectacle attracts the largest viewing figures of any sporting event in Great Britain, with a total worldwide audience in excess of a hundred million.*

Its popularity is not hard to fathom, for there can be no stiffer challenge for horse and jockey and a fairy-tale result seems to emerge every year. The number of fatalities is now thankfully on the decline following recent modifications to the fences, especially the notorious Becher's Brook.

The quality of racing is second only to the Cheltenham Festival and there is always a huge attendance, particularly on the day of the big race when tickets will need to be purchased in advance for certain sections of the course. After a gap of twenty years, 1992 saw the reintroduction of an autumn fixture, held towards the end of November and tremendously popular despite the inclement weather.

## FURTHER INFORMATION

Aintree Racecourse Co Ltd
Ormskirk Road, Aintree, Liverpool LP9 5AS
☎ 051-523 2600

## LOCATION AND HOW TO GET THERE

The course is on the outskirts of Liverpool on the A59, one mile south of its junction with the M57 and M58.
**Nearest Railway Station:** Aintree, adjacent to the course. From London Euston trains run to Liverpool Lime Street, from where there are local trains to Aintree.

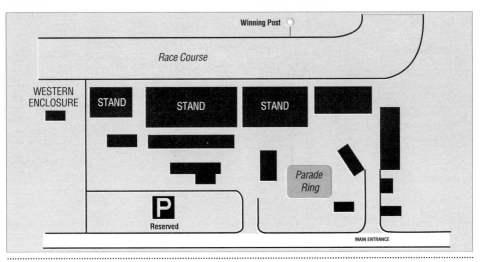

## ADMISSION

All classes of day ticket give access to full betting facilities, including Tote.

**Day Tickets:**
COUNTY £12 Thursday & Friday, £29 Saturday – access to bars and restaurants

PADDOCK £9 Thursay & Friday, £16 Saturday – access to bars, restaurant and raised viewing area

CENTRAL £9 Saturday – access to bars and refreshments

## COURSE FACILITIES

**Banks:**
there is a National Westminster Bank on the course, open normal bank hours; there are also cashpoint facilities.

**For families:**
picnic area with refreshment kiosk and toilets; no lost children centre as such, but there is a police station on the course.

## CALENDAR OF EVENTS

**April 7-9** – The Grand National Meeting; includes the Martell Cup Chase on Thursday, Mumm Melling Chase on Friday and the Martell Grand National on Saturday

**November 19**

## WHERE TO STAY

### HOTELS

**★★★★ 59% Liverpool Moat House**
Paradise Street,
☎ 051-709 0181, telex 627270, fax: 051-709 2706
251 bedrooms; double B&B £123
Credit cards 1 2 3 4 5

**★★★★ 54% Atlantic Tower**
Chapel Street
☎ 051-227 4444, telex 627070, fax: 051-236 3973
226 bedrooms; double bedroom £85
Credit cards 1 2 3 4 5

**★★★ 52% St George's**
St John's Precinct, Lime Street,
☎ 051-709 7090, fax: 051-709 0137
155 bedrooms
Credit cards 1 2 3 5

**★★ 63% Grange**
Holmfield Rd, Aigburth
☎ 051-427 2950, fax: 051-427 9055
25 bedrooms; double B&B £46.80-£60.85
Credit cards 1 2 3 5

**★★ 56% Green Park**
4/6 Greenbank Dr
☎ 051-733 3382
23 bedrooms; double B&B £38-£45
Credit cards 1 2 3 5

**Campanile**
Chaloner Street, Queens Dock
☎ 051-709 8104
82 bedrooms

### Around Liverpool

**★★ 65% Bridge Inn**
Bolton Rd, Port Sunlight, Bebington
☎ 051-645 8441
16 bedrooms
Credit cards 1 2 3 5

**Forte Travelodge**
New Chester Rd, Bebington
☎ 051-327 2489, Central Reservations:
(0800) 850950
31 bedrooms; double bedroom £31.95
Credit cards 1 2 3

**★★★ 62% Bowler Hat 2**
Talbot Rd, Oxton, Birkenhead
☎ 051-652 4931, telex 628761, fax: 051-653 8127
29 bedrooms; double B&B £52-£72
Credit cards 1 2 3 5

**★★ 61% Riverhill**
Talbot Rd, Oxton
☎ 051-653 3773, fax: 051-653 7162
16 bedrooms; double B&B £65.95
Credit cards 1 2 3 5

**★★★ 63% Blundellsands**
The Serpentine, Blundellsands
☎ 051-924 6515, fax: 051-931 5364
41 bedrooms; double B&B £70
Credit cards 1 2 3 5

**★★ 64% Tree Tops**
Southport Old Rd, Formby
☎ (07048) 79651
11 bedrooms
Credit cards 1 2 3 5

**★★★ 67% Beaufort**
High Ln, Burscough, Ormskirk
☎ (0704) 892655, fax: (0704) 895135
21 bedrooms; double B&B £69-£71
Credit cards 1 2 3 5

**★ 58% Rockland**
View Rd, Rainhill
☎ 051-426 4603, fax: 051-426 0107
10 bedrooms; double B&B £30-£49
Credit cards 1 3

### ★★★ 67% Forte Posthouse
Lodge Ln, Newton-le-Willows, St Helens
☎ (0942) 717878, fax: (0942) 718419
136 bedrooms; double bedrooms £39.50-£69.50
Credit cards 1 2 3 5

**★★ 67% Grove House**
Grove Rd, Wallasey
☎ 051-639 3947 & 051-630 4558,
fax: 051-630 0028
16 bedrooms; double bedroom £45.50
Credit cards 1 3

**★★ 66% Hill Crest**
75 Cronton Ln, Widnes
☎ 051-424 1616, telex 627098, fax: 051-495 1348
57 bedrooms
Credit cards 1 2 3 5

### BED AND BREAKFAST

**Aachen Hotel**
91 Mount Pleasant
☎ 051-709 3477 & 1126
Close to city centre; long established, popular hotel with friendly and efficient service.
17 bedrooms; double B&B £34-£44
Credit cards 1 2 3 5

**New Manx Hotel**
39 Catherine Street
☎ 051-708 6171, fax: 051-737 2206
Reasonably priced accommodation popular with students and musicians.
11 bedrooms; double B&B £35-£40
Credit cards 1 2 3 5

## WHERE TO STAY

### BED AND BREAKFAST

#### Around Liverpool

**Gronwen**
11 Willowbank Rd, Devonshire Park,
Birkenhead
☎ 051-652 8306
Small unpretentious guesthouse offering
modest accommodation in pleasant
surroundings.
5 bedrooms; double B&B £28-£30

### CAMPSITES

**►►► Abbey Farm Caravan Park**
Dark Ln, Ormskirk
☎ 0695 572686
North of Liverpool.

## WHERE TO EAT

### RESTAURANTS

**✿ Beadles**
15 Rosemount, Oxton,
Birkenhead
☎ 051-653 9010
Good, well cooked food in a busy,
intimate restaurant.
Dinner only: 7-9; from £24 à la carte
Credit cards 1 3

### PUBS

**Philharmonic Dining Rooms**
36 Hope St Liverpool
A historic and interesting pub, of which a
substantial part is Grade I listed, including
the interior woodwork, glass and ceramic
mosaics. A Tetley Walker pub with a range
of good-value, popular bar meals.
Afternoon tea also available. Children
allowed in restaurant and side room
daytime only.
Open: 11.30-11pm Monday to Friday;
11.30pm-3pm, 6-11pm Saturday; 12-3pm,
7-10.30pm Sunday
Bar food: daytime only, not available
evenings
Restaurant: daytime only, not available
evenings

# Ascot

*Set in the heart of beautiful Berkshire countryside, Ascot deserves to be recognised as the jewel in the crown of British racecourses, an appropriate metaphor, since it forms part of the Royal Estates.*

Facilities are among the best in the country, though inevitably this is reflected in admission prices, especially on Saturdays. Weekdays may lack atmosphere but are often cheaper and much better value for money. A word of warning - the 'no jeans' rule in the Members and Tattersalls enclosures is rigorously enforced by bowler-hatted gatemen.

Top-class action can be guaranteed throughout the year on Ascot's wide, triangular, galloping track. The highlight is the Royal meeting in mid-June which provides the best week's Flat racing of the season, and remains one of the major events in the social calendar. There is a vibrant fashion scene and plenty of pomp and circumstance, with members of the Royal Family parading down the course in open carriages before the first race. Other important Flat races are the King George VI and Queen Elizabeth Diamond Stakes at the end of July, and the Queen Elizabeth II Stakes, part of the Festival of British Racing in September.

## FURTHER INFORMATION

Racecourse Office,
Ascot Racecourse, Ascot, Berkshire SL5 7JN
☎ (0344) 22211

## LOCATION AND HOW TO GET THERE

The course is in Ascot town. From the south and east leave the M3 at junction 3 and take the A332 Bracknell Road; from the A30, take the A329 towards Bracknell; from the M4 eastbound, leave at junction 6 and take the A332 Windsor bypass; from the M4 westbound, leave at junction 10 and take the A329 towards Bracknell. The course is well signposted.

**Nearest railway Station:** Ascot; the station is less than a mile from the course, approximately seven minutes' walk.

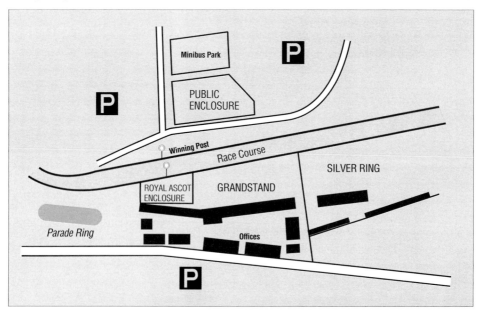

## ADMISSION

All classes of day ticket give access to full betting facilities, including Tote.

**Day Tickets:**
Accompanied children under 16 are admitted free to all enclosures, except at the Royal Meeting. Grandstand tickets must be booked in advance for the first three days of the Royal Meeting; members badges must be obtained in advance for Diamond Day.

MEMBERS/CLUB £11.50-£21, under 25s half price with proof of age – access to bars, restaurant, shops, champagne bars, excellent viewing, facilities for disabled racegoers

TATTERSALLS £7.50-£14 – access as for Members' Enclosure, plus creche and private boxes

SILVER RINGS £3 – access as for Members' Enclosure

**Transfers:** from the Grandstand to the Members Stand available on all racedays except for the Royal Meeting and Diamond Day.

## COURSE FACILITIES

**Banks:**
there is a Barclays Bank on the course, open during course opening hours, but no cashpoint facilities.

**For families:**
children's play area; free supervised creche

# CALENDAR OF EVENTS

**April 6** – National Hunt; The Daily Telegraph Day
**April 26-27** – Tuesday: National Hunt; The Ascot Spring Evening Meeting. Wednesday: flat; Insulpak Victoria Cup Day
**June 14-17** – Royal Meeting, includes St James's Palace Stakes, Coronation Stakes, Gold Cup and King's Stand Stakes; flat
**June 18** – flat; Heath Meeting The Sponsored Stakes
**July 22-23** – flat; includes Virginia Water Stakes on Friday; Diamond Day on Saturday

**September 22-24** – flat; Hoover Day on Thursday; Charity Raceday on Friday; The Festival at Ascot on Saturday
**October 7-8** – flat; includes Grunwick Day on Friday; Bovis Day on Saturday
**October 29** – National Hunt; United House Group Day
**November 18-19** – National Hunt; Coopers & Lybrand Day on Friday; The Gold Cup Steeplechase on Saturday
**December 17** – National Hunt; Betterware Day

## WHERE TO STAY

### HOTELS

**★★★★ 57% Berystede**
Bagshot Rd, Sunninghill
☎ (0344) 23311, fax: (0344) 872301
91 bedrooms; double bedroom £105-£112.
Credit cards 1 2 3 5

**★★ 67% Brockenhurst**
Brockenhurst Rd
☎ (0344) 21912, fax: (0344) 873252
11 bedrooms; double B&B £75-£100.
Credit Cards 1 2 3 5

**★★ 65% Highclere**
19 Kings Rd, Sunninghill
☎ (0344) 25220, fax: (0344) 872528
12 bedrooms; double B&B £55-£80.
Credit Cards 1 2 3

### Around Ascot

**★★★★ 76% Pennyhill Park**
London Rd, Bagshot
☎ (0276) 71774, fax: (0276) 73217
22 bedrooms
Credit Cards 1 2 3 4 5

**★★★ 65% Stirrups Country House**
Maidens Green, Winkfield
☎ (0344) 882284, fax: (0344) 882300
24 bedrooms; double B&B £50-£85.
Credit Cards 1 2 3 5

**★★★ 64% Burnham Beeches Moat House**
Grove Road, Burnham
☎ (0628) 603333, fax: (0628) 603994
75 bedrooms; double B&B £98-£103
Credit Cards 1 2 3 4 5

**★★★ 67% Frimley Hall**
Portsmouth Rd, Camberley
☎ (0276) 28321, telex 858446,
fax: (0276) 691253
66 bedrooms
Credit Cards 1 2 3 5

**★★★ 58% Lakeside International**
Wharf Rd, Frimley Green, Camberley
☎ (0252) 838000, telex 858095, fax:
(0252) 837857
97 bedrooms; double B&B £105.
Credit Cards 1 2 3 5

**★★★ 54% Waterloo**
Duke's Ride, Crowthorne
☎ (0344) 777711, fax: (0344) 778913
58 bedrooms; double bedroom £100 (room only)
Credit Cards 1 2 3 5

**★★ 54% The Manor**
The Village Green, Datchet
☎ (0753) 543442, fax: (0753) 545292
30 bedrooms; double B&B £70-£90
Credit Cards 1 2 3 5

**★★★★ 65% Runnymede**
Windsor Rd, Egham
☎ (0784) 436171, telex 934900,
fax: (0784) 436340
172 bedrooms; double bedroom £124-£137
(room only)
Credit Cards 1 2 3 5

**★★★ 64% Forte Crest**
Lynchford Rd, Farnborough
☎ (0252) 545051, telex 859637,
fax: (0252) 377210
110 bedrooms
Credit cards 1 2 3 4 5

## WHERE TO STAY

**★★ 70% Falcon**
Farnborough Rd, Farnborough
☎ (0252) 545378, fax: (0252) 522539
30 bedrooms; double B&B £45-£75
Credit cards 1 2 3 5

**★ 65% Alexandra**
144 Alexandra Rd, Farnborough
☎ (0252) 541050, fax: (0252) 371038
11 bedrooms; double B&B from £60
Credit Cards 1 2 3 5

**★★★★ 73% Fredrick's**
Shoppenhangers Rd, Maidenhead
☎ (0628) 35934, telex 849966,
fax: (0628) 771054
37 bedrooms; double B&B £155-£165
Credit Cards 1 2 3 5

**★★★ 63% Thames Riviera**
At the Bridge, Maidenhead
☎ (0628) 74057, telex 846687,
fax: (0628) 776586
34 bedrooms; double B&B £60-£125
Credit Cards 1 2 3 4 5

**★★★ 60% The Thames Lodge**
Thames St, Staines
☎ (0784) 464433, fax: (0784) 454858
44 bedrooms; double room £90-£105
(room only)
Credit cards 1 2 3 5

**★★★★★ (RED) Cliveden**
Taplow, signposted from all directions
☎ (0628) 668561, telex 846562, fax:
(0628) 661837
25 bedrooms
Credit cards 1 2 3 4 5

**★★★★ 73% Oakley Court**
Windsor Rd, Water Oakley, Windsor
☎ (0628) 74141, telex 849958, fax: (0628)
37011
65 bedrooms; double room £145-£375
(room only)
Credit cards 1 2 3 5

**★★★ 68% The Castle**
High St, Windsor
☎ (0753) 851011, telex 849220, fax:
(0753) 830244
104 bedrooms; double rooms £120-£140
(room only)
Credit cards 1 2 3 5

**★ 71% Aurora Garden**
14 Bolton Av, Windsor
☎ (0753) 868686, fax: (0753) 831394
14 bedrooms
Credit cards 1 2 3 5

**★★ 58% Ye Harte & Garter**
High St, Windsor
☎ (0753) 863426, fax: (0753) 830527
50 bedrooms; double B&B from £50
Credit Cards 1 2 3 5

**★★★ 66% Reading Moat House**
Mill Ln, Sindlesham
☎ (0734) 351035, telex 846360, fax:
(0734) 666530
96 bedrooms; double room £50-£110
(room only)
Credit cards 1 2 3 5

## BED AND BREAKFAST

**The Beeches**
19 The Avenue, Datchet
☎ (0753) 580722
Semi-detached, redbrick Victorian house providing comfortable bed and breakfast accommodation.
7 bedrooms; double B&B £45
Credit cards 1 3

**Colnbrook Lodge**
Bath Rd, Colnbrook
☎ (0753) 685958
Comfortable and well equipped detached house on the edge of the village of Colnbrook
8 bedrooms
Credit cards 1 3

**Clarence Hotel**
9 Clarence Rd, Windsor
☎ (0753) 864436, fax: (0753) 857060
Centrally placed old hotel offering attractive and well coordinated rooms.
21 bedroom; double B&B £49
Credit cards 1 2 3 5

**Melrose House**
53 Frances Rd, Windsor
☎ (0753) 865328
Elegant Victorian house offering bright, clean and very well equipped bedrooms.
9 bedrooms
Credit cards 1 3

**Glen Court**
St Johns Hill Rd, Woking
☎ (0483) 764154
Attractive Edwardian house set in 1.5 acres of woodland. 9 bedrooms

## CAMPSITES

**►►► California Chalet & Touring Park**
Nine Mile Ride, Finchampstead. Signposted
☎ (0734) 733928
Southwest of Ascot off B3016; pitch price £7.25 per night.

**►► Laleham Park Camping Site**
Thameside. Signposted
☎ (09325) 64149
Southeast of Ascot; pitch price £7.80 per night

## WHERE TO EAT

### RESTAURANTS

**🌸🌸🌸🌸 Waterside**
River Cottage, Ferry Rd, Bray
☎ (0628) 20691
Excellent French cuisine prepared by Michael Roux in picturesque riverside setting.
Lunch: 12-2 from £28 and à la carte
Dinner: 7-10 from £57.50 and à la carte

**🌸🌸 La Bonne Franquette**
5 High St, Egham
☎ (0784) 439494, fax: (0784) 431473
Eclectic carte and overall good quality food offered in this smart High Street restaurant.
Lunch: 12-2 from £14.50 and à la carte
Dinner: 7-9 from £27.50 and à la carte

**🌸🌸 New Mill**
New Mill Rd, Eversley
☎ (0734) 732277 fax: (0734) 328780
Sound cooking in a lovely old mill on the river.
Lunch: 12-2 from £19.50 and à la carte
Dinner: 7-10 from £25.50 and à la carte

**🌸🌸 Jade Fountain**
38 High St, Sunninghill
☎ (0344) 27070
Smart and friendly Chinese restaurant offering high standard Chinese cuisine.
Lunch: 12-1.50 from £14.50 and à la carte
Dinner: 7-10.30 from £14.50 and à la carte

### PUBS

**Bleak House**
Chertsey Road, Horsell, Woking
☎ (0483) 760717
Recently renovated pub where children are welcome anywhere away from the bar. Good food is mainly home made and there is a children's menu; list of 12 wines; Tetley, Burton and Youngs beer; three draught lagers.
Open: 11am-3pm, 5.30-11pm; Sunday 12-2.30pm, 7-10.30pm
Bar food: 12-2pm, 7-9.30pm; no food Monday evening

# Ayr

*This is without question the premier course in Scotland and it affords the only real opportunity for racegoers north of the border to see high-class horses in action.*

The Scottish Grand National in April always attracts a select field (Red Rum was a past winner) and the three-day Great Western Meeting in September is immensely popular and has formed the backdrop to many happy holidays over the years. The major betting race of the week is the Ayr Gold Cup, an ultra-competitive sprint handicap in which a low draw was traditionally a huge advantage, although recent drainage work on the turf appears to have rectified that problem. An extremely friendly track, renowned for its warm welcome and hospitality, it is also an ideal place to watch the horses being prepared for their races as the saddling boxes are situated right next to the parade ring. Catering facilities are excellent, and a visit is thoroughly recommended.

## FURTHER INFORMATION

The Western Meeting Club
Racecourse Office, 2 Whitletts Road, Ayr KA8 0JE
☎ (0292) 264179

## LOCATION AND HOW TO GET THERE

The course is in Whitletts Road, Ayr. Leave the A77 at the Whitletts Roundabout and follow signs for Ayr.
**Nearest railway Station:** Ayr, one mile from the course; there are connecting bus services to the course for major events only.

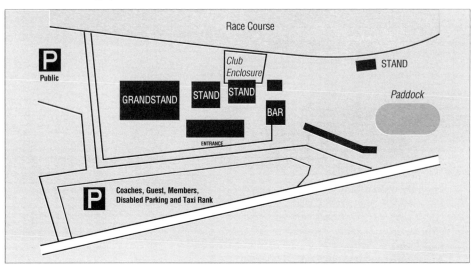

## ADMISSION

All classes of day ticket give access to full betting facilities, including Tote.

**Day Tickets:**
CLUBSTAND £12-£15 – access to bar, restaurant, private rooms

GRANDSTAND £6-£8, reduction for senior citizens and registered unemployed – access to bars, restaurant, private rooms

## COURSE FACILITIES

**Banks:**
there are various banks on the course during major events, open during racing, but no cashpoint facilities.

**For families:**
baby changing facilities; events are sometimes arranged for children.

## CALENDAR OF EVENTS

**April 14-16** – National Hunt; includes Scottish Champion Hurdle and Scottish National
**May 21** – flat
**May 23** – flat
**June 17-18** – flat
**July 16** – flat; evening meeting; includes Sprint Trophy
**July 18** – flat; includes Tennents Scottish Classic

**July 23** – flat
**August 6** – flat
**August 18** – flat
**September 15-17** – flat; includes Ladbrokes (Ayr) Gold Cup
**October 8** – National Hunt
**November 11-12** – National Hunt
**December 26** – National Hunt

## WHERE TO STAY

### HOTELS

**★★★ 64% Caledonian**
Dalblair Rd
☎ (0292) 269331, telex 776611, fax: (0292) 610722
114 bedrooms; double room £99 (room only)
Credit cards 1 2 3 5

**★★★ 60% Pickwick**
19 Racecourse Rd
☎ (0292) 260111, fax: (0292) 43174
15 bedrooms; double B&B £80-£90
Credit cards 1 2 3 5

**★★★ 57% Savoy Park**
16 Racecourse Rd
☎ (0292) 266112, fax: (0292) 611488
16 bedrooms; double B&B £55-£75
Credit cards 1 2 3

**★★ 69% Carrick Lodge**
46 Carrick Rd
☎ (0292) 262846
8 bedrooms; double B&B £60-£62
Credit cards 1 2 3

**★★ 68% Burns Monument**
Alloway
☎ (0292) 42466, fax: (0292) 43174
9 bedrooms; double B&B £70-£80
Credit cards 1 2 3 5

**★★ 66% Elms Court**
21 Miller Rd
☎ (0292) 264191 & 282332, fax: (0292) 610254
20 bedrooms; double B&B £50-£60
Credit cards 1 2 3

**★★ 64% Annfield**
49 Maybole Rd
☎ (0292) 41986 & 42368, fax: (0292) 43174
8 bedrooms; double B&B from £60
Credit cards 1 3

**★ 66% The Almont Hotel**
39 Charlotte St
☎ (0292) 263814
14 bedrooms

**★ 62% Aftongrange**
37 Carrick Rd
☎ (0292) 265679
8 bedrooms; double B&B £50

### Around Ayr

**★★★★ 53% Hospitality Inn**
Annick Rd, Annickwater, Irvine
☎ (0294) 74272, telex 777097, fax: (0294) 77287
128 bedrooms; double bedroom £79-£100 (room only)
Credit cards 1 2 3 4 5

**★★ Ladyburn**
Crosshill, Maybole
☎ (06554) 585, fax: (06554) 580
8 bedrooms; double B&B £130-£140
Credit cards 1 2 3

**★★★ 60% Carlton Toby Prestwick**
☎ (0292) 76811, telex 778740
39 bedrooms
Credit cards 1 2 3 5

**★★ 60% Parkstone Esplanade, Prestwick**
☎ (0292)77286
15 bedrooms; double B&B £56-£58
Credit cards 1 2 3

**★★ 60% St Nicholas**
41 Ayr Rd, Prestwick
☎ (0292) 79568
17 bedrooms; double B&B from £52
Credit cards 1 2 3 5

**★★★★ 65% Marine Highland**
Troon
☎ (0292) 314444, telex 777595, fax: (0292) 316922
72 bedroom; double B&B £132-£142
Credit cards 1 2 3 5

**★★★ 74% Lochgreen House**
Monktenhill Road, Southwood, Troon
☎ (0292) 313343 fax: (0292) 318661
7 bedrooms

**★★★ 67% Highgrove House**
Old Loans Rd, Troon
☎ (0292) 312511, fax: (0292) 318228
9 bedrooms

**★★★ 66% Piersland House**
Craigend Rd, Troon
☎ (0292) 314747, fax: (0292) 315613
15 bedrooms; double B&B £85-£110
Credit cards 1 2 3 5

**★★62% Craiglea**
South Beach, Troon
☎ (0292) 311366
20 bedrooms; double B&B £44-£60
Credit cards 1 2 3 5

**★★ 62% South Beach**
South Beach Rd, Troon
☎ (0292) 312033, fax: (0292) 318438
27 bedrooms
Credit cards 1 2 3

**★★ 59% Ardneil**
51 Saint Meddans, Troon
☎ (0292) 311611
9 bedrooms; double B&B £45-£60
Credit cards 1 2 3

**★★★ 66% Malin Court**
Turnberry
☎ (0655) 31457, fax: (0655) 31072
About 20 miles south of Ayr.
8 bedrooms
Credit cards 1 2 3 4 5

### BED AND BREAKFAST

**Arrandale Hotel**
2-4 Cassillis St
☎ (0292) 289959
Pleasant, enthusiastically run hotel, within walking distance of the seafront.
13 bedrooms

## WHERE TO STAY

**Brenalder Lodge**
39 Dunure, Doonfoot
☎ (0292) 43939
Attractive bedrooms
5 bedrooms; double B&B £50–£60

**Craggallan**
8 Queens Ter
☎ (0292) 264998
Attractive, nicely furnished bedrooms.
7 bedrooms; double B&B £28–£30

**Dargill**
7 Queens Ter
☎ (0292) 261955
4 bedrooms; double B&B £98–£105

**Glenmore**
35 Bellevue Crescent
☎ (0292) 269830
4 bedrooms; double B&B from £36

**Langley Bank**
39 Carrick Rd
☎ (0292) 264246
Substantial period house
6 bedrooms; double B&B £30–£45
Credit cards 1 3

**Windsor Hotel**
6 Alloway Place
☎ (0292) 264689
Full of character with 10 bright attractive bedrooms.
Credit Cards 1 3

**Lagg Farmhouse Dunure**
☎ (029250) 647
Attractive well maintained farmhouse.
3 bedrooms; double B&B from £26

**Boreland Farmhouse**
Hollybush
☎ (0292) 531228
Just off the main road south of the village
3 bedrooms; double B&B £26–£28

**Fairways Hotel**
19 Links Rd, Prestwick
☎ (0292) 70396
5 bedrooms; double B&B £41

**Fernbank**
213 Main Street, Prestwick
☎ (0292) 75027
7 bedrooms; double B&B £34–£36

**Golf View Hotel**
17 Links Rd, Prestwick
☎ (0292) 671234, fax: (0292) 671244
Overlooking golf course, friendly owners and high standard of bed and breakfast.
6 bedrooms; double B&B from £46
Credit Cards 1 3

**Kincraig Private Hotel**
39 Ayr Rd, Prestwick
☎ (0292) 79480
Spacious and well furnished bedrooms plus comfortable lounge and attractive dining room.
6 bedrooms; double B&B from £35

### CAMPSITES

**►► Crofthead Caravan Park**
Ayr
☎ (0292) 263516
Signposted; pitch price from £5 per night.

**►►►► Sundrum Castle Holiday Park**
Coylton
☎ (0292) 570057 & 570886
Ten minutes drive from the centre of Ayr off the A70; pitch price from £8.50 per night.

**►►► Camping & Caravanning Club Site**
Culzean
☎ (06556) 627 & (0203) 694995
South of Ayr off the A719; pitch price from £10.30 per night.

**► Skeldon Caravan Park**
Hollybush
☎ (029256) 202
Situated southeast of Ayr 2m from Dalrymple on B7034

**►►► Middlemuir Holiday Park**
Tarbolton
☎ (0292) 541647
Set in rolling farmland off the B743 Ayr-Mauchline road; pitch price from £5 per night.

## WHERE TO EAT

### RESTAURANTS

**❀ Fouters Bistro**
2A Academy St, Ayr
☎ (0292) 261391
Consistent quality and enthusiasm for new ideas characterises the cuisine offered here in this cosy basement restaurant.
Lunch: 12–2; from £7.50 and à la carte
Dinner: 7–10.30 from £10.75 and à la carte

# Bangor on Dee

*This charming rural track is set in a bowl beside the River Dee and the surrounding banks afford excellent viewing, not only from the paddock area but also from the course car parks.*

Due to its outstanding natural location, the management have never felt the need to built a grandstand, so be prepared for plenty of fresh air and a really enjoyable day out in the country. The best fixture is in late April, featuring a valuable three-mile handicap chase.

## FURTHER INFORMATION

Bangor-on-Dee Races Ltd
Chorlton Hall, Malpas, Cheshire SY14 7ET
☎ (0948) 860438 (0978 780323 on racedays)

## LOCATION AND HOW TO GET THERE

The course is 5 miles south of Wrexham off the A525 Wrexham-Whitchurch road. From the M53 take the A483 to bypass Wrexham; take the B5426 to Bangor, continue through Bangor village, then the B5069 Overton road for about a mile.

**Nearest railway Station:** Wrexham; there is no connecting bus service with the course.

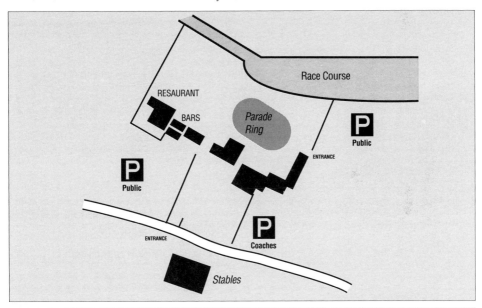

## ADMISSION

All classes of day ticket give access to full betting facilities, including Tote.

**Day Tickets:**
Children are admitted free to all enclosures.

PADDOCK £7 – access to bars, buffet bar, cafeteria, facilities for disabled racegoers, facilities for private parties

COURSE £3 – access to bar, fast food

**Annual membership:** £60 includes reciprocal arrangements for 10 days racing at other courses, reserved car park, access to Owners, Trainers and Members bar in the paddock.

## COURSE FACILITIES

**Banks:**
there are no banks or cashpoint facilities on the course.

**For families:**
picnic area with refreshment kiosk and toilets.

27

| | |
|---|---|
| April 16 | September 10 |
| April 29 – evening meeting | October 8 |
| May 14 | October 28 |
| July 29 | November 25 |
| August 13 | December 14 |

## WHERE TO STAY

### HOTELS

**Around Bangor-on-Dee**

**★★★ 62% Broxton Hall Country House**
Whitchurch Rd, Broxton
☎ (0829) 782321, fax: (0829) 782330
12 bedrooms; double B&B £65-£85
Credit Cards 1 2 3 5

**★★★✿ 60% Bryn Howel**
Llangollen
☎ (0978) 860331, fax: (0978) 860119
38 bedrooms
Credit cards 1 2 3

**★★★ 57% The Royal**
Bridge St, Llangollen
☎ (0978) 860202, fax: (0978) 861824
33 bedrooms; double room £65 (room only)
Credit cards 1 2 3 5

**★★ 61% Cross Lanes Hotel & Restaurant**
Cross Lanes, Marchwiel
☎ (0978) 780555, fax: (0978) 780568
18 bedrooms; double B&B from £59.50-£90
Credit cards 1 2 3 5

**★★★ 67% Wynnstay**
Church St, Oswestry
☎ (0691) 655261, fax: (0691) 670606
27 bedrooms; double room £39.95-£65 (room only)
Credit cards 1 2 3 4 5

**★★ 55% Sweeney Hall**
Morda, Oswestry
☎ (0691) 652450
9 bedrooms
Credit cards 1 3

**Forte Travelodge**
Mile End Service Area,
(junction A5/A483), Oswestry
☎ (0691) 658178 Central Reservations;
(0800) 850950
40 bedrooms; double bedroom £31.95
(room only) Credit cards 1 3

**★★★ 73% Llyndir Hall**
Rossett
☎ (0244) 571648, fax: (0244) 571258
38 bedrooms; double bedroom £103 (room only)
Credit cards 1 2 3 5

**★★★ 71% Rossett Hall**
Chester Rd, Rossett
☎ (0244) 571000, fax: (0244) 571505
30 bedrooms; double B&B £90
Credit cards 1 2 3 5

**★★ 56% Wynnstay Arms**
High St, Ruabon
☎ (0978) 822187
9 bedrooms; double B&B from £42
Credit cards 1 2 3 4 5

**★ 60% Ye Olde Boot Inn**
Whittington
☎ Oswestry (0691) 662250
6 bedrooms; double B&B from £38
Credit cards 1 3

**★★★ 64% Llwyn Onn Hall**
Cefn Rd, Wrexham
☎ (0978) 261225
13 bedrooms; double B&B £66-£72
Credit cards 1 2 3 5

**★★★ 63% Wynnstay Arms**
High St, Wrexham
☎ (0978) 291010, telex 61674, fax: (0978) 362138
76 bedrooms; double room £52.50-£57.50
(room only)
Credit cards 1 2 3 5

**Forte Travelodge**
Wrexham Bypass, Rhostyllen
☎ (0978) 365705, Central Reservations:
(0800) 850950
32 bedrooms; double room £31.95 (room only)
Credit cards 1 2 3

### BED AND BREAKFAST

**Buck Farmhouse**
Hanmer
☎ (094874) 339
Modest accommodation with wealth of charm and character situated midway between Wrexham and Whitchurch.
4 bedrooms

**Hillcrest**
Hill St, Llangollen
☎ (0978) 860208
Personally run private hotel located within a few minutes walk of the A5 and town centre.
7 bedrooms; double B&B £36

**Rhydonnen Ucha Rhewl**
Llangollen
☎ (0978) 860153
Simple but soundly maintained accommodation, with picturesque views across the Dee valley to the Berwyn Mountains.
4 bedrooms

**Tilston Lodge**
Malpas
☎ (0829) 250223
Delightful house well equipped, tastefully decorated, lovely public areas and friendly owners.
3 bedrooms; double B&B £36-£42

**Ashfield Country House**
Trefonen Rd, Oswestry
☎ (0691) 655200
Friendly, personally run small hotel; good reputation for home-made food and personal service.
12 bedrooms

**Bridge House**
Penley
☎ (097873) 763
Renovated former farmhouse with good quality modern accommodation, pretty gardens; 2 miles north of village.
3 bedrooms

## WHERE TO STAY

### CAMPSITES

**►►► Camping & Caravanning Club Site**
The Racecourse, Signposted
☎ (0978) 780740 & (0203) 694995
pitch price from £8.10 per night

**►►► Plassey Touring Caravan & Leisure Park**
Eyton
☎ (0978) 780277
Situated off the B5426; pitch price from £7

**►►► Ty-Ucha Farm**
Maesmawr Rd, Llangollen
☎ (0978) 860677
Close to A5, 1 mile east of Llangollen; pitch price from £7

**►►► Fernwood Caravan Park**
Lyneal (near Ellesmere)
☎ (094875) 221
Four miles southeast of Ellesmere off B5063; pitch price from £4

## WHERE TO EAT

### RESTAURANTS

**❀❀ Boat Inn**
Erbistock
☎ (0978) 780143, fax: (0978) 780312
Charming riverside restaurant offering interesting, enjoyable food.
Lunch: 12-2.15; from £10.95 and à la carte
Dinner: 7-9.30; from £14.95 and à la carte

# Bath

*Situated just three miles outside the famous Roman and Georgian city, with its architectural splendours, lies this lovely course on a beautiful hill-top setting which offers panoramic views of the surrounding countryside.*

A slight drawback is that it is fairly exposed to the elements, so be sure to wrap up well as a chill wind can blow even on the sunniest days. The track itself is very tight and a stiff uphill finish brings stamina into play. In sprint races, a low draw is absolutely vital as the course is constantly turning and lengths can be saved by hugging the rails.

There are about a dozen Flat meetings spread throughout the summer, with June and July probably the best time to go. The races are well supported by West Country folk and a good afternoon's entertainment is assured. As at most racecourses, private boxes or marquees can be hired for special occasions, but it is essential to book in advance.

### FURTHER INFORMATION
—🙰 ● 🙰—
The Bath Racecourse Co Ltd
Greenfields, Little Rissington, Cheltenham,
Gloucestershire GL54 2NA
☎ (0451) 20517

### LOCATION AND HOW TO GET THERE
—🙰 ● 🙰—
The course is two miles north of the city. Leave the M4 at junction 18 and take the A46 south for six miles; the course is signposted on racedays. **Nearest Railway Station:** Bath Spa; there is no connecting bus service to the course.

### ADMISSION

All classes of day ticket give access to full betting facilities, including Tote.

**Day Tickets:**
CLUB £10 – access to bar, luncheon room, boxes and private rooms

TATTERSALLS £7 – access to bar and snack bar

SILVER RING £3 – access to bar
COURSE £1 – access to bar

**Parking:** main parking free, central car park £3, including admission

### COURSE FACILITIES

**Banks:**
there are no banks or cashpoint facilities on the course.

**For families:**
picnic area with refreshment kiosk and toilets

## CALENDAR OF EVENTS

**April 26** – includes Tripleprint Stakes
**May 7** – includes James & Cowper Stakes
**May 16** – Timeform Day
**June 11** – includes Bonusprint Stakes; Electric Handicap and Rothmans Royal Handicap
**June 24** – evening meeting; includes Clifton Handicap
**July 2** – includes McKinnon & Clarke Handicap
**July 6** – includes Baxi Handicap
**July 18** – includes Tote Computer Stakes

**August 4** – includes Be Hopeful Handicap
**August 9** – includes Tripleprint Stakes and BBC Radio Bristol Handicap Stakes
**September 12** – includes Bathford Nursery
**September 26** – includes Morris Dancer Handicap Stakes and Tattersalls Stakes

## WHERE TO STAY

### HOTELS

**★★★★★ 68% Bath Spa**
Sydney Rd
☎ (0225) 444424, telex 449729, fax: (0225) 444006
100 bedrooms; double £50 (room only)
Credit cards 1 2 3 5

**★★★★★❀❀❀ 70% The Royal Crescent**
16 Royal Crescent
☎ (0225) 319090, telex 444251, fax: (0225) 339401
25 bedrooms; double B&B £152–£360
Credit cards 1 2 3 5

**★★★★❀❀ 66% Combe Grove Manor Hotel & Country Club**
Brassknocker Hill, Monkton Combe
☎ (0225) 834644, fax: (0225) 834961
10 bedrooms; double B&B £115–£260
Credit cards 1 2 3 5

**★★★❀❀ 80% The Priory**
Weston Rd
☎ (0225) 331922, telex 44612, fax: (0225) 448276
21 bedrooms, Credit cards 1 2 3 5

**★★★❀❀ 78% Queensberry**
Russel St
☎ (0225) 447928, telex 445628, fax: (0225) 446065
22 bedrooms; double B&B £84–£142
Credit cards 1 2 3 4

**★★★ 66% Lansdown Grove**
☎ (0225) 315891, fax: (0225) 448092
45 bedrooms; double B&B £90–£105
Credit cards 1 2 3 4 5

**★★★ 64% Bath Widcombe Basin**
☎ (0225) 338855, telex 445876, fax: (0225) 428941
96 bedrooms; double room £88–£94 (room only)
Credit cards 1 2 3 5

**★★★ 64% Francis Queen Square**
☎ (0225) 424257, telex 449162, fax: (0225) 319715
94 bedrooms; double room £100 (room only)
Credit cards 1 2 3 5

**★★★ 63% Compass**
North Pde
☎ (0225) 461603, telex 44812, fax: (0225) 447758
54 bedrooms; double B&B £79
Credit card 1 2 3 5

**★★★ 60% Pratts**
South Pde
☎ (0225) 460441, telex 444827, fax: (0225) 448807
48 bedrooms; double B&B £60–£75
Credit cards 1 2 3 5

**★★ 72% Duke's**
Great Pulteney St
☎ (0225) 463512, telex 449227, fax: (0225) 483733
21 bedrooms; double B&B £60–£70
Credit Cards 1 2 3

**★★ 64% Bailbrook Lodge**
35/37 London Rd West
☎ (0225) 859090
13 bedrooms; double B&B £45–£70
Credit cards 1 2 3 5

**★★ 62% Haringtons**
9/10 Queen St
☎ (0225) 461728
12 bedrooms; double B&B £44–£53
Credit cards 1 2 3

**★★ 60% Georges**
2-3 South Pde
☎ (0225) 464923, fax: (0225) 425471
19 bedrooms
Credit cards 1 2 3 5

### Around Bath

**★★★❀❀ 75% Woolley Grange**
Woolley Green, Bradford on Avon
☎ (0225) 864705, fax: (0225) 864059
14 bedrooms; double B&B £94–£175
Credit cards 1 2 3 5

**★★★★❀❀ 78% Manor House**
Castle Combe
☎ (0249) 782206, telex 449931, fax: (0249) 782159
12 bedrooms; double room £115–£250 (room only)
Credit cards 1 2 3 5

**★★❀ 73% Chelwood House**
Chelwood
☎ (0761) 490730,
11 bedrooms; double B&B £75–£99
Credit cards 1 3 5

**★★★❀ 66% Rudloe Park**
Leafy Ln, Corsham
☎ (0225) 810555, fax: (0225) 811412
11 bedrooms; double B&B £70–£100
Credit cards 1 2 3 4 5

**★★ 65% Methuen Arms**
High St, Corsham
☎ (0249) 714867, fax: (0249) 712004
19 bedrooms; double B&B £59–£75
Credit cards 1 3

**★★ 67% Country Ways**
Marsh Lane,
Farrington Gurney
☎ (0761) 452449, fax: (0761) 453360
6 bedrooms; double B&B £55–£65
Credit cards 1 3 5

**★★ 64% White Hart Inn**
Castle Combe, Ford
☎ (0249) 782213, fax: (0249) 783075
3 bedrooms; double B&B £59
Credit cards 1 2 3

## WHERE TO STAY

### ★★★🏵🏵 80% Homewood Park
Hinton Charterhouse
☎ (0225) 723731, fax: (0225) 723820
15 bedrooms; double B&B £105-£155
Credit cards 1 2 3 4 5

### ★★★🏵 67% Cliffe
Crowe Hill, Limpley Stoke
☎ (0225) 723226, fax: (0225) 723871
11 bedrooms; double B&B £87-£107
Credit cards 1 2 3 5

### ★★★🏵🏵 74% Beechfield House
Benacre, Melksham
☎ (0225) 703700, fax: (0225) 790118
20 bedrooms; double B&B £99-£112 (room only)
Credit cards 1 2 3 5

### ★★ 66% Shaw Country
Bath Rd, Shaw, Melksham
☎ (0225) 702836 & 790321, fax: (0225) 790275
13 bedrooms; double B&B £59-£78
Credit cards 1 2 3

### ★★ 63% Conigre Farm
Semington Rd, Melksham
☎ (0225) 702229
4 bedrooms
Credit cards 1 3

### ★★ 55% Kings Arms
Market Place, Melksham
☎ (0225) 707272, fax: (0225) 702085
14 bedrooms; double B&B £60
Credit cards 1 2 3 5

### ★★★ 68% Centurion
Charlton Ln, Midsomer Norton
☎ (0761) 417711, fax: (0761) 418357
44 bedrooms; double B&B £55-£77
Credit cards 1 2 3 5

### ★★ 64% Compass Inn
Tormarton
☎ (0454) 218242 & 218577, fax: (0454) 218741
31 bedrooms; double B&B £64.95-£82.50
Credit cards 1 2 3 5

## BED AND BREAKFAST

### Arden Hotel
73 Great Pulteney St
☎ (0225) 466601 & 330039, fax: (0225) 465548
Very elegant Grade I listed building, classically furnished and richly decorated.
10 bedrooms
Credit cards 1 3

### Arney
99 Wells Rd
☎ (0225) 310020
Small Victorian terraced house offering modest, value-for-money bed and breakfast accommodation.
7 bedrooms; double B&B £29-£32.01

### Ashley Villa Hotel
26 Newbridge Rd
☎ (0225) 421683 & 428887
Friendly small hotel with good range of modern facilities
14 bedrooms; double B&B £45-£59

### Astor House
14 Oldfield Rd
☎ (0225) 429134
Simple and functional good value-for-money accommodation in convenient location.
7 bedrooms; double B&B £30-£36

### The Bath Tasburgh
Warminster Rd, Bathampton
☎ (0225) 425096
Friendly hosts, individually styled and decorated rooms with superb views a mile from city centre.
13 bedrooms; double B&B £44-£68
Credit cards 1 2 3 5

### Bloomfield House
146 Bloomfield Rd
☎ (0225) 420105
Stylishly decorated Georgian house with period furniture on southern outskirts of Bath.
5 bedrooms; double B&B £35-£65
Credit cards 1 3

### Brocks
32 Brock St
☎ (0225) 338374
Bright and comfortable bedrooms, all individually decorated with modern facilities.
8 bedrooms; double B&B £40-£50

### Brompton House Hotel
St John's Rd
☎ (0225) 420972 & 48423
Renovated Victorian house providing modern standards of comfort in city-centre location.
19 bedrooms; double B&B £56-£69
Credit cards 1 3

### Carfax Hotel
Great Pulteney St
☎ (0225) 463089, fax: (0225) 443257
Upgraded bedrooms, bright comfortable public rooms on famous Bath street.
39 bedrooms; double B&B £40-£68
Credit cards 1 2 3

### Cedar Lodge
13 Lambridge, London Rd
☎ (0225) 423468
Comfortable and retaining much original character, including fine interior architecture.
3 bedrooms

### Cheriton House
9 Upper Oldfield Park
☎ (0225) 429862
Well equipped bedrooms and bathrooms with
some fine views over the city.
9 bedrooms; double B&B £47-£58
Credit cards 1 3

### Cranleigh
159 Newbridge Hill
☎ (0225) 310197
Spotlessly clean, airy and individually styled rooms in a friendly, family-run establishment.
4 bedrooms; double B&B £48-£58
Credit cards 1 3

### Devonshire House
143 Wellsway
☎ (0225) 312495
On the outskirts of the city with comfortable, individually styled bedrooms.
3 bedrooms; double B&B £38-£40
Credit cards 1 3

### Dorian House
1 Upper Oldfield Park
☎ (0225) 426336
In an elevated position off the A367, with fine views over city and well equipped bedrooms.
7 bedrooms; double B&B £49-£72
Credit cards 1 2 3 5

### Dorset Villa
14 Newbridge Rd
☎ (0225) 425975
Conveniently positioned on the main A4 to the west of the city; friendly atmosphere; comfortable bedrooms.
7 bedrooms; double B&B £38-£45
Credit cards 1 3

## WHERE TO STAY

### Eagle House Church
St, Bathford
☎ (0225) 859946
Modern well equipped bedrooms in very
attractive listed Georgian house.
6 bedrooms; double B&B £40-£62.50

### Edgar Hotel
64 Gt Pulteney St
☎ (0225) 420619
Comfortable bed and breakfast
accommodation close to city centre.
14 bedrooms: double B&B £35-£55
Credit cards 1 3

### Gainsborough Hotel
Weston Ln
☎ (0225) 3112380
16 bedrooms: double B&B £48-£60
Credit cards 1 2 3

### Grove Lodge
11 Lambridge, London Rd
☎ (0225) 310860
Regency building situated on A4 London
Road a mile from city centre.
8 bedrooms: double B&B £38-£45

### Haydon House
9 Bloomfield Park
☎ (0225) 444919, fax: (0225) 469020
Wealth of hospitality, elegance and comfort
offered within a building full of character
and charm.
4 bedrooms; double B&B £52-£65
Credit cards 1 3

### Highways House
143 Wells Rd
☎ (0225) 421238, fax: (0225) 481169
Comfortable and hospitable hotel.
7 bedrooms; double B&B £48-£58
Credit cards 1 3

### Holly Lodge
8 Upper Oldfield Park
☎ (0225) 424042, fax: (0225) 481138
Exceptionally comfortable, beautifully
decorated bedrooms in hospitable
establishment.
6 bedrooms; double B&B £65-£85
Credit cards 1 2 3 5

### Kennard Hotel
11 Henrietta St
☎ (0225) 310472, fax: (0225) 442456
Situated close to city centre, period house
offering bright, attractive bedrooms.
12 bedrooms; double B&B £40-£55

### Laura Place Hotel
3 Laura Place, Great Pulteney St
☎ (0225) 463815
Very convenient location, tastefully
decorated with some very large and well
equipped bedrooms.
8 bedrooms; double B&B £50-£80
Credit cards 1 2 3

### Leighton House
139 Wells Rd
☎ (0225) 314769
Fine Victorian residence in elevated
position, with high quality bedrooms.
8 bedrooms; double B&B £54-£62
Credit cards 1 3

### Meadowland
36 Bloomfield Park
☎ (0225) 311079
Bright and clean hotel in secluded grounds
on outskirts of city centre; charming
bedrooms.
3 bedrooms; double B&B £45-£55
Credit cards 1 3

### Monkshill
Shaft Rd, Monkton Combe
☎ (0225) 833028
On outskirts of city with superb views,
offering cosy, stylish bedrooms.
3 bedrooms; double B&B £40-£50

### Oldfields
102 Wells Rd
☎ (0225) 444471
Hospitable, friendly atmosphere with richly
furnished and equipped bedrooms.
14 bedrooms; double B&B £50-£58
Credit cards 1 3

### Old School House
Church St, Bathford
☎ (0225) 859593
Cosy, individually styled, well equipped
bedrooms and very welcoming, hospitable
hosts.
4 bedrooms; double B&B £59-£64
Credit cards 1 3

### Paradise House Hotel
Holloway
☎ (0225) 317723, fax: (0225) 482005
Beautiful Georgian house with excellent
view of city and particulary comfortable
bedrooms.
10 bedrooms; double B&B £48-£68
Credit cards 1 2 3

### Somerset House Hotel & Restaurant
35 Bathwick Hill
☎ (0225) 466451
Brightly decorated bedrooms in individual
styles in this listed property.
10 bedrooms
Credit cards 1 2 3

### Underhill Lodge
Warminster Rd,
Bathampton
☎ (0225) 464992
High standards provided with abundance of
personal touches throughout.
4 bedrooms
Credit cards 1 3

## Around Bath

### Bradford Old Windmill
4 Masons Ln, Bradford on Avon
☎ (0225) 866842
Unique converted windmill with wealth of
character and well equipped bedrooms.
4 bedrooms; double B&B £45-49

### Wildbrook Grange
Trowbridge Rd,
Bradford on Avon
☎ (02216) 3173 & 2899, fax: (02216)
2890
Set in rolling countryside, with very
comfortable, attractively furnished
bedrooms.
4 bedrooms; double B&B £49-£79

### Streets Hotel
The Street, Farmborough
☎ (0761) 471452
Set in picturesque village; well furnished
rooms with good modern facilities.
3 bedrooms; double B&B £42-£62
Credit cards 1 2 3

### Green Lane House
Green Ln, Hinton Charterhouse
☎ (0225) 723631
Cosy, comfortable guesthouse.
4 bedrooms; double B&B £34-£47
Credit cards 1 2 3

### Grasmere Court Hotel
22/24 Bath Rd
Keynsham
☎ (0272) 862662, fax: (0272) 862762
Situated on the edge of the town this hotel
offers well equipped bedrooms.
16 bedrooms; double B&B £48-£65
Credit cards 1 3

## WHERE TO STAY

### Wansdyke Cottage
Crosspost Ln, Marksbury
☎ (0225) 873674
Situated on A39/B3116 crossroads south of
Bath, this 18th-century stone cottage has
comfortable bedrooms.
4 bedrooms; double B&B £30-£40

### Longhope
9 Beanacre Rd, Melksham
☎ (0225) 706737
Attractive Victorian Bath stone house,
popular with business people and tourists
alike.
7 bedrooms; double B&B £30-£35

### Regency Hotel Restaurant
10-12 Spa Rd, Melksham
☎ (0225) 702971, fax: (0454) 776445
Well equipped, comfortable bedrooms,
bright public areas and a restaurant open to
non-smokers.
10 bedrooms; double B&B £36-£45
Credit cards 1 2 3 5

### Fosse Farmhouse Country Hotel
Nettleton Shrub
☎ (0249) 782286
Attractive 18th-century farmhouse with lots
of character, close to many areas of interest.
2 bedrooms
Credit cards 1 2 3

### Old Malt House Hotel & Licensed Restaurant
Radford, Timsbury
☎ (0761) 470106
Renovated former malting house. The
Horler family also operate a shire horse
stud adjacent to the house.
10 bedrooms; double B&B £33-£60
Credit cards 1 2 3 5

## CAMPSITES

### ►►► Piccadilly Caravan Site
Folly Ln, Chippenham
☎ (0249) 730260
East of Bath, 4 miles south of Chippenham;
pitch price from £6 per night.

## WHERE TO EAT

### RESTAURANTS

### 🏵 Popjoys Beau
Nash House, Sawclose
☎ (0225) 460494, fax: (0225) 446319
Mainly classical dishes with firm flavours
and good portions.
Lunch: 12-2; from £11.95
Dinner: 7-10.30; from £20 and à la carte

### 🏵🏵 Woods
9-13 Alfred St
☎ (0225) 314812
Excellently balanced flavours and generous
portions are offered in this popular local
venue.
Lunch: 12-2.30; from £12 and à la carte
Dinner: 7-10.30; from £18.95 and à la carte

### 🏵 Garlands
7 Edgar Buildings, George St
☎ (0225) 442283
Enjoyable, light cooking in intimate
surroundings.
Lunch: 12-2.15; from £11.75 and à la carte
Dinner: 7-10.30; from £17.50 and à la carte

### Around Bath

### 🏵 Box House
Box, Bath
☎ (0225) 744447, telex 831476,
fax: (0225) 743971
Enjoyable food is available at this former
vicarage.
Lunch: 12-2.30
Dinner 7-10.30

## PUBS

### The Crown
2 Bathford Hill, Bathford
☎ (0225) 852297
Large, elegant building on edge of town
with relaxed and friendly atmosphere.
Children's room available with magician on
Sunday lunchtimes. Ushers, Courage and
Bass beer on draught; stylishly presented
and generous portions of bar food. Garden
and terrace at rear.
Open: 11am-2.30, 6.30-11pm; Sundays
12-3pm, 7-10.30pm; closed Monday
lunchtimes, except Bank Holidays
Bar food: as opening hours, but not Sunday
evening

### The Crown
Kelston, near Bath
☎ (0225) 423032
Sixteenth-century roadside inn; candlelit
bars with dark wood and flagstone floors.
Smiles, Butcombe, Wadworth, Bass and
Guinness on draught; good range of
blended whiskies; Bar meals and separate
restaurant at weekends. Children are only
permitted in the garden.
Open 11.30am-3pm, 5-11pm; Sunday 12-
3pm, 7-10.30pm
Bar food: 12-2pm Monday to Saturday only
Restaurant: 7.30-9pm Thursday, Friday and
Saturday only

# Beverley

*There is a fine history behind this attractive venue - its track was initially laid out towards the end of the 17th century - and the site still possesses plenty of old-fashioned charm.*

The stands may be slightly outdated, but they are the subject of on-going modernisation and it would in any case be a great shame if the course were to lose its individual character.

The right-handed track is a galloping, roughly oval circuit. There is a separate chute for five-furlong races (horses drawn high have a distinct advantage) and this provides a stiff test of stamina for sprinters as the home straight rises steadily throughout. Lots of close finishes occur as a result and many a winner has triumphed with a late flourish.

### FURTHER INFORMATION

Beverley Race Company Ltd
The Grandstand, York Road, Beverley,
East Yorkshire HU17 8QZ
☎ (0482) 867488

### LOCATION AND HOW TO GET THERE

The course is signposted from the M62.
**Nearest Railway Station:** Beverley; there is a connecting bus service to the course on racedays.

---

### ADMISSION

All classes of day ticket give access to full betting facilities, including Tote.

**Day Tickets:**
Accompanied children under 16 admitted free.

CLUB £12, £8 junior (16-21 years) – access to bar, restaurant, boxes

TATTERSALLS £7 – access to bar and restaurant

SILVER RING £2.50 – access to bar and restaurant

NUMBER 3 RING £1.50

**Annual Membership:**
£70 single, £110 associate, £40 junior (under 25)

**Parking:** picnic parking £2 per car, plus £1.50 per person

### COURSE FACILITIES

**Banks:**
there are no banks or cashpoint facilities on the course.

**For families:**
picnic area with refreshment kiosk and toilets; children's play area

---

## CALENDAR OF EVENTS

**April 8-9** – flat
**April 21** – flat
**May 6-7** – flat
**May 17** – flat
**June 1-2** – flat; evening meeting on Wednesday
**June 8** – flat
**July 1-2** – flat; evening meeting on Friday

**July 18-19** – flat; evening meeting on Monday
**July 26** – flat
**August 10-11** – flat
**September 14-15** – flat

---

### WHERE TO STAY

**HOTELS**

**★★★ 66% Beverley Arms**
North Bar Within
☎ (0482) 869241, fax: (0482) 870907
57 bedrooms; double room from £85 (room only)
Credit cards 1 2 3 5

**★★★ 63% Tickton Grange**
Tickton
☎ (0964) 543666, fax: (0964) 542556
16 bedrooms; double B&B £33.50-£59.50
Credit cards 1 2 3 5

**★★ 71% Lairgate**
30-34 Lairgate
☎ (0482) 882141
23 bedrooms
Credit cards 1 3

## WHERE TO STAY

### Around Beverley

**★★ 67% Burton Lodge**
Brandesburton
☎ (0964) 542847, fax: (0964) 542847
8 Bedrooms; double B&B £38-£42
Credit cards 1 3

**★★★ 65% Bell**
46 Market Place, Great Driffield
☎ (0377) 46661, telex 52341, fax: (0377) 43228
14 Bedrooms; double B&B from £91
Credit cards 1 2 3 5

**★★ 57% Wold House Country**
Nafferton, Great Driffield
☎ (0377) 44242
10 bedrooms; double B&B £48-£60
Credit cards 1 3

**★★★★ 61% Forte Crest**
Castle St, Hull
☎ (0482) 225221, telex 592777, fax: (0482) 213299
99 bedrooms; double room £49.50-£80
(room only)
Credit cards 1 2 3 5

**★★★ 60% Valiant House**
11 Anlaby Rd, Hull
☎ (0482) 23299, fax: (0482) 214730
59 bedrooms; double B&B £45-£65
Credit cards 1 2 3 5

**★★ 64% Pearson Park**
Pearson Park, Hull
☎ (0482) 43043, fax: (0482) 447679
32 bedrooms; double B&B £60
Credit cards 1 2 3 5

**★★ 62% Waterfront**
Dagger Ln, Hull
☎ (0482) 227222
30 bedrooms; double bedroom £50-£80
(room only)
Credit card 1 2 3

**Campanile**
Beverley Rd, Freetown Way, Hull
☎ (0482) 25530, telex 592840, fax: (0482) 587538
50 bedrooms
Credit cards 1 2 3

**★★★ 65% Rowley Manor**
Rowley Rd, Little Weighton
☎ (0482) 848248, fax: (0482) 849900
16 bedrooms; double B&B £65-£80
Credit cards 1 2 3 5

**★★★ 73% Londesborough Arms**
44 High St, Market Weighton
☎ (0430) 872214
15 bedrooms; double B&B £80-£120
Credit cards 1 2 3

**★★★ 64% Forte Posthouse Hull**
Ferriby High Rd
☎ (0482) 645212, fax: (0482) 643332
97 bedrooms; double room £39.50-£49.50
(room only)
Credit cards 1 2 3 5

**★★★ Grange Park**
Main St, Willerby
☎ (0482) 656488, fax: (0482) 655848
109 bedrooms
Credit cards 1 2 3 5

**★★★ 70% Willerby Manor**
Well Ln, Willerby
☎ (0482) 652616, telex 592629, fax: (0482) 653901
36 bedrooms; double room £74.50-£82
(room only)
Credit cards 1 2 3

### BED AND BREAKFAST

**Earlsmere Hotel**
76/78 Sunny Bank, Spring Bank West, Hull
☎ (0482) 41977, telex 592729, fax: (0482) 473714
15 bedrooms; double B&B £41.12-£47
Credit cards 1 3

### CAMPSITES

**►► Silver Birches Tourist Park**
Waterside Rd, Barton upon Humber
☎ (0652) 32509
South of Beverley, close to the Humber Bridge; pitch price from £4.50 per night.

**►► Dacre Lakeside Park**
Brandesburton
☎ (0964) 543704
Northeast of Beverley; pitch price from £6.10 per night.

## WHERE TO EAT

### RESTAURANTS

**⚜ Cerutti's**
10 Nelson St, Hull
☎ (0482) 28501, fax: (0482) 587597
Fresh fish, competently cooked, in a pleasant waterside setting. Lunch: 12-2, Dinner: 7-9.30

### PUBS

**White Horse**
Hengate, Beverley
☎ (0482) 861973
Grade I listed building dating back to the 16th century with unspoilt interior. A Samuel Smiths pub serving tasty and substantial bar meals. Children are allowed in any of the rooms, except the one with the bar in. Open: 11am-11pm Monday to Saturday; 12-2 and 7-10.30 Sunday
Bar food: 12-2, 6-9 but not Sunday and Monday evenings

**Light Dragoon**
34 Main St, Etton
☎ (0430) 810282
Pleasant, comfortable pub with friendly atmosphere and small garden with swings and slide. A William Younger pub, and one of the few in the area open on Monday lunchtimes for food. Children are permitted in the pub. Open: 12-2.30pm, 7-11pm; Sunday 12-3pm, 7-10.30pm
Bar food: 12-2pm, 7-9.30pm

**Half Moon**
16 Main St, Skidby
☎ (0482) 843403
A John Smiths pub dating in parts back to the 17th century. Popular range of bar meals are plentiful and good value for money. Children are permitted in the pub and there is a garden with climbing nets, slides etc. Open: 11am-11pm; Sunday 12-2.30pm, 7-10.30pm
Bar food: 12-2pm, 7-10pm, except Sunday lunchtime

**Pipe and Glass**
West End, South Dalton
☎ (0430) 810246
Lovely old country inn with open fires and a pleasant garden. Beers include John Smiths, Ruddles, Castle Eden, Beamish and Guinness and the bar menu is original and well presented. Children are permitted in the restaurant and one of the bars. Open: 11.30am-2.30pm, 7-11pm, but closed Monday
Bar meals: Tuesday to Saturday lunchtimes
Restaurant: Tuesday to Saturday evenings; Carvery Sunday lunch

# Brighton

*The unique feature of this popular seaside course is its U-shaped track, one of the very few in Britain not to form a complete circuit. Consequently the start of long-distance contests (the furthest is 1.5 miles) is barely visible from the stands and much of the action will be missed without a good pair of binoculars (they can be hired).*

The finish is also interesting, because jockeys have to by pretty smart at pulling up as the course comes to an abrupt halt. In many other ways, the track resembled Epsom, with its long downhill stretch round a sharp left-hand bend before the ground rises again slightly in the final furlong. Look out for course specialists who have shown past ability at handling the unusual contours. With the Channel clearly visible in the background, except on the rare occasions when the sea mists roll in and obliterate everything, this is a very attractive setting. Nearly 20 fixtures are scheduled, with the three-day August meeting usually providing the best racing. Finding a seat in the stands is no problem, and for an exciting head-on view, try the open roof-top opposite the winning post.

## FURTHER INFORMATION

Brighton Raceground Lessees
Town Hall, Brighton, Sussex BN1 1JA
☎ (0273) 682912

## LOCATION AND HOW TO GET THERE

The course is on the hill above Brighton Marina. It is well signposted from both the A23 London-Brighton road and the A27.
**Nearest Railway Station:** Brighton; there is a connecting bus service to the course on racedays.

## ADMISSION

All classes of day ticket give access to full betting facilities, including Tote.

**Day Tickets:**
Accompanied children under 16 are admitted free to all enclosures, except Club.

CLUB £11 – access to restaurant, boxes, private rooms

TATTERSALLS £8 – access to snack bar, boxes, private rooms

SILVER RING £3.50 – access to bar and snack bar

**Annual membership:** £100

## COURSE FACILITIES

**Banks:**
there are no banks or cashpoint facilities on the course.

**For families:**
picnic area with refreshment kiosk and toilets; family room

## CALENDAR OF EVENTS

| | | |
|---|---|---|
| April 7 | June 13 | August 23-24 |
| April 18 | June 21 | September 21 |
| May 4 | June 30 | September 27 |
| May 12 | July 21 | |
| May 25-26 | August 2-4 | |

*36*

## WHERE TO STAY

### HOTELS

**★★★ 62% Norfolk Resort**
149 Kings Rd
☎ (0273)738201, fax: (0273) 821752
121 bedrooms; double room £66-£76
(room only)
Credit cards 1 2 3 5

**★★★ 61% Old Ship**
Kings Rd
☎ (0273) 29001, telex 877101,
fax: (0273) 820718
152 bedrooms; double B&B £75-£125
Credit cards 1 2 3 5

**★★★ 60% Excelsior**
205-209 Kingsway
☎ (0273) 773991, fax: (0273) 746363
58 bedrooms
Credit cards 1 2 3 5

**★★★ 58% Imperial First Av**
☎ (0273) 777320, fax: (0273) 777310
76 bedrooms; double B&B £80
Credit cards 1 2 3 5

**★★★ 58% Sackville**
Kingsway
☎ (0273) 736292, telex 877830,
fax: (0273) 205759
45 bedrooms

**★★★ 56% Courtlands**
19-27 The Drive
☎ (0273) 731055, fax: (0273) 28295
53 bedrooms; double B&B £60-£78
Credit cards 1 2 3 5

**★★❀❀ 75% Topps,**
17 Regency Square
☎ (0273) 729334, fax: (0273) 203679
14 bedrooms; double B&B £64-£99
Credit cards 1 2 3 4 5

**★★ 58% St Catherines Lodge**
Seafront, Kingsway
☎ (0273) 778181, fax: (0273) 774949
50 bedrooms; double B&B £50-£65
Credit cards 1 2 3 5

### Around Brighton

**★★❀ 70% Tottington Manor**
Edburton, Henfield
☎ (0903) 815757, fax: (0903) 879331
6 bedrooms
Credit cards 1 2 3 5

**★★ 68% Sussex Pad**
Old Shoreham Rd, Lancing
☎ (0273) 454647, fax: (0273) 453010
19 bedrooms
Credit cards 1 2 3 4 5

**★★★ 54% Shelleys**
High St, Lewes
☎ (0273) 472361, fax: (0273) 483152
21 bedrooms; double room £99-£120
(room only)
Credit cards 1 2 3 5

**★★ 58% White Hart**
55 High St, Lewes
☎ (0273) 474676 & 476694
telex 878468, fax: (0273) 476695
19 bedrooms
Credit cards 1 2 3 5

### BED AND BREAKFAST

**Adelaide Hotel**
51 Regency Square
☎ (0273) 205286, fax: (0273) 220904
Freshly decorated and tastefully furnished
bedrooms; the proprietors are welcoming.
12 bedrooms; double B&B £59-£75
Credit cards 1 2 3 5

**Allendale Hotel**
3 New Steine
☎ (0273) 675436, fax: (0273) 602603
Charming proprietors and smart, modern
bedrooms, exceptionally well equipped.
13 bedrooms; double B&B £54-£66
Credit cards 1 2 3 5

**Ambassador Hotel**
22 New Steine
☎ (0273) 676869, fax: (0273) 689988
Family-run hotel offers of a range of neat,
well equipped bedrooms.
9 bedrooms; double B&B £42-£57
Credit cards 1 2 3 5

**Arlanda Hotel**
20 New Steine,
☎ (0273) 699300, fax: (0273) 600930
Regency-style house offers a mixed style of
accommodation.
12 bedrooms; double B&B £38-£66
Credit cards 1 2 3 5

**Ascott House Hotel**
21 New Steine, Marine Pde
☎ (0273) 688085, fax: (0273) 623733
Small personally run hotel close to the
seafront, offering bright, freshly decorated
bedrooms
12 bedrooms; double B&B £50-£70
Credit cards 1 2 3 5

**Bannings**
14 Upper Rock Gardens, Kemptown
☎ (0273) 681403
Elegant town house with comfortable
bedrooms and offering a hearty breakfast.
6 bedrooms; double B&B £36-£44
Credit cards 1 2 3 5

**Claremont House**
Second Av
☎ (0273) 735161
Friendly and informal atmosphere;
bedrooms furnished to a high standard.
12 bedrooms
Credit cards 1 2 3 5

**George IV Hotel**
34 Regency Square
☎ (0273) 21196
Overlooking the gardens and sea, this hotel
provides smart bedrooms and every
conceivable convenience
8 bedrooms; double B&B £45-£65
Credit cards 1 2 3 5

**Gullivers**
10 New Steine
☎ (0273) 695415, fax: (0252) 372774
Attractive bedrooms feature in this Regency
residence close to the seafront.
9 bedrooms; double B&B £42-£54
Credit cards 1 2 3 5

**New Steine Hotel**
12a New Steine, Marine Pde
☎ (0273) 681546
Smart, comfortable accommodation.
11 bedrooms; double B&B £39-£42

## WHERE TO STAY

### Pier View Hotel
28 New Steine
☎ (0273) 605310, fax: (0273) 688604
The King family create a warm welcome here; freshly decorated rooms.
10 bedrooms; double B&B £39–£58
Credit cards 1 2 3

### Trouville Hotel
11 New Steine, Marine Pde
☎ (0273) 697384
Seafront, family-run guesthouse offering freshly decorated bedrooms.
9 bedrooms; double B&B £32–£46
Credit cards 1 2 3

### Twenty One
21 Charlotte St, Marine Pde
☎ (0273) 686450
Exceptionally well equipped bedrooms, each with its own charm.
6 bedrooms; double B&B £46–£68
Credit cards 1 2 3

### Around Brighton

### Harbour View
22 Mount Rd, Newhaven
☎ (0273) 512096
Situated on eastern edge of town, this guesthouse has a relaxed atmosphere
3 bedrooms

### Newhaven Marina Yacht Club Hotel
Fort Gate, Fort Rd, Newhaven
☎ (0273) 513976, fax: (0273) 517990
Fresh bedrooms with modern furniture
7 bedrooms; double B&B £42–£50
Credit cards 1 3

### Braemar House
Steyning Rd, Rottingdean
☎ (0273) 304263
Family run guesthouse offering simple but well kept accommodation.
16 bedrooms; double B&B £28–£30

### Corner House
Steyning Rd, Rottingdean
☎ (0273) 304533
Friendly proprietor and simple functional bedrooms.
6 bedrooms; double B&B £29–£30

### Avondale Hotel
4-5 Avondale Rd
☎ (0323) 890008
A family run hotel, close to town centre.
16 bedrooms; double B&B £30–£40
Credit cards 1 3

### CAMPSITES

### ►►► Downsview Caravan Park
Bramlands Ln, Woodmancote, Henfield
☎ (0273) 492801
North of Brighton; pitch price from £8.25 per night

### Harwoods Farm
West End Lane, Henfield
☎ (0273) 492820.
Unspoilt 'Venture' site for tents only, down narrow lane; pitch price from £3.50

### Gallops Farm
Streat Ln, Streat, Plumpton
☎ (0273) 890387
'Venture' site to the north of Brighton

## WHERE TO EAT

### RESTAURANTS

### ❀❀ Langan's Bistro
1 Paston Place
☎ (0273) 606933
Down to earth and flavoursome cooking in a relaxed friendly atosphere.
Lunch 12-2.15; from £15.70 and à la carte
Dinner 7-10.15; from £22 and à la carte

### ❀ Le Grandgousier
15 Western St
☎ (0273) 772005
Small cosy restaurant serving simple, good value bistro-style food.
Lunch: 12-1.30 £11.95
Dinner: 7-9.30 £11.95

### ❀❀ Whyte's
33 Western St, Brighton
☎ (0273 776618
Cosy, small restaurant near the seafront, serving sound, honest cooking in French and English styles.
Lunch: from £13.95
Dinner: 7-10; from £13.95–£16.95

### PUBS

### The Juggs
The Street, Kingston, nr Lewes
☎ (0273) 472523
Traditional Kentish-style building in attractive garden with a good play area.
Fairly standard pub meals; draught beers include Harveys and King & Barnes; wine list features around 30 bottles. Children are welcome anywhere in the pub and there is a children's menu.
Open: 10am-2.30pm, 6-10.45pm (11pm Friday and Saturday); Sunday 12-2.30pm, 7-10.45pm
Bar food: 12-2pm, 6-9.30pm; 7-9.30pm on Sunday
Restaurant: times as bar food

# Carlisle

*This friendly Cumbrian racecourse is situated between the Lake District and the Borders and is therefore an ideal place to visit for people wishing to explore the colourful countryside of the surrounding areas.*

Access is easy and a warm welcome is sure to be extended to any newcomers to the sport. Facilities are good, with a fair selection of bars and restaurants to choose from, and both the admission charges and catering prices are very reasonable.

There are 20 fixtures held here every year under both codes, with the highlight being the June meeting which features the Carlisle Bell and the Cumberland Plate, the two most important contests in the calendar. The roughly pear-shaped, undulating track provides an extremely stiff test of stamina and the general consensus among racing professionals is that it is the most demanding course in the north. The final home stretch rises steeply uphill and only the most resolute of gallopers are able to overcome this severe climb in heavy ground.

## FURTHER INFORMATION

Carlisle Racecourse Co Ltd
Grandstand Office, The Racecourse, Blackwell, Carlisle, Cumbria CA2 4TS
☎ (0228) 22973

## LOCATION AND HOW TO GET THERE

Carlisle racecourse is two miles south of the city at Blackwell. From M6 junction 42, follow signs on Dalston Road.
**Nearest Railway Station:** Carlisle; the number 66 bus runs between the station and the racecourse on racedays.

## ADMISSION

All classes of day ticket give access to full betting facilities, including Tote.

**Day Tickets:**
MEMBERS £10, £12 on Saturdays and Bank Holidays – access to members' stand with seating, bars and restaurants

TATTERSALLS £6, pensioners £3, accompanied children under 16 free – access to private rooms, bars and cafeteria

TRACKSIDE PARKING AND PICNIC AREA
£3, £5 Saturdays and Bank Holidays

**Annual membership:**
£75 single, £110 double, junior membership (under 21) £50 – includes admission to certain other racecourses on certain days in the year.

## COURSE FACILITIES

**Banks:**
There are no banks or cashpoint facilities on the course.

**For families:**
picnic area with toilet; children's play area and baby changing facilities on busy days only; lost children centre.

## CALENDAR OF EVENTS

**April 2** – jumping
**April 4** – jumping
**April 22** – flat
**May 5-6** – flat
**May 26** – flat
**June 22-23** – flat; includes Carlisle Bell and Cumberland Plate
**July 22** – flat

**August 17** – flat
**September 24** – jumping
**October 7** – jumping; Club Visitors Day
**October 10** – jumping
**November 7** – jumping
**November 24** – jumping
**December 29** – jumping

## WHERE TO STAY

### HOTELS

**★★★ 66% Cumbria Park**
32 Scotland Rd, Stanwix
☎ (0228) 22887, fax: (0228) 514796
49 bedrooms; double B&B £64–£110
Credit cards 1 2 3

**★★★ 64% Cumbrian**
Court Square
☎ (0228) 31951, telex 64287,
fax: (0228) 47799
70 bedrooms
Credit cards 1 2 3 5

**★★★ 63% Central Plaza**
Victoria Viaduct
☎ (0228) 20256, fax: (0228) 514657
84 bedrooms; double B&B £60–£75
Credit cards 1 2 3 5

**★★★ 62% Forte Posthouse**
Parkhouse Rd, Kingstown
☎ (0228) 31201, fax: (0228) 43178
93 bedrooms
Credit cards 1 2 3 4 5

**★★★ 59% Swallow Hilltop**
London Rd
☎ (0228) 29255, telex 64292,
fax: (0228) 25238
92 bedrooms; double B&B £72.50–£85

**★★ 65% County**
9 Botchergate
☎ (0228) 31316, fax: (0228) 515456
84 bedrooms; double room £39.95–£59.95
(room only)
Credit cards 1 2 3 5

**★★ 59% Pinegrove**
262 London Rd
☎ (0228) 24828, fax: (0228) 810941
28 bedrooms; double B&B £41–£51
Credit cards 1 3

**★★ 57% Woodlands**
264/266 London Rd
☎ (0228) 45643
15 bedrooms
Credit cards 1 2 3 5

**★ 58% Vallum House Garden**
Burgh Rd
☎ (0228) 21860
9 bedrooms
Credit cards 1 3

### Around Carlisle

**★★ 68% Solway Lodge**
Annan Rd, Gretna
☎ (0461) 38266, fax: (0461) 37791
3 bedrooms; double B&B £49–£75
Credit cards 1 2 3 5

**★★ 63% Gretna Chase**
Gretna
☎ (0461) 37517
9 bedrooms; double B&B £48–£80
Credit cards 1 2 3 5

**Forte Travelodge**
Gretna
☎ (0461) 37566, Central Reservations:
(0800) 850950
41 bedrooms; double room £31.95 (room
only)
Credit cards 1 2 3

**★★ 59% Wheyrigg Hall**
Wheyrigg, Wigton
☎ (06973) 61242, fax: (06973) 61020
10 bedrooms; double B&B £46
Credit card 1 2 3

**★★ 56% Greenhill Lodge**
Red Dial
☎ (06973) 43304
7 bedrooms; double B&B £45
Credit cards 1 3

### BED AND BREAKFAST

**Angus Hotel**
14 Scotland Rd
☎ (0228) 23546
Pleasant well run guesthouse offering
simple, well maintained accommodation.
12 bedrooms; double B&B £31–£42
Credit cards 1 3

**Crossroads House**
Brisco
☎ (0228) 28994
Modern detached house set in open
countryside.
5 bedrooms; double B&B from £32

**East View**
110 Warwick Rd
☎ (0228) 22112
Friendly, family owned and run guesthouse.
9 bedrooms; double B&B £25–£32

**Kenilworth Hotel**
34 Lazonby Ter
☎ (0228) 26179
A comfortable terraced Victorian house
offering good value for money.
6 bedrooms; double B&B £24–£26

**Kingstown Hotel**
246 Rd
☎ (0228) 515292
7 bedrooms; double B&B £37
Credit cards 1 3

**Blackwell Farmhouse**
☎ (0228) 24073
2 bedrooms; double B&B £28–£30

## WHERE TO STAY

### Around Carlisle

### The Beeches
Loanwath Rd, Gretna
☎ (0461) 37448
Panoramic views make this former
farmhouse special.
2 bedrooms; double B&B £32-£34

### Greenlaw
Gretna
☎ (0461) 38361
Generally compact modestly furnished
bedrooms.
8 bedrooms; double B&B £25-£26

### Surrone House
Annan Rd, Gretna
☎ (0461) 38341
This historic former farmhouse offers a
good standard of bedroom.
6 bedrooms

### New Pallyards Farm
Hethersgill, Longtown
☎ (0228) 577308
Nicely decorated farmhouse offers some
spacious bedrooms including a huge family
room.
5 bedrooms; double B&B £36-£38

### How End Farm
Thursby
☎ (06973) 42487
A farmhouse dating back to 1764 with
friendly, relaxed atmosphere.
2 bedrooms; double B&B £28-£30
Credit cards 1 3

## CAMPSITES

### ►► Dandy Dinmont Caravan Site
Blackford
☎ (022874) 611
North of Carlisle; pitch price from £4.50
per night

### ►►► Orton Grange Caravan & Camping Park
Orton Grange, Wigton Rd, Carlisle
☎ (0228) 710252
Pitch price from £5 per night

### ►►► Dalston Hall Caravan Park
Dalston Hall Estate, Dalston
☎ (0228) 710165
Southwest of Carlisle adjacent to the A35;
pitch price from £4.75 per night

### ►►► Braids Caravan Park
Annan Rd, Gretna
☎ (0461) 37409
On the old A75 to Annan north of Carlisle;
pitch price from £5 per night

### ►► Camelot Caravan Park
Sandysike, Longtown
☎ (0228) 791248
On the A7 north of Carlisle; pitch price from
£5.50

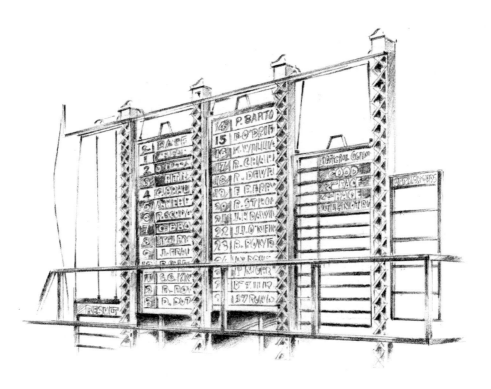

# Cartmel

*Amidst stunningly beautiful Lake District scenery, this delightful little course provides a truly idyllic site for jump racing. Even the journey to the course is a real pleasure, but allow lots of time because it is not a well-kept secret and crowds are always huge.*

Part of the reason for this is that only two meetings are run here every year, with five days' racing spread over the Spring Bank Holiday in May and the August Bank Holiday.

Fun is the order of the day, with plenty of other attractions besides the horses (these are often moderate due to firm ground, although fields are big and the exceptionally long run-in of half a mile usually witnesses exciting finishes). Exhibitions of hound-trailing are sometimes held before racing, and a fun-fair is always in attendance with the Ferris Wheel providing a unique perspective of the action as the runners pass virtually underneath. A charming course with a terrific atmosphere; it is well worth planning a holiday in the area around one of the meetings.

## FURTHER INFORMATION

Cartmel Steeplechases Ltd
Estate Office, Lowther, Penrith,
Cumbria CA10 2HG
☎ (0931712) 378

## LOCATION AND HOW TO GET THERE

The course is approximately 2 miles west of Grange over Sands. Leave the M6 at junction 36 and take the A590. Later turn left for Cartmel. **Nearest Railway Station:** Cark in Cartmel; there is a connecting bus service to the course on racedays.

## ADMISSION

All classes of day ticket give access to full betting facilities, including Tote.

**Day tickets:**
PADDOCK £8, senior citizens £4 – access to bar, restaurant and grandstand

COURSE £3, senior citizens £1.50 – access to bar

**Annual membership:** £70

**Parking:** free in Course Enclosure, £5 in Paddock Enclosure

## COURSE FACILITIES

**Banks:**
there are no banks or cashpoint facilities on the course.

## CALENDAR OF EVENTS

**May 25** – jumping
**May 28** – jumping

**May 30** – jumping
**August 27** – jumping

**August 29** – jumping

## WHERE TO STAY

### HOTELS

**★★ ✿ 70% Anysome Manor**
☎ (05395) 36653, fax: (05395) 366016
11 bedrooms; double B&B £77–£108
(including dinner)
Credit cards 1 2 3

### Around Cartmel

**★ 62% Wheatsheaf**
Milnthorpe, Beetham
☎ (05395) 62123
6 bedrooms; double B&B £40
Credit cards 1 3

**★★ 63% Royal Station**
Market St, Carnforth
☎ (0524) 732033 & 733636, fax: (0524) 733636
12 bedrooms; double B&B from £46
Credit cards 1 2 3 5

**★★★ 65% Grange**
Station Square,
Grange-over-Sands
☎ (05395) 33666, fax: (05393) 35064
41 bedrooms; double B&B from £72

**★★ 70% Netherwood**
Lindale Rd,
Grange-over-Sands
☎ (05395) 32552
32 bedrooms; double B&B £76.50–£99
Credit cards 1 3

**★★ 68% Graythwaite Manor**
Fernhill Rd, Grange-over-Sands
☎ (05395) 32001 & 33755,
fax: (05395) 35549
21 bedrooms; double B&B £80–£120
Credit cards 1 3

**★★ 66% Hampsfell House**
Hampsfell Rd, Grange-over-Sands
☎ (05395) 32567
8 bedrooms; double B&B £45–£55
Credit cards 1 3

**★ 68% Clare House**
Park Rd, Grange-over-Sands
☎ (05395) 33026 & 34253
17 bedrooms; double B&B £77–£82

**★★ 70% Grizedale Lodge**
Grizedale
☎ (05394) 36532
9 bedrooms; double B&B £75–£94
Credit cards 1 3

**★ 59% Silverdale**
Shore Rd
☎ (0524) 701206
10 bedrooms
Credit cards 1 3

**★★ ✿ 65% Virginia House**
Queen St, Ulverston
☎ (0229) 54844
7 bedrooms; double B&B £41.50–£49
Credit cards 1 2 3 5

### BED AND BREAKFAST

**Barrowfield Farm**
Brigsteer
☎ (04488) 336
Situated on a dairy farm, in a beautiful and peaceful area of lakeland.
3 bedrooms

**New Capernwray Farm**
Capernwray, Carnforth
☎ (0524) 734284
Very relaxed and informal, beautifully furnished bedrooms.
3 bedrooms; double £52–£58
Credit cards 1 3

**Crosthwaite House**
Crosthwaite
☎ (05395) 68264
Set in beautiful countryside; the house is well furnished and cared for.
6 bedrooms; double B&B £40–£44

**Birchleigh Kents**
Bank Rd, Grange-over-Sands
☎ (05395) 32592
Small, friendly guesthouse.
5 bedrooms; double B&B from £33

**Greenacres**
Lindale
☎ (05395) 34578
Attentive hosts, good location and thoughtful extras give excellent value for money
5 bedrooms

**Gilpin Bridge Hotel & Restaurant**
Bridge End
☎ (044852) 206
Just off the A590, offering good range of food and modern bedrooms.
10 bedrooms; double B&B £46

**Furness Fells**
Newby Bridge
☎ (05395) 31260
Friendly family-run guesthouse with well furnished, comfortable accommodation.
3 bedrooms.

**Tranthwaite Hall**
Underbarrow
☎ (04488) 285 due to change to
(05395) 68285
Lovely 14th-century farmhouse full of character and charm.
2 bedrooms; double B&B £27–£30

**The Bower**
Yealand Conyers
☎ (0524) 734585
Comfortable rooms with pine and antique furniture.
2 bedrooms; double B&B £44–£53

### CAMPSITES

**►► Oak Head Caravan Park**
Ayside
☎ (05395) 31475
Close to A590 north of Cartmel; pitch price from £4 per night

**►► Detron Gate Farm**
Bolton-le-Sands
☎ (0524) 732842 & 733617 (evening)
Overlooking Morecambe Bay off A6; pitch price from £4.60 per night

**► Bolton Holmes Farm**
Bolton-le-Sands
☎ (0524) 732854
South of Cartmel; pitch price from £3.50 per night

## WHERE TO STAY

### ► Black Beck Caravan Park Bouth
☎ (022986) 1274
Northwest of Cartmel

### ►► Old Hall Caravan Park
Capernwray
☎ (0524) 733276 & 732975
Situated southeast of Cartmel

### ►►► Waters Edge Caravan Park
Crooklands
☎ (05395) 67708
East of Cartmel

### ► Lambhowe Caravan Park
Crosthwaite
☎ (04488) 483 due to change to (05395) 68483
On A5074 between Lancaster and Windermere; pitch price from £8 per night.

### ►►► Lakeland Leisure Park
Moor Ln, Flookburgh
☎ (05395) 58235 & 58556
South of Cartmel; pitch price from £6 per night.

### ►►► Bigland Hall Caravan Park
Haverthwaite
☎ (05395) 31702
West of Cartmel; pitch price from £5 per night.

### ►►►► Fell End Caravan Park
Slackhead Rd, Hale, Milnthorpe
☎ (05395) 62122
East of Cartmel; pitch price from £7 per night.

### ►►► Holgate's Caravan Park
Cove Rd, Silverdale
☎ (0524) 701508
Southeast of Cartmel; pitch price from £12.50 per night.

### ►►► Bardsea Leisure Park
Priory Rd, Ulverston
☎ (0229) 54712
On southern edge of town off the A5087; pitch price from £3.95 per night.

## WHERE TO EAT

### RESTAURANTS

### ❀❀❀ Uplands
Haggs Lane, Cartmel
☎ (05395) 36248
Imaginative, consistently good cooking at very reasonable prices in a relaxed country-house hotel.
Lunch: 12-1; from £14.40
Dinner: 7-8; from £23.50

### ❀❀ Bay Horse Inn and Bistro
Ulverston
☎ (0229) 53972, fax: (0229) 580502
Sound, imaginative cooking at reasonable prices, superb views and a convivial atmosphere.
Lunch: 12-1.30; from £13.50 and à la carte.
Dinner: Last Dinner 7.30; from £17.65 and à la carte.

# Catterick Bridge

*Catterick offers a good mixture of Flat and National Hunt racing and is one of a select band of courses that stages a meeting in each month of the year.*

With over two dozen fixtures scheduled annually, there is every opportunity to catch local runners in action because the cards are always well supported by trainers from nearby Middleham, the major training centre in the north, whose size and popularity is increasing all the time thanks to the tremendous success that some of the handlers based there have been enjoying of late.

The course, like the area, makes no pretensions to grandeur, but there is a genuine country feel to the place which is most appealing. The undulating track is extremely sharp and the soil drains superbly so good ground can nearly always be guaranteed, even in very wet conditions. This means that races are run at an exceptionally fast pace, suiting the nippy type of horse who is able to lie handily or make all the running.

### FURTHER INFORMATION

The Racecourse Office
Catterick Racecourse, Catterick Bridge,
Richmond, North Yorkshire DL10 7PE
☎ (0748) 811478

### LOCATION AND HOW TO GET THERE

The racecourse is situated on the outskirts of Catterick village, approximately five miles south of Scotch Corner. Leave the A1 at the exit for Catterick and proceed through the village. **Nearest Railway Stations:** Darlington or Northallerton; there are connecting bus services to the course on racedays.

---

### ADMISSION

All enclosures have access to bookmakers and Tote points, but the Course Enclosure does not have access to the betting office or the Tote Credit Office.

**Day Tickets:**
MEMBERS £10 – access to parade ring, winners' enclosure, bar and bar meals, plus all facilities in Paddock (see below)

TATTERSALLS AND PADDOCK £6 – access to parade ring, winners' enclosure, bars, dining room, self-service restaurant, private rooms and facilities for disabled racegoers

COURSE £2 – access to bar and cafeteria; no access to winners enclosure

**Annual membership:**
£67 single, £114 joint, £33 junior (under 21)

**Parking:** there is free parking outside the course; on-course parking £2 per day or £26 for the year; parking for disabled racegoers in centre of course.

### COURSE FACILITIES

**Banks:**
there are no banks or cashpoint facilities on the course

**For families:**
baby changing facilities; lost children centre

---

## CALENDAR OF EVENTS

| | |
|---|---|
| **April 20** – flat | **October 14-15** – flat |
| **May 20-21** – flat | **November 19** – jumping |
| **June 3** – flat | **November 21** – jumping |
| **June 29-30** – flat | **November 30** – jumping |
| **July 13-14** – flat | **December 16-17** – jumping |
| **July 27** – flat | **December 31** – jumping |
| **August 12** – flat; evening meeting | |
| **September 17** – flat | |

## WHERE TO STAY

### HOTELS

**★★ 55% Bridge House**
☎ (0748) 818331
16 bedrooms; double B&B £44-£58
Credit cards 1 2 3 5

### Around Catterick Bridge

**★★ 62% Motel Leeming**
Great North Rd, Bedale
☎ (0677) 422122, fax: (0677) 424507
40 bedrooms; double B&B £49
Credit cards 1 2 3 5

**★★★ 71% Hallgarth Country House**
Coatham Mundeville, Darlington
☎ (0325) 300400, fax: (0325) 310083
29 bedrooms; double B&B £85-£90
Credit Cards 1 2 3 5

**★★★ 67% Headlam Hall**
Headlam, Gainford, Darlington
☎ (0325) 730238, fax: (0325) 730790
17 bedrooms; double B&B £65-£80
Credit cards 1 2 3

**★★★ 62% White Horse Darlington**
☎ (0325) 382121, telex 778704,
fax: (0325) 355953
40 bedrooms; double bedroom £49.50
Credit cards 1 2 3 5

**★★★ 61% Swallow King's Head**
Priestgate, Darlington
☎ (0325) 380222, telex 587112,
fax: (0325) 382006
86 bedrooms; double B&B £85-£100
Credit cards 1 2 3 5

**★★★ 73% Kirkby Fleetham Hall**
Kirkby Fleetham
☎ (0609) 748711, fax: (0609) 748747
22 bedrooms
Credit cards 1 2 3 4 5

**★★ 61% White Rose Leeming Bar**
☎ (0677) 422707 & 424941, fax: (0677)
425123
18 bedrooms; double B&B from £42
Credit cards 1 2 3 5

**★★ 64% The George Piercebridge**
☎ (0325) 374576, fax: (0325) 374577
22 bedrooms; double B&B £53-£63
Credit cards 1 2 3 5

**★★★ 65% Scotch Corner**
Scotch Corner
☎ (0748) 850900, telex 587447,
fax: (0748) 825417
90 bedrooms; double room £45-£65 (room
only)
Credit cards 1 2 3 5

**Forte Travelodge**
Skeeby, Scotch Corner
☎ (0748) 3768, Central Reservations:
(0800) 850950
40 bedrooms; double room £31.95 (room
only)
Credit cards 1 2 3

**Pavilion Lodge**
A1/A66 Middleton Tyas, Scotch Corner
☎ (0325) 377177, fax: (0325) 377890
50 bedrooms; double room £37 (room only)
Credit cards 1 2 3 5

### BED AND BREAKFAST

**Buck Inn Thornton**
Watlass
☎ (0677) 422461
6 bedrooms; double B&B £40-£46
Credit cards 1 2 3

**Blairgowrie Country House**
Crakehall, Bedale
☎ (0748) 811377
Friendly, charming farmhouse.
2 bedrooms; double B&B from £30

**The Countryman's Hunton**
Bedale
☎ (0677) 50554
Well appointed bedrooms in charming old
stone built inn.
6 bedrooms; double B&B £40
Credit cards 1 3

**Elmfield House**
Patrick Brompton, Bedale
☎ (0677) 50558 & 50557
Spacious, beautifully decorated and
furnished bedrooms with good views,
friendly hosts.
9 bedrooms; double B&B £38-£44

**Woodland**
63 Woodland Rd, Darlington
☎ (0325) 461908
Friendly, personal service with well
maintained bedrooms.
8 bedrooms; double from £32

**Clow Beck House**
Monk End Farm, Croft on Tees, Darlington
☎ (0325) 721075
Luxuriously furnished bedrooms
3 bedrooms; double B&B £37-£47

**Alverton**
26 South Pde, Northallerton
☎ (0609) 776207
Comfortably furnished rooms, in attractive
Victorian house.
5 bedrooms; double B&B £33.50-£37

**Porch House**
68 High St, Northallerton
☎ (0609) 779831
5 bedrooms; double B&B £42
Credit cards 1 3

**Windsor**
56 South Pde, Northallerton
☎ (0609) 774100
Thoughtfully furnished and equipped
bedrooms.
6 bedrooms; double B&B £30-£36
Credit cards 1 3

### CAMPSITES

**► Hutton Bonville Caravan Park**
Church Ln,
Hutton Bonville, Northallerton
☎ (060981) 416
Southeast of Catterick off the A167; pitch
price from £5.50 per night.

**Scotch Corner Caravan Park**
Scotch Corner
☎ (0748) 822530 & 826272
Off A6108 slightly north of Catterick; pitch
price from £7.75 per night.

## WHERE TO EAT

### RESTAURANTS

**⚜ Victors**
84 Victoria Rd, Darlington
☎ (0325) 480818
Imaginative cooking at reasonable prices in
a friendly town-centre restaurant.
Lunch: 12-2; from £7.50
Dinner: 7-10.30; from £18

**⚜ Black Bull**
Moulton
☎ (0325) 377289, fax: (0325) 377422
Four different settings in which to enjoy
honest, competently prepared food.
Lunch: 12-2; from £11.75 and à la carte
Dinner: 7-10.15; £15.25-£35 à la carte

# Cheltenham

*This is the undisputed Home of National Hunt Racing and a visit to the course is an absolute must for anyone remotely interested in the jumping game.*

Overlooked by the beautiful Cotswold Hills, it really is the perfect site to watch the best chasers and hurdlers in the world. Facilities match the setting, with improvements continually being made, such as the new saddling area and link tunnel to the parade ring. A recent innovation is the Cheltenham Hall of Fame, which tells the story of the racecourse's history and the illustrious figures, both equine and human, that have graced its turf over the years.

The track is best known for the National Hunt Festival in March, the top three-day meeting of the season which features the Gold Cup and Champion Hurdle and attracts some 50,000 spectators from all over Europe. Advance booking is advisable. Other high quality fixtures during the year including the Mackeson Gold Cup meeting in November.

## FURTHER INFORMATION

Cheltenham Racecourse
Prestbury Park, Cheltenham
Glos GL50 4SH
☎ ((0242) 513014

## LOCATION AND HOW TO GET THERE

The course is a mile north of Cheltenham on the A435. Leave the M5 at junction 10 southbound or 11 northbound.
**Nearest Railway Station:** Cheltenham Spa; there is a connecting bus service to the course on major racedays.

## ADMISSION

All classes of day ticket give access to full betting facilities, including Tote.

**Day Tickets:**
Accompanied children under 16 are admitted free to all enclosures, except during the National Hunt Festival in March, when full rates will apply. On feature days, Club and Tattersalls are one enclosure. There are substantial reductions for advance booking for the National Hunt Festival Meeting.

CLUB Feature days £10, junior £8; Premier days £15, junior £8; Mackeson Day £20, junior £10; National Hunt Festival £50 or £100 for three days, plus £20-£25 for a Guinness Grandstand Seat – access to viewing seats, restaurant, bars, buffets and boxes; during the National Hunt Festival the Tented Village is in the Club enclosure; seats should be booked in advance

TATTERSALLS Feature, Premier and Mackeson days £10; National Hunt Festival £20, plus £20-£25 for a Guinness Grandstand Seat – access to paddock, centre of course, viewing steps, restaurants, bars and boxes; during the National Hunt Festival extra seating, the Guinness Village and entertainments are provided

FOSTERS Feature and Premier days £3, Mackeson day £5; National Hunt Festival £7 – excellent viewing directly opposite the main stands, access to bars, buffets and snack bars; temporary stands, marquees and entertainments provided during National Hunt Festival

**Transfers:** Feature days – Tattersalls to Club £7; Premium days – Tattersalls to Club £5, Fosters to Tattersalls £7; Mackeson Day – Tattersalls to Club £12, Fosters to Tattersalls £6. There are NO transfers at the National Hunt Festival.

**Parking:** during the National Hunt Festival there is a charge of £5; advance purchase of parking vouchers provides a space nearest the entrance. At other meetings, parking is free, but can be reserved for a fee.

**Annual membership:**
Full: £110 plus £90 enrolment – includes free admission and parking on all racedays, admission to viewing seats, bars and buffet on Level 3 of the Grandstand on all Feature and Premier days, reciprocal arrangements with other racecourses on certain days. NB Members' Badges will NOT be honoured on the Cheltenham Sunday Best day in November, which benefits a number of charities, but car labels will be honoured.

## COURSE FACILITIES

**Banks:**
Bank of Ireland and Irish Bank at National Hunt Festival Meeting only (16-18 March); open 11am-4pm. There are no cashpoint facilities on the course.

**For families:**
lost children centre.

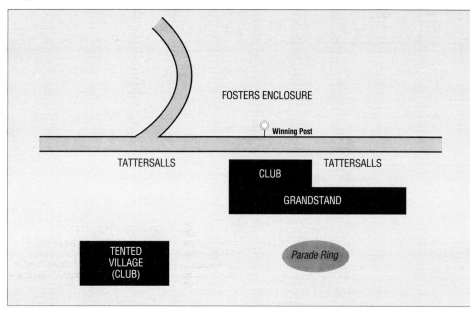

## CALENDAR OF EVENTS

**March 15-17** – National Hunt Festival; includes Smurfitt Champion Hurdle Day on Tuesday, Queen Mother Champion Chase on Wednesday and Tote Cheltenham Gold Cup on Thursday
**April 20** – includes South Wales Showers Chase and Howard E Perry Hunter Chase
**April 27** – evening meeting

**May 17** – Hunter Chase Evening Meeting
**September 29**
**October 26**
**November 11-12** – includes Mackeson Gold Cup on Saturday
**November 23**
**December 9-10**

## WHERE TO STAY

### HOTELS

**★★★★ 60% Golden Valley Thistle**
Gloucester Rd
☎ (0242) 232691, telex 43410,
fax: (0242) 221846
124 bedrooms; double bedroom from £90
Credit cards 1 2 3 4 5

**★★★★ 52% The Queen's**
Promenade
☎ (0242) 514724, telex 43381,
fax: (0242) 224145
74 bedrooms; double bedroom £100–£130
Credit cards 1 2 3 5

**★★★●● (RED) Greenway**
Shurdington
☎ (0242) 852352, fax: (0242) 862780
11 bedrooms; double B&B £120–£175
Credit cards 1 2 3 4 5

**★★★ 65% Carlton**
Parabola Rd
☎ (0242) 514453, fax: (0242) 226487
63 bedrooms; double B&B £60–£95
Credit cards 1 2 3 5

**★★★ 64% White House**
Gloucester Rd, Staverton
☎ (0452) 713226, telex 437382,
fax: (0452) 857590
50 bedrooms
Credit cards 1 2 3 5

**★★★ 62% The Prestbury House Hotel & Restaurant**
The Burgage, Prestbury,
☎ (0242) 529533, fax: (0242) 227076
9 bedrooms; double B&B £74.50
Credit cards 1 2 3

**★★★ 61% Hotel de la Bere**
Southam
☎ (0242) 237771, fax: (0242) 326016
32 bedrooms; double room £80–£95 (room only)
Credit cards 1 2 3 5

**★★●●● 77% On the Park**
38 Evesham Rd
☎ (0242) 518898, fax: (0242) 511526
8 bedrooms; double room £55–£80 (room only)
Credit cards 1 2 3 5

**★★ 68% Charlton Kings**
London Rd, Charlton Kings
☎ (0242) 231061, fax: (0242) 241900
14 bedrooms; double B&B £52–£78
Credit cards 1 3

## WHERE TO STAY

**★★ 67% George Hotel**
St George's Rd
☎ (0242) 235751, fax: (0242) 224359
39 bedrooms; double B&B £48–£64
Credit cards 1 2 3 5

**★★ 65% Wyastone**
Parabola Rd
☎ (0242) 516654 & 245549, fax: (0242) 522659
13 bedrooms; double B&B £50–£60
Credit cards 1 2 3 5

**★★ 62 Allards**
Shurdington
☎ (0242) 862498, fax: (0242) 863017
12 bedrooms; double B&B £48–£58
Credit cards 1 3

**★★ 59% Cotswold Grange**
Pittville Circus Rd
☎ (0242) 515119, fax: (0242) 241537
25 bedrooms
Credit cards 1 2 3

### Around Cheltenham

**★★★ 63% Royal George**
Birdlip
☎ (0452) 862506, telex 437238, fax: (0452) 862277
34 bedrooms; double B&B £77
Credit cards 1 2 3 5

**★★★ 61% Rising Sun**
Cleeve Hill
☎ (0242) 676281, telex 437410, fax: (0242) 673069
24 bedrooms; double B&B £70–£75
Credit cards 1 2 3 5

**★★★❀❀ 70% Corse Lawn House**
Corse Lawn
☎ (0452) 780479 & 780771, fax: (0452) 780840
19 bedrooms; double B&B from £90
Credit cards 1 2 3 5

**★★★❀❀ 76% Hatton Court**
Upton Hill, Upton St Leonards, Gloucester
☎ (0452) 617412, telex 437334, fax: (0452) 612945
17 bedrooms; double B&B £90–£99
Credit cards 1 2 3 5

**★★★ 69% Bowden Hall Resort**
Bondend Ln,
Upton St Leonards, Gloucester
☎ (0452) 614121, fax: (0452) 611885
72 bedrooms; double room £77–£87 (room only)
Credit card 1 2 3 5

**★★★ 68% Forte Crest**
Crest Way, Barnwood, Gloucester
☎ (0452) 613311, telex 437273, fax: (0452) 371036
123 bedrooms; double room £80 (room only)
Credit card 1 2 3 5

**★★★ 61% Hatherley Manor Down**
Hatherley Ln, Gloucester
☎ (0452) 730217, telex 437353, fax: (0452) 731032
56 bedrooms
Credit cards 1 2 3 4 5

**★★ 64% Twigworth Lodge**
Tewkesbury Rd, Gloucester
☎ (0452) 730266, fax: (0452) 730099
30 bedrooms; double B&B £50–£60
Credit cards 1 2 3 5

## WHERE TO STAY

### ★ 64% Rotherfield House
5 Horton Rd, Gloucester
☎ (0452) 410500
13 bedrooms; double B&B £39.50
Credit cards 1 2 3 5

### ★★★★֍֎ 74% Puckrup Hall
Puckrup
☎ (0684) 296200, fax: (0684) 850788
16 bedrooms; double B&B £77.50-£105
Credit cards 1 2 3 5

### ★★★ 66% Tewkesbury Park Golf & Country Club
Lincoln Green Ln, Tewkesbury
☎ (0684) 295405, telex 43563,
fax: (0684) 292386
78 bedrooms; double B&B £70-£85
Credit cards 1 2 3 4 5

### ★★★ 65% Royal Hop Pole Crest
Church St, Tewkesbury
☎ (0684) 293236, fax: (0684) 296680
29 bedrooms
Credit cards 1 2 3 5

### ★★★ 58%, Bell
Church St, Tewkesbury
☎ (0684) 293293, fax: (0684) 295938
25 bedrooms; double B&B £65-£110
Credit cards 1 2 3 5

### ★★ 65% Tudor House
High St, Tewkesbury
☎ (0684) 297755, fax: (0684) 290306
21 bedrooms; double B&B from £54
Credit cards 1 2 3 5

### ★★ 65% Old Manse
Victoria St, Bourton-on-the-Water
☎ (0451) 810381
Approximately 20 miles east of Cheltenham.
12 bedrooms
Credit cards 1 3

## BED AND BREAKFAST

### Battledown Hotel
125 Hales Rd
☎ (0242) 233881
Bright clean and comfortable bedrooms;
friendly hosts.
4 bedrooms; double £36-£44
Credit cards 1 3

### Beaumont House Hotel
56 Shurdington Rd
☎ (0242) 245986, fax: (0242) 245986
Attractive Victorian house with charm
and hospitality.
18 bedrooms; double B&B £43-£55
Credit cards 1 2 3

### Beechworth Lawn Hotel
133 Hales Rd
☎ (0242) 522583
Congenial guesthouse; excellent value for
money.
7 bedrooms; double B&B £36-£46

### Cleeve Hill Hotel
Cleeve Hill
☎ (0242) 672052
Good hospitality and tasteful, quality
surroundings provide excellent bed and
breakfast accommodation.
10 bedrooms; double B&B £50-£65
Credit cards 1 2 3

### Hannaford's
20 Evesham Rd
☎ (0242) 515181
Off the A435 Evesham road. Spacious
well equipped bedrooms.
10 bedrooms; double B&B £48-£60
Credit cards 1 3

### Hollington House Hotel
115 Hales Rd
☎ (0242) 519718, fax: (0242) 570280
Comfortable bedrooms; friendly relaxed
atmosphere.
9 bedrooms
Credit cards 1 2 3

### Lypiatt House
Lypiatt Rd
☎ (0242) 224994, fax: (0242) 224996
Elegant, charming Victorian house,
spotlessly clean bedrooms with original
features.
10 bedrooms; double B&B £62
Credit cards 1 3

### Milton House
12 Royal Pde, Bayshill Rd
☎ (0242) 582601, fax: (0242) 222326
Convenient location with individually styled
bedrooms.
9 bedrooms; double B&B £45-£60
Credit cards 1 2 3

### North Hall Hotel
Pittville Circus Rd
☎ (0242) 520589, fax: (0242) 261953
Central position, well equipped comfortable
bedrooms.
20 bedrooms; double B&B from £31
Credit Cards 1 3

### Regency House Hotel
50 Clarence Square
☎ (0242) 582718, fax: (0242) 262697
High ceilings, grand spiral stone staircase,
well equipped bedrooms.
8 bedrooms; double B&B £42-£48
Credit cards 1 3

### Stretton Lodge
Western Rd
☎ (0242) 528724 & 570771
Rich interior architecture, nicely
decorated bedrooms.
9 bedrooms; double B&B £50-£65
Credit cards 1 2 3

### Around Cheltenham

### The Old Manor House
43 Station Rd, Bishop's Cleeve
☎ (024267) 4127
Modest accommodation full of character.
6 bedrooms

### Colesbourne
Colesbourne
☎ (0242) 870376, fax: (0242) 870397
Former coaching inn steeped in history.
10 bedrooms; double B&B £49
Credit cards 1 2 3 5

### Claremont
135 Stroud Rd, Gloucester
☎ (0452) 529540 & 529270
Cosy guesthouse on the Stroud road.
6 bedrooms; double B&B £24-£27

### The Abbey Hotel
67 Church St, Tewkesbury
☎ (0684) 294247
Family-run hotel situated in the main
street.
16 bedroom
Credit cards 1 2 3

### Home Farm
Bredons Norton, Tewkesbury
☎ (0684) 72322
Attractive farmhouse with pretty bedrooms.
3 bedrooms.

## WHERE TO STAY

### CAMPSITES

**►► Caravan Club Site**
Cheltenham
☎ (0242) 523102
One and a half miles north of town on A435

**►► Longwillows Camping Site**
Station Rd, Woodmancote, Cheltenham
☎ (0242) 674113
Three and a half miles north of Cheltenham;
pitch price from £5.20 per night.

**►► Red Lion Caravan Park**
Wainlode Hill, Norton, Gloucester
☎ (0452) 730251
West of Cheltenham; pitch price from
£5 per night.

**►► Mill Avon Holiday Park**
Gloucester Rd, Tewkesbury
☎ (0684) 296876
North of Cheltenham alongside the River
Mill Avon.

## WHERE TO EAT

### RESTAURANTS

**🏵🏵🏵 Le Champignon Sauvage**
24 Suffolk Rd
☎ (0242) 573449
Predominantly classic French cooking in a
friendly relaxed style.
Lunch 12-1.30; from £17.50
Dinner 7-9.30; from £26

**🏵🏵 Cleeveway House**
Bishops Cleeve
☎ (0242) 672585
Small Cotswold manor house hotel with
reliable, straightforward cooking.
Lunch: 12-1.45; £15-£22 à la carte.
Dinner: 7-9.45; £15-£22 à la carte.

**🏵 Mayflower Chinese**
32-34 Clarence St
☎ (0242) 522426 & 511580,
fax: (0242) 511580
Comfortable and popular Chinese
restaurant, serving mainly Cantonese
dishes.
Lunch: 12-1.30; £6.20-£7 and à la carte
Dinner: 7-10.30; £14-£27 and à la carte

**🏵🏵 Staithes**
12 Suffolk Rd
☎ (0242) 260666
Enjoyable modern style food in a
comfortable, small restaurant.
Lunch by arrangement.

### PUBS

**Kilkeney Inn**
Andoversford, nr Cheltenham
☎ (0242) 820341
Long, low Cotswold stone building with a
pretty garden. Imaginative dishes are served
in generous portions. Draught beers
includes John Smiths, Ruddles Best,
Wadworth 6X and Kilkeney Drovers; there is
an extensive wine list and range of malt
whiskies.
Open: 11.30am-2.30pm, 6.30-11pm;
Sunday 12-2.3opm, 7-10.30pm
Bar food: 12-2pm, 7-9.30pm; Sunday 7-
9pm

# Chepstow

*Chepstow stands alone as the sole course in Wales, a surprising statistic considering the tremendous enthusiasm that the Welsh have for their racing. As a result, meetings attract sizeable turnouts with plenty of knowledgeable locals in evidence.*

Patrons are well served by a broad mixture of events under both codes, although the National Hunt cards tend to be of a much higher standard. This is particularly true around Christmas with the running of the Coral Welsh National, one of the major staying handicap chases of the seaon. Favourites have an outsanding record in this event as does top trainer Martin Pipe, who has monopolised the race virtually to the exclusion of all others in recent years.

Most Saturday jump meetings will stage at least one valuable contest, but traffic congestion can be notoriously bad on big days, with the Severn Bridge (vital for access) and nearby roundabouts sometimes grinding to a complete standstill, so set off early. Soft ground is usually prevalent, putting stamina at a premium, as does the undulating track that dips out of sight at the start of the home straight. Flat racing is of a lower calibre, but evening meetings are popular and feature many of the top jockeys.

### FURTHER INFORMATION

Chepstow Racecourse plc
The Racecourse, Chepstow, Gwent NP6 5YH
☎ (0291) 622260

### LOCATION AND HOW TO GET THERE

The course is on the northern edge of the town, off the A466. Leave the M4 at junction 22 on the western side of the Severn Bridge and take the A48 northwards, later taking the A446 Monmouth road.

**Nearest Railway Station:** Chepstow; there is a connecting bus service to the course on racedays.

---

## ADMISSION

All classes of day ticket give access to full betting facilities, including Tote

**Day Tickets:**
MEMBERS £11, £13 on Saturdays, £16 on Welsh National day – access to bars, restaurant, boxes, private rooms

TATTERSALLS £8, £9 on Saturdays, £11 on Welsh National day – access to bars, snack bar, facilities for disabled racegoers including special viewing

PUBLIC & CENTRE COURSE £4 – only available on April 12-13, May 31 and August 30; access to bar and snack bar

**Annual membership:** £108

## COURSE FACILITIES

**Banks:**
there are no banks or cashpoint facilities on the course

**For families:**
picnic area with refreshments kiosk and toilets

---

## CALENDAR OF EVENTS

**April 4-5** – jumping
**May 10** – jumping
**May 30** – flat
**June 4** – flat; evening meeting
**June 25** – flat
**June 28** – flat
**July 7** – flat; evening meeting
**July 14** – flat; evening meeting
**August 29** – flat

**September 10** – flat
**October 1** – jumping
**October 11** – flat
**October 18** – flat
**November 5** – jumping
**December 3** – jumping
**December 27** – jumping

## WHERE TO STAY

### HOTELS

**★★★ 69% St Pierre Hotel Golf & Country Club**
St Pierre Park.
☎ (0291) 625261, telex 497562, fax: (0291) 629975
106 bedrooms; double B&B £85-£100
Credit cards 1 2 3 5

**★★ 66% Castle View**
16 Bridge St
☎ (0291) 620349, fax: (0291) 627397
9 bedrooms; double B&B £59.50-£65
Credit cards 1 2 3 5

**★★ 62% The George**
Moor St
☎ (0291) 625363, fax: (0291) 627418
14 bedrooms; double bedroom from £73.50
Credit cards 1 2 3 5

### Around Chepstow

**★★ 68% Rangeworthy Court**
Church Ln, Wotton Rd, Rangeworthy
☎ (0454) 228347 & 228473, fax: (0454)228945
Approximately 16 miles east of Chepstow, via the M4.
16 bedrooms; double B&B £58-£72
Credit cards 1 2 3 5

**★★★★ 62% Aztec**
Aztec West Business Park, Almondsbury
☎ (0454) 201090, fax: (0454) 201593
88 bedrooms; double B&B £96-£126
Credit cards 1 2 3 5

**★★★ 72% Alveston House**
Alveston
☎ (0454) 415050, fax: (0454) 415425
30 bedrooms; double B&B £75.50-£89.50
Credit cards 1 2 3 5

**★★★ 62% Forte Posthouse**
Thornbury Rd, Alveston
☎ (0454) 412521, fax: (0454) 413920
74 bedrooms; double room £49.50-£69.50
(room only)
Credit cards 1 2 3 5

**★★ 62% Old Schoolhouse**
Canonbury St, Berkeley
☎ (0453) 811711
7 bedrooms
Credit cards 1 3

**★★★ 70% Stakis Bristol**
Woodlands Ln, Patchway, Bradley Stoke
☎ (0454) 201144, telex 445774, fax: (0454) 612022
111 bedrooms; double room £89-£99
(room only)
Credit cards 1 2 3 5

**★★★ 65% Clearwell Castle**
Church Rd, Clearwell
☎ (0594) 832320, fax: (0594) 835523
14 bedrooms
Credit cards 1 2 3

## WHERE TO STAY

★★★ **64% Wyndham Arms**
Clearwell
☎ (0594) 833666, fax: (0594) 836450
5 bedrooms; double B&B £55-£65
Credit cards 1 2 3 4 5

★★ **57% Park Hotel & Restaurant**
Falfield
☎ (0454) 260550
10 bedrooms; double B&B £45-£55
Credit cards 1 2 3

★★★★ **61% Cwrt Bleddyn Hotel & Country Club**
LLangybi
☎ (0633) 49521, fax: (0633) 49220
29 bedrooms; double B&B £97.50-£165
Credit cards 1 2 3 5

★★ **59% Feathers**
High St, Lydney
☎ (0594) 842815 & 842826
14 bedrooms
Credit cards 1 2 3

★★★✿✿ **Thornbury Castle**
Thornbury
☎ (0454) 281182, fax: (0454) 416188
18 bedrooms; double B&B £95-£195
Credit cards 1 2 3 5

★★ **64% Royal George**
Tintern
☎ (0291) 689205, fax: (0291) 689448
5 bedrooms; double B&B £57-£68
Credit cards 1 2 3 5

★★ **63% Parva Farmhouse Hotel & Restaurant**
Tintern
☎ (0291) 689411
9 bedrooms; double B&B £44-£66
Credit cards 1 3

★★ **62% Wye Valley**
Tintern
☎ (0291) 689441, fax: (0291) 689440
9 bedrooms; double B&B £48-£60
Credit cards 1 3

★★✿ **70% Crown at Whitebrook**
Whitebrook
☎ (0600) 860254, fax: (0600) 860607
12 bedrooms; double B&B £124-£138
(including dinner)
Credit cards 1 2 3 4 5

### BED AND BREAKFAST

**Abbotts Way**
Gloucester Rd, Almondsbury
☎ (0454) 613134
6 bedrooms; double B&B £40
Credit cards 1 3 5

**Greenacres**
Breadston, Berkeley
☎ (0453) 810348
Well situated; generous breakfasts.
4 bedrooms; double B&B £33-£35

**Tudor Farmhouse Hotel**
Clearwell
☎ (0594) 833046, fax: (0594) 837093
Listed Tudor farmhouse full of charm and character.
6 bedrooms; double B&B £49-£65
Credit cards 1 2 3

**Green Farm**
Falfield
☎ (0454) 260319
Situated on the A38 in its own pleasant grounds; soundly appointed bedrooms.
8 bedrooms; double B&B from £27

**Brown's Hotel & Restaurant**
Llandogo
☎ (0594) 530262
Set in beautful Wye Valley; good ensuite facilities in bedrooms.
7 bedrooms

**The Sloop**
Llandogo
☎ (0594) 530291
Modern well furnished bedrooms with good views.
4 bedrooms; double B&B £39-£47
Credit cards 1 2 3

**Lower Viney Country**
Viney Hill, Lydney
☎ (0594) 516000
Charming cottage-style guesthouse.
double B&B from £40
Credit cards 1 3

**Valley House**
Raglan Rd, Tintern
☎ (0291) 689652
Off the A466; situated in tranquil surroundings
with good standard rooms.
3 bedrooms; double B&B £35-£40

**Fountain**
Trellech Grange, Tintern
☎ (0291) 689303
Seventeenth century inn two miles west of the village.
5 bedrooms; double B&B £24-£28
Credit cards 1 3

### CAMPSITES

►►► **Salthouse Farm Caravan Site**
Severn Beach
☎ (0454) 632274
Adjacent to Severn Estuary and beach, off A403;
pitch price from £6.60

►►► **Christchurch Forest Park Camping Ground**
Coleford
☎ (0594) 833376
Northeast of Chepstow.

# Chester

*Chester has the oldest racecourse in the country - The Roodee - overlooked by the medieval walls of the city. The tight, circular track enables every spectator to get a close-up perspective of the action.*

It also means that runners are almost always on the turn which will not suit long-striding animals. Instead, the smaller, handy type of horse is greatly favoured here with speed out of the gate also a necessary attribute in sprint races.

The highlight of the racing calendar is the Festival Meeting in May huge crowds pack the grandstands in anticipation of seeing some potentially top-class horses. The County Stand, opened in 1988, provides excellent facilities and affords panoramic views. Indeed, about the only criticism that could be levelled at this delightful course is that there are not enough fixtures to satisfy demand.

## FURTHER INFORMATION

Chester Racecourse Co Ltd
Steam Mill, Steam Mill Street, Chester CH3 5AN
☎ (0244) 348976 or 323170

## LOCATION AND HOW TO GET THERE

The racecourse is within easy walking distance of the centre of Chester. By road, join the Inner Ring road and take the A548 Queensferry Road. The racecourse and car parks are on the left hand side, immediately beyond the city walls.

**Nearest Railway Station:** Chester General; there are frequent bus services to the city centre from where the course can be reached by walking down Watergate Street, across the Inner Ring Road and through the Watergate.

## ADMISSION

All classes of day ticket give access to full betting facilities, including Tote.

**Day Tickets:**
COUNTY ENCLOSURE Adult £12, Junior (up to 17 years) £2, seats free; May Festival Meeting £17-£22 per day or £45 for 3 days, Junior £3 per day, reserved seats £15 for 3 days – access to bars, restaurant, boxes, tented village during May Festival Meeting.

TATTERSALLS AND PADDOCK £7; May Festival Meeting £9-£11 – access to new entrance building, bars, fast food

DEE STANDS £4 – access to open bars, fast food

COURSE £1

**Parking:** £1; £2.50 for 3 days reserved parking during May Festival Meeting.

**Annual membership:**
£100 including free parking

## COURSE FACILITIES

**Banks:**
there are no banks or cashpoint facilities on racecourse.

**For families:**
Picnic area with refreshment kiosk and toilets, baby changing facilities, lost children centre.

## CALENDAR OF EVENTS

**May 3-5** – Festival Meeting including Dalham Chester Vase, Ladbroke Chester Cup, Dee Stakes and Ormonde EBF Stakes
**June 22** – evening meeting
**July 8-9** – evening meeting on Friday

**July 22**
**August 19-20**
**September 21**

## WHERE TO STAY

**HOTELS**

**★★★★⊛⊛⊛ The Chester Grosvenor**
Eastgate St
☎ (0244) 32024, telex 61240, fax: (0244) 313246
86 bedrooms; double bedroom £195-£225
Credit cards 1 2 3 4 5

**★★★★ 71% Moat House International**
Trinity St
☎ (0244) 322330, telex 61251, fax: (0244) 316118
150 bedrooms; double B&B £95-£145
Credit Cards 1 2 3 4 5

**★★★★ 62% Mollington Banastre**
Parkgate Rd
☎ (0244) 851471, telex 61686, fax: (0244) 851165
64 bedrooms; double B&B £85-£105
Credit cards 1 2 3 5

**★★★⊛⊛ 78% Crabwall Manor**
Parkgate Rd, Mollington
☎ (0244) 851666, telex 61220, fax: (0244) 851400
48 bedrooms; double bedroom from £135
Credit cards 1 2 3 5

**★★★ 66% Rowton Hall**
Whitchurch Road, Rowton
☎ (0244) 335262, telex 61172, fax: (0244) 335464
42 bedrooms; double B&B £95-£105
Credit cards 1 2 3 5

**★★★ 64% Hoole Hall**
Warrington Rd, Hoole Village
☎ (0244) 350011, telex 61292, fax: (0244) 320251
99 bedrooms; double B&B from £82.50
Credit cards 1 2 3

**★★★ 63% Forte Posthouse**
Wrexham Rd
☎ (0244) 680111, fax: (0244) 674100
105 bedrooms; double room £39.50-£69.50 (room only)
Credit cards 1 2 3 5

**★★★ 62% Blossoms**
Saint John St
☎ (0244) 323186, telex 61113, fax: (0244) 346433
64 bedrooms; double room £85-£110 (room only)
Credit cards 1 2 3 5

**★★★ 60% Royal Oak**
Warrington Rd, Mickle Trafford
☎ (0244) 301391, telex 61536
36 bedrooms
Credit cards 1 2 3 5

**★★★ 56% Plantation Inn**
Liverpool Rd
☎ (0244) 374100, telex 61263, fax: (0244) 379240
75 bedrooms
Credit cards 1 2 3 5

**★★ 72% Green Bough**
60 Hoole Rd
☎ (0244) 326241, fax: (0244) 326265
14 bedrooms; double B&B £52-£56
Credit cards 1 3

**★★ 63% Brookside**
Brook Ln
☎ (0244) 381943, fax: (0244) 379701
26 bedrooms; double B&B £54-£68
Credit cards 1 3

**★★ 63% Cavendish**
42-44 Hough Green
☎ (0244) 675100, fax: (0244) 679942
18 bedrooms; double B&B £49.50-£65
Credit cards 1 2 3

**★★ 62% Dene**
Hoole Rd
☎ (0244) 321165, fax: (0244) 350277
41 bedrooms; double B&B £49-£51
Credit cards 1 3

**★ 62% Leahurst Court**
74 Hoole Rd, Hoole
☎ (0244) 327542, fax: (0244) 344889
7 bedrooms; double B&B from £38
Credit cards 1 3

**★ 61% Weston House**
82 Hoole Rd
☎ (0244) 326735
8 bedrooms
Credit cards 1 3

**Around Chester**

**★★★ 67% Cromwell**
High St, Bromborough
☎ 051-334 2917, telex 628225, fax: 051-346 1175
31 bedrooms; double B&B £70-£77
Credit cards 1 2 3 5

**★★★ 62% Broxton Hall Country House**
Whitchurch Rd, Broxton
☎ (0829) 782321, fax: (0829) 782330
12 bedrooms; double B&B £65-£85
Credit cards 1 2 3

**★★★ 66% The Woodhey**
Welsh Rd, Little Sutton, Ellesmere Port
☎ 051-339 5121, fax: 051-339 3214
53 bedrooms
Credit cards 1 2 3 5

**★★ 62% Berni Royal**
Childer Thornton, Ellesmore Port
☎ 051-339 8101
47 bedrooms
Credit cards 1 2 3 5

**★★★★⊛ 70% St David's Park**
St Davids Park, Ewloe
☎ (0244) 520800, fax: (0244) 520930
121 bedrooms; double room £83-£130 (room only)
Credit cards 1 2 3 5

**★★★ 64% Forest Hill Hotel & Leisure Complex**
Overton Hill, Frodsham
☎ (0928) 35255, fax: (0928) 35517
58 bedrooms; double room £49-£71 (room only)
Credit cards 1 2 3 5

**★★ 64% Bryn Awel**
Denbigh Rd, Mold
☎ (0352) 758622, fax: (0352) 758625
7 bedrooms; double B&B from £48
Credit cards 1 2 3 5

**★★★⊛ 79% Soughton Hall**
Northop
☎ (035286) 811, fax: (035286) 382
12 bedrooms; double B&B £80-£190
Credit cards 1 2 3

**★★★ 64% The Chequers Country House Hotel**
Chester Rd, Northop Hall
☎ (0244) 816181, fax: (0244) 814661
27 bedrooms; double B&B £60-£70
Credit cards 1 2 3

**★★★ 60% Autolodge**
Gateway Services A55 Westbound, Northop Hall
☎ (0244) 550011, fax: (0244) 550763
38 bedrooms; double room £34.95 (room only)
Credit cards 1 2 3

## WHERE TO STAY

**★★★ 73% Llyndir Hall**
Rossett
☎ (0244) 571648, fax: (0244) 571258
38 bedrooms; double room £103 (room only)
Credit cards 1 2 3 5

**★★★ 71% Rossett Hall**
Chester Rd, Rossett
☎ (0244) 571000, fax: (0244) 571505
30 bedrooms; double B&B £90
Credit cards 1 2 3 5

### BED AND BREAKFAST

**Chester Court Hotel**
48 Hoole Rd
☎ (0244) 320779 & 311098, fax: (0244) 344795
Modernised hotel, smartly furnished bedrooms. 8 bedrooms
Credit cards 1 2 3 5

**Chester Town House**
23 King St
☎ (0244) 350021
Quaint old house with rooms individually decorated to a high standard.
3 bedrooms; double B&B £45
Credit cards 1 3

**Green Gables**
11 Eversley Park
☎ (0244) 372243, fax: (0244) 376352
Fully modernised small hotel on outskirts with smart bedrooms.
4 bedrooms; double B&B £33-£35

**Redland Private Hotel**
64 Hough Green
☎ (0244) 671024
Former gentleman's residence retaining much of the original character.
13 bedrooms

**Vicarage Lodge**
11 Vicarage Rd, Hoole
☎ (0244) 319533
Welcoming proprietors and warm cosy bedrooms.
4 bedrooms; double B&B from £27

### Around Chester

**Golborne Manor**
Platts Ln, Hatton Heath
☎ (0829) 70310
Beautifully preserved Victorian country house.
2 bedrooms; double B&B £35

**Hill Farmhouse**
Llong, Mold
☎ (0244) 550415
Well maintained, comfortable accommodation.
3 bedrooms; double B&B £26-£30

### CAMPSITES

**► Woodbine Cottage Caravan & Camping Park**
Acton Bridge
☎ (0606) 852319 & 77900
Northeast of Chester off the A49.

**►►► Camping & Caravanning Club Site**
Bangor-on-Dee
☎ (0978) 780740 & (0203) 694995
On the A525 south of Chester; pitch price from £8.10 per night.

**►►► Plassey Touring Caravan & Leisure Park**
Eyton
☎ (0978) 780277
South of Chester; pitch price from £7 per night.

## WHERE TO EAT

### RESTAURANTS

🏵🏵 Craxton Wood
Parkgate Rd, Puddington
☎ 051-339 4717, fax: 051-339 1740
Classical food and attentive service in a hotel restaurant.
Lunch: 12-2; from £17.85-£21.80 and à la carte
Dinner: 7-10; from £21.75-£26.70 and à la carte

### PUBS

**Ye Olde Kings Head**
48-50 Lower Bridge Street, Chester
☎ (0244) 324855
A charming black and white listed building. Fresh bar menu every day. Draught beers include Davenports, Thomas Greenhall Original, Stones; selection of whiskies, range of wines and champagne available. No children under 14 in the bars.
Open: 11am-11pm; Sunday 12-3, 7-10.30
Bar food: 12-2pm
Restaurant: 12-2pm, 6-9.30pm; Sunday 12-9pm
Accommodation: double B&B £50-£60

# Doncaster

*This Yorkshire venue has undergone a major programme of improvements in recent years after being the subject of some justified criticism in the 80s for its boring atmosphere and lack of soul.*

Nearly £10million has been sunk into its redevelopment and the construction of a spanking new grandstand has done much to change its image and restore its reputation as a Grade One racecourse. Facilities have been similarly refurbished and there is now a splendid selection of restaurants and bars to suit all needs.

The quality of racing on this flat, galloping track has never been in question. Doncaster boasts a fine tradition as home to the fifth and oldest Classic, the St Leger, the highlight of a vibrant four-day meeting in September. Its late March fixture also holds an important place in the calendar as it heralds the opening of the new Flat season, with the Lincoln, a lottery of a handicap, as the principle race. Several major two-year-old contests take place during the summer and it also plays host to the last important Flat meeting of the year in early November before jumping fans get a chance to see some action during the winter months.

## FURTHER INFORMATION

International Racecourse Management Ltd
Doncaster Racecourse, Grand Stand, Leger Way
Doncaster DN2 6BB
Tel (0302) 320066/7

## LOCATION AND HOW TO GET THERE

The course is on the southeastern outskirts of Doncaster, alongside the M18 (junctions 3 and 4). The M18 connects directly with the M1, A1(M), M180 and M62.

**Nearest Railway Station:** Doncaster. Doncaster airport is adjacent to the course and there is a helicopter landing pad.

## ADMISSION

All classes of day ticket give access to full betting facilities, including Tote.

**Day Tickets:**
MEMBERS £14-£16, St Leger Festival £18 Wednesday, Thursday and Friday, £24 Saturday, or £60 for a 4-day ticket – access to bar, restaurant, boxes, private rooms

GRANDSTAND £8-£10, St Leger Festival £10 Wednesday, Thursday and Friday, £14 Saturday, or £34 for a 4-day ticket – access to bar, restaurant, boxes, private rooms

FAMILY £3-£5, St Leger Festival £5 – access to bar, restaurant, boxes, private rooms

**Annual membership:** £160 single, £220 dual, £75 junior, includes exclusive use of 'Flying Fox' room, reciprocal days at other courses for certain meetings

## COURSE FACILITIES

**Banks:**
Co-op Bank on course during the St Leger Meeting only, but no cashpoint facilities

**For families:**
baby-changing facilities, lost children centre, creche at Saturday meetings for children over 2 years, children's entertainment at summer meetings

## CALENDAR OF EVENTS

**May 2** – flat
**May 28** – flat
**May 30** – flat
**June 4** – flat
**June 24-25** – flat; evening meeting on Saturday

**July 20-21** – flat; evening meeting on Thursday
**September 7-10** – flat
**October 21-22** – flat; includes Racing Post Trophy
**November 4-5** – flat; includes William Hill November Handicap
**December 9-10** – jumping

## WHERE TO STAY

### HOTELS

**★★★ 67% Doncaster Moat House**
Warmsworth
☎ (0302) 310331, telex 547963, fax: (0302) 310197
100 bedrooms
Credit cards 1 2 3 4 5

**★★★ 62% Danum Swallow**
High St
☎ (0302) 342261, telex 547533, fax: (0302) 329034
66 bedrooms
Credit cards 1 2 3 5

**★★★ 60% Grand St Leger**
Bennetthorpe
☎ (0302) 364111, fax: (0302) 329865
21 bedrooms; double B&B £50-£90
Credit cards 1 2 3 5

**★★ 69% Regent**
Regent Square
☎ (0302) 364180 & 364336, telex 54480, fax: (0302) 322331
50 bedrooms; double B&B £45-£65
Credit cards 1 2 3 4 5

**Campanile**
Doncaster Leisure Park Bawtry Rd
☎ (0302) 370770, telex 547942, fax: (0302) 370813
50 bedrooms
Credit cards 1 2 3

### Around Doncaster

**Forte Travelodge**
Great North Rd, Carcroft
☎ (0302) 330841, Central Reservations: (0800) 850950
40 bedrooms; double bedroom £31.95
Credit cards 1 2 3

**★★ 70% Earl of Strafford**
Doncaster Rd, Hooton Roberts
☎ (0709) 852737, fax: (0709) 851903
27 bedrooms; double B&B £67-£77
Credit cards 1 2 3 5

**★★★ 64% Mount Pleasant**
Great North Rd, Rossington
☎ (0302) 868696 & 868219, fax: (0302) 865130
32 bedrooms; double B&B £62.50-£72
Credit cards 1 2 3 5

**★★ 67% Belmont Horsefair**
Thorne
☎ (0405) 812320, telex 54480, fax: (0405) 740508
23 bedrooms; double B&B £56.50-£70
Credit cards 1 2 3 5

## BED AND BREAKFAST

**Almel Hotel**
20 Christchurch Rd,
☎ (0302) 365230, fax: (0302) 341434
Town centre guesthouse with light, quite compact rooms.
30 bedrooms; double B&B £34-£38
Credit cards 1 2 3

**Nelsons Hotel**
Cleveland St
☎ (0302) 344550, fax: (0302) 341596
Small town centre privately owned hotel with
nicely decorated bedrooms.

### CAMPSITES

**►► Hatfield Marina Water Sports Centre**
Hatfield
☎ (0302) 841572
Situated northeast of Doncaster; pitch price from £2.60 per night.

## WHERE TO EAT

### RESTAURANTS

**❀❀ Greenhead House**
84 Buncross Rd, Chapeltown
☎ (0742) 469004
Enjoyable French-based cooking in cottage-style restaurant.
Lunch: by prior arrangement only.
Dinner: 7-9; from £27

# Edinburgh

*Although it is officially called Edinburgh, the site of this racecourse is actually some eight miles to the east of Scotland's capital city at Musselburgh. Its location, the the sea-shore whose beaches overlook the Firth of Forth, usually helps to protect the course from extremes of weather and racing is rarely abandoned here.*

Indeed, it has even been known for a meeting to go ahead when neighbouring areas are completely covered under a blanket of snow, so favoured by a mild climate is this coastal venue. The sharp mile and a quarter oval circuit is very level, suiting front-runners who accordingly have an excellent record at the track. It was originally devoted solely to Flat racing until the decision was taken to develop it into a dual purpose course with the successful introduction of jump meetings in 1987. Unfortunately, the standard of racing has remained fairly moderate over the years but admission charges are cheap compared to most southern racetracks.

## FURTHER INFORMATION

Lothian Racing Syndicate Ltd
Racecourse Office, 2 Whitletts Road
Ayr KA8 0JE
☎ (0292) 264179

## LOCATION AND HOW TO GET THERE

The course is east of the city at the Musselburgh, off the A1. Leave the M8 at junction 2, take the A8 towards Edinburgh, then follow the ring road. **Nearest Railway Station:** Musselburgh; there is no connecting bus service to the course.

## ADMISSION

All classes of day ticket give access to full betting facilities, including Tote

**Day Tickets:**
CLUB £11 – access to bar, restaurant, private rooms

GRANDSTAND £6, senior citizens £3 – access to bar, restaurant and snack bar

**Annual membership:** £90

## COURSE FACILITIES

**Banks:**
there are no banks or cashpoint facilities on the course

**For families:**
picnic area; children play area; lost children centre

## CALENDAR OF EVENTS

**April 18** – flat
**May 4** – flat
**May 16** – flat
**June 10** – flat; evening meeting
**June 13** – flat
**June 20** – flat
**July 4** – flat
**July 11-12** – flat

**July 29** – flat; evening meeting
**August 25** – flat
**September 19** – flat
**November 3** – flat
**December 5** – jumping
**December 10** – jumping
**December 19** – jumping

## WHERE TO STAY

### HOTELS

**★★★★★ 69% Caledonian**
Princes St
☎ 031-225 2433, telex 72179,
fax: 031-225 6632
239 bedrooms; double bedroom £225-£295
Credit cards 1 2 3 5

**★★★★ 66% Balmoral**
Princes St
☎ 031-556 2414, telex 727282,
fax: 031-557 3747
189 bedrooms; double bedroom £150-£175
Credit cards 1 2 3 5

**★★★★ 68% Carlton Highland**
North Bridge
☎ 031-556 7277, telex 727001, fax: 031-556 2691
197 bedrooms; double B&B £138-£149
Credit cards 1 2 3 4 5

**★★★★ 65% Dalmahoy Hotel, Golf & Country Club**
Kirknewton
☎ 031-333 1845, fax: 031-335 3203
116 bedrooms; double B&B £120-£170
Credit cards 1 2 3 5

**★★★★ 63% George Hotel Inter-Continental**
19-21 George St
☎ 031-225 1251, telex 72570, fax: 031-226 5644
195 bedrooms; double bedroom £155-£165
Credit cards 1 2 3 5

**★★★ 73% Norton House**
Ingliston
☎ 031-333 1275, fax: 031-333 5305
47 bedrooms; double B&B £95-£150
Credit cards 1 2 3 5

**★★★ 70% Channings**
South Learmonth Gardens
☎ 031-315 2226, fax: 031-332 9631
48 bedrooms; double B&B £80-£115
Credit cards 1 2 3 5

**★★★ 70% King James Thistle**
107 Leith
☎ 031-556 0111, telex 727200, fax: 031-557 5333
147 bedrooms; double bedroom £95-£125
Credit cards 1 2 3 5

**★★★ 69% The Howard**
Great King St
☎ 031-557 3500, telex 727887, fax: 031-557 6515
16 bedrooms
Credit cards 1 2 3 5

**★★★ 67% Barnton Thistle**
Queensferry Rd, Barnton
☎ 031-339 1144, telex 727928, fax: 031-339 5521
50 bedrooms; double room from £85 (room only)
Credit cards 1 2 3 5

**★★★ 67% Bruntsfield**
69/74 Bruntisfield Place
☎ 031-229 1393, telex 727897, fax: 031-229 5634
50 bedrooms; double B&B £70-£100
Credit cards 1 2 3 5

**★★★ 66% Roxburghe**
Charlotte Square
☎ 031-225 3921, telex 727054, fax: 031-220 2518
75 bedrooms; double B&B £90-£140
Credit cards 1 2 3 5

**★★★ 65% Capital Moat House**
Clermiston Rd
☎ 031-334 3391, telex 728284, fax: 031-334 9712
111 bedrooms; double bedroom £94.50
Credit cards 1 2 3 5

**★★★ 65% Forte Posthouse**
Corstorphine Rd
☎ 031-334 0390, fax: 031-334 9237
200 bedroom
Credit cards 1 2 3 5

**★★★ 65% Royal Scot**
111 Glasgow Rd
☎ 031-334 9191, telex 727197, fax: 031-316 4507
259 double B&B from £117.50
Credit cards 1 2 3 5

**★★★ 64% Mount Royal**
53 Princes St
☎ 031-225 7161, telex 727641, fax: 031-220 4671
159 bedrooms
Credit cards 1 2 3 5

**★★★ 63% Learmonth**
Learmonth Ter,
☎ 031-343 2671, fax: 031-315 2232
62 bedrooms; double B&B £92
Credit cards 1 2 3 5

**★★★ 63% Stakis Grosvenor**
Grosvenor St,
☎ 031-226 6001, telex 72445, fax: 031-220 2387
136 bedrooms; double room £89-£99 (room only)
Credit cards 1 2 3 5

**★★★ 60% Donmaree**
21 Mayfield Gardens
☎ 031-667 3641, fax: 031-667 9130
17 bedrooms
Credit cards 1 2 3 5

**★★★ 59% Braid Hills**
134 Braid Rd, Braid Hills
☎ 031-447 8888, telex 72311, fax: 031-452 8477
68 bedrooms; double B&B £89
Credit cards 1 2 3 52

**★★★ 59% Old Waverley**
Princes St
☎ 031-556 4648, telex 727050, fax: 031-557 6316
66 bedrooms; double B&B £115-£124
Credit cards 1 2 3 5

**★★★ 54% Ellersly House**
4 Ellersly Rd
☎ 031-337 6888, telex 727239, fax: 031-313 2543
57 bedrooms
Credit cards 1 2 3 5

**★★ 65% Murrayfield**
18 Corstorphine Rd
☎ 031-337 1844, fax: 031-346 8159
23 bedrooms; double B&B £65-£70
Credit cards 1 2 3 5

**★★ 60% Harp Toby**
St John's Rd, Corstorphine
☎ 031-334 4750
27 bedrooms
Credit cards 1 2 3 5

## WHERE TO STAY

### ★★ 60% Suffolk Hall
10 Craigmillar Park
☎ 031-668 4333, fax: 031-668 4506
12 bedrooms; double B&B £55-£60
Credit cards 1 2 3

### ★★ 58% Rothesay
8 Rothesay Place
☎ 031-225 4125, telex 727025, fax: 031-220 4350
35 bedrooms; double B&B £40-£75
Credit cards 1 2 3 5

### ★★ 50% Clarendon
Grosvenor St
☎ 031-337 7033, telex 72450, fax: 031-346 7606]
51 bedrooms; double B&B £93-£100
Credit cards 1 2 3 5

### ★ 61% Iona
Strathearn Place
☎ 031-447 6264 & 031-447 5050, fax: 031-452 8574
17 bedrooms; double B&B £55-£61.50
Credit cards 1 3

### Forte Travelodge
Dreghorn Link
☎ 031-441 4296, Central Reservations: (0800) 850950
40 bedrooms; double room £31.95 (room only)
Credit cards 1 2 3

### Around Edinburgh

### ★★ 67% Woodside
High St, Aberdour
☎ (0383) 860328, fax: (0383) 860920
21 bedrooms; double B&B £48-£77
Credit cards 1 2 3 5

### ★★ 65% Inchview Hotel
69 Kinghorn Rd, Burntisland
☎ (0592) 872239, fax: (0592) 874866
12 bedrooms; double B&B £60-£72.50
Credit cards 1 2 3

### ★★ 66% Eskbank Motor
29 Dalhousie Rd, Dalkeith
☎ 031-663 3234, fax: 031-660 4347
16 bedrooms; double B&B £45-£60
Credit cards 1 2 3 5

### Granada Lodge
A1 Old Craighall, Musselburgh
☎ 031-653 2427, fax: 031-653 6106
44 bedrooms; double room £34.95 (room only)
Credit cards 1 2 3 5

### ★★★ 70% Queensferry Lodge
St Margaret's Head, North Queensferry
☎ (0383) 410000, fax: (0383) 419708
32 bedrooms; double B&B £55-£70
Credit cards 1 2 3

### ★★★ 60% Forth Bridges Moat House
Forth Bridge, South Queensferry
☎ 031-331 1199, telex 727430, fax: 031-319 1733
108 bedrooms; double room £50-£100 (room only)
Credit cards 1 2 3 5

## BED AND BREAKFAST

### The Adria Hotel
11-12 Royal Ter
☎ 031-556 7875
Relaxed spacious atmosphere, offering spacious accommodation.
28 bedrooms

### Allison House
15/17 Mayfield Gardens
☎ 031-667 8049, fax: 031-667 5001
Popular guesthouse situated in a residential area beside the A7.
24 bedrooms; double B&B £40-£60
Credit cards 1 3

### Ashdene House
23 Fountainhall Rd
☎ 031-667 6026
Compact guesthouse situated in a quiet residential area.
5 bedrooms; double B&B £32-£44

### Brunswick Hotel
7 Brunswick St
☎ 031-556 1238
Family-run guesthouse with pleasant, well decorated bedrooms.
10 bedrooms; double B&B £40-£60
Credit cards 1 2 3

### Dorstan Private Hotel
7 Priestfield Rd
☎ 031-667 6721
Bright, fresh plain decor in the bedrooms, and dining room full of character.
14 bedrooms; double B&B £40-£50
Credit cards 1 3

### Ellesmere House
11 Glengyle Ter
☎ 031-229 4823
Delightful, cheery proprietor and spacious, individually decorated bedrooms.
6 bedrooms; double B&B £30-£50

### Glenora Hotel
14 Rosebery Crescent
☎ 031-337 1186
Close to the town centre, providing attractive, well furnished bedrooms.
10 bedrooms
Credit cards 1 3

### Greenside Hotel
9 Royal Ter
☎ 031-557 0022
Friendly, family-run hotel offering good-value bed and breakfast.
12 bedrooms; double B&B £41-£55

### Grosvenor
1 Grosvenor Gardens
☎ 031-337 4143, fax: 031-346 8732
In desirable residential area in West End; well equipped, comfortable bedrooms.
8 bedrooms
Credit cards 1 2 3

### International
37 Mayfield Gardens
☎ 031- 667 2511
Friendly atmosphere and good value bed and breakfast accommodation.
7 bedrooms; double B&B £30-£50

### The Lodge Hotel
6 Hampton Ter, West Coates
☎ 031-337 3682
Impeccably maintained Georgian town house hotel, with bright airy bedrooms, individually decorated.
10 bedrooms; double B&B £50-£75
Credit cards 1 3

### The Newington
18 Newington Rd
☎ 031-667 3356
Delightful accommodation with lots of character.
8 bedrooms

### Parklands
20 Mayfield Gardens
☎ 031-667 7184
Solid, terraced house with comfortable, mainly spacious bedrooms.
6 bedrooms; double B&B £36-£44

### Ravensneuk
11 Blacket Av
☎ 031-667 5347
A tastefully restored semi-detached Victorian house in a quiet avenue on the south side of the city.
6 bedrooms; double B&B £30-£44

## WHERE TO STAY

### Salisbury Hotel
45 Salisbury Rd
☎ 031-667 1264
Friendly, family-run guesthouse; cheery bright bedrooms.
12 bedrooms; double £36-£44

### Salisbury View Hotel
64 Dalkeith Rd
☎ 031-667 1133
Accommodation throughout is tastefully decorated and fitted with comfort in mind.
8 bedrooms; double B&B £42-£54
Credit cards 1 3

### Stra'ven
3 Brunstane Rd North, Joppa
☎ 031-669 5580
Fine semi-detached Victorian house close to beach and 3 miles east of city centre.
7 bedrooms; double B&B £30-£44

### Stuart House
12 East Claremont St
☎ 031-557 9030, fax: 031-557 0563
North of city; well appointed bedrooms.
7 bedrooms
Credit cards 1 3

### Thrums Private Hotel
14 Minto St, Newington
☎ 031-667 5545
Full of character and with a comfortable lounge; bedrooms in the modern annexe are large and lofty.
8 bedrooms

### Around Edinburgh

### Fairways
17 Manse St, Aberdour
☎ (0383 860478
Family-run establishment offering simply furnished bedrooms and attractive breakfast room.
5 bedrooms; double B&B from £30

### Barley Bree Motel
3 Easthouses Rd, Dalkeith
☎ 031-663 3105
Half a mile off the B6482 of the A68; bright cheerful bedrooms; also has an Indian restaurant.
4 bedrooms; double B&B £35
Credit cards 1 3 5

### Whitecroft East Calder
☎ (0506) 881810, fax: (0506) 884327
Fine views, friendly owners, compact accommodation.
3 bedrooms; double B&B from £28

### Forth Craig Private Hotel
90 Hope St, Inverkeithing
☎ (0383) 418440
Small popular purpose-built hotel offering practical accommodation.
5 bedrooms; double B&B £32-£36
Credit cards 1 3

### Long Boat
107 Pettycur Rd, Kinghorn
☎ (0592) 890625
Magnificent views; attractive bedrooms; good bars.
6 bedrooms
Credit cards 1 2 3 5

### Olde Original Rosslyn
4 Main St, Roslin
☎ 031-440 2384
Attractive village inn, 7 miles from Edinburgh;
pretty well appointed bedrooms.
6 bedrooms
Credit cards 1 2 3

### CAMPSITES

### ►►► Monksmuir Caravan Park
Haddington
☎ (0620) 860340
Off the A1 Edinburgh-Dunbar road; pitch price from £10 per night.

## WHERE TO EAT

### RESTAURANTS

### ✿✿ L'Auberge
56 Saint Mary St, Edinburgh
☎ 031-556 5888
Elegant, stylish food – and good value at lunchtime.
Lunch: 12-2; from £11.50 and à la carte
Dinner: 7-9.30; from £21 and à la carte

### ✿✿✿ Martins
70 Rose St, North Lane, Edinburgh
☎ 031-225 3106
Great warmth and friendliness, and satisfying modern British food with an organic emphasis.
Lunch: 12-2; from £10.50 and à la carte
Dinner: 7-10; from £22.50 à la carte

### ✿✿ The Vintners Room
The Vaults, 87 Giles St, Leith
☎ 031-554 8423 & 031-554 6767
Confident, highly enjoyable provincial French and
modern cooking in atmospheric, relaxed period setting.
Lunch: 12-2.30; from £9
Dinner: 7-10.30

### PUBS

### Bennets Bar
8 Leven Street
☎ 031-229 5143
Next door to the Kings Theatre; beautiful old city pub with stained glass windows. A Scottish Newcastle pub with a range of draught beer, lager and cider and over 100 malt whiskies. Fairly standard bar menu. Children are permitted in the lounge only for lunch.
Open: all day Monday to Saturday; Sunday 7pm-midnight
Bar food: 12-2pm Monday to Saturday

### Guildford Arms
1-5 West Register Street
☎ 031-556 4312
Fine 18th-century building. Not one for the children, but adults will relish the choice of ten draught beers and 16 malt whiskies. Bar meals are fairly standard choices.
Open: all day, every day
Bar food: 12-2pm; snacks available all day

### The Tattler
23 Commercial Street, Leith
☎ 031-554 9999
A pleasant and cosy pub near the harbour and river. Range of real ales and excellent wine list. Bar menu includes good fish dishes. Children are permitted into pub, but not allowed to stand at the bar.
Open: all day, every day
Bar food: 12-2pm, 6-10pm; Saturday and Sunday 12-10pm
Restaurant: hours as bar food

# Epsom Downs

*Epsom is, of course, famous as the home of the Derby, the most prestigious contest in the British racing calendar and an event which has been run over this course for some 200 years.*

Derby Day traditionally falls on the first Wednesday in June, when huge crowds always pack the beautiful downs, lining the rails several deep right down to Tattenham Corner. There is a real carnival atmosphere with open-topped buses, fun-fairs, a tented village and plenty of gypsies gazing into their crystal balls. The course also plays host to the fillies' Classic, the Oaks (run on the Saturday of the four-day meeting), as well as the Coronation Cup, an important Group One event for older horses. Sadly though, spectators are few, as at the other meetings staged here, and this is a track which really only comes alive once a year.

The huge white building of the Queen's Stand opened in 1992, offers superb facilities and a spectacular view of the racing. Its design did not meet with universal approval (likened by some to an ocean liner), but it is certainly a substantial improvement on the previous antiquated structure. One other point to note is that there is a very long walk from the stands to the parade ring - jockeys are driven there in a van.

### FURTHER INFORMATION

United Racecourses (Holdings) Ltd
The Grandstand, Epsom Downs
Surrey KT18 5LQ
☎ (0372)726311

### LOCATION AND HOW TO GET THERE

The course is two miles south of Epsom on the B290. From M25 junction 8 take the A217; from junction 9 take the A24.
**Nearest Railway Stations:** Epsom, Epsom Downs or Tattenham Corner; there are connecting bus services to the course on racedays. There are two trains an hour from Waterloo or Victoria to Epsom (half an hour); there is one train an hour from Victoria to Epsom Downs Station (47 minutes) and to Tattenham Corner Station (52 minutes) and two trains an hour from Charing Cross to Tattenham Corner Station (45-55 minutes). There is a 15-minute helicopter service from London Heliport and from Sandown Park Racecourse in Esher (tel: (0279 814632 or 502513 for details).

---

### ADMISSION

All classes of day ticket give access to full betting facilities, including Tote.

**Day Tickets:**
QUEEN'S STAND £13, £22 Oaks Day, £50 Derby Day (limited to members and their guests by voucher only on Derby Day) – access to bar, restaurant, boxes, private rooms; morning dress required on Derby Day

GRANDSTAND £9, £13 Oaks Day, £20 Derby Day – access to paddock (extra £4 on Derby Day, otherwise free), Anglesey Seats (except Derby Day), bar, restaurant, boxes, private rooms

LONSDALE, TATTENHAM AND WALTON £3-£10 – access to bars; Lonsdale enclosure is opposite the Grandstand, for good head-on views of racing and final furlong rails position

ANGLESEY STAND £40 Derby Day – all seats must be booked in advance; access also to the Grandstand and Paddock

**Transfers** to the Queen's Stand are available on all days, space permitting, apart from Derby Day.

**Annual membership:** £120

### COURSE FACILITIES

**Banks:**
National Westminster bank on course during Derby Week only; open 10.30am-4.30pm on Derby Day, 11.30am-4.30pm other days; there are no cashpoint facilities on the course.

**For families:**
picnic area with refreshment kiosk and toilets.

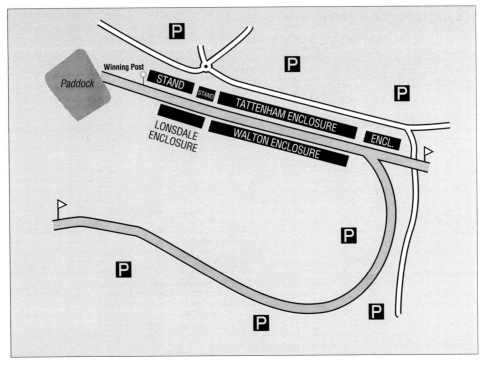

## CALENDAR OF EVENTS

**June 1-4** – Derby Week, including the Ever Ready Derby; the Ever Ready Coronation Cup, International Day and the Energizer Oaks
**June 29** – evening meeting

**July 27** – evening meeting
**August 29-30** – includes Moet & Chandon Silver Magnum

## WHERE TO STAY

### HOTELS

#### Around Epsom

**★★ 62% Heathside**
Brighton Rd, Burgh Heath
☎ (0737) 353355, fax: (0737) 370857
73 bedrooms; double B&B £75-£85
Credit cards 1 2 3 5

**★★★★ 60% The Burford Bridge**
Burford Bridge, Box Hill, Dorking
☎ (0306) 884561, fax: (0306) 880386
48 bedrooms; double bedroom £105-£120.
Credit cards 1 2 3 5

**★★★ 56% The White Horse**
High St, Dorking
☎ (0306) 881138, fax: (0306) 887241
36 bedrooms; double bedroom £85
Credit cards 1 2 3 5

**Forte Travelodge**
Reigate Rd, Dorking
☎ (0306) 740361, Central Reservations:
(0800) 850950
29 bedrooms; double room £31.95
Credit cards 1 2 3

**★★★❀ 61% Thatchers Resort**
Epsom Rd, East Horsley
☎ (04865) 4291, fax: (04865) 4222
36 bedrooms; double room £80-£90 (room only)
Credit cards 1 2 3 5

**★★★★❀65% Cannizaro House**
West Side, Wimbledon Common, London SW19
☎ 081-879 1464, telex 9413837, fax: 081-879 7338
46 bedrooms; double room from £118 (room only)
Credit cards 1 2 3 4 5

**★★★❀❀ 74% Nutfield Priory**
Nutfield
☎ (0737) 822066, fax: (0737) 823321
52 bedrooms; double B&B from £110-£140
Credit cards 1 2 3 5

## WHERE TO STAY

### ★★★ 65% Reigate Manor Hotel
Reigate Hill, Reigate
☎ (0737) 240125, fax: (0737) 223883
51 bedrooms; double B&B £78–£88
Credit cards 1 2 3 5

### ★★★ 61% Bridge House
Reigate Hill, Reigate
☎ (0737) 246801 & 244821, telex 268810,
fax: (0737) 223756
40 bedrooms; double B&B £50–£90
Credit cards 1 2 3 5

### ★★★✿ 72% Woodlands Park
Woodlands Ln, Stoke D'Abernon
☎ (037284) 3933, telex 919246
59 bedrooms
Credit cards 1 2 3 5

### BED AND BREAKFAST

### Around Epsom

### Kings Lodge
5 Kings Rd, London SW19
☎ 081-545 0191, fax: 081-545 0381
Bedrooms furnished to very high standard.
7 bedrooms;
Credit cards 1 2 3 5

### Trochee Hotel
21 Malcolm Rd, London SW19
☎ 081-946 1579 & 3924,
fax: 081-785 4058
Old-fashioned but soundly maintained guesthouse.
17 bedrooms; double B&B £49
Credit cards 1 3

### Wimbledon Hotel
78 Worple Rd, London SW19
☎ 081-946 9265, fax: 081-946 1581
Detached Victorian house offering a choice to suit everyone.
Credit cards 1 3 5

### Worcester House
38 Alwyne Rd, London SW19
☎ 081-946 1300, fax: 081-785 4058
Choice of brightly decorated bedrooms, all equipped with modern amenities.
9 bedrooms; double B&B £59.50
Credit cards 1 3 5

### Woods Hill Country
Village St, Newdigate
☎ (030677) 437
Simple compact accommodation. Full English breakfast available on request.
4 bedrooms; double B&B from £54
Credit cards 1 3

### Ashleigh House Hotel
39 Redstone Hill, Redhill
☎ (0737) 764763
Modestly furnished bedrooms; hospitable owners; ideally located for town centre and station.
8 bedrooms; double B&B £38–£55
Credit cards 1

### Beechwood Hotel
39 Hatchlands Rd, Redhill
☎ (0737) 761444 & 764277
Providing hotel standards of accommodation, 10 minutes walk from the railway station.
9 bedrooms; double B&B £45–£55
Credit cards 1 3

### Lynwood House
50 London Rd, Redhill
☎ (0737) 766894 & 762804
Clean and comfortable rooms in a friendly small guesthouse.
10 bedrooms; double B&B £34–£45
Credit cards 1 3

### Cranleigh Hotel
41 West St, Reigate
☎ (0737) 223417, fax: (0737) 223734
Ideally located for town centre, with many orginal features; attractive bedrooms.
10 bedrooms; double B&B £59.50–£65
Credit cards 1 2 3 5

### CAMPSITES

### ►► Laleham Park Camping Site
Laleham
☎ (09325) 64149]
Northwest of Epsom beside the Thames; pitch price from £7.80 per night

### ►► Long Acres Farm Caravan & Camping
Newchapel Rd, Lingfield
☎ (0342) 833205
Southeast of Epsom; pitch price from £8.25 per night

## WHERE TO EAT

### RESTAURANTS

#### 🌸🌸 Le Raj
211 Firtree Rd,
☎ (0737 371371
Excellent Indian cuisine in stylish air
conditioned restaurant.
Lunch 12-2.30
Dinner: 7-11

### Around Epsom

#### 🌸🌸 Partners
West Street 2,3 & 4 West St, Dorking
☎ (0306) 882826
Stylish and unpretentious modern cooking
with decor to match, at reasonable prices.
Lunch: 12-2; from £13.25
Dinner: 7-9.30; from £16

#### 🌸🌸 Michels
13 High St, Ripley
☎ (0483) 224777 & 222940
Stylish town house where the cooking
shows more than a dash of flair.
Lunch: 12-1.45; from £17 and à la carte
Dinner: 7-9; from £20 and à la carte

#### 🌸🌸🌸🌸🌸 Harvey's
2 Bellevue Road, London SW17
☎ 081-672 0114/5
Highly accomplished and at times dazzling
modern French cooking in elegant,
comfortable surroundings.
Lunch: 12-2.50; from £24
Dinner: 7-11; from £48

### PUBS

#### City Arms
5-6 Portsmouth Rd, Long Ditton,
nr Surbiton
☎ 081-398 2471
Comfortable riverside pub. Webster's
Yorkshire, Courage Best, Wadworth 6X and
a selection of imported lagers available.
Home made dishes available and there is a
non-smoking restaurant. Children are
permitted in restaurant only and have their
own menu.
Open: 11am-11pm; Sunday 12-3pm, 7-
10.30pm
Bar food: 11am-2.30pm, 5.30-10pm;
Sunday 12-2.30pm, 7-10pm
Restaurant: times as bar food

#### Cricketers
Downside Cobham
☎ (0932) 862105
Pretty and cottage-like 16th-century pub
with an atmosphere of civilised calm,
overlooking common. Ruddles County and
Best, Courage Best and Webster's Yorkshire
beers available. Spacious restaurant with
table d'hote lunch and a la carte menu;
blackboard menu offers cheaper
alternatives.
Open 11am-2.30pm, 6-11pm; Sunday 12-
2.30pm, 7-10.30pm
Bar food: 12-2pm, 7-10pm
Restaurant: times as bar food, but closed
Sunday evening and all day Monday

# Exeter

*This is a majestic country venue in the heart of Devon that thoroughly merits a visit. Situated on the top of Haldon Hill, the breathtaking landscape can provide a welcome distraction if backing a winner is proving too difficult.*

It is also not unknown for stags to jump out of the nearby woods and, on an infamous occasion, one even changed the result of a race by knocking over the leading horse which was 15 lengths clear at the time. As it was a foggy day, this incident was not visible from the stands and so everyone thought the jockey was suffering from concussion when he proffered his explanation for not completing the course. In fact, he had almost been sent to hospital by the time the other riders backed up his bizarre but true story.

Such a freak occurrence is unlikely to be repeated but racegoers can be sure of seeing some exciting jumping action on this big, galloping track. Viewing is pretty good, apart from a slight dip in the back straight where the horses momentarily pass out of sight, and the catering is first rate. The only disappointment is that, with the exception of the valuable Plymouth Gin Gold Cup Chase in early November, the course does not attract the calibre of runner it deserves due to the lack of prize money. Nevertheless, the early season meetings in August are a wonderful occasion when the sun is shining and the New Year's Day fixture always attracts a good turnout.

## FURTHER INFORMATION

Exeter Racecourse
Haldon Hill, Kennford, Nr Exeter, Devon
☎ (0392) 832599

## LOCATION AND HOW TO GET THERE

The course is five miles west of Exeter. From the end of the M5, continue on the A38 Plymouth road the course is two miles east of Chudleigh. **Nearest Railway Station:** Exeter St Davids; there is no connecting bus service to the course.

## ADMISSION

All classes of day ticket give access to full betting facilities, including Tote.

**Day Tickets:**
Accompanied children under 16 are admitted free to all enclosures.

GRANDSTAND AND PADDOCK £9 – access to bar, restaurant, boxes, hospitality rooms

COURSE £4 – access to bar and snacks

**Annual membership:** £75

## COURSE FACILITIES

**Banks:**
there are no banks or cashpoint facilities on the course.

**For families:**
picnic area with toilets; lost children centre.

## CALENDAR OF EVENTS

| | | |
|---|---|---|
| January 3 | August 24 | **November 1** – includes the Plymoth Gin |
| March 23 | September 7 | Haldon Gold Cup |
| April 27 | September 14 | **December 2** |
| May 2 | September 27 | **December 14** |
| May 19 | October 12 | |
| August 3 | October 19 | |

*68*

## WHERE TO STAY

### HOTELS

**★★★ 65% Edgemoor**
Haytor Rd, Bovey Tracey
☎ (0626) 832466, fax: (0626) 834760
12 bedrooms
Credit cards 1 2 3 5

**★★ 61% Riverside Inn**
Fore St, Bovey Tracey
☎ (0626) 832293, fax: (0626) 833880
10 bedrooms; double B&B £39.50
Credit cards 1 2 3

**★★ 60% Coombe Cross**
Coombe Cross, Bovey Tracey
☎ (0626) 832476, fax: (0626) 835298
26 bedrooms; double £50–£60
Credit cards 1 2 3 5

**★★ 61% Old Coaching House**
25 Fore St, Chudleigh
☎ (0626) 853270
14 bedrooms; double B&B £55–£65
Credit cards 1 3

**★★★ 60% Langstone Cliff**
Dawlish Warren, Dawlish
☎ (0626) 865155, telex 57515, fax: (0626) 867166
64 bedrooms; double B&B £104
Credit cards 1 2 3 5

**★★★★ 67% Forte Crest**
Southernhay East
☎ (0392) 412812, telex 42717, fax: (0392) 413549
110 bedrooms; double room £80 (room only)
Credit cards 1 2 3 5

**★★★ 70% Royal Clarence**
Cathedral Yard
☎ (0392) 58464, telex 42551, fax: (0392) 439423
56 bedrooms; double B&B £80–£140
Credit cards 1 2 3 5

**★★★ 67% Rougemont**
Queen St
☎ (0392) 54982, telex 42455, fax: (0392) 420928
90 bedrooms; double B&B from £79
Credit cards 1 2 3 5

**★★★★●● 66% St Olaves Court**
Mary Arches St
☎ (0392) 217736, fax: (0392) 413054
15 bedrooms; double B&B £70–£80
Credit cards 1 2 3 5

**★★★ 64% Buckerell Lodge**
Topsham Rd
☎ (0392) 52451, telex 42410, fax: (0392) 412114
54 bedrooms; double room £59–£79 (room only)
Credit cards 1 2 3 5

**★★★ 64% White Hart**
66 South St
☎ (0392) 79897, telex 42521, fax: (0392) 50159
59 bedrooms; double B&B £44–£78
Credit cards 1 2 3 5

**★★★ 63% Granada**
Moor Ln, Sandygate
☎ (0392) 74044, fax: (0392) 410406
76 bedrooms; double room £49 (room only)
Credit cards 1 2 3 5

**★★★ 61% Countess Wear Lodge**
Topsham Rd, Exeter Bypass
☎ (0392) 875441, telex 42551, fax: (0392) 876174
44 bedrooms
Credit cards 1 2 3 5

**★★★ 59% Gipsy Hill**
Pinhoe, Exeter
☎ (0392) 65252, telex 57515, fax: (0392) 64302
20 bedrooms; double B&B £56–£72
Credit cards 1 2 3

**★★★ 55% Devon Motel**
Exeter Bypass, Exeter
☎ (0392) 59268, telex 42551, fax: (0392) 413142
4 bedrooms; double B&B £60–£70
Credit cards 1 2 3 5

**★★★ 50% Exeter Arms Toby**
Rydon Ln, Middlemoor, Exeter
☎ (0392) 435353, fax: (0392) 420826
37 bedrooms
Credit cards 1 2 3 5

**★★ 67% St Andrews**
28 Alphington Rd, Exeter
☎ (0392) 76784, fax: (0392) 50249
17 bedrooms
Credit cards 1 2 3

**★★ 58% Red House**
2 Whipton Village Rd, Exeter
☎ (0392) 56104, fax: (0392) 435708
12 bedrooms; double B&B £40–£48
Credit cards 1 3

**★★★ 64% Royal Beacon**
The Beacon, Exmouth
☎ (0395) 264886, fax: (0395) 268890
35 bedrooms; double B&B £72.60–£78.40
Credit cards 1 2 3 4 5

**★★★ 61% The Imperial**
The Esplanade, Exmouth
☎ (0395) 274761, fax: (0395) 265161
57 bedrooms; double bedroom £85–£100
Credit cards 1 2 3 5

**★★ 66% Barn**
Foxholes Hill, Exmouth
☎ (0395) 224411
11 bedrooms; double B&B £58–£66
Credit cards 1 3

**★★ 58% Manor**
The Beacon, Exmouth
☎ (0395) 272549 & 274477, fax: (0395) 225519
38 bedrooms; double B&B £50–£60
Credit cards 1 2 3

**★ 58% Aliston House**
58 Salterton Rd, Exmouth
☎ (0395) 274119
12 bedrooms; double B&B £44–£48

**★★ 62% Fairwinds**
Kennford
☎ (0392) 832911
8 bedrooms; double B&B £49–£52
Credit cards 1 3

**★★★ 71% Passage House**
Hackney Ln, Kingsteignton
☎ (0626) 55515, fax: (0626) 63336
39 bedrooms; double B&B £85–£95
Credit cards 1 2 3 5

## WHERE TO STAY

**★★ 68% The White Hart**
The Square, Moretonhamstead
☎ (0647) 40406, fax: (0647) 40565
20 bedrooms; double B&B £63-£65
Credit cards 1 2 3 5

**★★ 59% Queens**
Queen St, Newton Abbot
☎ (0626) 63133 & 54106, fax: (0626) 55179
24 bedrooms; double B&B £48-£58
Credit cards 1 2 3

**★ 64% Hazelwood**
33A Torquay Rd, Hazelwood
☎ (0626) 66130 & 65021
7 bedrooms; double B&B £41-£49
Credit cards 1 3

**★★★❀ 68% Barton Cross Hotel & Restaurant**
Huxham, Stoke Canon
☎ (0392) 841245 & 841584, fax: (0392) 841942
6 bedrooms; double B&B £83.50-£90.50
Credit cards 1 2 3 5

**★★ 65% Ness House**
Marine Dr, Shaldon, Teignmouth
☎ (0626) 873480, fax: (0626) 873486
7 bedrooms; double B&B £68-£78
Credit cards 1 2 3

**★ 63% Belvedere**
Parnpark Rd, Teignmouth
☎ (0626) 774561
13 bedrooms; double B&B £38-£44
Credit cards 1 3

**★ 63% Glenside**
Ringmoor Rd, Shaldon, Teignmouth
☎ (0626) 872448
10 bedrooms; double B&B £35-£45

**★ 58% Bay**
Sea Front, 15 Powerham Ter, Teignmouth
☎ (0626) 774123
18 bedrooms
Credit cards 1 2 3 5

**★★❀ 69% Ebford House**
Exmouth Rd, Teignmouth
☎ (0392) 877658, fax: (0392) 874424
18 bedrooms; double B&B £58-£80
Credit cards 1 2 3

### BED AND BREAKFAST

**East Burne**
Bickington
☎ (0626) 821496
Grade II listed medieval house full of character.
3 bedrooms; double B&B £30-£40

**Blenheim Hotel**
Brimley Rd, Bovey Tracey
☎ (0626) 832422
Fine detached Victorian property.
7 bedrooms; double B&B £49-£56

**Willmead Bovey Tracey**
☎ (06477) 214
Charming 15th-centry thatched cottage.
3 bedrooms; double B&B from £40

**Mimosa**
11 Barton Ter, Dawlish
☎ (0626) 863283
Family-run guesthouse, close to town centre and beaches.
9 bedrooms

**The Old Vicarage**
Cofton Hill, Cockwood, Dawlish
☎ (0626) 891354
3 bedrooms; double B&B £35-£45

**Braeside**
21 New North Rd, Exeter
☎ (0392) 56875
Easy walk from city centre, offering simple furnished bedrooms.
7 bedrooms

**The Edwardian**
30/32 Heavitree Rd, Exeter
☎ (0392) 76102 & 54699
Convenient location, with simply furnished bedrooms.
13 bedrooms; double B&B £32-£44
Credit cards 1 3

**Hotel Gledhills**
32 Alphington Rd, Exeter
☎ (0392) 430469 & 71439
En suite comfortable bedrooms in this hotel situated on the edge of the city.
12 bedrooms; double B&B £39-£43
Credit cards 1 3

**Park View Hotel**
8 Howell Rd, Exeter
☎ (0392) 71772 & 53047
Particularly well equipped bedrooms feature in this hotel close to the city centre.
10 bedrooms; double B&B £35-£45
Credit cards 1 3

**Sunnymede**
24 New North Rd, Exeter
☎ (0392) 73844
Georgian house providing bright, well equipped rooms.
9 bedrooms; double B&B £29-£31

**Telstar Hotel**
77 St Davids Hill, Exeter
☎ (0392) 72466
Clean comfortable bedrooms; close to the city centre.
9 bedrooms; double B&B £24-£30

**Trees Mini Hotel**
2 Queen's Crescent, York Rd, Exeter
☎ (0392) 59531
Immaculate bedrooms, close to city centre and with friendly resident proprietors.
10 bedrooms
Credit cards 1 3

**Trenance House Hotel**
1 Queen's Crescent, York Rd, Exeter
☎ (0392) 73277
Small family-run hotel offering simple accommodation.
15 bedrooms; double B&B £25-£33
Credit cards 1 3

## WHERE TO STAY

### Blenheim
39 Morton Rd, Exmouth
☎ (0395) 264230
Small, modest, personally run guesthouse
close to the seafront.
6 bedrooms
Credit cards 1 3

### Carlton Lodge Hotel
Carlton Hill, Exmouth
☎ (0395) 263314
Friendly service, relaxed atmosphere, very
well equipped bedrooms.
6 bedrooms; double B&B £36-£48
Credit cards 1 3

### Cookshayes
33 Court St, Moretonhampstead
☎ (0647) 40374
Welcoming proprietors, comfortable old
fashioned bedrooms, beautifully kept
gardens.
8 bedrooms; double B&B £32-£39
Credit cards 1 2 3

### Moorcote
Moretonhampstead
☎ (0647) 40966
Individually decorated bedrooms with
character and charm.
6 bedrooms; double B&B from £30

### Wooston
Moretonhampstead
☎ (0647) 40367
Glorious open views across the moors.
Tastefully decorated bedroom with
thoughtful extras.
3 bedrooms; double B&B £29-£36

### Lamorna
Ideford Combe, Newton Abbot
☎ (0626) 65627
Attractive rural views from this cosy modern
guesthouse.
6 bedrooms; double B&B £32-£36

### Fonthill
Torquay Rd, Shaldon, Teignmouth
☎ (0626) 872344
The Graeme family warmly welcome non-
smoking guests to their home.
3 bedrooms; double B&B £36-£42

### Hill Rise Hotel
Winterbourne Rd, Teignmouth
☎ (0626) 773108
Edwardian house offering light, airy
accommodation.
8 bedrooms; double B&B £25-£35

### Lyme Bay House Hotel
Den Promenade, Teignmouth
☎ (0626) 772953
A large Victorian house overlooking the sea.
9 bedrooms; double B&B from £42

### Rathlin House Hotel
Upper Hermosa Rd, Teignmouth
☎ (0626) 774473
In quiet residential area, with well
presented, simply furnished bedrooms.
10 bedrooms

### Thomas Luny House
Teign St, Teignmouth
☎ (0626) 772976
Bedrooms furnished with great flair and
thoughtful touches. A lovely house, restored
to its 18th-century style.
4 bedrooms; double B&B £55-£60

### Pierce's
Upton Pyne
☎ (0392) 841252
Sixteenth century oak beamed farmhouse
with friendly hosts.
2 bedrooms; double B&B £34-£38

### Rowhorne House
Whitestone
☎ (0392) 74675
Splendid rural views, spacious bedrooms.
3 bedrooms; double B&B £27
Credit cards 1 2 3 5

### CAMPSITES

#### ►►► Lemonford Caravan Park
Bickington
☎ (0626) 821242
West of Exeter off the A382; pitch price from
£7.90 per night

#### ►►►► Finlake Leisure Park
Chudleigh
☎ (0626) 853833
West of Exeter off the A38; pitch price from
£6 per night.

#### ►►► Holmans Wood Tourist Park
Chudleigh
☎ (0626) 853785
West of Exeter off the A38; pitch price from
£8.45 per night.

#### ►►► Clifford Bridge Park
Clifford Bridge
☎ (0647) 24226
West of Exeter; pitch price from £7.45 per
night.

#### ►►►► Cofton Farm Caravan & Camping Park
Dawlish
☎ (0626) 890358
South of Exeter on A379; pitch price from
£6.40 per night.

#### ►►►► Kennford International Caravan Park Kennford
☎ (0392) 833046
Just west of Exeter off the A38; pitch price
from £7.50 per night.

#### ►►►► Dornafield
Dornafield Farm Newton Abbot
☎ (0803) 812732
Situated off the A381; pitch price from £9
per night.

#### ►►►► Stover International Caravan Park
Lower Staple Hill, Newton Abbot
☎ (0626) 821446
Situated off the A382; pitch price from
£6.55 per night.

#### ►►► Springfield Holiday Park
Tedburn Rd, Tedburn St Mary
☎ (0647) 24242
One and a half miles east of Tedburn; pitch
price from £7.30 per night.

## WHERE TO EAT

### RESTAURANTS

#### ❀❀ River House
The Strand, Lympstone
☎ (0395) 265147
Accomplished light, modern cooking, with plenty of fish, in a pretty waterside location.
Lunch: 12-1.30; from £29.75
Dinner: 7-9.30; from £29.75

### PUBS

#### Nobody Inn
Doddiscombsleigh
☎ (0647) 52394
A combination of 260 whiskies, a superior wine list, Nobody Beer, Bass, a guest beer and local farm cider; well cooked, reasonably priced bar meals.
Open: 12-2.30pm, 6-11pm; Sun 12-3pm, 7-10.30pm
Bar food: 12-2pm, 7-10pm
Restaurant: Tuesday-Saturday 7.30-9pm
Accommodation: double B&B £33-£53

#### Double Locks
Canal Banks Exeter
Simple, traditional pub beside the canal, with large grassed area to the rear incorporating a play area for children. A range of real ales and generous portions of freshly cooked bar meals.
Open: 11am-11pm; Sunday 12-2pm, 7-10.30pm
Bar food: 11am-10.30pm; Sunday 12-2pm, 7-10pm

#### Turf
Turf Lock, Exminster
Informal pub in a beautiful setting on the Exe estuary; ideal for families. Range of real ales on draught and superb home-cooked dishes; outdoor barbecue menu available in summer. Morning coffee and afternoon tea available.
Open: 11am-11pm July and August; 11am-3pm, 6-11pm April to June and September; closed January and February; rest of year, lunchtimes only
Bar food: 12-2pm, 6-9pm, (7pm Sunday)
Accommodation: from £22.50 per person

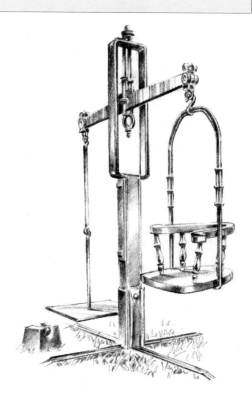

# Fakenham

*Hidden away in the peaceful surroundings of rural Norfolk lies this small, friendly course. Opportunities to visit are limited, however, as there are only half a dozen National Hunt meetings run here every year, the most popular fixtures being held on Bank Holidays in April and May when a large attendance is as certain as the warm reception you will receive.*

There is always an appealing atmosphere at Fakenham that draws spectators from a wide circumference.

Facilities are relatively sparse and this is an ideal place to take a picnic - drive into the centre of the track (known as the course enclosure) and make a proper day of it with all the family. Entrance fees are comparatively cheap and should certainly not break the budget. The action is fast and furious round the sharp, left-handed circuit, with horses galloping flat out all the way. Long-striding animals are not suited to the tight turns, so look out for small, nippy types who will be able to scoot round the bends.

### FURTHER INFORMATION

Fakenham Racecourse Ltd
The Racecourse , Fakenham, Norfolk NR21 7NY
☎ (0328) 862388

### LOCATION AND HOW TO GET THERE

The course is a mile from the outskirts of Fakenham on the B146 Dereham road. It is signposted from all main junctions on the approach to Fakenham.
**Nearest Railway Station:** King's Lynn or Norwich; there are no connecting bus services to the racecourse.

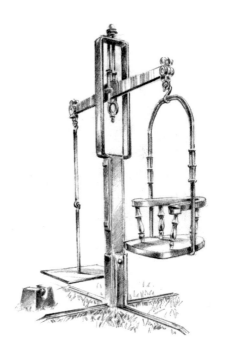

## ADMISSION

All classes of day ticket give access to full betting facilities, including Tote.

**Day Tickets:**
Accompanied children under 16 are admitted free to all enclosures.

MEMBERS £8–£10 – access to bar, restaurant, viewing stand for disabled racegoers

GRANDSTAND/PADDOCK £4-£7 – access to bar and restaurant

COURSE £3.50-£4 – access to bar and snack bar

Transfers: Paddock to Members £3-£4; Course to Grandstand/Paddock £3.50

**Annual membership:** £25 single, £36 double rising to £30 single, £45 double from 1 July 1993

## COURSE FACILITIES

**Banks:**
There are no banks or cashpoint facilities on the course.

**For families:** picnic area with refreshment kiosk and toilets.

73

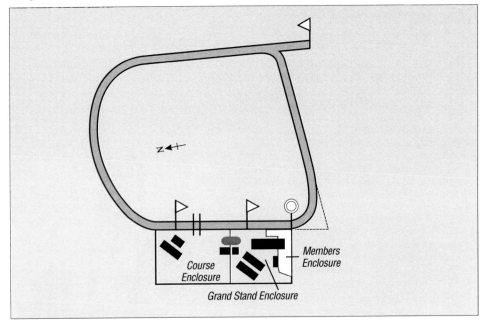

Members
Enclosure

Course
Enclosure

Grand Stand Enclosure

## CALENDAR OF EVENTS

**April 4**
**May 7** – West Norfolk Hunt Point-to-Point
**May 20** – evening meeting

**June 25** – Arab Horse Society Flat Races
**October 21**
**December 8**

## WHERE TO STAY

### HOTELS

**Around Fakenham**

**★★★ 68% Blakeney**
The Quay, Blakeney
☎ Cley (0263) 740797, fax: (0263) 740795
50 bedrooms; double B&B £94-£144
Credit cards 1 2 3 5

**★★ 鍏鍏 76% Morston Hall**
Morston, Blakeney
☎ (0263) 741041
4 bedrooms; double B&B £50-£70
Credit cards 1 2 3

**★★ 61% Manor Blakeney**
☎ (0263) 740376, fax: (0263) 741116
8 bedrooms; double B&B £54-£78

**★★★ 鍏 64% Burnham Beeches Moat House**
Grove Rd, Burnham
☎ (0628) 603333, fax: (0628) 603994
75 bedrooms; double B&B £98-£103
Credit cards 1 2 3 4 5

**★ 57% Crown**
The Buttlands, Wells-next-the-Sea
☎ (0328) 710209
15 bedrooms; double B&B £58-£68
Credit cards 1 2 3 5

### BED AND BREAKFAST

**The Old Brick Kilns**
Little Barney, Barney
☎ (0328) 878305
Hospitality is assured at this immaculate guesthouse, with period furniture in the bedroom.
3 bedrooms; double B&B £36-£42

**Flintstones**
Wiveton, Blakeney
☎ (0263) 740337
In quiet village setting; modern bedrooms, with bright, fresh decor.
5 bedrooms; double B&B £34

## WHERE TO STAY

### Kings Head Hotel
Crossroads, North Elmham
☎ (0362) 668856
Small country inn dating back to 16th-century. Enthusiastic management encourages a relaxed atmosphere.
2 bedrooms
Credit cards 1 2 3

### Rookery Farm
Thurning
☎ (0263) 860357
Seventeenth century, detached red-brick farmhouse; spacious and comfortable bedrooms.
2 bedrooms; double B&B £28

### Mill House
Northfield Ln, Wells-next-the-Sea
☎ (0328) 710739
Splendid red-brick Georgian house; cheerful proprietor; charming, warm bedrooms.
7 bedrooms; double B&B £30-£45

### The Normans Invaders Court
Standard Rd, Wells-next-the-Sea
☎ (0328) 7107657
Lovely red-brick Georgian house with cobbled courtyard at front.
7 bedrooms; double B&B £33-£44

### Scarborough House
Clubbs Ln, Wells-next-the-Sea
☎ (0328) 710309 & 711661
Close to the quay; furnished comfortably and attractively with antiques and collectables.
11 bedrooms; double B&B £36-£54

### CAMPSITES

### ►►► Caravan Club Site
Fakenham
☎ (0328) 862388
Southeast of Fakenham off A1065 Swaffham road.

### ►►►► The Old Brick Kilns
Little Barney, Barney
☎ (0328) 878305
East of Barney off A148; pitch price from £8 per night.

## WHERE TO EAT

### RESTAURANTS

### 🏵 Tollbridge
Dereham Rd, Guist
☎ (036284) 359
Unpretentious service and food in a floodlit riverside restaurant.
Lunch: Sundays only; from £8.95
Dinner: 7-9; from £20.95 and à la carte

### 🏵🏵 Moorings
6 Freeman St, Wells-next-the-Sea
☎ Fakenham 0328 710949
Fresh, local ingredients cooked with free-ranging imagination – and served with charm.
Lunch: 12-1.45; from £12
Dinner: 7-8.45; from £15.10

### PUBS

### White Horse Inn
East Barsham, nr Fakenham
☎ (0328) 820645
Rambling, whitewashed brick and flint inn, dating from the 17th century. Draught beers include Woodfordes, Boddingtons, Tolly Cobbold and Greene King Abbot; also a fantastic range of liqueurs from all over the world. Extensive menu with some unusual dishes. There is a family room.
Open: 11am-3pm, 7-11pm; open all day Monday to Saturday during the summer
Bar food: 12-2pm, 7-10pm
Restaurant: times as bar food
Accommodation: double B&B £45

# Folkestone

*A duel purpose, bread-and-butter type course, whose main virtue is its easy access from all parts of the country, thanks to the M25 (traffic jams permitting) and M20. Situated on the southeast coast, not far from Dover, this Kent track is rightly famous for the excellence of its fish stalls with delicious fresh seafood and tasty fish and chips at very reasonable prices – one definite advantage of a seaside venue.*

There is never any shortage of runners and, though they may not be of the highest quality, there is the occasional prestigious contest sprinkled among the mixed calendar of events. One of the biggest crowds of the year is always seen at the United Hunts meeting, an evening fixture in mid-May to which local point-to-point enthusiasts flock in droves. All the participants are amateurs, creating a very warm and friendly atmosphere, and displays of various other country pursuits help to provide an interesting evening's entertainment with the post race celebrations of winning connections often extending long into the night.

## FURTHER INFORMATION

Pratt & Company
11 Boltro Road, Haywards Heath,
West Sussex RH16 1BP.
☎ (0444) 441111

## LOCATION AND HOW TO GET THERE

The course is six miles west of Folkestone at Westenhanger, near Stanford. Leave the M20 at junction 11 and take the A20 southwards towards Sellindge and Stanford, following AA signposting. **Nearest Railway Station:** Westenhanger; there is no connecting bus service to the course.

## ADMISSION

**Day Tickets:**
MEMBERS £10, children 12-15 £2 – access to Westenhanger Club, Members' bar and Members' dining room

TATTERSALLS £8.50, accompanied children under 16 free – access to grandstand, bars, restaurant, boxes, Orchard Suite and Tote

COURSE £3, car £3, accompanied children under 16 free – access to bar, hot and cold snacks. There is no betting shop in the Course Enclosure.

**Annual membership:** £120

## COURSE FACILITIES

**Banks:**
there are no banks or cashpoint facilities on the course.

**For families:**
picnic area with refreshment kiosk and toilets; children's play area at certain meetings; lost children in weighing room.

## CALENDAR OF EVENTS

| | |
|---|---|
| **April 11** – flat | **September 8** – flat |
| **April 19** – flat | **September 19** – flat |
| **May 10** – steeplechasing; evening meeting | **September 28** – flat |
| **May 24** – flat | **October 17** – flat |
| **June 28** – flat | **November 7** – flat |
| **July 12** – flat | **November 21** – steeplechasing |
| **July 19** – flat | **December 13** – steeplechasing |
| **August 12** – flat | **December 30** – steeplechasing |
| **August 16** – flat | |

## WHERE TO STAY

### HOTELS

**★★★ 62% Clifton**
The Leas, Folkestone
☎ (0303) 851231, telex: 57515
80 bedrooms; double B&B £68-£78
Credit cards 1 2 3 5

**★★ 61% Wards**
39 Earls Av, Folkestone
☎ (0303) 245166, fax: (0303) 254480
10 bedrooms; double B&B £57.50-£86.50
Credit cards 1 2 3 5

**★★★★ (RED) ❀❀ Eastwell Park**
Boughton Lees, Ashford
☎ (0233) 635751, telex: 966281, fax: (0233) 635530
23 bedrooms; double B&B £115-£255
Credit cards 1 2 3 5

**★★★★ 67% Ashford International**
Simone Weil Av, Ashford
☎ (0233) 611444, telex: 96498, fax: (0233) 627708
200 bedrooms; double B&B £90.95-£245.25
Credit cards 1 2 3 5

**★★★ 62% Forte Posthouse**
Canterbury Rd, Ashford
☎ (0233) 625790, fax: (0233) 643176
60 bedrooms; double bedroom £39.50-£49.50
Credit cards 1 2 3 5

**★★★ 58% Master Spearpoint**
Canterbury Rd, Kennington, Ashford
☎ (0233) 636863, telex: 965978, fax: (0233) 610119
36 bedrooms; double B&B from £49.50
Credit cards 1 2 3 5

**★★★★ 68% The Hythe Imperial**
Princes Pde, Hythe
☎ (0303) 267441, telex: 965082, fax: (0303) 264610
100 bedrooms; double B&B £117-£149
Credit cards 1 2 3 5

**★★★ 69% Stade Court**
West Pde, Hythe
☎ (0303) 268263, telex: 965082, fax: (0303) 261803
42 bedrooms; double B&B £80-£98
Credit cards 1 2 3 5

### BED AND BREAKFAST

**Croft Hotel**
Canterbury Rd, Kennington, Ashford
☎ (0233) 622140
Well kept grounds and a choice of well equipped bedrooms; friendly hosts.
15 bedrooms; double B&B £42.50-£50
Credit cards 1 3

**Chantry Hotel**
Sycamore Gardens, Dymchurch
☎ (0303) 873137
Situated off the A259; most bedrooms retain period character; friendly proprietors.
6 bedrooms
Credit cards 1 3

**Waterside**
15 Hythe Rd, Dymchurch
☎ (0303) 872253
Attractive detached roadside building with extensive rear views over Romney Marsh.
7 bedrooms; double B&B £28-£32

**The White House**
27 Napier Gardens, Hythe
☎ (0303) 266252
Close to the sea, with individually furnished bedrooms and friendly service.
3 bedrooms; double B&B £32-£34

**Blue Dolphins Hotel & Restaurant**
Dymchurch Rd, New Romney
☎ (0679) 63224
Historic small hotel with candlelit à la carte restaurant; friendly and helpful service.
8 bedrooms
Credit cards 1 3

**The Old Poor House**
Kake St, Petham
☎ (0227) 700413, fax: 071-247 1873
Delightful 18th century house set in its own grounds, with attractive bedrooms and a restaurant (see Where to Eat below).
4 bedrooms; double B&B £50
Credit cards 1 3

**New Flying Horse**
Upper Bridge St, Wye
☎ (0223) 812297, fax: (0233) 813487
This is a popular village inn.
4 bedrooms; double B&B £41-£46
Credit cards 1 2 3

### CAMPSITES

**►► Caravan Club Site**
Folkestone Racecourse, Westenhanger
☎ (0303) 261761
Pitch price from £8.80 per night.

**►► Black Horse Farm**
Canterbury Rd, Densole
☎ (030389) 2665
Adjoining A260 Folkestone-Canterbury road; pitch price from £7.50 per night.

**►►► Little Satmar Holiday Park**
Winehouse Ln, Capel Le Ferne, Folkestone
☎ (0303) 251188
Two miles west, off A20; pitch price from £5 per night.

**►► Camping and Caravanning Club Site**
The Warren, Folkestone
☎ (0303) 255093 & 694995
pitch price £10.30-£12

**►►► Broad Hembury Farm**
Steeds Ln, Kingsnorth
☎ (0233) 620859
Four miles from Ashford off the B2070; pitch price from £10

## WHERE TO EAT

### RESTAURANTS

**❀ The Old Poor House**
Kake St, Petham
☎ Canterbury 0227 700413
Lunch: 12-1.30; from £10.99 and à la carte
Dinner: 7-9.30; from £10.99 and à la carte

# Fontwell Park

*This must be one of the very best courses in Britain for first-time racegoers to visit. Newcomers to the sport are welcomed with open arms and nothing is too much trouble for the courteous and ever helpful staff. Facilities are compact and the catering is of a high standard.*

Unfortunately, it is not the easiest place to reach, but the route is well signposted and it is well worth the effort.

Racing is over the sticks and the chase course is one of only two in the country (the other is at Windsor) to be run on a figure-of-eight circuit. Consequently, runners are never far out of sight and for a really exciting close-up view of the action, walk over to the centre of the track where it is possible to see the horses jumping the first obstacle in the back straight before moving across to watch them negotiate the final fence. Meetings are well supported by the top trainers and all the necessary ingredients are present for an enjoyable day's racing.

### FURTHER INFORMATION

Pratt & Company
11 Boltro Road, Haywards Heath, West Sussex
RH16 1BP
☎ (0444) 441111

### LOCATION AND HOW TO GET THERE

The course is mid-way between Arundel and Chichester at the junction of the A27 with the A29.

**Nearest Railway Station:** Barnham; there is a connecting bus service to the course on racedays.

### ADMISSION

All classes of day ticket give access to full betting facilities, including Tote.

**Day Tickets:**
CLUB £11 – access to bars, restaurant and private boxes

TATTERSALLS AND PADDOCK £8 – access to bars, seafood bar, mobile catering, boxes and private rooms

SILVER RING £3.50 – access to bar, mobile catering, picnic area (£3.50 per car, plus £3.50 per occupant)

**Annual membership:** £90, plus £10 for car badge if required

### COURSE FACILITIES

**Banks:**
there are no banks or cashpoint facilities on the course.

**For families:**
picnic area with refreshment kiosk and toilets; children's play area on Bank Holidays and August Meeting only.

## CALENDAR OF EVENTS

| | | |
|---|---|---|
| April 21 | August 31 | November 8 |
| May 2 | September 26 | Novenber 29 |
| May 30 | October 10 | December 29 |
| August 10 | October 26 | |

## WHERE TO STAY

### HOTELS

**Forte Travelodge**
Fontwell
☎ (0243) 543973, Central Reservations:
(0800) 850950
32 bedrooms; double room £31.95 (room
only)
Credit cards 1 2 3

### Around Fontwell

**★★★ ❀❀ 77% Amberley Castle**
Amberley
☎ (0798) 831992, fax: (0798) 831998
14 bedrooms; double room £130-£225
(room only)
Credit cards 1 2 3 5

**★★★ 62% Norfolk Arms**
High St, Arundel
☎ (0903) 882101, fax: (0903) 884275
21 bedrooms; double B&B £60
Credit cards 1 2 3 4 5

**★ 62% Burpham Country**
Old Down, Burpham, Arundel
☎ (0903) 882160
10 bedrooms; double B&B £60-£68
Credit cards 1 3

**★ 62% Black Mill House**
Princess Av, Aldwick, Bognor Regis
☎ (0243) 821945 & 865596, fax: (0243)
821316
22 bedrooms; double B&B £46-£68
Credit cards 1 2 3 5

**★★ ❀ 73% The Millstream**
Bosham Ln, Bosham
☎ (0243) 573234, fax: (0243) 573459
29 bedrooms; double B&B £89-£99
Credit cards 1 2 3 5

**★★★ 64% Chichester Resort**
Westhampnett, Chichester
☎ (0243) 786351, fax: (0243) 782371
77 bedrooms; double room £75-£85 (room
only)
Credit cards 1 2 3 5

**★★★ 61% The Dolphin & Anchor**
Chichester
☎ (0243) 785121, fax: (0243) 533408
49 bedrooms; double room £80-£95 (room
only)
Credit cards 1 2 3 5

**★★ 68% Suffolk House**
3 East Row, Chichester
☎ (0243) 778899 & 778924, fax: (0243)
787282
9 bedrooms; double B&B £79
Credit cards 1 2 3 5

**★★ 62% Ship**
North St, Chichester
☎ (0243) 782028, fax: (0243) 774254
37 bedrooms; double B&B £48-£88
Credit cards 1 3

**★ 64% Bedford**
Southgate, Chichester
☎ (0243) 785766, fax: (0243) 533175
24 bedrooms; double B&B £48.50-£61.50
Credit cards 1 2 3 5

**★★★ 66% Goodwood Park**
Goodwood,
☎ (0243) 775537, fax: (0243) 533802
89 bedrooms; double B&B £96-£146
Credit cards 1 2 3 5

**★★★ ❀❀ 75% Angel**
North St, Midhurst
☎ (0730) 812421, fax: (0730) 815928
17 bedrooms; double B&B £60-£90
Credit cards 1 2 3

**★★★❀ 67% Spread Eagle**
South St, Midhurst
☎ (0730) 816911, fax: (0730) 815668
37 bedrooms; double B&B £83-£150
Credit cards 1 2 3 5

**★★ 68% Chequers**
Church Place, Midhurst
☎ (0798) 872486, telex: 67596, fax: (0798)
872715
11 bedrooms; double B&B £65-£75
Credit cards 1 2 3 5

**★★ 65% Arun Cosmopolitan**
87 Lower St
☎ (0798) 872162, fax: (0798) 872935
6 bedrooms; double B&B £60-£80
Credit cards 1 2 3 5

**★★★ ❀❀ 74% Abingworth Hall**
Storrington Rd, Thakeham
☎ (0798) 813636, fax: (0798) 813914
21 bedrooms; double B&B £96-£164
Credit cards 1 3 4

### BED AND BREAKFAST

**Cherrymead**
Station Rd, Angmering
☎ (0903) 782119
Personally run, pleasant guesthouse set in
pretty well tended gardens.
5 bedrooms; double B&B £54-£58
Credit cards 1 3

**Arden**
4 Queens Ln, Arundel
☎ (0903) 882544
Quietly situated off the main road; freshly
decorated, neat, well equipped bedrooms.
8 bedrooms; double B&B £30-£37

**Bridge House**
18 Queen St, Arundel
☎ (0903) 882142 & 882779
Bedrooms of various sizes; good views of
the castle.
16 bedrooms; double B&B £28-£40
Credit cards 1 3

**Swan Hotel**
High St, Arundel
☎ (0903) 882314, fax: (0798) 831716
Popular free house; bedrooms are modern
in style.
13 bedrooms; double B&B £55
Credit cards 1 2 3 5

**The Park House Hotel**
Pebton
☎ (0730) 813543, fax: (0730) 815643
Dating back to 17th-century, with charm and
tranquility throughout.
10 bedrooms; double B&B £90-£99
Credit cards 1 3

## WHERE TO STAY

### Kenmore
Claigmar Rd, Rustington
☎ (0903) 784634
Located in quiet residential area with well
equipped rooms.
7 bedrooms
Credit cards 1 2 3

### The White Horse
Sutton
☎ (07987) 221, fax: (07987) 291
Attractive surroundings, friendly staff fresh
food, real ales and five splendid bedrooms.
5 bedrooms; double B&B £54
Credit cards 1 3

### CAMPSITES

#### ►► Caravan Club Site
Fontwell Park Racecourse
Fontwell
☎ (0243) 542497
Pitch price from £9 per night.

#### ►►► Maynards Caravan & Camping Park
Crossbush, Arundel
☎ (0903) 882075
Half a mile east on A27; pitch price from
£7.50 per night.

#### ►►► Southern Leisure
Lakeside Village
Vinnetrow Rd, Chichester
☎ (0243) 787715
West of Fontwell

#### ►► Caravan Club Site
Goodwood Racecourse, Goodwood
☎ (0243) 774486
Five miles north of Chichester; pitch price
from £9.20 per night.

#### ► Camping & Caravanning Club Site
Great Bury, Graffham
☎ (07986) 476 & (0203) 694995
From A285 towards Petworth, first left after
Duncton; pitch price from £8.10 per night.

#### ►►► White Rose Touring Park
Littlehampton
☎ (0903) 716176
Close to Arundel; pitch price from £9 per
night.

## WHERE TO EAT

### RESTAURANTS

#### ✿✿ George & Dragon
Burpham, Arundel
☎ (0903) 883131
Honest, tasty cooking with good use of
fresh local produce in warm friendly
atmosphere.
Lunch: 12-2; from £14.50
Dinner: 7-9.45; from £17 and à la carte

#### ✿ Cliffords Cottage
Bracklesham Ln, Bracklesham
☎ (0243) 670250
Reasonably priced traditional French-style
food in a charming 17th-century thatched
cottage.
Lunch: Sunday only; from £11.50
Dinner: 7-9; from £16.50 and à la carte

#### ✿ Comme Ca
Broyle Rd, Chichester
☎ (0243) 788724, fax: (0243) 530052
Simple French dishes in a prettily Gallicised
country inn.
Lunch: 12-1.45; from £10.50 and à la carte
Dinner: 7-10.45; from £14.50 à la carte

#### ✿✿ White Horse Inn
Chilgrove
☎ (024359) 219 & 251, fax: (024359) 301
Popular, pretty country inn with skilful,
unpretentious cooking and an exceptional
wine list.
Lunch: 12-1.45; from £16.50
Dinner: 7-9.30; from £22

#### ✿✿ Stane Street Hollow
Codmore Hill, Pulborough
☎ (0798) 872819
Traditional, carefully cooked Swiss and
French dishes, in a relaxed country setting.
Lunch: 12-1.15; from £11.75 and à la carte
Dinner: 7-9; from £16.25 à la carte

#### ✿✿✿ Manleys
Manleys Hill, Storrington
☎ (0903) 742331
Rich, imaginative European cooking and
friendly, professional service in elegant
intimate atmosphere.
Lunch: 12-2; from £18.60
Dinner: 7-9.30; from £26

# Goodwood

*There is no course in the country that can match this marvellous setting on a summer's day. With the beautiful South Downs providing an idyllic backdrop, this magical venue offers a near perfect combination of top-class racing and outstanding facilities.*

One of the most enjoyable week's racing to be found anywhere in the world is the six-day 'Glorious Goodwood' meeting run here in late July, a fixture which rivals Royal Ascot in importance. The cards are a great mixture of competitive handicaps and conditions events. The two-year-old maidens are nearly always won by potential Classic horses while the Richmond Stakes attracts many of the best juveniles. The undoubted highlight of the week, however, is the Sussex Stakes, arguably Europe's most important mile race for older horses. A meeting and a course not to be missed.

## FURTHER INFORMATION

Goodwood Racecourse Ltd
Goodwood, Chichester, West Sussex PO18 0PX
☎ (0243) 774107

## LOCATION AND HOW TO GET THERE

Four miles north of Chichester, signposted from A27 2 miles south and from A285 2 miles north. **Nearest Railway Station:** Chichester; special bus service from the station to the course on racedays.

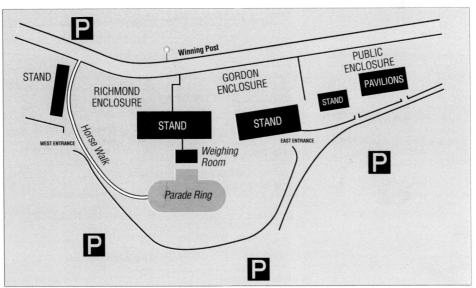

## ADMISSION

All classes of day ticket give access to full betting facilities, including Tote.

**Day Tickets:**
RICHMOND ENCLOSURE £14, July meeting £30 (available to members only during July meeting) – access to Charlton Hunt Restaurant, bars and boxes.

GORDON ENCLOSURE £9, July meeting £15 – access to Gordon Restaurant (July meeting), fast food bar and private rooms.

PUBLIC ENCLOSURE £4, July meeting £5 – access to bars and fast food areas.

**Annual membership:** £120 (£30 joining fee)

## COURSE FACILITIES

**Banks:**
Barclays Bank is open 1 hour before the first race until the start of the penultimate race. There are no cashpoint facilities on the course.

**For families:**
picnic area with toilets; children's play area; baby changing facilities; lost children centre in Operations HQ.

 ○*GOODWOOD*

## CALENDAR OF EVENTS

**May 17-19** – includes A R Dennis Bookmakers Predominate Stakes (Derby Trial) and Tripleprint Lupe Stakes (Oaks Trial). Members and over 65's day on Thursday

**June 3** – evening meeting; Southampton Evening Echo Stakes

**June 10** – evening meeting; BBC Local Radio & TV Race Night

**June 17** – evening meeting; Festival of Speed Stakes

**June 24** – evening meeting; Midsummer Race Night

**July 26-30** – Festival Meeting – includes William Hill Cup, Sussex Stakes, Schweppes Golden Mile, Schroders Glorious Stakes and Vodac Stewards Cup

**August 26-27** – includes Prestige Stakes and Tripleprint Celebration Mile

**September 9-10** – includes Abtrust Select Stakes. Pub 'n' Club Day on Saturday

**September 30** – includes Supreme Stakes

**October 1** – includes City of Portsmouth Stakes

**October 8** – Arab Horse Society Races

(information subject to confirmation)

## WHERE TO STAY

### HOTELS

**Around Goodwood**

**Forte Travelodge**
Fontwell
☎ (0243) 543973, Central Reservations: (0800) 850950
32 bedrooms; double room £31.95 (room only)
Credit cards 1 2 3

**★★★ ❀❀ 77% Amberley Castle**
Amberley
☎ (0798) 831992, fax: (0798) 831998
14 bedrooms; double bedroom £130-£225
Credit cards 1 2 3 5

**★★★ 62% Norfolk Arms**
High St, Arundel
☎ (0903) 882101, fax: (0903) 884275
21 bedrooms; double B&B £60
Credit cards 1 2 3 4 5

**★ 62% Burpham Country**
Old Down, Burpham, Arundel
☎ (0903) 882160
10 bedrooms; double B&B £60-£68
Credit cards 1 3

**★ 62% Black Mill House**
Princess Av, Aldwick, Bognor Regis
☎ (0243) 821945 & 865596, fax: (0243) 821316
22 bedrooms; double B&B £46-£68
Credit cards 1 2 3 5

**★★ ❀ 73% The Millstream**
Bosham Ln, Bosham
☎ (0243) 573234, fax: (0243) 573459
29 bedrooms; double B&B £89-£99
Credit cards 1 2 3 5

**★★★ 64% Chichester Resort**
Westhampnett, Chichester
☎ (0243) 786351, fax: (0243) 782371
77 bedrooms; double room £75-£85 (room only)
Credit cards 1 2 3 5

**★★★ 61% The Dolphin & Anchor**
Chichester
☎ (0243) 785121, fax: (0243) 533408
49 bedrooms; double room £80-£95 (room only)
Credit cards 1 2 3 5

**★★ 68% Suffolk House**
3 East Row, Chichester
☎ (0243) 778899 & 778924, fax: (0243) 787282
9 bedrooms; double B&B £79
Credit cards 1 2 3 5

**★★ 62% Ship**
North St, Chichester
☎ (0243) 782028, fax: (0243) 774254
37 bedrooms; double B&B £48-£88
Credit cards 1 3

**★ 64% Bedford**
Southgate, Chichester
☎ (0243) 785766, fax: (0243) 533175
24 bedrooms; double B&B £48.50-£61.50
Credit cards 1 2 3 5

**★★★ 64% Brookfield**
Havant Rd, Emsworth
☎ (0243) 373363 & 376383, fax: (0243) 376342
41 bedrooms; double B&B £63-£68
Credit cards 1 2 3 5

**★★ 64% The Crown**
8 High St, Emsworth
☎ (0243) 372806, fax: (0243) 370082
9 bedrooms
Credit cards 1 2 3 4 5

**★★★ 66% Goodwood Park**
Goodwood,
☎ (0243) 775537, fax: (0243) 533802
89 bedrooms; double B&B £96-£146
Credit cards 1 2 3 5

**★★★ 61% The Bear**
East St, Havant
☎ (0705) 486501, telex: 869136, fax: (0705) 470551
42 bedrooms; double B&B £67-£81
Credit cards 1 2 3 5

**★★★ ❀❀ 75% Angel**
North St, Midhurst
☎ (0730) 812421, fax: (0730) 815928
17 bedrooms; double B&B £60-£90
Credit cards 1 2 3

**★★★ ❀ 67% Spread Eagle**
South St, Midhurst
☎ (0730) 816911, fax: (0730) 815668
37 bedrooms; double B&B £83-£150
Credit cards 1 2 3 5

**★★★ 63% Southdowns**
Trotton
☎ (0730) 821521, fax: (0730) 821790
22 bedrooms; double B&B £60-£90
Credit cards 1 2 3

## WHERE TO STAY

### BED AND BREAKFAST

**Arden**
4 Queens Ln, Arundel
☎ (0903) 882544
Quietly situated off the main road; freshly decorated, neat, well equipped bedrooms.
8 bedrooms; double B&B £30-£37

**Bridge House**
18 Queen St, Arundel
☎ (0903) 882142 & 882779
Bedrooms of various sizes; good views of the castle.
16 bedrooms; double B&B £28-£40
Credit cards 1 3

**Swan Hotel**
High St, Arundel
☎ (0903) 882314, fax: (0798) 831716
Popular free house; bedrooms are modern in style.
13 bedrooms; double B&B £55
Credit cards 1 2 3 5

**The Park House**
Hotel Bepton
☎ (0730) 813543, fax: (0730) 815643
Dating back to 17th-century, with charm and tranquility throughout.
10 bedrooms; double B&B £90-£99
Credit cards 1 3

**Jingles Hotel**
77 Horndean Rd, Emsworth
☎ 0243 373755
Bright well-kept bedrooms and garden with rural views.
13 bedrooms; double B&B from £40
Credit cards 1 3

**Merry Hall Hotel**
73 Horndean Rd, Emsworth
☎ (0243) 372424
Small privately owned hotel with compact but well equipped bedrooms.
10 bedrooms
Credit cards 1 3

**Holland House**
33 Bedhampton Hill, Emsworth
☎ (0705) 475913, fax: (0705) 470134
Neat tidy guesthouse.
4 bedrooms; double B&B £27-£34

**Mizzards Farm**
Rogate
☎ (0730) 821656
Lovely 16th-century house in tranquil rural setting. High standard of bedrooms.
3 bedrooms; double B&B £42-£46

**Trotton Farmhouse**
Trotton, Rogate
☎ (0730) 813618, fax: (0730) 816093
Converted farmhouse with beams, antique pine and a friendly family atmosphere.
3 bedrooms; double B&B £35-£40

**The White Horse**
Sutton
☎ (07987) 221, fax: (07987) 291
Attractive surroundings, friendly staff fresh food, real ales and five splendid bedrooms.
5 bedrooms; double B&B £54
Credit cards 1 3

## WHERE TO STAY

### Mill Farmhouse
Trotton
☎ (0730) 813080
Overlooking attractive open countryside, the house has a comfortable family atmosphere.
2 bedrooms

### CAMPSITES

#### ►► Caravan Club Site
Fontwell Park Racecourse
Fontwell
☎ (0243) 542497
Pitch price from £9 a night

#### ►►► Maynards Caravan & Camping Park
Crossbush, Arundel
☎ (0903) 882075
Half a mile east on A27; pitch price from £7.50 per night.

#### ►►► Southern Leisure
Lakeside Village
Vinnetrow Rd, Chichester
☎ (0243) 787715
South of Goodwood.

#### ►► Caravan Club Site
Goodwood Racecourse, Goodwood
☎ (0243) 774486
Five miles north of Chichester; pitch price from £9.20 per night.

#### ► Camping & Caravanning Club Site
Great Bury, Graffham
☎ (07986) 476 & (0203) 694995
From A285 towards Petworth, first left after Duncton; pitch price from £8.10 per night.

#### ►►► White Rose Touring Park
Littlehampton
☎ (0903) 716176
Close to Arundel; pitch price from £9 per night.

## WHERE TO EAT

### RESTAURANTS

#### 🏵🏵 George & Dragon
Burpham, Arundel
☎ (0903) 883131
Honest, tasty cooking with good use of fresh local produce in warm friendly atmosphere.
Lunch: 12-2; from £14.50
Dinner: 7-9.45; from £17 and à la carte

#### 🏵 Cliffords Cottage
Bracklesham Ln, Bracklesham
☎ (0243) 670250
Reasonably priced traditional French-style food in a charming 17th-century thatched cottage.
Lunch: Sunday only; from £11.50
Dinner: 7-9; from £16.50 and à la carte

#### 🏵 Comme Ca
Broyle Rd, Chichester
☎ (0243) 788724, fax: (0243) 530052
Simple French dishes in a prettily Gallicised country inn.
Lunch: 12-1.45; from £10.50 and à la carte
Dinner: 7-10.45; from £14.50 à la carte

#### 🏵🏵 White Horse Inn
Chilgrove
☎ (024359) 219 & 251, fax: (024359) 301
Popular, pretty country inn with skilful, unpretentious cooking and an exceptional wine list.
Lunch: 12-1.45; from £16.50
Dinner: 7-9.30; from £22

#### 🏵🏵 On The Quay
47 South St, Emsworth
☎ (0243) 375592 & 372257
Innovative French cooking served with modern presentation in a quayside restaurant.
Lunch: 12-2; from £9.95 and à la carte
Dinner: 7-10; 7-10 £27.50 and à la carte

# Hamilton Park

*A small track, this is very much overshadowed by its near neighbour Ayr and, given the massive local catchment area that this Scottish venue has to draw upon, it must be said that attendances are generally disappointing, except at the summer evening meetings where there is a much happier atmosphere altogether.*

The compact facilities contain plenty of bars and families are well catered for.

Racing is restricted to the Flat with meetings being staged from April right through to October. The standard of competition is fairly ordinary and top northern trainer Jack Berry usually dominates the two-year-old events. One positive aspect about the track is that it is possible to see the start of long distance races close up, with the horses being loaded into the stalls right in front of the stands. This is because of the unusual configuration of the course which consists of a six furlong straight with a pear-shaped loop attached. Runners in contests of around a mile and a half therefore begin by racing away from the winning post before going round the loop and heading back towards the stands.

## FURTHER INFORMATION

Hamilton Park Racecourse Co Ltd
Penrose Hill, Moffat, Dumfriesshire DG10 9BX
☎ (0683) 20131

## LOCATION AND HOW TO GET THERE

The course is on Bothwell Road, Hamilton. Leave the M74 at junction 5 and follow signs to Hamilton. **Nearest Railway Station:** Hamilton West; there is no connecting bus service to the course.

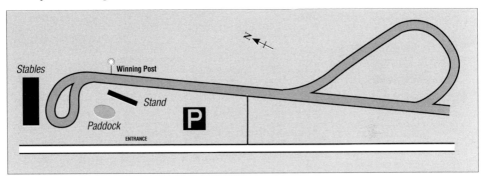

## ADMISSION

All classes of day ticket give access to full betting facilities, including Tote.

**Day Tickets:**
CLUB £12, £20 per couple* – access to bars, restaurant, private rooms

TATTERSALLS AND PADDOCK £7, £10 per couple*, senior citizens and registered unemployed £4 – access to bars, cafeteria, fast food

**Annual membership:** £100 single, £150 per couple*
(* the term 'couple' applies only to a man and a woman)

## COURSE FACILITIES

**Banks:** there are no banks or cashpoint facilities on the course.

**For families:**
children's play area; lost children centre in the racecourse office.

## CALENDAR OF EVENTS

**April 28-29**
**May 5** – evening meeting
**May 14** – evening meeting
**May 20**
**May 25**
**June 8-9** – evening meeting on Wednesday – Saints and Sinners
   Charity Meeting

**June 27** – evening meeting
**July 14-15** – evening meetings
**July 21**
**July 28** – evening meeting
**August 15**
**September 5**
**September 26**

## WHERE TO STAY

### HOTELS

**Roadchef Lodge**
M74 Northbound,
☎ (0698) 891904, fax: (0698) 891682
36 bedrooms; double room £45 (room only)
Credit cards 1 2 3 5

**Around Hamilton**

**★★★ 61% Bothwell Bridge**
89 Main St, Bothwell
☎ (0698) 852246, telex: 776838, fax:
(0698) 854686
76 bedrooms; double B&B £68-£73
Credit cards 1 2 3 5

**★★ 58% Silvertrees**
Silverwells Crescent, Bothwell
☎ (0698) 852311
7 bedrooms; double B&B £66-£77
Credit cards 1 2 3 5

**★★★★ ⚘ 66% Westpoint**
Stewartfield Way, East Kilbride
☎ (03552) 36300, fax: (03552) 33552
74 bedrooms; double B&B £115-£130
Credit cards 1 2 3 5

**★★★ 61% Bruce Swallow**
Cornwall St, East Kilbride
☎ (03552) 29771, telex: 778428, fax:
(03552) 42216
79 bedrooms; double B&B £45-£72
Credit cards 1 2 3 5

**★★★ 60% Stuart**
2 Cornwall Way, East Kilbride
☎ (03552) 21161, telex: 778504, fax:
(03552) 64410
39 bedrooms; double B&B £68-£80
Credit cards 1 2 3 5

**★★ 67% Crutherland Country House**
Strathaven Rd, East Kilbride
☎ (03552) 37633
19 bedrooms
Credit cards 1 2 3

**★★★ 63% Macdonald Thistle**
Eastwood Toll, Giffnock
☎ 041-638 2225, telex: 779138, fax: 041-
638 6231
56 bedrooms
Credit cards 1 2 3 4 5

**★★★★ ⚘ 69% Moat House International**
Congress Rd, Glasgow
☎ 041-204 0733, telex: 776244, fax: 041-
221 2022
284 bedrooms; double room £70-£115
(room only)
Credit cards 1 2 3 4 5

**★★★★ 62% Glasgow Marriott**
Argyle St, Anderston, Glasgow
☎ 041-226 5577, telex: 776355, fax: 041-
221 9202
298 bedrooms; double room £115-£130
(room only)
Credit cards 1 2 3 4 5

**★★★★ 60% Forte Crest**
Bothwell St, Glasgow
☎ 041-248 2656, telex: 77440, fax: 041-
221 8986
251 bedrooms; double room £80 (room
only)
Credit cards 1 2 3 5

**★★★★ 60% Stakis Grosvenor**
1/10 Grosvenor Ter,
Great Western Rd, Glasgow
☎ 041-339 8811, telex: 776247, fax: 041-
334 0710
95 bedrooms; double room £94-£104
(room only)
Credit cards 1 2 3 4 5

**★★★★ 58% Hospitality Inn**
36 Cambridge St, Glasgow
☎ 041-332 3311, telex: 777334, fax: 041-
332 4050
307 bedrooms; double room £95-£105
(room only)
Credit cards 1 2 3 4 5

**★★★ (RED) ⚘⚘ One Devonshire Gardens**
1 Devonshire Gardens, Glasgow
☎ 041-339 2001 & 041-334 9494, fax:
041-337 1663
27 bedrooms; double room £150-£160
(room only)
Credit cards 1 2 3 4 5

**★★★ ⚘ 77% Devonshire**
5 Devonshire Gardens, Glasgow
☎ 041-339 7878, fax: 041-339 3980
14 bedrooms; double B&B £95-£140
Credit cards 1 2 3 5

**★★★ ⚘ 71% Town House West**
George St, Glasgow
☎ 041-332 3320, fax: 041-332 9756
34 bedrooms; double room £91-£133
(room only)
Credit cards 1 2 3 5

## WHERE TO STAY

★★★ **70% Copthorne Hotel**
George Square, Glasgow
☎ 041-332 6711, telex: 778147, fax: 041-332 4264
141 bedrooms; double room £100-£112 (room only)
Credit cards 1 2 3 5

★★★ **66% Tinto Firs Thistle**
470 Kilmarnock Rd, Glasgow
☎ 041-637 2353, telex: 778329, fax: 041-633 1340
28 bedrooms; double room £80-£90 (room only)
Credit cards 1 2 3 4 5

★★★ **63% Kelvin Park Lorne**
923 Sauchiehall St, Glasgow
☎ 041-334 4891, telex: 778935, fax: 041-337 1659
98 bedrooms; double room £49.50-£75 (room only)
Credit cards 1 2 3 4 5

★★★ **62% Swallow**
517 Paisley Rd, Glasgow
☎ 041-427 3146, telex: 778795, fax: 041-427 4059
119 bedrooms; double B&B £88-£98
Credit cards 1 2 3 5

★★★ **61% Sherbrooke Castle**
11 Sherbrooke Av, Pollokshields, Glasgow
☎ 041-427 4227, fax: 041-427 5685
21 bedrooms; double B&B from £79.50
Credit cards 1 2 3 5

★★★ **60% Jurys Pond**
Great Western Rd, Glasgow
☎ 041-334 8161, telex: 776573, fax: 042-334 3846
134 bedrooms; double room £59.50 (room only)
Credit cards 1 2 3 5

★★★ **60% Stakis Ingram**
Ingram St, Glasgow
☎ 041-248 4401, telex: 776470, fax: 041-226 5149
90 bedrooms; double room £69-£79 (room only)
Credit cards 1 2 3 5

★★★ **59% Central**
99 Gordon St, Glasgow
☎ 041-221 9680, telex: 777771, fax: 041-226 3948
221 bedrooms; double room £66-£75.50 (room only)
Credit cards 1 2 3 5

★★★ **59% Glasgow Crest**
377 Argyle St, Glasgow
☎ 041-248 2355, telex: 779652, fax: 041-221 1014
121 bedrooms
Credit cards 1 2 3 5

★★★ **55% The Buchanan**
185 Buchanan St, Glasgow
☎ 041-332 7284, fax: 041-333 0635
60 bedrooms; double B&B £55
Credit cards 1 2 3 5

★★ **66% Ewington**
132 Queens Dr, Queens Park, Ewington
☎ 041-423 1152, fax: 041-422 2030
43 bedrooms; double B&B £75-£95
Credit cards 1 2 3 5

★★★ **63% Popinjay**
Lanark Rd, Rosebank
☎ Crossford 055586 441,fax: 055586 204
38 bedrooms; double B&B £ 55-£ 66
Credit cards 1 2 3 5

★★★ **64% Garfield House**
Cumbernauld Rd, Stepps
☎ 041-779 2111
27 bedrooms
Credit cards 1 2 3 5

★★★ 🌸 **60% Strathaven**
Hamilton Rd, Strathaven
☎ (0357) 21778, fax: (0357) 20789
10 bedrooms; double B&B £50-£71
Credit cards 1 2 3

★★ **64% Redstones**
8-10 Glasgow Rd, Uddingston
☎ (0698) 813774 & 814843, fax: (0698) 815319
18 bedrooms; double B&B £70-£79.50
Credit cards 1 2 3 5

### BED AND BREAKFAST

**Around Hamilton**

**Rosslee**
107 Forrest St, Airdrie
☎ 0236 765865
Run by enthusiastic owners and catering for both tourist and commercial trade.
6 bedrooms; double B&B £35-£43

**Ambassador**
7 Kelvin Dr, Glasgow
☎ 041-946 1018, fax: 041-945 5377
Tastefully furnished and decorated hotel; very well equipped bedrooms.
16 bedrooms; double B&B £45-£50
Credit cards 1 3

**Dalmeny Hotel**
62 St Andrews Dr, Nithsdale Cross, Glasgow
☎ 041-427 1106 & 6288
Small family-run hotel with thoughtfully equipped bedrooms.
8 bedrooms
Credit cards 1 2 3

**Hotel Enterprise**
144 Renfrew St, Glasgow
☎ 041-332 8095
In the heart of the city offering a good standard of accommodation.
6 bedrooms; double B&B £50-£70
Credit cards 1 3

**Albion Hotel**
405-407 North Woodside Rd, Kelvin Bridge, Glasgow
☎ 041-339 8620
Two minutes from the underground; friendly service, well equipped bedrooms.
16 bedrooms
Credit cards 1 2 3

**Botanic Hotel**
1 Alfred Ter, Great Western Rd, Glasgow
☎ 041-339 6955
Spacious, commfortable bedrooms are a feature of this well run hotel.
11 bedrooms; double B&B £37-£49
Credit cards 1 3

## WHERE TO STAY

### Braidenhill Farm
Braidenhill, Glenmavis
☎ (0236) 872319
Unassuming working farm, modest
accommodation and cheery hospitality from
Mrs Dunbar.
3 bedrooms; double B&B from £26

### Dykecroft
Kirkmuirhill
☎ (0555) 892226
A modern bungalow situated 1.5m west of
Kirkmuirhill. Compact cosy accommodation
in friendly environment.
3 bedrooms; double B&B £26-£28

### Springvale Hotel
18 Letham Rd, Strathaven
☎ (0357) 21131
Personal, friendly service, well equipped
bedrooms; cheerful dining room with nice
view.
14 bedrooms.

### CAMPSITES

#### Around Hamilton

►►► **Strathclyde Park Caravan Site**
Bothwellhaugh Rd, Bothwell
☎ (0698) 66155
Junction 5 of M74; pitch price from £5.65
per night.

## WHERE TO EAT

### RESTAURANTS

#### Around Hamilton

🌑🌑 **Buttery**
652 Argyle St, Glasgow
☎ 041-221 8188, fax: 041-204 4639
An atmospheric Victorian setting for plush
modern cooking.
Lunch: 12-2.30; from £14.25 and à la carte
Dinner: 7-10.30; from £21.30 à la carte
Credit cards 1 2 3 5

🌑🌑 **Rogano**
11 Exchange Place, Glasgow
☎ 041-248 4055 & 041-248 4913,
fax: 041-248 2608
A stylish Thirties setting for skilful modern
cooking with an emphasis on fish.
Lunch: 12-2.30; from £16.50 and à la carte
Dinner: 7-10.30; from £25 à la carte
Credit cards 1 2 3 5

🌑 **Crannog Seafood**
28 Cheapside St, Glasgow
☎ 041-221 1727
Lunch: 12-2.30; from £7.50 and à la carte
Dinner: 7-9.30; from £16 à la carte
Credit cards 1 3

# Haydock Park

*Haydock Park is the top course in the northwest of England, offering an excellent standard of racing under both codes at the 28 meetings that are held here throughout the year. The facilities at this Grade One venue match the high quality of competition.*

The catering is especially praiseworthy as there is a broad range of dining areas, serving everything from fast foods to à la carte cuisine. The viewing from the large stands is outstanding and the place always seems to be buzzing with excitement and eager anticipation - the crowds get really involved in the contests, giving their fancies lots of vociferous support.

The oval track is galloping in nature and the very stiff fences will catch out any shoddy jumpers. January and February see two important handicaps run over these imposing obstacles in the shape of the Peter Marsh Chase and Greenalls Gold Cup, while the mixed May Bank Holiday card features the last valuable contest of the jumps season, the Swinton Handicap Hurdle. Connoisseurs of the Flat, meanwhile, get the opportunity to sample some high-class racing during the summer. Particularly attractive is the three-day fixture at the start of July which culminates on the Saturday with the Old Newton Cup and Lancashire Oaks. Best of all, though, is the Haydock Sprint Cup in early September, a contest which regularly attracts the cream of Europe's speed merchants.

## FURTHER INFORMATION
—•—

The Haydock Park Racecourse Co Ltd
Newton-le-Willows, Lancashire WA12 0HQ
☎ (0942) 725963

Clubcall is a recorded message service giving information on
1. Going report and trainers information
2. Previews of next meeting
3. prices and facilities
☎ (0891) 800828 (calls are charged at 36p per minute cheap rate, 48p at other times)

## LOCATION AND HOW TO GET THERE
—•—

Between Manchester and Liverpool. Leave the M6 at junction 23 then take the A49; it is possible that, up to an hour before racing, the police may direct the majority of traffic from the M6 down the A580 to enter the racecourse at the eastern end. Because of the one way system in the car park, it may not be possible for cars to reach the Owners and Trainers, or A, B, C, or D Car Parks, and an alternative area is provided.
**Nearest Railway Station:** Wigan or Newton le Willows; from Wigan take bus number 320.

## ADMISSION

All classes of day ticket give access to full betting facilities, including Tote.

**Day Tickets:**
Accompanied children under 16 and wheelchair users are admitted free; senior citizens are admitted into Tattersalls and Newton Enclosures at half price. On ladies evenings, ladies are admitted at half price.

COUNTY STAND £13 – access to boxes, private rooms, restaurant, several bars and dining areas.

TATTERSALLS £7 – access to several bars and snack kiosks

NEWTON £3 – access to bar and cafe

**Annual membership:** £140, Junior (under 21) £50, includes free and reserved parking and reciprocal arrangements at certain other courses on certain days. A supplement of £10 per day is charged for admission to the Park Suite.

## COURSE FACILITIES

**Banks:**
There are no banks or cashpoint facilities on the course.

**For families:**
children's play area; lost children centre.

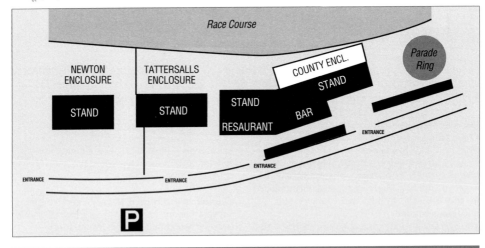

**April 2** – flat; Family Day; includes Field Marshal Stakes
**April 30** – flat; includes Halliwell Landau Spring Trophy
**May 2** – jumping; includes Swinton Hurdle
**May 27-28** – flat; Spinal Injuries Association Raceday on Friday; Saturday racing includes Tote Credit Silver Bowl and Sandy Lane Stakes
**June 3-4** – flat; First Ladies Evening on Friday. Saturday racing includes The John Gaunt Stakes
**June 30-July 2** – flat; The Chippendales Evening on Thursday, includes July Trophy. Saturday racing includes Lancashire Oaks and Old Newton Cup
**August 5-6** – flat; Second Ladies Evening on Friday. Saturday racing includes Burtonwood Brewery Rose of Lancaster Stakes

**August 12** – flat; Newcomers Evening
**September 2-3** – flat;includes Hazlewood Foods Sprint Cup
**September 23-24** – flat; Stanley Leisure Raceday on Friday; Saturday racing includes Akzo Group Handicap
**October 5-6** – flat; Tommy Wallis Handicap on Wednesday; RNLI Raceday on Thursday
**November 2** – jumping; Open Morning
**November 16-17** – jumping; includes Edward Hanmer Handicap Chase
**December 7-8** – jumping; includes Tommy Whittle Chase, Waterloo Hurdle and The Ronnie Johnston Handicap Chase

## WHERE TO STAY

### HOTELS

**★★★★ 61% Haydock Thistle**
Penny Ln, Haydock
☎ (0942) 272000, telex: 67304, fax: (0942) 711092
139 bedrooms; double room from £89 (room only)
Credit cards 1 2 3 4 5

**★★★ 67% Forte Posthouse**
Lodge Ln, Newton-Le-Willows, Haydock
☎ (0942) 717878, fax: (0942) 718419
136 bedrooms; double room from £39.50-£69.50 (room only)
Credit cards 1 2 3 5

**Forte Travelodge**
Piele Rd, Haydock
☎ (0942) 272055, Central Reservations: (0800) 850950
40 bedrooms; double room £31.95 (room only)
Credit cards 1 2 3

**Forte Travelodge**
London Rd South, Adlington
☎ (0625) 875292, Central Reservations: (0800) 850950
32 bedrooms; double room £31.95 (room only)
Credit cards 1 2 3

**Forte Travelodge**
Burtonwood Motorway Service (M62)
☎ Central Reservations (0800) 850950
40 bedrooms; double room £31.95 (room only)
Credit cards 1 2 3

**★★★ 68% Lord Daresbury**
Chester Rd, Daresbury
☎ (0925) 267331, fax: (0925) 265615
141 bedrooms; double B&B £95-£115
Credit cards 1 2 3 5

**★★ 66% Swallowfield**
Chorley New Rd, Horwich
☎ (0204) 697914, fax: (0204) 68900
31 bedrooms
Credit cards 1 3

## WHERE TO STAY

### ★★★ 59% Lymm
Whitbarrow Rd, Lymm
☎ (092575) 2233, fax: (092575) 6035
22 bedrooms; double B&B £80-£94
Credit cards 1 2 3 5

### ★★ 59% Kirkfield
2-4 Church St, Newton-le-Willows
☎ (0925) 228196 & 220489
17 bedrooms
Credit cards 1

### ★★ 66% Holland Hall
6 Lafford Ln, Upholland
☎ (0695) 624426, fax: (0695) 622433
29 bedrooms
Credit cards 1 2 3 5

### ★★ 59% The Pied Bull
58 High St, Newton-le-Willows
☎ (0925) 224549, fax: (0442) 843745
11 bedrooms; double B&B £32-£38
Credit cards 1 3

### ★ 58% Rockland
View Rd, Rainhill
☎ 051-426 4603, fax: 051-426 0107
10 bedrooms; double B&B £30-£49
Credit cards 1 3

### ★★ 71% Old Vicarage
Stretton Rd, Stretton
☎ (0925) 730706, fax: (0925) 730740
26 bedrooms; double B&B from £60
Credit cards 1 2 3

### ★★★ 63% Fir Grove
Knutsford Old Rd, Warrington
☎ (0925) 267471, fax: (0925) 601092
40 bedrooms; double B&B £35-£66
Credit cards 1 2 3 5

### ★★ 70% Rockfield
Alexandra Rd, Grappenhall
☎ (0925) 262898, fax: (0925) 263343
6 bedrooms; double B&B £40-£55
Credit cards 1 3 5

### ★★ 55% Paddington House
514 Old Manchester Rd, Warrington
☎ (0925) 816767
37 bedrooms; double B&B from £49.95
Credit cards 1 3

### ★ 68% Kenilworth
2 Victoria Rd, Grappenhall, Warrington
☎ (0925) 262323 & 268320
17 bedrooms; double B&B £36-£45
Credit cards 1 3

### ★ 57% Ribblesdale
Balmoral Rd, Grappenhall, Warrington
☎ (0925) 601197, fax: (0925) 62135
14 bedrooms
Credit cards 1 2 3

### ★★ 66% Hill Crest
75 Cronton Ln, Widnes
☎ 051-424 1616, telex: 627098,
fax: 051-495 1348
57 bedrooms
Credit cards 1 2 3 5

## BED AND BREAKFAST

### Aalton Court
23 Upper Dicconson St, Wigan
☎ (0942) 322220
Compact but well equipped bedrooms;
conveniently situated Victorian terraced
house.
6 bedrooms

## CAMPSITES

### ►►► Holly Bank Caravan Park
Warburton Bridge Rd, Rixton
☎ 061-775 2842
Off A57 close to the Manchester Ship Canal;
pitch price from £7.50

## WHERE TO EAT

### RESTAURANTS

### ❀❀ High Moor
Highmoor Ln, Wrightington
☎ (0257) 252364
Careful, unpretentious cooking and a cosy
period style setting for a formal but relaxing
evening out.
Lunch: 12-1.45 Sunday only; from £11.95
Dinner: 7-9.45; from £20 a la carte

# Hereford

*A nice little National Hunt course which has always found wide favour among jumping enthusiasts. Part of the reason for its popularity is that the stands, parade ring and saddling boxes are all situated within a short distance of each other, eliminating the need to rush about madly in order to see all the action.*

Rather, this is a place where everything can be done at a leisurely pace, allowing plenty of time to savour the friendly, easy-going atmosphere that makes this such an appealing venue.

The hilly track is unusual in that it is almost square-shaped, with the turn into the home straight being particularly sharp, a feature which tends to suit front-runners. Fields will, by and large, consist of moderate horses, but do not be put off by that as the programmes have been deliberately structured to create competitive racing, albeit of a lesser quality. There are some 15 fixtures scheduled here annually and a trip to one of the evening meetings in May or August will probably prove most rewarding.

## FURTHER INFORMATION

Hereford Racecourse Company Ltd
Shepherd's Meadow, Eaton Bishop
Hereford HR2 9UA
☎ (0981) 250436

## LOCATION AND HOW TO GET THERE

The course is on the northern outskirts of the city, a quarter of a mile west of the A49 at its junction with the northern Roman Road Ring Road. **Nearest Railway Station:** Hereford; there is no connecting bus service to the course.

## ADMISSION

**Day Tickets:**
There is free access to racing for those staying on the adjacent campsite – see under Where to Stay.

CLUB £11 – access to excellent viewing, bar, restaurant, cloakrooms, private boxes, toilets for the disabled.

TATTERSALLS £8 – access to excellent viewing, bar, snack restaurant, private boxes

COURSE £4 – access to grandstand, bar and Tote facilities. Racecourse betting is only available in the course enclosure on Bank Holidays.

## COURSE FACILITIES

**Banks:**
there are no banks or cashpoint facilities on the course

**For families:**
picnic area with toilets

## CALENDAR OF EVENTS

April 4
April 9
April 30
May 11
May 26
May 30
**August 17** – evening meeting

**August 27** – evening meeting
October 17
November 16
December 2
December 20

## WHERE TO STAY

### HOTELS

**★★★ 67% Hereford Moat House**
Belmont Rd,
☎ (0432) 354301, fax: (0432) 275114
28 bedrooms; double B&B £79.50
Credit cards 1 2 3 5

**★★★ 59% The Green Dragon**
Broad St,
☎ (04342) 272506, telex: 35491,
fax: (0432) 352139
88 bedrooms; double room £80 (room only)
Credit cards 1 2 3 5

**★★ 69% Merton Hotel & Governors Restaurant**
Commercial Rd
☎ (0432) 265925, fax: (0432) 354983
15 bedrooms; double B&B £70-£75
Credit cards 1 2 3 5

**★★ 65% Dormington Court Country House**
Dormington
☎ (0432) 850370
7 bedrooms
Credit cards 1 3

**★★ 65% Munstone House**
Munstone
☎ (0432) 267122
6 bedrooms
Credit cards 1 3 5

**★★ 63% Somerville**
12 Bodenham Rd
☎ (0432) 273991, fax: (0432) 266723
10 bedrooms; double B&B £42-£51
Credit cards 1 2 3

**★★ 59% Castle Pool**
Castle St
☎ (0432) 356321
26 bedrooms; double B&B £70-£82
Credit cards 1 2 3 5

**Around Hereford**

**★★ 65% Green Man Inn**
Fownhope
☎ (0432) 860243, fax: (0432) 860207
10 bedrooms
Credit cards 1 2 3

**★★ 63% How Caple Grange**
How Caple
☎ (098986) 208, fax: (098986) 301
26 bedrooms

### BED AND BREAKFAST

**Hermitage Manor**
Canon Pyon
☎ (0432) 760317
Impressive manor house with magnificent oak panelling and spacious accommodation. It is surrounded by 11 acres of grounds bordering woodland.
3 bedrooms; double B&B from £38

**Ferncroft Hotel**
144 Ledbury Rd
☎ (0432) 265538
Attractive family hotel with modern facilities, set in pleasant grounds.
11 bedrooms; double B&B from £30

**Hopbine Hotel**
Roman Rd
☎ (0432) 268722
Simple and modest, but well equipped accommodation to the north of the city centre.
10 bedrooms; double B&B from £28

**Sink Green Farm**
Rotherwas
☎ (0432) 870223
16th-century ivy-clad farmhouse with lots of exposed timbers and excellent bedrooms, including one four-poster.
3 bedrooms; double B&B from £34

### CAMPSITES

**►► Caravan Club Site**
Hereford Racecourse
☎ (0432) 272364
Quiet, well maintained sloping grass site on the perimeter of the racecourse. Free access to racing on racedays.

## WHERE TO EAT

### PUBS

**Around Hereford**

**Ancient Camp**
Ruckhall Common, nr Hereford
☎ (0981) 250449
High above the Wye Valley, with one of the most outstanding views in the country, particularly from the terrace. Wood Parish Bitter and West Country Pale Ale, a choice of malt whiskies and an above-average wine list; food on offer is of good quality and variety. Children welcome anywhere during the day, but in the evening only if eating; no children under eight accommodated overnight.
Open: Tuesday to Saturday 12-2.30pm, 6-11pm; Sunday 12-2.30pm, 7-10.30pm; Monday 6-11pm
Bar food: Tuesday to Saturday 12-2pm, 7-9.30pm
Restaurant: times as bar food
Accommodation: double B&B £48-£55

# Hexham

*Hexham is quite simply a delight. Its location in the heart of the unspoilt Northumberland countryside, just a short distance south of Hadrian's Wall, is one of the most attractive to be found anywhere in Britain.*

It is a great place to leave behind the hustle and bustle of Newcastle's city life (some twenty miles to the east) and escape to a different world where peace and tranquillity reign in a charming, rural venue. This is also one of the highest sites where racing is held as the course is some 800 feet above sea level, the upshot being that it is totally open to the elements, so be sure to take plenty of extra layers of clothing to keep warm.

On account of its exposed setting, this National Hunt track has very sensibly taken the decision not to stage any meetings during the bleak winter months of January and February, preferring instead to concentrate most of its fixtures from March through to May with a few more in the autumn. The mile and a half circuit is considered to be exceptionally testing due to its steep undulations and races finish on a separate spur which runs along right in front of the stands. For a great day out in the country where a cracking atmosphere is ensured, this is the place to come.

## FURTHER INFORMATION

Hexham Steeplechase Co Ltd
The Ridings, Hexham, Northumberland
NE46 4PF
☎ (0434) 606881

## LOCATION AND HOW TO GET THERE

The course is 1½ miles south of Hexham. It is signposted from the Bridge End Roundabout on the A69, which connects with the M6 at Carlisle and with the A1 at Newcastle.
**Nearest Railway Station:** Hexham; there is a free connecting bus service to and from the course.

## ADMISSION

All classes of day ticket give access to full betting facilities, including Tote.

**Day Tickets:**
There is a reduced rate for caravanners using the adjacent caravan site on racedays.

CLUB £9 – access to bars and exclusive viewing area

TATTERSALLS £6 – access to bars and restaurant

## COURSE FACILITIES

**Banks:**
There are no banks or cashpoint facilities on the course.

**For families:**
picnic area with refreshment kiosk and toilets, children's play area.

## CALENDAR OF EVENTS

**April 23** – evening meeting; jumping
**April 25** – evening meeting; jumping
**April 30** – evening meeting; jumping
**May 28** – jumping
**May 31** – evening meeting; jumping
**September 30** – jumping

**October 13** – jumping
**November 4** – jumping
**November 23** – jumping
**December 9** – jumping
**December 21** – jumping

## WHERE TO STAY

### HOTELS

#### ★★★ 65% Beaumont
Beaumont St
☎ (0434) 602331
23 bedrooms; double room £80 (room only)
Credit cards 1 2 3 5

#### ★★ 64% Country
Priestpopple
☎ (0434) 602030
9 bedrooms; double B&B £58
Credit cards 1 2 3

#### ★★ 63% Royal Priestpopple
☎ (0434) 602270
24 bedrooms; double B&B £52-£62
Credit cards 1 2 3 5

#### Around Hexham

#### ★★ ● 70% Bishopfield Country House
Allendale
☎ Hexham (0434) 683248, fax: (0434) 683830
13 bedrooms; double B&B £76
Credit cards 1 3

#### ★ 67% Vallum Lodge
Military Rd, Twice Brewed, Bardon Mill
☎ (0434) 344248
7 bedrooms; double B&B £36-£53

#### ★★ ● 69% Lord Crewe Arms
Blanchland
☎ (0434) 675251, fax: (0434) 675337
8 bedrooms; double B&B £100
Credit cards 1 2 3 5

#### ★★★ ● 71% George
Chollerford
☎ (0434) 681611, fax: (0434) 681727
50 bedrooms; double B&B from £95
Credit cards 1 2 3 5

#### ★★ 65% The Lion of Corbridge
Bridge End, Corbridge
☎ (0434) 632504, fax: (0434) 632571
14 bedrooms
Credit cards 1 2 3 5

#### ★★ 59% Angel Inn
Main St, Corbridge
☎ (0434) 632119
5 bedrooms
Credit cards 1 2 3 5

#### ★ 66% Riverside
Main St, Corbridge
☎ (0434) 632942
10 bedrooms

#### ★★ 60% Anchor John
Martin St, Haydon Bridge
☎ (0434) 684227, fax: (0434) 684586
12 bedrooms; double B&B £44-£58
Credit cards 1 3

#### ★★ 58% Highlander Inn
Ovington,
☎ (0661) 832016
5 bedrooms; double B&B £38-£47
Credit cards 1 2 3

### BED AND BREAKFAST

#### Rye Hill Farm
Hexham
☎ (0434) 673259
Converted barn and cow shed; bright,
modern and sensibly furnished, including
lovely family room.
6 bedrooms; double B&B from £33

#### Westbrooke Hotel
Allendale Rd
☎ (0434) 603818
The bedrooms are adequately furnished and
there is a public bar as part of the hotel.
11 bedrooms
Credit cards 1 3

#### Morningside
Riding Mill, Corbridge
☎ (0434) 682350
Delightful old stone-built house in the heart
of the village; comfortable well furnished
bedrooms.
5 bedrooms; double B&B from £28

#### Beggar Bog Housesteads
☎ (0434) 344320
Delightful public rooms; Hadrian's Wall and
a Roman fort are nearby; uninterrupted
views of moorlands.
3 bedrooms; double B&B £32

#### The Stanegate
Newbrough
☎ (0434) 674241
In the centre of a peaceful village, the
Stanegate provides comfortable
accommodation and a popular restaurant.
3 bedrooms
Credit cards 1 3

#### Crookhill Farm
Newton
☎ (0661) 843117
Set in elevated position overlooking open
countryside, close to A69; friendly service.
3 bedrooms; double B&B £28

### CAMPSITES

#### ►►► Caravan Club Site
Hexham Racecourse,
☎ (0434) 606847
Overlooking Hexham Moors; pitch price
from £8.40 per night.

#### ►►► Causey Hill Caravan Park
Benson's Fell Farm,
☎ (0434) 602834 & 604647
Pitch price from £7.75 per night

#### ► Ascroft Farm
Bardon Mill
☎ (0434) 344409
Adjacent to A69 between Haltwhistle and
Hexham; pitch price from £2 per night.

# Huntingdon

*A pretty market town whose most famous son is Oliver Cromwell, although it has more recently come to prominence as the constituency of the current Prime Minister, John Major. He is an occasional visitor to the track and his daughter even rode in a charity race here, unfortunately falling off near the finish due to exhaustion.*

The racecourse lies just outside Huntingdon itself by the small village of Brampton and is set in the flat fen lands that are so typical of this Cambridgeshire area. This has resulted in a level, sharp circuit which places a greater premium on speed than stamina, while a particularly nice feature is the siting of an open ditch in front of the grandstand, providing an added spectacle for spectators.

The fifteen or so jumps meetings regularly draw large crowds of enthusiastic racegoers with the two highest attendances normally being seen at the Boxing Day and Easter Monday fixtures. The standard of the runners on both these occasions is usually nothing to write home about, but the course has begun to go slightly more up-market in recent years and there are now a growing number of valuable contests. In February, the Chatteris Fen Hurdle and Sidney Banks Memorial Hurdle are two important Cheltenham trials for novices, but most pretigious of all is the Peterborough Chase, a Grade Two event in late November that carries nearly £20,000 in prize money.

## FURTHER INFORMATION

Huntingdon Racecourse
Brampton, Huntingdon, Cambs PE18 8NN
☎ (0840) 453373/454610

## LOCATION AND HOW TO GET THERE

The course is at Brampton near Huntingdon. From the end of the M11 continue on the A604, turning off at Spitals Link (signposted). From the A1, take the A604 east for a mile.

**Nearest Railway Station:** Huntingdon; there are no connecting bus services to the course.

## ADMISSION

All classes of day ticket give access to full betting facilities, including Tote.

**Day Tickets:**
MEMBERS £11 – access to bar dining room, restaurant, private rooms, boxes

TATTERSALLS £8 – access to bars, restaurants, dining rooms

COURSE CENTRE £4 – access to bar and restaurant

**Annual membership:** £70 single, £110 double

## COURSE FACILITIES

**Banks:**
there are no banks or cashpoint facilities on the course

**For families:**
picnic area with toilets

## CALENDAR OF EVENTS

| | |
|---|---|
| April 4 | October 22 |
| April 27 – evening meeting | November 11 |
| May 11 – evening meeting | November 22 – includes the Peterborough Chase |
| May 30 | November 30 |
| August 29 | December 26 |
| September 16 | |

## WHERE TO STAY

### ★★★ 72% The Old Bridge
Huntingdon
☎ (0480) 52681, fax: (0480) 411017
26 bedrooms; double B&B £96.50-£115.50
Credit cards 1 2 3 5

### ★★★ 61% The George
George St
☎ (0480) 432444, fax: (0480) 453130
24 bedrooms; double room £80-£95 (room only)
Credit cards 1 2 3 5

### ★★ 61% Alconbury House
Alconbury Weston, Alconbury
☎ (0480) 890807, fax: (0480) 891259
24 bedrooms
Credit cards 1 2 3 5

### ★★ 64% Grange
115 High St, Brampton
☎ (0480) 459516
9 bedrooms; double B&B £52.50-£55
Credit cards 1 3

### Forte Travelodge
A604 Huntingdon Rd, Fenstanton
☎ (0954) 30919, Central Reservations: (0800) 850950
40 bedrooms; double room £31.95 (room only)
Credit cards 1 2 3

### ★★★ 66% Olivers Lodge
Needingworth Rd, St Ives
☎ (0480) 63252, fax: (0480) 61150
11 bedrooms; double B&B £48-£58
Credit cards 1 3

### ★★★ 64% Slepe Hall
Ramsey Rd, St Ives
☎ (0480) 63122, fax: (0480) 300706
16 bedrooms; double B&B from £70
Credit cards 1 2 3 5

### ★★★ 62% Dolphin
Bridge Foot, St Ives
☎ (0480) 66966, fax: (0480) 495597
31 bedrooms; double B&B from £70
Credit cards 1 2 3 5

### ★★ 64% St Ives Motel
London Rd, St Ives
☎ (0480) 63857, fax: (0480) 492027
16 bedrooms
Credit cards 1 2 3 5

### ★★ 64% Abbotsley Golf
Eynesbury Hardwicke, St Neots
☎ (0480) 474000, fax: (0480) 403280
15 bedrooms; double B&B £62-£68
Credit cards 1 3

## BED AND BREAKFAST

### Cross Keys
Molesworth
☎ (08014) 283
Archetypal village inn; with friendly proprietor; high standard of accommodation and good bar meals.
4 bedrooms; double B&B from £38
Credit cards 1 3

## CAMPSITES

### ►►► Park Lane Touring Park
Godmanchester, Huntingdon
☎ (0480) 453740
Just off the B1043 between Godmanchester and Huntingdon; pitch price from £8 per night.

### ►►► Quiet Waters Caravan Park
Hemingford Abbots
☎ (0480) 63405
One mile from the A604; pitch price from £7 per night.

### ►► Houghton Mill Caravan & Camping Park
Mill St, Houghton
☎ (0480) 62413 & 492811
East of Huntingdon; pitch price from £8.50 per night.

### ►► Camping & Caravanning Club Site
Rush Meadow, St Neots
☎ (0480) 474404 & (0203) 694995
South of Huntingdon; pitch price from £8.10 per night.

## WHERE TO EAT

### RESTAURANTS

### ❀ Pheasant Inn
Keystone
☎ (08014) 241
Competent modern cooking with some exotic flavours in a cosy, beamed pub restaurant.
Lunch: 12-2; from £21 a la carte
Dinner: 7-10; from £21 a la carte

### PUBS

### Old Ferry Boat Inn
Holywell, nr St Ives
☎ (0480) 63227
Low-built, whitewashed and thatched pub claiming to be the oldest in Britain (documents show that liquor was sold here as long ago as AD560, though foundations have been dated even earlier). Draught beers include Stones IPA, Green King Abbot Ale, Adnams Broadside and Fullers London Pride. Varied menu of interesting dishes. Children's area and children's menu available.
Open: 11am-3pm, 6-11pm; Sunday 12-3pm, 7-10.30pm
Bar food: 12-2pm, 6.30-9.30pm
Accommodation: double B&B £49.50-£68

# Kelso

*The glorious Scottish Border country is home to Kelso, one of the most picturesque racecourses in Britain. Far removed from any major urban settlements, this small venue is full of character.*

For instance, the old grandstand was originally constructed in 1822 and is still going strong today, albeit with most of the original amenities having been replaced over the intervening 160 years. Even so, an old-fashioned feel has deliberately been preserved with special touches like the lighting of log fires to provide extra warmth during the winter.

This is real jumping country and the love of National Hunt racing is deeply ingrained in the local psyche. The track is quite wide (there is enough room for a golf course to have been located in its centre) and the extremely long and demanding run-in of two furlongs has seen many a clear leader swallowed up by the chasing pack in the closing stages. This is definitely not a course where it is safe to start counting the winnings until the horses have passed the post. The best fixture is in early February and features a couple of decent races, the Bollinger Rutherford Chase and Morebattle Hurdle.

## FURTHER INFORMATION

Kelso Racecourse
18-20 Glendale Road, Wooler, Northumberland
NE71 6DW
☎ (0668) 81611

## LOCATION AND HOW TO GET THERE

The racecourse is just north of the town on the A698. Take the A6089 from Edinburgh, or the A699 from the west.
**Nearest Railway Station:** Berwick-upon-Tweed; there are no connecting bus services to the racecourse.

## ADMISSION

All classes of day ticket give access to full betting facilities, including Tote.

**Day Tickets:**
Accompanied children under 16 are admitted free.

MEMBERS £10-£12 – access to full facilities including restaurant, bars, snack bar, corporate rooms and facilities for disabled racegoers.

TATTERSALLS £6, senior citizens £3 – access to restaurant, bars and fast food.

**Annual membership:** £50 single, £90 double, £40 senior citizens – includes reciprocal arrangements with certain other courses on certain days.

## COURSE FACILITIES

**Banks:**
there are no banks or cashpoint facilities on the course, but the Secretary will cash cheques.

**For families:**
baby changing facilities, lost children centre.

## CALENDAR OF EVENTS

| | |
|---|---|
| April 11 | November 2 |
| April 27 | November 10 |
| October 1 | November 28 |
| October 15 | December 15 |

*98*

## WHERE TO STAY

### HOTELS

**★★★ ❀❀ 75% Sunlaws House**
Heiton
☎ (05735) 331, fax: (05735) 611
22 bedrooms; double B&B £82-£128
Credit cards 1 2 3 5

**★★★ 64% Ednam House**
Bridge St
☎ (0573) 224168, fax: (0573) 226319
32 bedrooms
Credit cards 1 3

**★★★ 63% Cross Keys**
36-37 The Square
☎ (0573) 223303, fax: (0573) 225792
24 bedrooms; double B&B £49.80-£58.90
Credit cards 1 2 3 5

### BED AND BREAKFAST

### Around Kelso

**The Spinney**
Langlee Jedburgh
☎ (0835) 63525, due to change to 863525
Delightful house 2 miles south of Jedburgh;
inviting, individually decorated bedrooms.
3 bedrooms; double B&B from £34

**Froylehurst Friars**
Jedburgh
☎ (0835) 62477, due to change to 862477
Handsome Victorian house in quiet area;
attractive fabrics individually deocrated
bedrooms.
5 bedrooms; double B&B from £27

**Kenmore Bank Hotel**
Oxnam Rd, Jedburgh
☎ (0835) 62369, due to change to 862369
Off the A68, friendly family-run guesthouse.
Compact brightly decorated and furnished
bedrooms.
6 bedrooms; double B&B £33-£38
Credit cards 1 3

**Willow Court**
Willow Court, The Friars, Jedburgh
☎ (0835) 63702, due to change to 863702
Standing in 2 acres of gardens above the
town centre. Warm and welcoming
atmosphere.
4 bedrooms; double B&B £30-£36

**Ferniehirst Mill Lodge**
Jedburgh
☎ (0835) 63279, due to change to 863279
Modern purpose-built lodge; compact neat
bedrooms.
11 bedrooms; double B&B £42
Credit cards 1 3

### CAMPSITES

**▶▶▶ Camping & Caravanning Club Site**
Elliot Park, Edinburgh Rd, Jedburgh
☎ (0835) 63393 & (0203) 694995
North of Jedburgh off A68; pitch price from
£8.10 per night.

**▶▶▶ Springwood Caravan Park**
Kelso
☎ (0573) 224596
One mile west of town

**▶▶ Kirkfield Caravan & Camping Site**
Yetholm
Seven miles south of Kelso on B6352

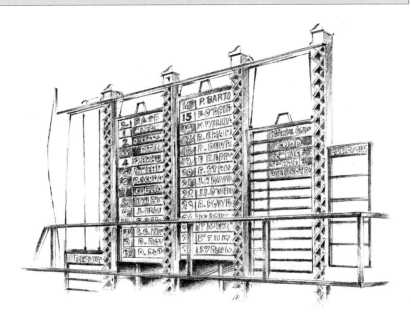

# Kempton Park

*Located just 15 miles from central London, this first-rate venue has some of the finest facilities of any racecourse in the country. Every enclosure has undercover viewing in spacious stands and there are 21 superb private boxes, 16 of them having the added bonus of balconies that overlook the track.*

There is a wide selection of places ot eat, varying from the main restaurant, which offers an excellent three-course meal, to the numerous snack bars serving light refreshments. And for those who want to toast their good fortune or drown their sorrows, there is a broad range of well-stocked bars from which to choose.

If the facilities are good, then the quality of the racing is even better. The majority of the fixtures are run on the Flat with the Easter Saturday meeting featuring a couple of significant Classic trials. At the height of summer, a gala evening in June combines an interesting card with a spectacular fireworks display and musical programme, while the September Stakes sometimes gives a few pointers towards the Arc result. Although they are fewer in number, it is with the jumps meetings that this delightful course really excels itself. One of the main highlights of the National Hunt season is the two-day Christmas Festival which starts on Boxing Day and includes the King George VI Chase, a race which the now retired Desert Orchid virtually made his own in recent years. Not surprisingly, massive crowds flock to see this prestigious contest, causing horrible tail-backs on the roads, so allow twice the normal time for your journey.

## FURTHER INFORMATION

The Club Secretary,
Kempton Park Racecourse, Sunbury on Thames,
Middlesex TW16 5AQ
☎ (0932) 782292

## LOCATION AND HOW TO GET THERE

Fifteen miles from central London via the A316 and A308. From outside London, leave the M3 at junction 1 and take the A308 towards Kingston-upon-Thames.
**Nearest Railway Station:** Kempton Park; there is an excellent service from Waterloo.

## ADMISSION

All classes of day ticket give access to full betting facilities, including Tote.

**Day Tickets:**
Accompanied children under 16 are admitted free to all enclosures.

CLUBHOUSE – reserved exclusively for Annual Members and their guests. No children under 10.

MEMBERS – £13 normal days, £15 premium days, £20 feature days; junior (16 – 25 years) £10 normal days, £11 premium days, £14 feature days – access to viewing terrace encircling parade ring and winners enclosure, bar, restaurant, snack bar, Tote

GRANDSTAND – £9 normal days, £10 premium days, £13 feature days – access to viewing terrace, bar, restaurant, snack bar, Tote

SILVER RING – £4 normal and premium days, £6 feature days – access to bar, restaurant, snack bar, Tote.

Parking: – main car park £2, Silver Ring and Centre free.

**Annual membership:** £160, junior £65 includes free Members Car Park label and reciprocal visits to certain other race meetings.

## COURSE FACILITIES

**Banks:**
there are no banks or cashpoint facilities on the course. Cheques may be cashed at racecourse office and Tote betting vouchers may be purchased with banker's card.

**For families:**
Picnic area with refreshment kiosk and toilets; children's play area; baby changing facilities; lost children centre; creche

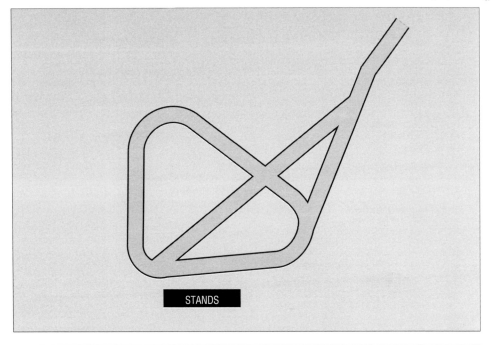

STANDS

## CALENDAR OF EVENTS

**April 2** – flat; includes Bonusprint Easter Stakes, Bonusprint Masaka Stakes
**April 4** – flat; includes Rosebery Handicap
**April 20** – flat; evening meeting
**May 2** – flat; includes Jubilee Handicap
**May 21** – flat; evening meeting
**May 28** – flat; includes Crawley Warren Heron Stakes
**June 8** – flat; evening meeting
**June 22** – flat; Gala Evening
**July 6** – flat; The City Evening

**August 3** – flat; evening meeting
**August 17** – flat; evening meeting
**September 2-3** – flat; Milcars Day on Friday; Bonusprint September Stakes on Saturday
**September 20** – flat
**October 15** – jumping; Charisma Gold Cup
**November 2** – jumping
**November 16** – jumping
**December 26-27** – jumping; includes King George VI Tripleprint Chase and Bonusprint Christmas Hurdle

## WHERE TO STAY

### HOTELS

#### Around Kempton Park

★★ **54% The Manor**
The Village Green, Datchet
☎ (0753) 543442, fax: (0753) 545292
30 bedrooms; double B&B £70–£90
Credit cards 1 2 3 5

★★★ ✿ **61% Thatchers Resort**
Epsom Rd, East Horsley
☎ (04865) 4291, fax: (04865) 4222
36 bedrooms; double room £80–£90 (room only)
Credit cards 1 2 3 5

★★★★ **65% The Excelsior**
Bath Rd, West Drayton
☎ 081-759 6611, telex: 24525, fax: 081-759 3421
839 bedrooms; double room £95–£120 (room only)
Credit cards 1 2 3 5

★★★★ **65% Heathrow Sterling**
Terminal 4, Heathrow Airport
☎ 081-759 7755
400 bedrooms
Credit cards 1 2 3 5

★★★★ **62% Forte Crest**
Sipson Road, West Drayton
☎ (0895) 445555, telex: 934518, fax: (0895) 445122
380 bedroom; double room £120–£150 (room only)
Credit cards 1 2 3 4 5

## WHERE TO STAY

**★★★★ 54% Heathrow Penta**
Bath Rd, Heathrow Airport
☎ 081-897 6363, telex: 934660, fax: 081-897 1113
636 bedrooms; double room £127.50-£150 (room only)
Credit cards 1 2 3 5

**★★★ 62% Forte Posthouse**
Bath Rd, Heathrow Airport
☎ 081-759 2552, telex: 21777, fax: 081-564 9265
180 bedrooms; double room from £49.50 (room only)
Credit cards 1 2 3 5

**★★ 50% Hotel Ibis Heathrow**
112/114 Bath Rd, Heathrow Airport
☎ 081-759 4888, telex: 929014, fax: 081-564 7894
354 bedrooms; double bedroom £55
Credit cards 1 2 3 5

**★★★ 62% Master Brewer**
Western Av, Hillingdon,
☎ (0895) 251199, telex: 946589, fax: (0895) 810330
106 bedrooms; double room £72-£87 (room only)
Credit cards 1 2 3 5

**★★★★★ 🌸 65% Cannizaro House**
West Side, Wimbledon Common, London SW19
☎ 081-879 1464, telex: 9413837, fax: 081-879 7338
46 bedrooms; double room from £118 (room only)
Credit cards 1 2 3 4 5

**★★★ 🌸 67% Carnarvon,**
Ealing Common, London W5
☎ 081-992 5399, telex: 935114, fax: 081-992 7082
145 bedrooms; double room from £104 (room only)
Credit cards 1 2 3 5

**★★★★ 64% Heathrow/Slough Marriott**
Ditton Road, Langley, Slough
☎ (0753) 544244, telex: 848646, fax: (0753) 540272
350 bedrooms; double room £125-£130 (room only)
Credit cards 1 2 3 5

**★★★★ 🌸 63% Copthorne**
400 Cippenham Ln, Slough
☎ (0753) 516222, fax: (0753) 516237
219 bedrooms
Credit cards 1 2 3 5

**★★★ 🌸 72% Woodlands Park**
Woodlands Ln, Stoke D'Abernon
☎ (037284) 3933, telex: 919246
59 bedrooms
Credit cards 1 2 3 5

**★★★★ 🌸🌸 73% Oakley Court**
Windsor Road, Water Oakley, Windsor
☎ (0628) 74141, telex: 849958, fax: (0628) 37011
65 bedrooms; double room £145-£375 (room only)
Credit cards 1 2 3 5

**★★★ 🌸 68% The Castle**
High St, Windsor
☎ (0753) 851011, telex: 849220, fax: (0753) 830244
104 bedrooms; double room £120-£140 (room only)
Credit cards 1 2 3 5

**★ 71% Aurora Garden**
14 Bolton Av, Windsor
☎ (0753) 868686, fax: (0753) 831394
14 bedrooms
Credit cards 1 2 3 5

**★★ 58% Ye Harte & Garter**
High St, Windsor
☎ (0753) 863426, fax: (0753) 830527
50 bedroom; double B&B £89
Credit cards 1 2 3 5

## BED AND BREAKFAST

**The Beeches**
19 The Avenue, Datchet
☎ (0753) 580722
Recently upgraded Victorian house providing comfortable bed and breakfast accommodation.
7 bedrooms; double B&B £45
Credit cards 1 3

**Epsom Downs Hotel**
9 Longdown Rd, Epsom
☎ (0372) 740643, fax: (0372) 723259
Charming hotel located in peaceful residential area; modern, well equipped accommodation.
14 bedrooms; double B&B £43.45-£71.50
Credit cards 1 2 3 5

**The White House**
Downs Hill Rd, Epsom
☎ (0372) 722472, fax: (0372) 744447
15 bedrooms
Credit cards 1 3

**Kings Lodge**
5 Kings Rd, London SW19
☎ 081-545 0191, fax: 081-545 0381
Bedrooms furnished to very high standard.
7 bedrooms;
Credit cards 1 2 3 5

**Trochee Hotel**
21 Malcolm Rd, London SW19
☎ 081-946 1579 & 3924, fax: 081-785 4058
Traditional, well maintained guesthouse.
17 bedrooms; double B&B £49
Credit cards 1 3

**Wimbledon Hotel**
78 Worple Rd, London SW19
☎ 081-946 9265, fax: 081-946 1581
Detached Victorian house offering a choice to suit everyone.
Credit cards 1 3 5

**Worcester House**
38 Alwyne Rd, London SW19
☎ 081-946 1300, fax: 081-785 4058
Choice of brightly decorated bedrooms, all equipped with modern amenities.
9 bedrooms; double B&B £59.50
Credit cards 1 3 5

**Chiswick Hotel**
73 Chiswick High Rd, London W4
☎ 081-994 1712, fax: 081-742 2585
Well equipped accommodation, furnished in modern style.
33 bedrooms; double B&B from £82.50
Credit cards 1 2 3 5

## WHERE TO STAY

### Wellmeadow Lodge
24 Wellmeadow Rd, London W7
☎ 081-567 7294, fax: 081-556 3468
Charming little guesthouse, quietly situated
and personally supervised.
5 bedrooms; double B&B £61-£70
Credit cards 1 2 3

### Colnbrook Lodge
Bath Rd, Colnbrook, Slough
☎ (0753) 685958
Comfortable, well equipped bedrooms with
double-glazing to combat air-traffic noise.
8 bedrooms
Credit cards 1 3

### Clarence Hotel
9 Clarence Rd, Windsor
☎ (0753) 864436, fax: (0753) 857060
Centrally placed in Windsor, old building
with bedrooms of variety of shapes and
sizes.
21 bedrooms; double B&B £49
Credit cards 1 2 3 5

### Melrose House
53 Frances Rd, Windsor
☎ (0753) 865328
Elegant, detached house in residential area.
Clean, well equipped bedrooms; friendly
proprietor.
9 bedrooms
Credit cards 1 3

### Glen Court
St John's Hill Rd, Woking
☎ (0483) 764154
Attractive Edwardian house; spacious
comfortable bedrooms, traditionally
furnished.
12 bedrooms
Credit cards 1 3

## CAMPSITES

### ►► Laleham Park Camping Site
Laleham
☎ (09325) 64149
Northwest of Epsom beside the Thames;
pitch price from £7.80 per night.

## WHERE TO EAT

### RESTAURANTS

### 🏵🏵 Le Raj
211 Firtree Rd, Epsom
☎ (0737) 371371
Excellent Indian cuisine in stylish air-
conditioned restaurant.
Lunch 12-2.30
Dinner: 7-11

### 🏵 Khamwan
5 White Hart Ln, Barnes, London SW13
☎ 081-876 3335
Mainly modern cuisine; daily changing
menu and informal attentive service.
Lunch: 12-3; from £6.95
Dinner: 7-11.45
Credit cards 1 2 3

### 🏵 Riva
169 Church Rd, Barnes, London SW13
☎ 081-748 0434
Regional Italian cooking in small attractive
urban restaurant.
Lunch: 12-2.30
Dinner: 7-11
Credit cards 1 3

### 🏵🏵 Sonny's
94 Church Rd, Barnes, London SW13
☎ 081-748 0393, fax: 081-748 2698
Reliable imaginative modern cooking in
stylish informal brasserie-type restaurant.
Lunch: 12-2.30; from £11.95
Dinner: 7-11.30; from £11.95 and à la carte
Credit cards 1 3

### 🏵🏵 Crowthers
481 Upper Richmond Rd West, East Sheen,
London SW14
☎ 081-876 6372
Popular local restaurant with good modern
cooking and a warm welcome.
Lunch: 12-1.45
Dinner: 7-10.45
Credit cards 1 2 3

### 🏵🏵 Maxim
153-155 Northfield Av, Ealing, London W13
Popular local Chinese restaurant with
Peking specialists and consistent standards.
Lunch: 12-2.30; from £8 and à la carte
Dinner: 7-12pm; from £8
Credit cards 1 2 3 5

### 🏵🏵 Michels
13 High St, Ripley
☎ (0483) 224777 & 222940
Stylish town house where the cooking
shows more than a dash of flair.
Lunch: 12-1.45; from £17 and à la carte
Dinner: 7-9; from £20 and à la carte
Credit cards 1 2 3

# Leicester

*The standard of racing that is held throughout the year at this Midlands venue is fairly average although fields are generally large because trainers like to introduce their inexperienced horses on the wide, galloping track.*

This can get very soft during the winter, particularly in the dip in the back straight, and the testing conditions will invariably expose any runners with stamina limitations. It is also a regular occurrence to witness the jockeys bringing their mounts extremely wide into the home straight in search of better ground. In fact, the turf was once so badly cut up on the inside that a certain winner stumbled and unseated his rider just yards from the finishing line.

One of the best fixtures to attend here is the two-day meeting which traditionally sees out the Old Year and welcomes in the new. What better way to cure the hangover blues than by spending the afternoon in the brisk open air, watching some exciting jumping action. There are also plenty of indoor bars for those preferring the alternative method of the 'hair of the dog'. In summer, it can make a pleasant change to take along a picnic to the Silver Ring car park that overlooks the course, while the evening meetings are always lovely occasions.

## FURTHER INFORMATION

Leicester Racecourse Co Ltd
2 Lower Mounts, Northampton NN1 3DE
☎ (0604) 30757 or (0533) 716515 on racedays

## LOCATION AND HOW TO GET THERE

The course is adjacent to the A6, two miles south of the city centre. From the M1 leave at junction 21 and take the A46 towards Leicester. After half a mile follow signs to the Outer Ring Road/Leicester East A563.
**Nearest Railway Station:** Leicester; there is a connecting bus service on racedays.

## ADMISSION

All classes of day ticket give access to full betting facilities, including Tote.

**Day Tickets:**
CLUB £11 – includes racecard and parking; access to bars, boxes and private rooms

TATTERSALLS £8 – includes racecard and parking; access to bars and restaurant

SILVER RING £4 includes racecard and parking, or £14 for a car and four occupants to Silver Ring Car Park overlooking the track – access to bar

## COURSE FACILITIES

**Banks:**
there are no banks or cashpoint facilities on the course.

**For families:**
picnic area with refreshment kiosk and toilets in Silver Ring Car Park; no specific play area, but a bouncy castle and climbing frame with 100m slide are provided for evening and Bank Holiday meetings.

## CALENDAR OF EVENTS

**April 7** – flat
**April 23** – flat
**May 23** – flat
**May 30-31** – flat
**June 11** – flat; evening meeting
**July 4** – flat
**July 11** – flat; evening meeting
**July 27** – flat; evening meeting
**August 8** – flat; evening meeting

**September 6** – flat
**September 12** – flat
**October 10-11** – flat
**October 24-25** – flat
**November 14** – jumping
**November 18** – jumping
**November 29** – jumping
**December 30** – jumping

## WHERE TO STAY

### HOTELS

**★★★★ 66% Stakis Country Court**
Braunstone
☎ (0533) 630066, telex: 34429, fax: (0533) 630627
141 bedrooms; double room £94 (room only)
Credit cards 1 2 3 5

**★★★★ 60% Holiday Inn**
St Nicholas Circle
☎ (0533) 531161, telex: 341281, fax: (0533) 513169
188 bedrooms; double room £95–£100 (room only)
Credit cards 1 2 3 4 5

**★★★ ❀ 72% Belmont House**
De Montfort
☎ (0533) 544773, fax: (0533) 470804
46 bedrooms; double B&B £77–£85
Credit cards 1 2 3 5

**★★★ 65% Leicester Forest Moat House**
Hinckley Rd, Leicester Forest East
☎ (0533) 394661, fax: (0533) 394952
34 bedrooms; double room £52–£62 (room only)
Credit cards 1 2 3 5

**★★★ 65% Leicestershire Moat House**
Wigston Rd
☎ (0533) 719441, telex: 34474, fax: (0533) 720559
57 bedrooms; double room £77–£88 (room only)
Credit cards 1 2 3 5

**★★★ 63% Forte Posthouse**
Braunstone Ln
☎ (0533) 630500, fax: (0533) 823623
172 bedrooms; double room £39.50–£49.50 (room only)
Credit cards 1 2 3 5

**★★★ 63% Stage**
299 Leicester Rd, Wigston Fields
☎ (0533) 886161, fax: (0533) 811874
79 bedrooms; double B&B £45–£79
Credit cards 1 2 3 4 5

**★★★ 60% Hotel Saint James**
Abbey St
☎ (0533) 510666, fax: (0533) 515183
72 bedrooms; double room £40–£45 (room only)
Credit cards 1 2 3 5

**★★★ 55% Park International**
Humberstone Rd
☎ (0533) 620471, telex: 341460, fax: (0533) 514211
220 bedrooms; double room £36.80–£67 (room only)
Credit cards 1 2 3 5

**★★ 69% Red Cow**
Hinckley Rd, Leicester Forest East
☎ (0533) 387878
31 bedrooms; double room £28.50–£39.50 (room only)
Credit cards 1 3

**★★ 64% Old Tudor Rectory**
Main St, Glenfield
☎ (0533) 320220, fax: (0533) 876002
14 bedrooms; double B&B £53–£54
Credit cards 1 2 3

**★★ 59% Gables**
368 London Rd
☎ (0533) 706969
31 bedrooms
Credit cards 1 2 3 5

### Around Leicester

**★ 66% Brant Inn**
Leicester Rd, Groby
☎ (0533) 872703, fax: (0533) 875292
10 bedrooms
Credit cards 1 3 5

**★★ 65% Castle Hotel & Restaurant**
Main St, Kirby Muxloe
☎ (0533) 395337, fax: (0533) 387868
4 bedrooms; double B&B £45–£50
Credit cards 1 2 3

**★★★ 71% Field Head**
Markfield Ln, Markfield
☎ (0530) 245454, telex: 342296, fax: (0530) 243740
28 bedrooms; double B&B £52–£71
Credit cards 1 2 3 5

**★★ 63% Charnwood**
48 Leicester Rd, Narborough
☎ (0533) 862218, fax: (0533) 750119
20 bedrooms
Credit cards 1 2 3

**★★ 61% Johnscliffe Hotel & Restaurant**
73 Main St, Newtown Linford
☎ (0530) 242228 & 243281, fax: (0533) 312767
15 bedrooms; double B&B £55–£75
Credit cards 1 2 3

**★★★ 71% Rothley Court**
Westfield Ln, Rothley
☎ (0533) 374141, fax: (0533) 374483
15 bedrooms; double room from £85 (room only)
Credit cards 1 2 3 5

**★★ 63% Mill on the Soar**
Coventry Rd, Sutton in the Elms
☎ (0455) 282419, fax: (0455) 285937
20 bedrooms; double room £28.50–£39.50 (room only)
Credit cards 1 2 3 5

**Forte Travelodge**
Green Acres Filling Station, (A46 Southbound), Thrussington
☎ (0664) 424525, Central Reservations: (0800) 850950
32 bedrooms; double room £31.95 (room only)
Credit cards 1 2 3

### BED AND BREAKFAST

**Burlington Hotel**
Elmfield Av
☎ (0533) 705112, fax: (0533) 704207
Small, family-run hotel, retaining much of its Victorian character; well maintained bedrooms.
16 bedrooms; double B&B £32–£40
Credit cards 1 3

## WHERE TO STAY

### Croft Hotel
3 Stanley Rd
☎ (0533) 703220, fax: (0533) 706067
One mile south of city centre. Dinner (by prior arrangement) offers good value for money.
26 bedrooms; double B&B £34-£38
Credit cards 1 3

### Daval Hotel
292 London Road, Stoneygate
☎ (0533) 708234
On the busy A6; predominantly used by commercial guests.
14 bedrooms
Credit card 1

### Scotia Hotel
10 Westcotes Dr
☎ (0533) 549200
Small family-run guesthouse undergoing upgrading, including refurbished lounge with licensed bar.
11 bedrooms; double B&B £40-£45

### The Stanfre House Hotel
265 London Rd
☎ (0533) 704294
Small, friendly, family-run guesthouse. Simply furnished, brightly decorated bedrooms.
12 bedrooms; double B&B £30

### Stoneycroft Hotel
5/7 Elmfield Av
☎ (0533) 707605, fax: (0533) 706067
Large cream-washed building in a quiet residential road.
44 bedrooms; double B&B £38
Credit cards 1 3

### Around Leicester

### Ambion Court Hotel
The Green, Dadlington, Hinckley
☎ (0455) 212292, fax: (0455) 213141
Set in a quiet village overlooking the green. All rooms have modern facilities and furniture.
2 bedrooms; double B&B £45-£60
Credit cards 1 3

### Woodside Farm
Ashby Rd, Stapleton, Hinckley
☎ (0455) 291929
Georgian farmhouse; Well maintained and equipped bedrooms; home-cooked meals.
6 bedrooms; double B&B from £32.50
Credit cards 1 2 3

### The Limes Hotel
35 Mountsorrel Ln, Rothley
☎ (0533) 302531
Friendly, efficiently run hotel with comfortable bedrooms and pleasant bars.
12 bedrooms
Credit cards 1 2 3

### Knaptoft House Farm & The Greenway
Bruntingthorpe Rd, Shearsby
☎ (0533) 478388
Surrounded by open countryside, friendly family farm with light, cheerful bedrooms.
3 bedrooms; double B&B from £32

### CAMPSITES

### Kilworth Caravan Park North
Kilworth
☎ (0858) 880385 & 880597
South of Leicester off the A427. No tents.

# Lingfield Park

*This pretty Surrey course used to be known as 'leafy Lingfield' because of its beautiful countryside setting, but that epithet is rarely applied nowadays. The reason is that the site was completely restructured a couple of years back with the addition of a ten-furlong all weather track inside the grass circuit.*

This new dirt surface is incredibly resilient to the vagaries of the British winter, allowing racing to continue here when other venues would be forced to abandon. The trouble is that the concept has totally failed to catch on with the public and as a result, crowds can be poor - horses almost outnumber the spectators sometimes.

Turf meetings are a completely different kettle of fish. These are much more popular and the standard of competition is also quite good. Over the jumps, there are a couple of decent cards at the beginning of December and the end of March but the highlight of the year is the Flat fixture in early May which features two important trials for the Derby and Oaks. It should also be pointed out that the course does possess some top-class facilities. The paddock and pre-parade ring are attractively sited in a natural setting among the trees and there are several fine restaurants as well as an excellent seafood bar.

## FURTHER INFORMATION

The Racecourse Office
Lingfield Park, Lingfield, Surrey RH7 6PQ
☎ (0342) 834800

## LOCATION AND HOW TO GET THERE

Leave the M25 at junction 6 and take the A22 southbound for approximately 4 miles. At Blindley Heath, after the filling station, turn sharp left onto the B2029 and continue for about 2 miles, passing through the village to reach the racecourse.

**Nearest Railway Station:** Lingfield; the station is a short walk from the racecourse.

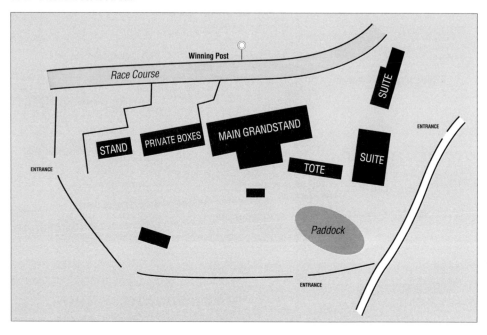

## ADMISSION

All classes of day ticket give access to full betting facilities, including Tote.

**Day Tickets:**
There is no reduction for senior citizens, but a £2 catering voucher is given, valid on the day of issue.

CLUB £12 – £15 – access to bar, restaurant, boxes, private rooms

FAMILY £7 – £9 – access to bar, restaurant, boxes, private rooms

**Annual membership:** £150 – includes Club Car Park.
Executive Club £500 – includes 71 race days, including 17 VIP days inclusive of catering, one free guest badge, parking, race card and guest's catering discount. Other race days include free parking and 10% catering discount.

## COURSE FACILITIES

**Banks:**
there are no banks or cashpoint facilities on the course

**For families:**
children's play area, lost children centre

## CALENDAR OF EVENTS

| | |
|---|---|
| April 8 | September 29 |
| May 6-7 | October 24 |
| May 14 – evening meeting | November 3 |
| May 21 | November 9 |
| May 28 – evening meeting | November 11 |
| June 11 – evening meeting | November 26 |
| June 18 – evening meeting | November 28 |
| June 24-25 – evening meeting on Saturday | December 1 |
| July 8-9 | December 7 |
| July 16 – evening meeting | December 10 |
| July 25 | December 14 |
| August 6 – evening meeting | December 17 |
| August 13 – evening meeting | December 19-20 |
| August 25 | December 31 |
| September 6 | |
| September 15 | |

## WHERE TO STAY

### HOTELS

**★★★ (RED) ❀❀❀ Gravetye Manor**
East Grinstead
☎ (0342) 810567, fax: (0342) 810080
18 bedrooms; double room £106-£212 (room only)

**★★★ ❀ 64% Woodbury House**
Lewes Rd, East Grinstead
☎ (0342) 313657, fax: (0342) 314801
13 bedrooms
Credit cards 1 2 3 4 5

**★★★★ 66% Copthorne Effingham Park**
West Park Road, Copthorne
☎ (0342) 714994, telex: 95649, fax: (0342) 716039
122 bedrooms; double room £108-£128 (room only)
Credit cards 1 2 3 5

**★★★ 65% Copthorne**
Copthorne Rd, nr Gatwick Airport (on A264)
☎ (0342) 714971, telex: 95500, fax: (0342) 717375
227 bedrooms; double room £108-£128 (room only)
Credit cards 1 2 3 5

**★★★ 64% Forte Posthouse**
Povey Cross Rd, Gatwick Airport
☎ (0293) 771621, fax: (0293) 771054
210 bedrooms; double room £39.50-£49.50 (room only)
Credit cards 1 2 3 5

**★★★ 62% Chequers Thistle**
Brighton Road, Horley
☎ (0293) 786992, telex: 877550, fax: (0293) 820625
78 bedrooms; double room from £89 (room only)
Credit cards 1 2 3 4 5

**★★★ 59% Gatwick Concorde**
Church Rd, Lowfield Heath
☎ (0293) 533441, telex: 87287, fax: (0293) 535369
121 bedrooms; double bedroom £56-£90
Credit cards 1 2 3 5

**★★★ 57% Goffs Park**
45 Goffs Park Road, Crawley
☎ (0293) 535447, telex: 87415, fax: (0293) 542050
37 bedrooms
Credit cards 1 2 3 5

**★★★ 56% The George**
High St, Crawley
☎ (0293) 524215, fax: (0293) 548565
86 bedrooms; double room £80-£95 (room only)
Credit cards 1 2 3 5

## WHERE TO STAY

### ★★ 61% Gatwick Manor
London Rd, Lowfield Health, Crawley
☎ (0293) 526301 & 535251, telex: 87529,
fax: (0293) 513077
30 bedrooms; double B&B £50-£70
Credit cards 1 2 3 5

### ★ (RED) ❀ Langshott Manor
Ladbroke Rd, Crawley
☎ (0293) 786680, fax: (0293) 783905
5 bedrooms
Credit cards 1 2 3 5

### ★★★ ❀❀ 74% Nutfield Priory
Nutfield
☎ (0737) 822066, fax: (0737) 823321
52 bedrooms; double B&B £110-£140
Credit cards 1 2 3 5

### ★★★ 63% Kings Arms
Market Square, Westerham
☎ (0959) 562990, fax: (0959) 561240
16 bedrooms; double room £70-£90 (room
only)
Credit cards 1 2 3 5

### BED AND BREAKFAST

### Cranfield Lodge Hotel
Maypole Rd, East Grinstead
☎ (0342) 321251 & 410371
Set in a residential area, close to all
amenities; well maintained accommodation.
11 bedrooms
Credit cards 1 2 3

### Bolebroke Watermill
Perry Hill, Edenbridge Rd, Hartfield
☎ (0892) 770425
Charming watermill with a history dating
back to 1086.
2 bedrooms; double B&B £48-£58
Credit cards 1 2 3

### Chalet
77 Massetts Rd, Horley
☎ (0293) 821666, fax: (0293) 821619
Small friendly guesthouse; beautifully clean
bedrooms with fresh decor.
6 bedrooms; double B&B from £40
Credit cards 1 3

### Gainsborough Lodge
39 Massetts Rd, Horley
☎ (0293) 783982
Attractive house offering comfortable en
suite bedrooms.
13 bedrooms; double B&B £38.50-£46.50
Credit cards 1 2 3

### The Lawn
30 Massetts Rd, Horley
☎ (0293) 775751
Charming Victorian house situated close to
the town centre.
7 bedrooms; double B&B £35-£42
Credit cards 1 2 3 5

### Vulcan Lodge
27 Massetts Rd, Horley
☎ (0293) 771522
Stylishly furnished, individually decorated
bedrooms in 17th century farmhouse.
4 bedrooms; double B&B £40-£44
Credit cards 1 3

### CAMPSITES

### ►► Long Acres Farm Caravan & Camping
Newchapel Rd, Lingfield
☎ (0342) 833205
Pitch price from £8.25 per night.

## WHERE TO EAT

### RESTAURANTS

### ❀❀ Honours Mill
87 High St, Edenbridge
☎ (0732) 866757
Generous portions of expensive, mainly
French food served in a converted watermill.
Lunch: 12-2; from £32.95
Dinner: 7-9; from £32.95
Credit cards 1 3

### ❀❀ La Bonne Auberge
Tilburstow Hill, South Godstone
☎ (0342) 892318, fax: (0342) 893435
Interesting French country cooking in a
quiet rural setting.
Lunch: 12-2; from £17.50
Dinner: 7-10; from £26.50
Credit cards 1 2 3 5

# Ludlow

*Located close to the Welsh border in some pretty Shropshire countryside is this homely track in the centre of which is a nine-hole golf course. Crowds include a fair proportion of local farmers who know and love their sport and there is a tremendous country feel to the place.*

This is enhanced by outlets selling freshly baked home-made food, while a more traditional sit-down meal can be obtained in the main grandstand.

All twelve jump meetings are held mid-week and usually feature a long-distance handicap chase as the main event. A peculiarity of the course is that six lines of coconut matting have to be put down to cover the roads that cut across it. On one infamous occasion, jockeys were alarmed to discover that they had an even trickier obstacle to negotiate in the shape of a car that had been inadvertently parked on the track! Miraculously, everyone safely avoided the vehicle. Such bloomers by officials are thankfully a thing of the past, and Ludlow is now a very professionally run course which at the same time still manages to retain its informal character.

## FURTHER INFORMATION

Ludlow Race Club Ltd
Shepherd's Meadow, Eaton Bishop, Hereford
HR2 9UA
☎ (0981) 250052

## LOCATION AND HOW TO GET THERE

The course is about 2 miles north of Ludlow on the B4365, just off the A49 Shrewsbury-Hereford road. From the M5 junction 6 take the A449 towards Kidderminster; turn left onto the A4025 to Stourport on Severn; leave Stourport on the B4195 Bewdley road, then turn left onto the A456. Branch right onto the A4117 and later turn right to join the Ludlow bypass. From the M54 junction 7 take the A5 towards Shrewsbury, then take the A49 southwards to Ludlow.
**Nearest Railway Station:** Ludlow; there is no connecting bus service to the course.

## ADMISSION

## ADMISSION

Tote Credit Office available in Members' Enclosure only; Betting shop available in Members' and Tattersalls only.

**Day Tickets:**
MEMBERS £12 – access to bars, restaurants, private rooms and toilet for disabled racegoers

TATTERSALLS £8 – access to bar and snack bar

COURSE £3 – access to bar and snacks, railside parking and picnic area

**Annual membership:** £65, junior (16-21) £32.50

## COURSE FACILITIES

**Banks:**
there are no banks or cashpoint facilities on the course.

**For families:**
picnic area with refreshment kiosk and toilets; baby changing facilities

## CALENDAR OF EVENTS

| | |
|---|---|
| April 6 | October 14 |
| April 22 – evening meeting | November 17 |
| May 2 | December 5 |
| October 6 | December 21 |

## WHERE TO STAY

### HOTELS

**★★★ ❀ 70% Dinham Hall**
Ludlow
☎ (0584) 876464, fax: (0584) 876019
13 bedrooms; double B&B £89.50-£112.50
Credit cards 1 2 3

**★★★ ❀ 69% Overton Grange**
☎ (0584) 873500, fax: (0584) 873524
16 bedrooms; double B&B £56-£88
Credit cards 1 2 3 5

**★★★ 68% The Feathers at Ludlow**
Bull Ring
☎ (0584) 875261, fax: (0584) 876030
40 bedrooms; double B&B £104-£124
Credit cards 1 2 3 4 5

**★★ 65% Dinham Weir**
Dinham Bridge
☎ (0584) 874431
7 bedrooms; double B&B £60-£65
Credit cards 1 2 3 5

**★★ 64% Cliffe**
Dinham
☎ (0584) 872063
10 bedrooms; double B&B from £35-£42
Credit cards 1 2 3

### Around Ludlow

**★★ 71% Mynd House**
Little Stretton, Church Stretton
☎ (0694) 722212, fax: (0694) 724180
8 bedrooms; double B&B £52-£100
Credit cards 1 2 3

**★★★ 57% Talbot**
West St, Leominster
☎ (0568) 616347, fax: (0568) 614880
20 bedrooms; double B&B £68-£76
Credit cards 1 2 3 5

**★★ 56% Royal Oak**
South St, Leominster
☎ (0568) 612610, fax: (0568) 612710
17 bedrooms; double B&B £45-£47.50
Credit cards 1 2 3 5

**★ (RED) Marsh Country**
Eyton, Leominster
☎ (0568) 613952
6 bedrooms; double B&B £100-£110
Credit cards 1 2 3

**Forte Travelodge**
Woofferton
☎ (058472) 695, Central Reservations:
(0800) 850950
32 bedrooms; double room £31.95 (room only)
Credit cards 1 2 3

### BED AND BREAKFAST

**Cecil**
Sheet Rd
☎ (0584) 872442
Very well maintained modern bungalow; friendly proprietors; home cooked meals.
10 bedrooms; double B&B £33-£38
Credit cards 1 2 3

**No 28 Lower Broad St**
☎ (0584) 876996
Attractive half-timbered town house; welcoming proprietors and well equipped bedrooms.
2 bedrooms; double B&B £60-£70

**The Church**
The Buttercross
☎ (0584) 872174
Smart little town centre hotel. Prettily decorated rooms with modern facilities.
8 bedrooms; double B&B £40
Credit cards 1 3

### Around Ludlow

**Chadstone**
Aston Munslow
☎ (058476) 675
Modern bungalow in a small hamlet, with views of the countryside. Friendly owners.
5 bedrooms; double B&B £40-£44

**Seifton Court**
Culmington
☎ (058473) 214
Delightful 18th-century farmhouse; with particularly nice loft bedrooms.
3 bedrooms

**The Glebe**
Diddlebury
☎ (058476) 221
Impressive Elizabethan farmhouse with exposed wall timbers, full of charm and character throughout.
3 bedrooms; double B&B £36-£54

**Withenfield**
South St, Leominster
☎ (0568) 612011
Warmth and hospitality offered by owners, spacious bedrooms furnished with antiques.
4 bedrooms
Credit cards 1 3

**The Hills**
Leysters, Leominster
☎ (056887) 205
Fifteenth-century farmhouse with old timbers and lots of character; friendly owners.
2 bedrooms; double B&B £36-£38

**Knapp House**
Luston, Leominster
☎ (0568) 615705
Impressive 16th-century black and white timbered house; magnificent sitting room.
2 bedrooms

**Wharton Bank Farm**
Leominster
☎ (0568) 612575
A warm welcome is assured; bedrooms are well decorated.
4 bedrooms

**Strefford Hall**
Strefford
☎ (0588) 672383
Imposing Victorian house with 3 spacious bedrooms; set in its own pretty gardens.
3 bedrooms; double B&B from £32

**Compasses Hotel**
Wigmore
☎ (056886) 203
Ivy-clad village inn; abundance of ceiling beams and wall timbers.
3 bedrooms; double B&B from £40
Credit cards 1 2 3 5

## WHERE TO STAY

### CAMPSITES

► **Engine & Tender Inn**
Broome
☎ (05887) 275
Northwest of Ludlow

►► **Glebe Farm**
Diddlebury
☎ (058476) 221
North of Ludlow, off the B4368; pitch price
from £3.50 per night.

## WHERE TO EAT

### RESTAURANTS

✿✿ **Poppies Roebuck Inn**
Brimfield
☎ (058472) 230
Highly skilled, appetizing cooking in a
bright, hospitable restaurant attached to a
popular village inn.
Lunch: 12-2; from £8.50 a la carte
Dinner: 7-10; from £8.50 a la carte

### PUBS

**Roebuck**
Brimfield, nr Leominster
☎ (0584) 711230
The food is exceptionally good here,
certainly among the best pub food in
Britain, and draught beers include Ansells
Best, Tetley Bitter and Wood Traditional (a
local brew). Surroundings are comfortable
and club-like in style. Children are welcome
anywhere away from the bar.
Open: 12-2pm, 7-11pm; Sunday 12-2pm,
7-10.30pm
Bar food: Tuesday to Saturday 12-2pm, 7-
10pm; no food on Sunday or Monday
Accommodation: double B&B £60

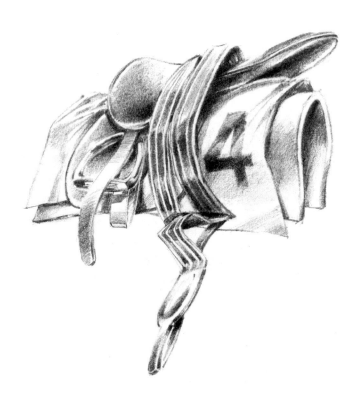

# Market Rasen

*Market Rasen is the sole surviving course in Lincolnshire. The lack of local competition has helped this friendly track to grow and prosper in recent times so that meetings are always well attended even though its location is fairly isolated. The grandstand has undergone a steady programme of improvements and offers some of the best viewing that can be found on any racecourse.*

There is a wide selection of bars and restaurants, with the standard of catering being exceptionally high. It is also an excellent venue for families, as there is a particularly good children's playground which should keep the youngsters occupied.

The racing is over the jumps on a sharp oval circuit. Most of the fences are relatively soft although the second last is a notorious exception, causing all manner of mishaps in recent years. Fixtures take place here throughout the National Hunt season and sizeable crowds are always in evidence on Boxing Day and Easter Monday. Easily the most popular occasions, though, are the summer Saturday evening meetings which include the final fixture of the season in June, a card that features the appropriately titled Last Chance Selling Hurdle.

## FURTHER INFORMATION

The Racecourse Office
Market Rasen Racecourse Ltd, Legsby Road, Market Rasen, Lincs LN8 3EA
Telephone (0673) 843434

## LOCATION AND HOW TO GET THERE

The course is in Legsby Road, Market Rasen and is reached via the A46 and the A631.
**Nearest Railway Station:** Market Rasen; there is no connecting bus service to the course.

## ADMISSION

All classes of day ticket give access to full betting facilities, including Tote.

**Day Tickets:**
Accompanied children under 16 are admitted free.

MEMBERS £10, £12 evening meetings and Bank Holidays – access to carvery restaurant, champagne and seafood bar, members' bar, boxes.

TATTERSALLS £7 – access to bars, snack bars, information kiosk and facilities for disabled racegoers.

SILVER RING £3.50 – access to bars, fish and chip restaurant, toilets for disabled racegoers

**Annual membership:** £90 single, £150 dual (husband and wife) £50 junior (16-24 years)

## COURSE FACILITIES

**Banks:**
there are no banks or cashpoint facilities on the course.

**For families:**
picnic area, children's play area

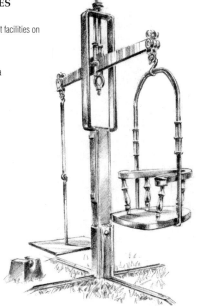

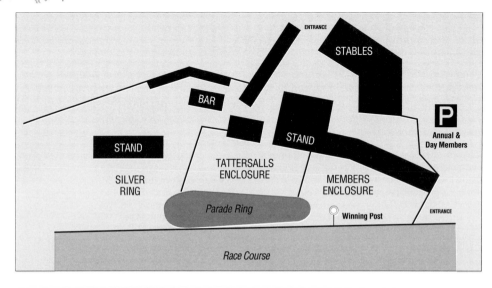

## CALENDAR OF EVENTS

| | |
|---|---|
| **April 4** | **September 24** |
| **April 23** | **October 5** |
| **May 6** – evening meeting | **November 4** |
| **June 4** – evening meeting | **November 19** |
| **July 30** – evening meeting | **December 16** |
| **August 20** – evening meeting | |
| **September 17** | |

## WHERE TO STAY

### HOTELS

**★★ 62% Four Seasons**
Scothern Ln,
☎ (0673) 860108, fax: (0673) 862784
24 bedrooms
Credit cards 1 2 3

**★★★★ 62% The White Hart**
Bailgate, Lincoln
☎ (0522) 526222, fax: (0522) 531798
50 bedrooms; double room £100–£110
(room only)
Credit cards 1 2 3 5

**★★★ 68% Washingborough Hall
Country House**
Church Hill, Washingborough
☎ (0522) 790340, fax: (0522) 792936
14 bedrooms; double B&B £69–£88
Credit cards 1 2 3 5

**★★★ 63% Forte Crest**
Eastgate
☎ (0522) 520341, telex: 56316, fax: (0522)
510780
70 bedrooms; double room £70 (room only)
Credit cards 1 2 3 5

**★★ 70% Hillcrest**
15 Lindum Ter
☎ (0522) 510182
17 bedrooms; double B&B £59.50
Credit cards 1 2 3

**★★ 56% Castle**
Westgate
☎ (0522) 538801, fax: (0522) 510291
15 bedrooms; double B&B £60–£65
Credit cards 1 2 3 5

**★★★ 62% Beaumont**
Victoria Rd, Louth
☎ (0507) 605005, fax: (0507) 607768
17 bedrooms; double room £65–£85 (room
only)
Credit cards 1 2 3

**★★ 65% Priory**
Eastgate, Louth
☎ (0507) 602930
12 bedrooms; double B&B £45–£59
Credit cards 1 3

## WHERE TO STAY

### BED AND BREAKFAST

**The Old Vicarage**
School Ln, Hainton
☎ (0507) 313660
Quiet, relaxing guesthouse, friendly
proprietors, brightly decorated bedrooms.
3 bedrooms; double B&B £29-£32

**D'Isney Place Hotel**
Eastgate, Lincoln
☎ (0522) 538881, fax: (0522) 511321
Georgian town house; excellent spacious
bedrooms, furnished in period style
18 bedrooms; double B&B £62-£72
Credit cards 1 2 3 5

**Carline**
1-3 Carline Rd, Lincoln
☎ (0522) 530422
Good quality accommodation; attractive,
comfortable bedrooms.
9 bedrooms

**Ferncliffe House Hotel**
2 St Catherines, Lincoln
☎ (0522) 522618
High ceilings, spacious bedrooms,
individually and attractively furnished with
comfort in mind.
5 bedrooms
Credit cards 1 2 3

**Minster Lodge Hotel**
3 Church Ln, Lincoln
☎ (0522) 513220, fax: (0522) 513220
Located in the upper part of the city, with
high standards of housekeeping.
6 bedrooms
credit cards 1 2 3

**Tennyson Hotel**
7 South Park, Lincoln
☎ (0522) 521624 & 513684
Extremely well kept, comfortable
guesthouse.
8 bedrooms; double B&B £40-£42
Credit cards 1 2 3

**Brierley House Hotel**
54 South Park, Lincoln
☎ (0522) 526945 & 522945
South of city centre with generally well
portioned rooms.
11 bedrooms

### CAMPSITES

**►►► Walesby Woodlands Caravan
Park**
Walesby Rd, Market Rasen
☎ (0673) 843285
Pitch price from £7.25 per night.

**►► Caravan Club Site**
Legsby Rd, Market Rasen
☎ (0673) 842307
One mile southeast of town centre off
A63 Louth road.

## WHERE TO EAT

### RESTAURANTS

**❀ Wig & Mitre**
29 Steep Hill, Lincoln
☎ (0522) 535190 & 523705, fax: (0522)
532402
English food, ranging from light to
substantial, served in a convivial medieval
inn.
Lunch: from £8.50 a la carte
Dinner: Last dinner 11pm; from £10 a la
carte

# Newbury

*This is one of the foremost racing venues in this country and it is very rare for anyone to leave this wonderful course disappointed. Newbury caters for virtually every requirement with some superb facilities in the new Berkshire Stand which was completed in October 1992.*

The terrific range of restaurants would do justice to a first-rate hotel and there are also plenty of stalls selling seafood and snacks for those who want a quicker bite to eat. Another major advantage here is the almost unparalleled view of the action that can be obtained from the top of stands. Indeed, maybe the only drawback with this site is that is great appeal inevitably leads to huge crowds and terrible traffic problems on the big days, so either set off early or go by train.

The wide oval track finds almost universal favour among trainers and consequently runners tend to be of the highest quality at the 27 fixtures that are held here under both codes. The list of important races is long, but a couple that warrant a special mention are the Fred Darling and Greenham Stakes, both important Classic trials that are run at a two-day meeting in mid-April. Over the jumps, the Tote Gold Trophy in February is always a competitive contest, but the course really saves the best to last in the shape of the Hennessy Gold Cup in late November, one of the most prestigious handicap chases of the entire season.

## FURTHER INFORMATION

Newbury Racecourse
Newbury, Berkshire RG14 7NZ
☎ (0635) 40015/41485

## LOCATION AND HOW TO GET THERE

The course is in the town, just off the A34. Racegoers from the London direction should leave the M4 at junction 12 (Theale) and continue to Newbury on the A4; those from the west should leave at junction 13 and continue south on the A34. **Nearest Railway Station:** Newbury Racecourse; the station is a few yards from the course and has a special raceday timetable. Special inclusive tickets are available from London which include entrance to Tattersalls or Silver Ring and return rail fare. By air: the racecourse has a landing strip suitable for light aircraft – ☎ (0635) 40015.

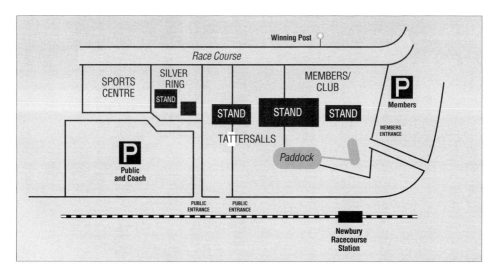

## ADMISSION

All classes of day ticket give access to full betting facilities, including Tote.

**Day Tickets:**
Accompanied children under 17 admitted free; senior citizens half price in Silver Ring; parking free, except Picnic Car Park.

MEMBERS OR CLUB £13 – £15, £20 for Hennessy Cognac Gold Cup Day on Nov 27; Seat £5 on Feature and Premium Days – access to Berkshire Stand, Hampshire Stand, paddock, winners enclosure, saddling up boxes, bars, restaurants, lift and wheelchair viewing for disabled racegoers.

TATTERSALLS £8 – £10, £12 on Hennessy Cognac Gold Cup Day – access to paddock and winners' enclosure, stepped viewing and 2nd floor viewing deck on Berkshire Stand, bars, grill room, fish bar, and other refreshments, large private room for hire

SILVER RING £3, £4 on Hennessy Cognac Gold Cup Day – access to viewing within last furlong before winning post, parking beside rails, bars, refreshments.

PICNIC CAR PARK £3, £4 on Hennessy Cognac Gold Cup Day – access as Silver Ring.

**Annual membership:** Single £145, double £190; £290 to include one non-transferable badge and one transferable badge; junior member £70; annual bench reservation £60; annual seat reservation £50 – includes car park label and reciprocal arrangements with certain other courses, including Arlington International Racecourse, Chicago.

## COURSE FACILITIES

**Banks:**
There are no banks or cashpoint facilities on the course.

**For families:**
Picnic area with refreshment kiosk and toilets, children's play area, baby changing facilities, lost children centre, Rocking Horse Nursery, opening in 1993, provides creche for patrons of Club, Tattersalls and Silver Ring.

## CALENDAR OF EVENTS

**April 15-16** – flat; includes Gainsborough Stud Fred Darling Stakes, Lanes End John Porter Stakes, Singer and Friedlander Greenham Stakes and Ladbroke Spring Cup

**May 13-14** – flat; includes Juddmonte Lockinge Stakes, Vodafone Group Fillies Trial Stakes, Quantel Aston Park Stakes, London Gold Cup and Winchester Stakes

**May 25** – evening meeting; flat; includes Castrol Stakes, Burmah Stakes and Kenneth Robertson Stakes

**June 9** – flat; includes Coopers and Lybrand Summer Stakes, Kingsclere Stakes, Cork Gully Apprentice Stakes, Ballymacoll Stud Stakes

**June 21** – flat; evening meeting; includes Kingston Smith Stakes and Wimpey Hobbs Fillies Stakes

**July 15-16** – flat; includes Hackwood Stakes, Mtoto Donnington Castle Stakes, Arlington International Racecourse Stakes

**August 12-13** – flat; includes Gardner Merchant Hungerford Stakes, Washington Singer Stakes, Ibn Bey Geoffrey Freer Stakes, St Hugh's Stakes, Eurolink Silver Trophy Stakes

**September 16-17** – flat; includes Haynes Hanson and Clark Stakes, Trinfold Silver Clef Trophy, Rokeby Farms Mill Reef Stakes, Courage Stakes, Tote Autumn Cup

**October 20-22** – flat Thursday and Saturday, jumping Friday; includes Vodafone Horris Hill Stakes, Glynwed International Chase, Castrol St Simon Stakes, Burmah Stakes

**November 9** – jumping; jumping; includes Tom Masson Trophy Hurdle, Lional Vick Memorial Chase, Halloween Chase

**November 25-26** – jumping; Hennessy Cognac Gold Cup Meeting

**December 30-31** – jumping; Old Year Chase

## WHERE TO STAY

### HOTELS

**★★★★ 68% Donnington Valley**
Old Oxford Rd, Donnington
☎ (0635) 551199, fax: (0635) 551123
58 bedrooms; double B&B £55-£155
Credit cards 1 2 3 5

**★★★★ 62% Foley Lodge**
Stockcross
☎ (0635) 528770, fax: (0635) 528398
69 bedrooms
Credit cards 1 2 3 5

**★★★ 72% Millwaters**
London Rd
☎ (0635) 528838, telex: 83343, fax: (0635) 523406
32 bedrooms; double B&B £60-£140
Credit cards 1 2 3 5

**★★★ 60% The Chequers**
Oxford St
☎ (0635) 38000, fax: (0635) 37170
45 bedrooms; double room £90 (room only)
Credit cards 1 2 3 5

**Around Newbury**

**★★★ ❀❀ 74% Elcot Park Resort**
Elcot
☎ (0488) 58100, fax: (0488) 58288
57 bedrooms; double room £90-£120 (room only)
Credit cards 1 2 3 5

**★★★ ❀❀ 84% Hollington House**
Woolton Hill, nr Highclere
☎ (0635) 255100, fax: (0635) 255075
20 bedrooms; double B&B £105-£250
Credit cards 1 2 3

**★★★ 61% The Bear**
Charnham St, Hungerford
☎ (0488) 682512, telex: 47757, fax: (0488) 684357
12 bedrooms; double room £75-£85 (room only)
Credit cards 1 2 3 5

**★★ 66% Three Swans**
117 High St, Hungerford
☎ (0488) 682721, fax: (0488) 681708
15 bedrooms; double B&B £54
Credit cards 1 2 3 5

**★★❀ 74% Esseborne Manor**
Hurstbourne Tarrant
☎ (0264) 76444, fax: (0264) 76473
12 bedrooms; double B&B £115
Credit cards 1 2 3 4 5

**★★★ 70% Padworth Court**
Bath Rd, Padworth
☎ (0734) 714411, fax: (0734) 714442
50 bedrooms; double B&B £56-£81
Credit cards 1 2 3 5

**★★★ 61% Romans**
Little London Rd, Silchester
☎ (0734) 700421, fax: (0734) 700691
24 bedrooms; double B&B £75-£85
Credit cards 1 2 3 5

**★★★★ 63% Regency Park**
Bowling Green Rd, Thatcham
☎ (0635) 871555, telex: 847844, fax: (0635) 871571
50 bedrooms; double room £80-£90 (room only)
Credit cards 1 2 3 5

**★★ ❀❀ 73% Royal Oak**
The Square, Yattendon
☎ (0635) 201325, fax: (0635) 201926
5 bedrooms; double B&B £70-£80
Credit cards 1 2 3 4 5

### BED AND BREAKFAST

**Marshgate Cottage Hotel**
March Ln, Hungerford
☎ (0488) 682307, fax: (0488) 685475
Cosy bedrooms and public areas full of character; informal friendly atmosphere.
9 bedrooms; double B&B from £39.50
Credit cards 1 2 3

### CAMPSITES

**►► Riverside Caravan & Camping Site**
Wallingford
☎ (0491) 35351 ext 3260
North of Newbury; pitch price from £5 per night.

## WHERE TO EAT

### RESTAURANTS

#### ✿✿ The Dew Pond
Old Burghclere
☎ (063527) 408
Reasonably priced, imaginative use of local
ingredients in and off-the-beaten-path
location.
Lunch 12-2: from £16
Dinner: 7-10; from £23
Credit cards 1 3

### PUBS

#### Bell Inn
Aldworth
☎ (0635) 578272
Established in 1314 and run by the same
family for some 200 years, this fascinating
pub is remarkably unchanged, with stone
floors and huge fireplaces. There is an
attractive garden, backing onto open fields.
Draught beers include Arkell Bitter, Badger
Best, Morrell Dark Mild, Hook Norton Best
and Kingsdown Bitter; bar food is simple –
hot crusty rolls with various fillings – but
very popular. Children are welcome.
Open: 11am-3pm, 6-11pm; Sunday 12-
3pm, 7-10.30pm; closed Monday, except
Bank Holidays
Bar food: as opening times

#### Bell
Lambourn Rd, Boxford
☎ (048838) 721
Roomy pub dating back to Tudor times with
an attractive garden. Beers include
Whitbread Best Bitter, Flowers Original,
Boddington Bitter and Wadworth 6X and
there is a reasonable list of French and
German wines. Daily blackboard specials
can be eaten in the bar or the small
restaurant. Children are welcome.
Occasional jazz evenings when the races are
on.
Open: 11am-2.30pm, 6-11pm (closes
10.30pm on Sunday)
Bar food: as opening hours
Restaurant: as opening hours
Accommodation: double B&B £48

#### Pot Kiln
Frilsham, nr Yattendon
☎ (0635) 201366
Secluded 17th-century pub in traditional
style. Beers include Arkell, Morland Bitter or
Old Speckled Hen and menu includes
vegetarian dishes, but on Sunday and
Tuesday, only rolls are available. Children
are welcome.
Open: 12-2.30pm, 6.30-11pm; Sunday 12-
2.30pm, 7-10.30pm
Bar food: 12-1.45pm, 7-9.45pm; Tuesday
and Sunday (rolls only) 12-2pm, 7-10pm

#### Swan
East Ilsley
☎ (063528) 238
Roomy 16th-century coaching inn in
peaceful village location. Beers include
Morland or Charles Wells and the menu
includes traditional favourites. There is a
spacious garden with play area and children
are welcome in the pub.
Open: 10.30am-2.30pm, 6-11pm; Sunday
12-3pm, 7-10.30pm
Bar food: 12-2pm, 6.15-10pm; Sunday 12-
2pm, 7-10pm
Restaurant: as opening hours
Accommodation: double B&B £42-£49

#### Dundas Arms
53 Station Rd, Kintbury
☎ (0488) 58263 and 58559
This charming pub is right beside the
Kennet and Avon canal, with lots of tables
and chairs by the water's edge. Beers
include Morland Original, Thomas Hardy
and Charles Wells Bombadier and the menu
is varied and interesting. Children are
welcome.
Open: 11am-2.30pm, 6.30-11pm; Sunday
12-2.30, 7-10.30pm
Bar food: as opening times, but no food on
Sunday or on Monday evening.
Restaurant: as bar food
Accommodation: double B&B £55-£65

#### Bull
Stanford Dingley
☎ (0734) 744409
This delightful village inn, dating from the
15th century, offers above average bar food
and a friendly welcome. Beers include
Brakspear Ordinary and Bass Charrington.
Children are welcome and there is outdoor
seating.
Open: Tuesday to Saturday 12-3pm, 7-
11pm; Sunday 12-3pm, 7-10.30pm;
Monday 7-11pm.
Bar food: as opening hours

#### Harrow
West Ilsley
☎ (0635) 28260
An imaginative menu of country dishes,
including a renowned rabbit pie, are on offer
here together with beers such as Morland
Original, Old Masters and Old Speckled
Hen. The building is very old, with lots of
character in the comfortable bar, and there is
a pleasant garden.
Open: 11am-3pm, 6-11pm; Sunday 12-
3pm, 7-10.30pm
Bar food: 12-2.15pm, 6-9.15pm; Sunday
12-2.15pm, 7-9.15pm

# Newcastle

*Like most things in life, the Geordies are passionate about their racing, and well-backed favourites are sure to receive plenty of vocal encouragement from the stands at the northeast venue.*

Known locally as Gosforth Park, the course is one of many whose facilities have been significantly upgraded in recent times, a particularly necessary improvement here as it used to be a fairly depressing site. The whole place is much brighter now, thanks to an extensive programme of redecoration and the improved amenities, combined with the genuine warmth of the people, should leave visitors with happy memories.

Decent racing is to be found at all times of the year. The highlight of the summer is the Saturday fixture in late June (25th in 1994) featuring the Northumberland Plate, an extremely valuable two-mile handicap. Loads of runners make the long journey up from their southern training centres to participate, resulting in a huge field and open betting market. Jumping fans, meanwhile, get the chance to see some of the top hurdlers in action in the Fighting Fifth, one of the major early season trials for the Champion Hurdle.

## FURTHER INFORMATION

High Gosforth Park plc
High Gosforth Park, Newcastle upon Tyne
NE3 5HP
☎ 091-236 2020 and 5508

## LOCATION AND HOW TO GET THERE

The course is north of the city, beyond Gosforth and is easily accessible from the A1; from the A19 northbound, about 4 miles beyond North Shields, turn left onto the A1056, crossing the A189 to reach the course.

**Nearest Railway Station:** Newcastle Central; from here transfer to Metro train to Regent Centre or Four Lane End stations, from where buses or taxis run to the course.

## ADMISSION

CLUB £12-£17 - access to restaurant and bar

TATTESALLS £8 - access to restaurant, bar, snack bar, fast food

SILVER RING £3 - only available during June meeting, Easter Monday and August Bank Holiday; access to snacks, bar and fast food

## COURSE FACILITIES

**Banks:**
there are no banks or cashpoint facilities on the course.

**For families:**
picnic area

## CALENDAR OF EVENTS

April 4-5 – flat
May 2 – flat
May 7 – jumping; evening meeting
May 19 – flat
June 24-25 – flat; evening meeting on Friday; includes the
    Northumberland Plate
July 23 – flat
July 25 – flat
August 27 – flat
August 29 – flat
September 27 – flat
October 19 – jumping
October 31 – flat
November 5 – jumping
November 26 – jumping
November 29 – jumping
December 28 – jumping

## WHERE TO STAY

### HOTELS

**★★★★ 67% Swallow Gosforth Park**
High Gosforth Park, Gosforth
☎ 091-236 4111, telex: 53655, fax: 091-236 8192
178 bedrooms; double B&B £115-£120
Credit cards 1 2 3 5

**★★★★ 64% The Copthorne Newcastle**
The Close, Quayside
☎ 091-222 0333, telex: 53340, fax: 091-230 1111
156 bedrooms; double room £102.50-£117 (room only)
Credit cards 1 2 3 5

**★★★ 67% County Thistle**
Neville St
☎ 091-232 2471, telex: 537873, fax: 091-232 1285
115 bedrooms; double room £85-£125 (room only)
Credit cards 1 2 3 4 5

**★★★ 66% Forte Crest**
New Bridge St
☎ 091-232 6191, telex: 53467, fax: 091-2612 8529
166 bedrooms; double room from £70 (room only)
Credit cards 1 2 3 5

**★★★ 64% Novotel Newcastle**
Ponteland Rd, Kenton
☎ 091-214 0303, telex: 53675, fax: 091-214 0633
126 bedrooms
Credit cards 1 2 3 5

**★★★ 63% Swallow**
Newgate Arcade
☎ 091-232 5025, telex: 538230, fax: 091-232 8428
93 bedrooms; double B&B £60-£82
Credit cards 1 2 3 5

**★★★ 61% New Kent Hotel**
Osborne Rd
☎ 091-281 1083, fax: 091-281 3369
32 bedrooms; double B&B £56-£79
Credit cards 1 2 3 4 5

**★★★ 59% Imperial**
Jesmond Rd
☎ 091-281 5511, fax: 091-281 8472
129 bedrooms; double B&B £84
Credit cards 1 2 3 5

**★★★ 54% Hospitality Inn**
64 Osborne Rd, Jesmond
☎ 091-281 7881, telex: 53636, fax: 091-281 6241

**★★ 59% Whites**
38-40 Osborne Road, Jesmond
☎ 091-281 5126
25 bedrooms
Credit cards 1 2 3 5

**★★ 58% Cairn**
97/103 Osborne Road, Jesmond
☎ 091-281 1358, fax: 091-281 9031
51 bedrooms; double B&B £62.50-£65
Credit cards 1 2 3 5

**★ 64% Osborne**
Osborne Road, Jesmond
☎ 091-281 3385
25 bedrooms; double B&B from £44
Credit cards 1 2 3 5

### Around Newcastle

**★★★ 64% Friendly**
Witney Way, Boldon Business Park, Boldon
☎ 091-519 1999, fax: 091-519 0655
84 bedrooms; double room £66-£76.50 (room only)
Credit cards 1 2 3 5

**★★ 60% Bay**
Front St, Cullercoats
☎ 091-252 3150
17 bedrooms; double B&B from £35
Credit cards 1 2 3 5

**Forte Travelodge**
Leam Ln, Wardley, Whitemare Pool, Felling
☎ 091-438 3333, Central Reservations: (0800) 850950
41 bedrooms; double room £31.95 (room only)
Credit cards 1 2 3

**★★★ 66% Swallow**
High West St, Gateshead
☎ 091-477 1105, telex: 53534, fax: 091-478 7214
103 bedrooms; double B&B £82-£105
Credit cards 1 2 3 4 5

**★★ 🏵🏵 76% Eslington Villa**
8 Station Rd, Low Fell, Gateshead
☎ 091-487 6017, fax: 091-482 2359
12 bedrooms
Credit cards 1 2 3 5

**★★★ 64% Airport Moat House**
Woolsington
☎ (0661) 24911, telex: 537121, fax: (0661) 860157
100 bedrooms; double B&B £50-£79
Credit cards 1 2 3 5

**★★★★ 54% Holiday Inn**
Great North Rd, Seaton Burn
☎ 091-236 5432, telex: 53271, fax: 091-236 8091
150 bedrooms; double room £78-£115 (room only)
Credit cards 1 2 3 4 5

**★★★ 60% Sea**
Sea Rd, South Shields
☎ 091-427 0999, fax: 091-454 0500
33 bedrooms; double B&B £63-£77
Credit cards 1 2 3 5

**★★★ 58% Park**
Grand Pde, Tynemouth
☎ 091-257 1406, fax: 091-257 1716
49 bedrooms; double B&B £58-£65
Credit cards 1 2 3 5

**★★★ 60% Newcastle Moat House**
Coast Rd, Wallsend
☎ 091-262 8989 & 091-262 7044, telex: 53583, fax: 091-263 4172
150 bedrooms; double B&B £40-£68
Credit cards 1 2 3 5

## WHERE TO STAY

### ★★★ 65% Washington Moat House
Stone Cellar Rd, District 12, High Usworth, Washington
☎ 091-417 2626, telex: 537143, fax: 091-415 1166
106 bedrooms; double room £68-£80 (room only)
Credit cards 1 2 3 5

### ★★★ 61% Forte Posthouse
Emerson District 5, Washington
☎ 091-416 2264, fax: 091-415 3371
138 bedrooms; double room £39.50-£49.50 (room only)
Credit cards 1 2 3 4 5

### ★★★ 71% Gibside Arms
Front St, Whickham
☎ 091-488 9292, fax: 091-488 8000
45 bedrooms; double B&B from £51
Credit cards 1 2 3 5

### ★★ 68% High Point
The Promenade, Whitley Bay
☎ 091-251 7782, fax: 091-251 6318
14 bedrooms

### ★★ 67% Windsor
South Pde, Whitley Bay
☎ 091-251 8888, fax: 091-297 0272
64 bedrooms; double B&B £48-£65
Credit cards 1 2 3 5

### ★★ 60% Park Lodge Hotel
160-164 Park Av, Whitley Bay
☎ 091-253 0288 & 091-252 6879, fax: 091-297 1006
16 bedrooms; double B&B £50-£60
Credit cards 1 2 3 5

### ★★ 59% Holmedale
106 Park Av, Whitley Bay
☎ 091-251 3903 & 091-253 1162, fax: 091-253 0053
18 bedrooms; double B&B from £40
Credit cards 1 2 3 5

### ★ 57% Cavendish
51 Esplanade, Whitley Bay
☎ 091-253 3010
11 bedrooms
Credit cards 1 3

### BED AND BREAKFAST

### Chirton House Hotel
46 Clifton Rd
☎ 091-273 0407
Individually decorated bedrooms; cosy bar and comfortable lounges.
11 bedrooms; double B&B from £40
Credit cards 1 3

### The Rise
The Rise, Woolsington
☎ 091-286 4963
Individually styled bedrooms. Restful and relaxing atmosphere.
5 bedrooms.

### The George Hotel
88 Osborne Rd, Jesmond
☎ 091-281 4442, fax: 091-281 8300
14 bedrooms.

### Around Newcastle

### Burnbrae
Leazes Villas, Burnopfield
☎ (0207) 70432
Handsome Edwardian house; appealing bedrooms.
6 bedrooms
Credit cards 1 3

### Portobello Lodge
Durham Rd, Birtley
☎ 091-410 2739
Good standard of newly refurbished bedrooms.
11 bedrooms; double B&B from £30
Credit cards 1 2 3

### Victoria
681 Durham Rd, Lowfell, Gateshead
☎ 091-482 3172
Close to the motorway, with neat, unpretentious, individually styled bedrooms.
6 bedrooms
Credit cards 1 2 3 5

### Walkerville
125 Ocean Rd, South Shields
☎ (091456) 5931
Close to seafront, parks and amusements; friendly service and modest but neat accommodation.
8 bedrooms; double B&B from £28

### Hope House
47 Percy Gardens, Tynemouth
☎ 091-257 1989
Antiques feature in all rooms in this spacious Victorian house overlooking the sea.
3 bedrooms; double B&B £37.50-£47.50
Credit cards 1 2 3

### Marlborough Hotel
20-21 East Pde, Central Promenade, Whitley Bay
☎ 091-251 3628
Family-owned hotel with spacious accommodation.
15 bedrooms; double B&B £40-£45
Credit cards 1 3

### York House Hotel
30 Park Pde, Whitley Bay
☎ 091-252 8313 & 091-251 3953
Family-run guesthouse offering sound accommodation.
8 bedrooms; double B&B £36-£40
Credit cards 1 2 3

### Cherrytree House
35 Brook St, Whitley Bay
☎ 091-251 4306
Close to the seafront; neat accommodation and friendly service.
4 bedrooms; double B&B £26-£36

### Lindisfarne Hotel
11 Holly Av, Whitley Bay
☎ 091-251 3954 & 091-297 0579
Small, friendly gueshouse with fresh, bright bedrooms.
9 bedrooms; double B&B £28-£56
Credit cards 1 3

### White Surf
8 South Pde, Whitley Bay
☎ 091-253 0103
Light and airy accommodation.
7 bedrooms; double B&B £31-£33
Credit cards 1 2 3

## WHERE TO STAY

### CAMPSITES

**►►► Caravan Club Site**
Gosforth Park Racecourse, High Gosforth Park, Newcastle-upon-Tyne
☎ 091-236 3258
Off the B1318 Morpeth road next to the racecourse.

**►►► Derwent Park Caravan Site**
Rowlands Gill
☎ (0207) 543383
Southwest of Newcastle; pitch price from £4.50 per night.

**► Lizard Lane Caravan & Camping Site**
Lizard Ln, South Shields
☎ 091-454 4982
Two miles south of town centre on A183 Sunderland road.

**► Sand Haven**
Bents Park Rd, South Shields
☎ 091-454 5594
Situated on A183.

## WHERE TO EAT

### RESTAURANTS

**❀❀❀ 21 Queen Street**
Quayside
☎ 091-222 0755, fax: 091-230 5875
A busy, modern restaurant serving a fashionably eclectic mix of food cooked with great style.
Lunch: 12-2; from £15.50 and a la carte
Dinner: 7-10.45; from £27 a la carte
Credit cards 1 2 3 5

**❀❀ Fishermans Lodge**
Jesmond Dene, Jesmond,
☎ 091-281 3281 & 091-281 3724, fax: 091-281 6410
A speciality seafood restaurant serving light, modern dishes in an elegant setting.
Lunch: 12-2; £16-£18 and a la carte
Dinner: 7-11; £25-£35 a la carte
Credit cards 1 2 3 5

**❀ Courtneys**
5-7 The Side
☎ 091-232 5537
Lunch 12-2; £13.95 and a la carte
Dinner 7-10.30 £20-£30 a la carte
Credit cards 1 2 3

### PUBS

**Shiremoor House**
Middle Engine Lane, New York, North Shields
☎ 091-257 6302
An imaginative conversion of an old stone farm building now houses this pleasant pub offering good value meals which are both substantial and interesting. Beers include Stones, Theakstons, Courage Directors and draught Bass. Children are allowed in granary and restaurant only.
Open: 11am-11pm; Sunday 12-3pm, 7-10.30pm
Bar food: 12-2.30pm, 6-9.30pm (7-9.30pm on Sunday)
Restaurant: 12-1.30pm, 7-8.30pm

**Black Bull**
Matfen
☎ (0661) 886330
Attractive stone village-centre pub offering a wide choice of good-value food. Real ale includes Theakstons Best Bitter and a guest beer. Children are allowed in family room and restaurant only.
Open: 11am-3pm, 6-11pm; Sunday 12-3pm, 7-10.30pm
Bar food: as opening hours
Restaurant: as opening hours

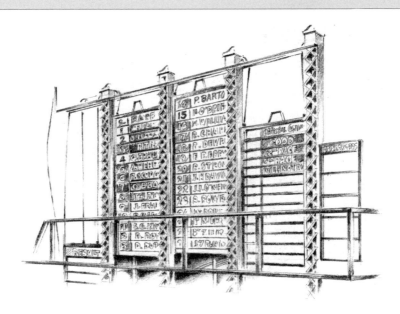

# Newmarket

*Acknowledged as the 'Horseracing Capital of the World, Newmarket has been the home of the sport of Kings since 1605, when James I and his nobles established racing on the springy turf of Newmarket Heath.*

There are two racecourses here - The Rowley Mile, named after King Charles II's favourite hack, Rowley, and the July Course, one of the most beautiful racecourses in the world. Racing on the Rowley Mile is divided into a spring and an autumn session, the spring session featuring the first two classics of the season - the 1000 and 2000 Guineas Stakes. The July Course takes over for the summer months, beginning with the important three-day July Meeting, featuring the Carroll Foundation July Cup, a Group 1 international race which is the most valuable six furlong race in Europe. There are also three very popular evening meetings with a barbeque and live entertainment by top performers immediately after the last race.

### THE NATIONAL HORSERACING MUSEUM
The story of the development of horseracing is told in this museum's five permanent galleries. There is a collection of videos of classic races and displays are changed each year.
Open: end of Mar to beginning of Dec, 10am-5pm Tue to Sat, 2-5pm Sun (12-5 on Sun in Jul and Aug); closed Mon, except during Jul and Aug and Bank Hols.

### THE NATIONAL STUD
This is one of the most prestigious centres of racehorse breeding and tours are available to visitors, taking in modern purpose-built stable units and, of course, some of the racing stars of the past and the future.
Open: by appointment only: Apr to Oct, Mon to Fri 11.15am and 2.30pm, also Sat mornings when there is racing at Newmarket and most Suns at 3pm. Admission: £2.75, £1.50 for senior citizens, students and children over 5.
☎ (0638) 663464 during office hours

### LOCATION AND HOW TO GET THERE
The course is on the western edge of the town. From the M11 (south), take the A11 at junction 9, then at the start of the Newmarket bypass (A45) turn right onto the A1304; from the A1 take the A45 eastwards.
**Nearest Railway Station:** Newmarket (unmanned halt) or Cambridge; there is a free bus service to and from Newmarket station, and a service from Cambridge station.

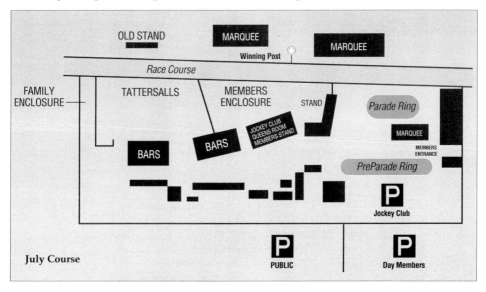

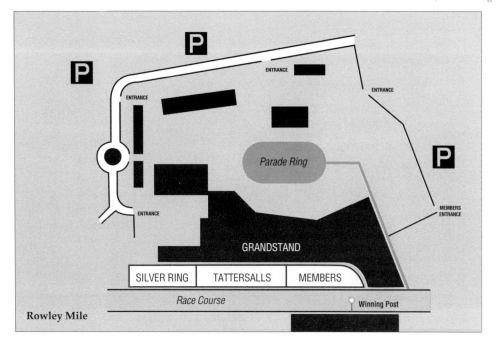

Rowley Mile

## ADMISSION

All classes of day ticket give access to full betting facilities, including Tote.

**Day Tickets:**

MEMBERS £13 normal days, £17 July Meeting, £20 for 1000 Guineas, 2000 Guineas, William Hill Cambridgeshire and Tote Cesarewitch Days - access to restaurants, bars, private boxes and luncheon rooms

GRANDSTAND AND PADDOCK £9 normal days, £11 special days as listed above - access to bars, snacks and fast food

SILVER RING (FAMILY ENCLOSURE ON JULY COURSE) £2.50 July Course, £3 Rowley Mile, £5 for special days (see Members Enclosure details) - access to bars, snacks, fast food, childrens supervised adventure playground

**Annual membership:** £160

## COURSE FACILITIES

**Banks:**
there is a Barclays Bank on the course, but no cashpoint facilities.

**For families:**
picnic area with refreshment kiosk and toilets in the Family Enclosure on the July Course; children's play area, lost children centre.

## CALENDAR OF EVENTS

**April 12-14** – Craven Meeting; includes Shadwell Stud Nell Gwyn Stakes, European Free Handicap and Craven Stakes
**April 28-30** – includes Madagans 1000 Guineas, 2000 Guineas and The Jockey Club Stakes
**May 20-21** – includes the Coral Handicap
**June 17** – evening meeting
**June 24-25** – includes Tartan International Day and Van Geest Criterion Stakes
**July 5-7** – includes the Princess of Wales Stakes, the Falmouth Stakes and July Cup
**July 15-16** – Veuve Cliquot Evening Meeting on Friday, Food Brokers Trophy on Saturday

**July 29-30** – includes the Colman's of Norwich Stakes
**August 5-6** – evening meeting on Friday; includes Brierley Group New Zealand Handicap on Saturday
**August 26-27** – includes the Hopeful Stakes
**September 28-October 1** – includes the Tattersalls Houghton Sales Stakes, the Shadwell Stud Cheveley Park Stakes, the Somerville Tattersall Stakes and the William Hill Cambridgeshire Handicap
**October 13-15** – includes the Challenge Stakes, the Dewhurst Stakes, the Dubai Champion Stakes and the Tote Cesarewitch
**October 28-29** – includes the Ladbroke Autumn Handicap

## WHERE TO STAY

### HOTELS

#### ★★★ 67% Bedford Lodge
Bury Road
☎ (0638) 663175, fax: (0638) 667391
56 bedrooms; double B&B £75-£120
Credit cards 1 2 3 5

#### ★★★ ⊛ 65% Newmarket Moat House
Moulton Rd
☎ (0638) 667171, fax: (0638) 666533
47 bedrooms; double B&B £80-£95
Credit cards 1 2 3 5

#### Around Newmarket

#### Forte Travelodge
A11, Barton Mills
☎ (0638) 717675, Central Reservations:
(0800) 850950
32 bedrooms; double room £31.95 (room only)
Credit cards 1 2 3

#### ★★★★ ⊛ 70% Garden House
Granta Place, Mill Ln, Cambridge
☎ (0223) 63421, fax: (0223) 316605
118 bedrooms; double B&B £120-£168
Credit cards 1 2 3 5

#### ★★★★ 59% Holiday Inn
Downing St, Cambridge
☎ (0223) 464466, fax: (0223) 464440
199 bedrooms; double room £115-£120
(room only)
Credit cards 1 2 3 4 5

#### ★★★★ 56% University Arms
Regent St, Cambridge
☎ (0223) 351241, fax: (0223) 315256
115 bedrooms; double B&B £80£110
Credit cards 1 2 3 5

#### ★★★ 66% Gonville
Gonville Pl, Cambridge
☎ (0223) 66611
62 bedrooms; double B&B from £82
Credit cards 1 2 3 4 5

#### ★★★ 70% Royal Cambridge
Trumpington St, Cambridge
☎ (0223) 351631, telex: 329265, fax:
(0223) 352972
46 bedrooms; double B&B £82
Credit cards 1 2 3 5

#### ★★ 70% Cambridge Lodge
Huntingdon Rd, Cambridge
☎ (0223) 352833, fax: (0223) 355166
11 bedrooms; double B&B £80
Credit cards 1 2 3 5

#### ★★ 69% Centennial
63-71 Hills Rd, Cambridge
☎ (0223) 314652, fax: (0223) 315443
39 bedrooms; double B&B £70-£80
Credit cards 1 2 3 5

#### ★★ 68% Arundel House
53 Chesterton Rd, Cambridge
☎ (0223) 67701, fax: (0223) 67721
66 bedrooms; double B&B £54-£72.50
Credit cards 1 2 3 5

#### ★★ ⊛ 67% Regent
41 Regent St, Cambridge
☎ (0223) 351470, fax: (0223) 356220
25 bedrooms; double B&B £55-£67.50
Credit cards 1 2 3 5

#### ★★ 71% Rosery Country House
15 Church St, Exning
☎ (0638) 577312
11 bedrooms
Credit cards 1 2 3 5

#### ★★★ 64% Forte Posthouse
Lakeview, Bridge Rd, Impington
☎ (0223) 237000, fax: (0223) 233426
118 bedrooms; double room £39.50-£69.50
(room only)
Credit cards 1 2 3 5

#### ★★★ 65% Smoke House Inn
Beck Row, Mildenhall
☎ (0638) 713223, fax: (0638) 712202
105 bedrooms; double B&B £77-£85

#### ★★★ ⊛ 62% Riverside
Mill St, Mildenhall
☎ (0638) 717274, fax: (0638) 715997
21 bedrooms; double B&B £70-£74
Credit cards 1 2 3 5

#### ★★ 62% Bell
High St, Mildenhall
☎ (0638) 717272, fax: (0638) 717057
17 bedrooms; double B&B £55-£65
Credit cards 1 2 3 5

#### ★★★ 72% Swynford Paddocks
Six Mile Bottom
☎ (063870) 234, fax: (063870) 283
15 bedrooms; double B&B £107-£140
Credit cards 1 2 3 5

### BED AND BREAKFAST

#### Helen Hotel
167-169 Hills Rd, Cambridge
☎ (0223) 246465, fax: (0223) 214406
About a mile east of the city centre; well
equipped accommodation of a good
standard, run by friendly Italian couple.
22 bedrooms; double B&B £50-£55
Credit cards 1 3

#### Lensfield Hotel
53 Lensfield Rd, Cambridge
☎ (0223) 355017, telex: 818183, fax:
(0223) 312022
Friendly, family run hotel on the ring road
with a restaurant offering English, French
and Greek dishes.
36 bedrooms; double B&B £58-£68
Credit cards 1 2 3 5

#### Sorrento Hotel
196 Cherry Hinton Rd, Cambridge
☎ (0223) 243533, fax: (0223) 213463
Welcoming guesthouse with well equipped
accommodation and a well-stocked bar.
24 bedrooms
Credit cards 1 2 3 5

#### Suffolk House Private Hotel
69 Milton Rd, Cambridge
☎ (0223) 352016
Fresh, attractive bedrooms and high
standards of housekeeping are offered at
this hotel to the north of the city centre.
10 bedrooms; double B&B £45-£65
Credit cards 1 3

#### Assisi
193 Cherry Hinton Rd, Cambridge
☎ (0223) 211466 & 246648
East of the city centre; well equipped
accommodation and friendly atmosphere.
17 bedrooms; double B&B £35-£38
Credit cards 1 2 3

#### Avimore
310 Cherry Hinton Rd, Cambridge
☎ (0223) 410956
Small, family run guesthouse near the ring
road.Evening meals available with prior
notice.
4 bedrooms; double B&B £30-£36
Credit cards 1 3

## WHERE TO STAY

### Benson House
24 Huntingdon Rd, Cambridge
☎ (0223) 311594
Modest, rather compact bedrooms; close to the city centre on the A604.
5 bedrooms; double B&B £35-£40

### Bon Accord House
20 St Margarets Sq, Cambridge
☎ (0223) 411188 & 246568
In a quiet cul-de-sac off the Cherry Hinton road; comfortable accommodation; no smoking.
9 bedrooms; double B&B £33-£42
Credit cards 1 3

### Brooklands
95 Cherry Hinton Rd, Cambridge
☎ (0223) 242035
Cosy, family run guesthouse with pretty bedrooms and comfortable lounge.
6 bedrooms; double B&B £32-£42
Credit cards 1 2 3 5

### Cristina's
47 St Andrews Rd, Cambridge
☎ (0223) 65855 & 327700
North of the city centre; bright, clean accommodation and helpful proprietors.
6 bedrooms; double B&B £34-£40

### Fairways
141-143 Cherry Hinton Rd, Cambridge
☎ (0223) 246063, fax: (0223) 212093
Good standard of accommodation, and always improving range of facilities; bar meals and small a la carte selection available in the evening.
16 bedrooms; double B&B £32-£40
Credit cards 1 3

### De Freville House
166 Chesterton Rd, Cambridge
☎ (0223) 354993, fax: (0223) 321890
Friendly atmosphere in a Victorian house maintained in its original style; pleasant basement dining room.
9 bedrooms; double B&B £32-£42

### Hamilton Hotel
156 Chesterton Rd, Cambridge
☎ (0223) 65664
Popular, good-value accommodation with a range of services including bar, snacks and bar meals.
10 bedrooms
Credit card 3

### Hamden
89 High St, Cherry Hinton
☎ (0223) 413263
Very good accommodation in village location; professionally run by Italian proprietors.
4 bedrooms; double B&B £35-£40

### Hill Farm
Kirtling
☎ (0638) 730253
Traditional 16th-century farmhouse with modern exterior and comfortable accommodation.
3 bedrooms; double B&B £40

### Live & Let Live
76 High St, Stetchworth
☎ (0638) 508153
Less than a mile south of Newmarket, this former inn has lovely colour-coordinated rooms; great care and attention are provided by the proprietors.
7 bedrooms; double B&B £36-£38
Credit cards 1 3

### CAMPSITES

### ►► Barron Cove Caravan & Camping Site
Weirs Rd, Burwell
☎ (0638) 741547
About 4 miles northwest of Newmarket on the B1103

## WHERE TO EAT

### RESTAURANT

### ❀❀❀ Midsummer House
Midsummer Common, Cambridge
☎ (0223) 69299
Excellent food in a charming restaurant with four distinctive dining rooms; you would be well advised to book in advance - and get directions.
Last lunch: 2pm; £12.95-£38
Last dinner: 9.30pm; £23-£38
Credit cards 1 2 3 5

### PUBS

### Plough & Fleece
High Rd, Horningsea
☎ (0223) 860795
A 300-year-old pub on the edge of the village with beams, quarry tiles and a collection of farm implements. Excellent home-made food is on offer and beers include Greene King IPA and Abbott Ale.
Open: 11am-2.30pm, 7-11pm; Sunday 12-2pm, 7-10.30pm
Bar food: 12-2pm; Sunday 12-1.30pm
Restaurant: 12-2pm, 7-9.30pm; Sunday 12-1.30pm; closed Monday evening.

### Free Press
Prospect Row, Cambridge
☎ (0223) 68337
This town pub has engagingly old-fashioned decor with cricketing and rowing memorabilia. Good traditional dishes are served and beers include Green King IPA and Abbott Ale. There is a sunny patio and small garden. Children welcome anywhere.
Open: 12-3pm, 6-11pm; Sunday 12-3pm, 7-10.30pm
Bar food: 12-2pm, 6-8.30pm; Sunday 12-2pm, 7-8.30pm

# Newton Abbot

*This is a friendly little West Country course (the furthest west in England) where a high priority has been placed on the creation of a pleasant, laid-back atmosphere. It makes no pretensions to being a glamorous, up-market track; instead, there is an unassuming, down-to-earth feel and it is all the better for that.*

The quality of racing may perhaps suffer as a result, but prize money has been substantially boosted in recent seasons and the standard of competition is getting better all the time. In particular, champion trainer Martin Pipe is always a great supporter of meetings here and his runners always merit respect.

August and September are Newton Abbot's busiest time of the year with a cluster of fixtures scheduled during those late summer months in order to attract holiday-makers from the nearby Torbay resorts. Entrance fees are amongst the lowest in the land and it is one of a small band of courses which does not have a separate Members enclosure, presumably due to its lack of space. Facilities are closely grouped together with only a short walk from the paddock to the stands while the tight track provides excellent viewing and means binoculars are not essential. All in all, it is well worth paying a visit if taking a holiday in the area.

### FURTHER INFORMATION

Newton Abbot Races Ltd
The Racecourse, Kingsteignton Rd
Newton Abbot, Devon TQ12 3AF
☎ (0626) 53235

### LOCATION AND HOW TO GET THERE

The course is between Newton Abbot and Kingsteignton. From the end of the M5 continue south, taking the A380 towards Torbay. The Newton Abbot turn-off is thirteen miles from the end of the motorway.

---

### ADMISSION

**Day tickets:**

COURSE £4 - access to restaurants, bars

**transfers:** Course to Paddock £4.50

### COURSE FACILITIES

**Banks:**
there are no banks or cashpoint facilities on the course

**For families:**
picnic area; lost children centre

---

## CALENDAR OF EVENTS

April 2 – jumping
April 4 – jumping
April 20 – jumping; evening meeting
April 29 – jumping
May 3 – jumping
May 13 – jumping; evening meeting
July 30 – jumping
August 1 – jumping
August 11 – jumping
August 29 – jumping
August 31 – jumping
September 8 – jumping
October 4 – jumping
October 25 – jumping
November 15 – jumping
December 12 – jumping
December 26 – jumping

## WHERE TO STAY

### HOTELS

### Around Newton Abbot

**★★ ⚜ 71% Holne Chase**
Ashburton
☎ (03643) 471, fax: (03643) 453
12 bedrooms; double B&B £82–£111
Credit cards 1 2 3 5

**★★ 67% Tugela House**
68-70 East St, Ashburton
☎ (0364) 52206
7 bedrooms; double B&B from £40
Credit cards 1 3

**★★ 63% Dartmoor Lodge**
Peartree Cross, Ashburton
☎ (0364) 52232, fax: (0364) 53990
30 bedrooms; double room £34.95–£51
(room only)
Credit cards 1 2 3

**★★★ 62% Sefton**
Babbacombe Downs Rd, Babbacombe
☎ (0803) 328728 & 326591
47 bedrooms
Credit cards 1 2 3

**★★ 55% Norcliffe**
7 Babbacombe Downs Rd, Babbacombe
☎ (0803) 328456 & 328023
28 bedrooms; double B&B £55–£80
Credit cards 1 3

**★★ 61% Morningside**
Babbacombe Downs
☎ (0803) 327025
14 bedrooms
Credit cards 1 3

**★ 62% Ashley Rise**
18 Babbacombe Rd, Babbacombe
☎ (0803) 327282
25 bedrooms; double B&B £40–£50

**★ 58% Sunray**
Aveland Rd, Babbacombe
☎ (0803) 328285
22 bedrooms; double B&B £40–£52
Credit cards 1 3

**★★★ 65% Edgemoor**
Haytor Rd, Bovey Tracey
☎ (0626) 832466, fax: (0626) 834760
12 bedrooms
Credit cards 1 2 3 5

**★★ 61% Riverside Inn**
Fore St, Bovey Tracey
☎ (0626) 832293, fax: (0626) 833880
10 bedrooms; double B&B £39.50
Credit cards 1 2 3

**★★ 60% Coombe Cross**
Coombe Cross, Bovey Tracey
☎ (0626) 832476, fax: (0626) 835298
26 bedrooms; double B&B £50–£60
Credit cards 1 2 3 5

**★★★ 60% Quayside**
King St, Brixham
☎ 0803 855751, telex: 336682, fax: 0803 882733
29 bedrooms
Credit cards 1 2 3 5

**★ 57% Smugglers Haunt**
Church Hill East, Brixham
☎ (0803) 853050 & 859416, fax: (0803) 858738
14 bedrooms; double B&B £48–£54
Credit cards 1 2 3 5

**★★ 61% Old Coaching House**
25 Fore St, Chudleigh
☎ (0626) 853270
14 bedrooms; double B&B £55–£65
Credit cards 1 3

**★★★ 60% Langstone Cliff**
Dawlish Warren, Dawlish
☎ (0626) 865155, telex: 57515, fax: (0626) 867166
64 bedrooms; double B&B £104
Credit cards 1 2 3 5

**★★ 62% Fairwinds**
Kennford
☎ (0392) 832911
8 bedrooms; double B&B £49–£52
Credit cards 1 3

**★★★ 71% Passage House**
Hackney Ln, Kingsteignton
☎ (0626) 55515, fax: (0626) 63336
39 bedrooms; double B&B £85–£95
Credit cards 1 2 3 5

**★★ 68% The White Hart**
The Square, Moretonhampstead
☎ (0647) 40406, fax: (0647) 40565
20 bedrooms; double B&B £63–£65
Credit cards 1 2 3 5

**★ 64% Hazelwood**
33A Torquay Rd, Hazelwood
☎ (0626) 66130 & 65021
7 bedrooms; double B&B £41–£49
Credit cards 1 3

## WHERE TO STAY

**★★★ 65% Redcliffe**
Marine Dr, Paignton
☎ (0803) 526397, fax: (0803) 528030
59 bedrooms
Credit cards 1 2 3 5

**★★★ 58% The Palace**
Esplanade Rd, Paignton
☎ (0803) 555121, fax: (0803) 527974
52 bedrooms; double room from £80 (room
only)
Credit cards 1 2 3 5

**★★ 68% Sunhill**
Alta Vista Rd, Paignton
☎ (0803) 557532, fax: (0803) 663850
28 bedrooms; double B&B £58-£76
Credit cards 1 2 3

**★★ 63% Preston Sands**
10/12 Marine Pde, Paignton
☎ (0803) 558718
31 bedrooms; double B&B £38-£50
Credit cards 1 2 3

**★★ 62% Dainton**
95 Dartmouth Rd, Three Beaches,
Goodrington, Paignton
☎ (0803) 550067 & 525901
11 bedrooms
Credit cards 1 3

**★ 68% Oldway Links Hotel**
21 Southfield Rd, Paignton
☎ (0803) 559332
13 bedrooms
Credit cards 1 3

**★ 59% South Sands**
Alta Vista Rd, Paignton
☎ (0803) 557231 & 529947
19 bedrooms
Credit cards 1 3

**★ 67% Sea Trout Inn**
Staverton
☎ (080426) 274, due to change to (0803)
762274,
fax: (080426) 506, due to change to (0803)
762506
10 bedrooms; double B&B £48-£52
Credit cards 1 2 3

**★★★ 71% Gabriel Court**
Stoke Gabriel
☎ (080428) 206 & 267, fax: (080428) 333
20 bedrooms; double B&B from £71
Credit cards 1 2 3 5

**★★ 65% Ness House**
Marine Dr, Shaldon, Teignmouth
☎ (0626) 873480, fax: (0626) 873486
7 bedrooms; double B&B £68-£78
Credit cards 1 2 3

**★ 63% Belvedere**
Parnpark Rd, Teignmouth
☎ (0626) 774561
13 bedrooms; double B&B £38-£44
Credit cards 1 3

**★ 63% Glenside**
Ringmoor Rd, Shaldon, Teignmouth
☎ (0626) 872448
10 bedrooms; double B&B £35-£45

**★ 58% Bay**
Sea Front, 15 Powerham Ter, Teignmouth
☎ (0626) 774123
18 bedrooms
Credit cards 1 2 3 5

**★★ ✿ 69% Ebford House**
Exmouth Rd, Teignmouth
☎ (0392) 877658, fax: (0392) 874424
18 bedrooms; double B&B £58-£80
Credit cards 1 2 3

**★★★★Y 58% The Imperial**
Park Hill Rd, Torquay
☎ (0803) 294301, telex: 42849, fax: (0803)
298293
167 bedrooms; double B&B £150-£180
Credit cards 1 2 3 5

**★★★★ 56% Palace**
Babbacombe Rd, Torquay
☎ (0803) 200200, fax: (0803) 299899
141 bedrooms; double B&B £110-£152
Credit cards 1 3 5

**★★★★ 53% Grand**
Sea Front, Torquay
☎ (0803) 296677, fax: (0803) 213462
112 bedrooms; double B&B £95-£130
Credit cards 1 3

**★★★ ✿ 70% Orestone Manor**
Rockhouse Ln, Maidencombe
☎ (0803) 328098 & 328099, fax: (0803)
328336
18 bedrooms; double B&B £70-£180
Credit cards 1 2 3 5

**★★★ 69% Corbyn Head**
Torquay Rd, Sea Front, Livermead, Torquay
☎ (0803) 213611, fax: (0803) 296152
51 bedrooms; double B&B £80-£110
Credit cards 1 2 3 5

**★★★ 68% Abbey Lawn Hotel**
Scarborough Rd, Torquay
☎ (0803) 299199, fax: (0803) 291460
56 bedrooms
Credit cards 1 2 3 5

**★★★ 68% Homers**
Warren Rd, Torquay
☎ (0803) 213456, fax: (0803) 213458
14 bedrooms
Credit cards 1 2 3 5

**★★★ 67% Livermead Cliff**
Torbay Rd, Torquay
☎ (0803) 299666 & 292881, telex: 42424,
fax: (0803) 294496
64 bedrooms; double B&B £58-£104
Credit cards 1 2 3 5

**★★★ 63% Belgrave**
Seafront, Torquay
☎ (0803) 296666, fax: (0803) 211308
68 bedrooms; double B&B £74-£100
Credit cards 1 3 5

**★★★ 60% Kistor**
Belgrave Rd, Torquay
☎ (0803) 212632, fax: (0803) 293219
56 bedrooms; double B&B £72-£96
Credit cards 1 2 3

**★★★ 60% Toorak**
Chestnut Av, Torquay
☎ (0803) 291444, 42885, fax: (0803)
291666
91 bedrooms; double B&B £54-£88
Credit cards 1 3

**★★★ 57% Devonshire**
Parkhill Rd, Torquay
☎ (0803) 291123, fax: (0803) 291710
59 bedrooms; double B&B £65-£86
Credit cards 1 3 4 5

**★★★ 54% Livermead House**
Torbay Rd, Torquay
☎ (0803) 294361, telex: 42918, fax: (0803)
200758
62 bedrooms; double B&B £56-£96
Credit cards 1 2 3 5

**★★ 67% Coppice**
Barrington Rd, Torquay
☎ (0803) 297786
40 bedrooms; double B&B £40-£48

**★★ 67% Frognel Hall**
Higher Woodfield Rd, Torquay
☎ (0803) 298339
27 bedrooms; double B&B £39-£59
Credit cards 1 3

## WHERE TO STAY

**★★ 66% Burlington**
462-466 Babbacombe Rd, Torquay
☎ (0803) 294374, fax: (0803) 200189
55 bedrooms; double B&B £48-£65
Credit cards 1 3

**★★ 66% Chelston Tower**
Rawlyn Rd, Torquay
☎ (0803) 607351
23 bedrooms; double B&B £51-£73
Credit cards 1 3

**★★ 66% Gresham Court**
Babbacombe Rd, Torquay
☎ (0803) 293007 & 293658
30 bedrooms; double B&B £43-£55
Credit cards 1 3

**★★ 66% Red House**
Rousdown Rd, Chelston, Torquay
☎ (0803) 607811, fax: (0803) 200592
10 bedrooms; double B&B £45-£70
Credit cards 1 3

**★★ 65% Albaston House**
27 St Marychurch Rd, Torquay
☎ (0803) 296758
13 bedrooms
Credit cards 1 3

**★★ 65% Dunstone**
Lower Warberry Rd, Torquay
☎ (0803) 293185
14 bedrooms
Credit cards 1 3

**★★ 65% Hunsdon Lea**
Hunsdon Rd, Torquay
☎ (0803) 296538
12 bedrooms

**★★ 65% Oscar's Hotel & Restaurant**
56 Belgrave Rd, Torquay
☎ (0803) 293653
12 bedrooms
Credit cards 1 3 4

**★★ 64% Seascape**
8-10 Tor Church Rd, Torquay
☎ (0803) 292617
63 bedrooms; double B&B £26-£54
Credit cards 1 3

**★★ 63% Bute Court**
Belgrave Rd, Torquay
☎ (0803) 293771, fax: (0803) 213429
48 bedrooms; double B&B £36-£55
Credit cards 1 2 3 5

**★★ 62% Ansteys Lea**
Babbacombe Rd, Wellswood, Torquay
☎ (0803) 294843
24 bedrooms; double B&B £53-£70
Credit cards 1 3

**★★ 61% Roseland**
Warren Rd, Torquay
☎ (0803) 213829, fax: (0803) 291266
34 bedrooms; double B&B £57-£75
Credit cards 1 3

**★★ 61% Hotel Sydore**
Meadfoot Rd, Torquay
☎ (0803) 294758, fax: (0803) 294489
13 bedrooms; double B&B £41-£75
Credit cards 1 3

**★★ 60% Bancourt**
Avenue Rd, Torquay
☎ (0803) 295077
46 bedrooms; double B&B £54-£74
Credit cards 1 2 3

**★★ 58% Hotel Balmoral**
Meadfoot Sea Rd, Torquay
☎ (0803) 293381 & 299224
24 bedrooms; double B&B £44-£60
Credit cards 1 2 3

**★★ 58% Carlton**
Falkland Rd, Torquay
☎ (0803) 291166
32 bedrooms
Credit cards 1 3

**★★ 58% Lansdowne**
Babbacombe Rd, Torquay
☎ (0803) 299599, fax: (0803) 290344
27 bedrooms; double B&B £43.50-£71
Credit cards 1 3

**★★ 52% Vernon Court**
Warren Rd, Torquay
☎ (0803) 292676
29 bedrooms; double B&B £33-£64
Credit cards 1 2 3 5

**★ 70% Fairmount House**
Herbert Road, Chelston
☎ (0803) 605446
8 bedrooms; double B&B £47-£53
Credit cards 1 2 3

**★ 66% Shelley Court**
Croft Rd, Torquay
☎ (0803) 295642, fax: (0803) 2157963
28 bedrooms; double B&B £34-£54
Credit cards 1 3

**★ 66% Westwood**
111 Abbey Rd, Torquay
☎ (0803) 293818
26 bedrooms; double B&B £32-£40
Credit cards 1 3

**★ 64% Sunleigh**
Livermead Hill, Torquay
☎ (0803) 607137
20 bedrooms; double B&B £50-£60
Credit cards 1 2 3

**★ 62% Hotel Fluela**
15-17 Hatfield Rd, Torquay
☎ (0803) 297512, fax: (0803) 296261
13 bedrooms; double B&B £29-£45
Credit cards 1 3

**★★ 61% Royal Seven Stars**
Totnes
☎ (0803) 862125 & 863241, fax: (0803) 867925
18 bedrooms; double B&B £49.50-£69.50
Credit cards 1 3 5

### BED AND BREAKFAST

**Lamorna**
Ideford Combe, Newton Abbot
☎ (0626) 65627
Attractive rural views from this cosy modern guesthouse.
6 bedrooms; double B&B £32-£36

**Gages Mill**
Buckfastleigh Rd, Ashburton
☎ (0364) 52391
Former 14th-century wool mill; warm, relaxed, cosy atmosphere.
8 bedrooms; double B&B £39-£41

**Brembridge Farm**
Woodland, Ashburton
☎ (0364) 52426, fax: (0364) 53589
Simply appointed farmhouse; welcoming proprietors.
5 bedrooms; double B&B £33-£37

**East Burne Farm**
Bickington
☎ (0626) 821496
Grade II listed medieval house full of character.
3 bedrooms; double B&B £30-£40

**Blenheim Hotel**
Brimley Rd, Bovey Tracey
☎ (0626) 832422
Fine detached Victorian property.
7 bedrooms; double B&B £49-£56

## WHERE TO STAY

### Willmead Farm
Bovey Tracey
☎ (06477) 214
Charming 15th-century thatched cottage.
3 bedrooms; double B&B from £40

### Harbour Side
65 Berry Head Rd, Brixham
☎ (0803) 858899
Friendly guesthouse with beautiful views.
5 bedrooms; double B&B £27-£35

### Woodlands
Parkham Rd, Brixham
☎ (0803) 852040
Neat guesthouse for non-smokers,
overlooking Brixham.
5 bedrooms; double B&B £35-£39
Credit cards 1 3

### Raddicombe Lodge
105 Kingswear Rd, Brixham
☎ (0803) 882125
Friendly guesthouse with views of the
countryside and the sea.
8 bedrooms; double B&B £31-£44
Credit cards 1 3

### Ranscombe House Hotel
Ranscombe Rd, Brixham
☎ (0803) 882337
Views over the harbour; comfortable and
well equipped bedrooms.
9 bedrooms; double B&B £42-£54
Credit cards 1 2 3

### Sampford House
59 Kings St, Brixham
☎ (0803) 857761
Cosy family-run terraced period house
overlooking the inner harbour.
6 bedrooms; double B&B £28-£32

### Harbour View Hotel
65 King St, Brixham
☎ (0803) 853052
Former home of a harbour master; simply
furnished.
9 bedrooms; double B&B £30-£35

### Furzeleigh Mill Country Hotel
Dart Bridge, Buckfast
☎ (0364) 43476
A 16th-century converted mill house in a
pleasant rural spot.
15 bedrooms
Credit cards 1 2 3

### Dartbridge Manor
20 Dartbridge Rd, Buckfastleigh
☎ (0364) 43575
Four hundred year old manor house full of
character and charm.
10 bedrooms.

### Cott Inn
Dartington
☎ (0803) 863777, fax: (0803) 866629
A delightful thatched country inn dating back
to 1324.
6 bedrooms; double B&B from £55
Credit cards 1 2 3

### Mimosa
11 Barton Ter, Dawlish
☎ (0626) 863283
Family-run guesthouse, close to the town
centre and beaches.
9 bedrooms

### The Old Vicarage
Cofton Hill, Cockwood, Dawlish
☎ (0626) 891354
3 bedrooms; double B&B £35-£45

### Ford Farm
Harberton
☎ (0803) 863539
Cottage with attractively coordinated
bedrooms.
3 bedrooms; double B&B £34-£40

### Wellpritton Farm
Holne
☎ (03643) 273
Warm welcoming atmosphere in Devonshire
longhouse. Bedrooms have many thoughtful
extras.
4 bedrooms; double B&B £32-£34

### Beresford
5 Adelphi Rd, Paignton
☎ (0803) 551560
Sound accommodation and personal
service is provided by this small, friendly
guesthouse.
8 bedrooms; double B&B from £40

### Clennon Valley Hotel
1 Clennon Rise, Paignton
☎ (0803) 550304 & 557736
Brightly decorated bedrooms, several of
which offer family accommodation.
12 bedrooms
Credit cards 1 3

### Danethorpe Hotel
23 St Andrews Rd, Paignton
☎ (0803) 551251
Short walk from the seafront and harbour;
nicely equipped bedrooms.
10 bedrooms
Credit cards 1 2 3

### Redcliffe Lodge Hotel
1 Marine Dr, Paignton
☎ (0803) 551394
Beside the safe, sandy beach and green;
relaxed atmosphere.
17 bedrooms; double B&B £40-£60
Credit cards 1 3

### Hotel Retreat
43 Marine Dr, Paignton
☎ (0803) 550596
Comfortable private hotel, family owned, set
in pleasant grounds in a secluded position
on the seafront.
13 bedrooms; double B&B £32-£40

### St Weonard's Private Hotel
12 Kernou Rd, Paignton
☎ (0803) 558842
Close to town centre; warm and welcoming.
8 bedrooms; double B&B £26-£37

### The Sealawn Hotel
Sea Front, 20 Esplanade Rd, Paignton
☎ (0803) 559031
Four-storey establishment affording views
across the greens to the sea.
13 bedrooms; double B&B £36-£48

### Torbay Sands Hotel
16 Marine Pde, Preston Sea, Paignton
☎ (0803) 525568
Hospitable atmosphere, with panoramic
views of the bay.
14 bedrooms; double B&B £26-£34
Credit cards 1 3

### Fonthill
Torquay Rd, Shaldon, Teignmouth
☎ (0626) 872344
The Graeme family warmly welcome non-
smoking guests to their home.
3 bedrooms; double B&B £36-£42

### Hill Rise Hotel
Winterbourne Rd, Teignmouth
☎ (0626) 773108
Edwardian house offering light, airy
accommodation.
8 bedrooms; double B&B £25-£35

## WHERE TO STAY

**Lyme Bay House Hotel**
Den Promenade, Teignmouth
☎ 0626 772953
A large Victorian house overlooking the sea.
9 bedrooms; double B&B from £42

**Rathlin House Hotel**
Upper Hermosa Rd, Teignmouth
☎ 0626 774473
In quiet residential area, with well
presented, simply furnished bedrooms.
10 bedrooms

**Thomas Luny House**
Teign St, Teignmouth
☎ (0626) 772976
Bedrooms furnished with great flair and
thoughtful touches. Restored to its 18th-
century style.
4 bedrooms; double B&B £55-£60

**Glenorleigh Hotel**
26 Cleveland Rd, Torquay
☎ (0803) 292135
This friendly family holiday hotel has won
many awards, both for its hospitality and for
its beautifully kept gardens.
16 bedrooms; double B&B £32-£54

**Kingston House**
75 Avenue Rd, Torquay
☎ (0803) 212760
Cheerful hosts; high standard of
accommodation; delightful place to stay.
6 bedrooms; double B&B £23-£35
Credit cards 1 3

**Barn Hayes Country Hotel**
Brim Hill, Maidencombe, Torquay
☎ (0803) 327980
Standing in pretty sloping gardens with
spectacular views.
10 bedrooms; double B&B £40-£48
Credit cards 1 3

**The Berburry Hotel**
64 Bampfylde Rd, Torquay
☎ (0803) 297494
Well equipped, pretty bedrooms; friendly
and attentive service.
10 bedrooms
Credit cards 1 3

**Braddon Hall Hotel**
Braddons Hill Rd East, Torquay
☎ (0803) 293908
High standard accommodation and a warm
welcome are offered here.
11 bedrooms.

**Burley Court Hotel**
Wheatridge Lane, Livermead, Torquay
☎ (0803) 607879
Comfortable hotel with fresh local produce
prepared and presented by the chef/patron.
11 bedrooms; double B&B £54-£64
Credit cards 1

**Chesterfield Hotel**
62 Belgrave Rd, Torquay
☎ (0803) 292318
Four minutes walk from the seafront and
gardens.
12 bedrooms; double B&B £24-£42
Credit cards 1 3

**Hotel Concorde**
26 Newton Rd, Torquay
☎ (0803) 292330
Well equipped bedrooms; outdoor heated
pool.
22 bedrooms
Credit cards 1 3

**Craig Court Hotel**
10 Ash Hill Rd, Castle Circus, Torquay
☎ (0803) 294400
Victorian detached house with views of
Torquay and beyond. Narrow gauge railway
track in the garden.
10 bedrooms; double B&B £32-£44

**Cranborne Hotel**
58 Belgrave Rd, Torquay
☎ (0803) 290846
A regular award winner; food, puddings in
particular, are of a good standard.
12 bedrooms; double B&B £38-£42
Credit cards 1 3

**Cranmore**
89 Avenue Rd, Torquay
☎ (0803) 298488
Bedrooms are well equipped and have
orthopaedic beds.
9 bedrooms; double B&B £24-£32
Credit cards 1 2 3

**Daphne Court Hotel**
Lower Warberry Rd, Torquay
☎ (0803) 212011
Bedrooms are comfortable and nicely
appointed and there is a cheerful and
friendly atmosphere throughout.
16 bedrooms
Credit cards 1 3

**Elmdene Hotel**
Rathmore Rd, Torquay
☎ (0803) 294940
12 bedrooms; double B&B £37-£48
Credit cards 1 3

**Grosvenor House Hotel**
Falkland Rd, Torquay
☎ (0803) 294110
Small, friendly and comfortable hotel.
11 bedrooms; double B&B £34-£42
Credit cards 1 3

**Hotel Trelawney**
48 Belgrave Rd, Torquay
☎ (0803) 296049
Bright and airy bedrooms are all en suite.
14 bedrooms; double B&B £32-£44
Credit cards 1 3 5

**Lindum Hotel**
Abbey Rd, Torquay
☎ (0803) 292795
Long-established, centrally situated hotel
with nicely furnished bedrooms.
20 bedrooms; double B&B from £24

**Mapleton Hotel**
St Lukes Rd North, Torquay
☎ (0803) 292389
This well managed hotel has a lively,
convivial atmosphere.
11 bedrooms; double B&B from £30
Credit cards 1 3

**Olivia Court**
Upper Braddons Hill Rd, Torquay
☎ (0803) 292595
Grade II listed Victorian villa set in a quiet
residential area close to the town centre.
13 bedroom; double B&B £35-£41
Credit cards 1 2 3

**Rawlyn House Hotel**
Rawlyn Road, Chelston, Torquay
☎ (0803) 605208
This hotel has an attractive heated
swimming pool, and the comfortable
bedrooms are individually furnished.
17 bedrooms; double B&B from £52

**Richwood Hotel**
20 Newton Rd, Torquay
☎ (0803) 293729
Popular family holiday hotel with a relaxed
atmosphere.
21 bedrooms; double B&B £24-£40
Credit cards 1 3

## WHERE TO STAY

### Seaway Hotel
Chelston Rd, Torquay
☎ (0803) 605320
A spacious Victorian house with
comfortable lounge
and bar.14 bedrooms
Credit cards 1 3

### Sevens Hotel
27 Morgan Av, Torquay
☎ (0803) 293523
Relaxed, informal, comfortable atmosphere.
12 bedrooms; double B&B £28-£40

### Villa Marina Hotel
Cockington Ln, Livermead, Torquay
☎ (0803) 605440
A modern holiday hotel, with very well
equipped bedrooms.
26 bedrooms
Credit cards 1 3

### Westgate Hotel
Falkland Rd, Torquay
☎ (0803) 295350
This relaxed and friendly holiday hotel has
comfortable bedrooms.
13 bedrooms; double B&B £38-£46
Credit cards 1 3

## CAMPSITES

### ►►► Ashburton Caravan Park
Waterleat, Ashburton
☎ (0364) 52552
Off the A38 west of Newton Abbot; pitch
price from £9 per night.

### ►►► Lemonford Caravan Park
Bickington
☎ (0626) 821242
West of Exeter off the A382; pitch price from
£7.90 per night

### ►►► Galmpton Park Camping Site
Greenway Rd, Brixham
☎ (0803) 842066
Overlooking the River Dart.

### ►►► Hillhead Holiday Camp
Brixham
☎ (0803) 853204
On B3205 between Brixham and Kingswear.

### ►► Neara Farm Campsite
Colston Rd, Buckfastleigh
☎ (0364) 42234
Off the A38; pitch price from £4.50 per
night.

### ►►►► Finlake Leisure Park
Chudleigh
☎ (0626) 853833
North of Newton Abbot; pitch price from £6
per night.

### ►►► Holmans Wood Tourist Park
Harcombe Cross, Chudleigh
☎ (0626) 853785
North of Newton Abbot; pitch price from
£8.45 per night.

### ►►►► Cofton Farm Caravan & Camping Park
Dawlish
☎ (0626) 890358
South of Exeter on A379; pitch price from
£6.40 per night.

### ►►►► Kennford International Caravan Park
Kennford
☎ (0392) 833046
Just west of Exeter off the A38; pitch price
from £7.50 per night.

### ►►►► Dornafield
Dornafield Farm, Newton Abbot
☎ (0803) 812732
Situated off the A381; pitch price from £9
per night.

### ►►►► Stover International Caravan Park
Lower Staple Hill, Newton Abbot
☎ (0626) 821446
Situated off the A382; pitch price from
£6.55 per night.

### ►►►►► Beverley Parks Caravan & Camping Park
Goodrington Rd, Paignton
☎ (0803) 843887
Pitch price from £9 per night.

### ►►►► Byslades Camping Park
Totnes Rd, Paignton
☎ (0803) 555072
Pitch price from £5.60 per night.

### ►►►► Grange Court Holiday Centre
Grange St, Paignton
☎ (0803) 558010
Pitch price from £6.50 per night.

### ►►►► Widend Camping Park
Berry Pomeroy Rd, Marldon, Paignton
☎ (0803) 550116
Pitch price from £5.50

### ►►►► Lower Yalberton Farm Holiday Park
Long Rd, Paignton
☎ (0803) 558127
Pitch price from £5.85 per night.

### ►►► Marine Park Holiday Centre
Grange Rd, Paignton
☎ (0803) 843887
Pitch price from £8.50 per night.

### ►►► Orchard Park
Totnes Rd, Paignton
☎ (0803) 550504
Pitch price from £6 per night.

### ►►►► Paignton International Touring & Camping Park
Totnes Rd, Paignton
☎ (0803) 521684
Pitch price from £6 per night.

### ►►►► Ramslade Touring Park
Stoke Rd, Stoke Gabriel
☎ (0803) 782575
Between Paignton and Stoke Gabriel.

## WHERE TO EAT

### RESTAURANTS

### ❀❀❀ The Table
135 Babbacombe Rd, Torquay
☎ (0803) 324292
Fresh, honest cooking in a small restaurant
on the outskirts of town.
Lunch: Not Served
Dinner: 7-10; from £24
Credit cards 1 3

### PUBS

See under Exeter Racecourse –
Where to Eat.

# Nottingham

*A pretty bleak picture used to be painted of this Midlands course, but much work has been carried out to correct that image in recent times and its great potential is finally beginning to be realised.*

For instance, a new grandstand has risen phoenix-like from the ashes after a previous structure was ravaged by fire in an arson attack a few years back. This has led to a significant improvement in the facilities that are on offer to patrons with the result that there is a far jollier atmosphere about the place nowadays.

The track itself is one of the fairest in the country and there can be few excuses for beaten horses here. Many of the top Newmarket trainers, most notably Henry Cecil, take advantage of the wide, galloping circuit to introduce some of their better unraced two-year-olds and there is always the possibility that a new star will be born at one of the late season Flat meetings. Nottingham also has a rich jumping history as the site of former jockey Stan Mellor's 1000th winner over the sticks. Now retired, he was the first National Hunt jockey ever to reach that figure and the feat is suitably commemorated with a race named in his honour. By far the best fixture of the year is run on a Saturday in late February and features a couple of important trials for the Cheltenham Festival.

## FURTHER INFORMATION

Nottingham Racecourse Co Ltd
Colwick Park, Colwick Road, Nottingham NG2 4BE
☎ (0602) 580620

## LOCATION AND HOW TO GET THERE

The course is on the southwestern edge of Nottingham, on the B686 at Colwick. From the M1 junction 25, take the A52 east; from the A1 south take the A52 west, or from the north take the A46 from Newark to join the A52, then continue west. **Nearest Railway Station:** Nottingham; there is no connecting bus service to the course.

## ADMISSION

All classes of day ticket give access to full betting facilities, including Tote.

**Day Tickets:**
CENTENARY STAND £12 - access to bar, light snacks, boxes, balcony viewing, facilities for disabled racegoers

TATTERSALLS £8 - access to bar, restaurant, roof-top bar, private rooms

SILVER RING £3 - access to paddock bar and light snacks

**Annual membership:** £125 single, £200 double, £45 National Hunt

## COURSE FACILITIES

**Banks:**
there are no banks or cashpoint facilities on the course

**For families:**
picnic area with toilets; children's play area (unsupervised)

## CALENDAR OF EVENTS

| | |
|---|---|
| **April 4** – flat | **August 3** – flat; evening meeting |
| **April 18** – flat | **August 13** – flat; evening meeting |
| **April 26** – flat | **August 22** – flat |
| **May 13** – flat | **September 19-20** – flat |
| **May 27** – flat | **October 17** – flat |
| **June 6** – flat | **October 27** – flat |
| **June 13** – flat; evening meeting | **November 12** – National Hunt |
| **June 27** – flat | **November 24** – National Hunt |
| **July 1** – flat; evening meeting | **December 17** – National Hunt |
| **July 25** – flat; evening meeting | **December 31** – National Hunt |

## WHERE TO STAY

### HOTELS

**★★★★ 64% Royal Moat House International**
Wollaton St
☎ (0602) 414444, telex: 37101, fax: (0602) 475667
201 bedrooms; double room £87 (room only)
Credit cards 1 2 3 5

**★★★★ 60% Forte Crest**
Saint James's St, Nottingham
☎ (0602) 470131, telex: 37211, fax: (0602) 484366
139 bedrooms; double room from £70 (room only)
Credit cards 1 2 3 5

**★★★ 70% Nottingham Gateway**
Cinderhill
☎ (0602) 794949, fax: (0602) 794744
108 bedrooms
Credit cards 1 2 3 5

**★★★ 69% Nottingham Moat House**
Mansfield Rd,
☎ (0602) 602621, fax: (0602) 691506
172 bedroom; double room £72-£77 (room only)
Credit cards 1 2 3 5

**★★★ 69% Swan Hotel & Restaurant**
84-90 Radcliffe Rd, West Bridgford
☎ (0602) 814042, fax: (0602) 455745
31 bedrooms; double B&B £35-£59.50
Credit cards 1 2 3 5

**★★★ 61% Strathdon Thistle**
Derby Rd
☎ (0602) 418501, telex: 377185, fax: (0602) 483725
69 bedrooms; double room £84-£92 (room only)
Credit cards 1 2 3 4 5

**★★★ 59% Stakis Victoria**
Milton St
☎ (0602) 419561, telex: 37401, fax: (0602) 484736
166 bedrooms; double room £59-£69 (room only)
Credit cards 1 2 3 5

**★★★ 59% Waltons**
2 North Road, The Park,
☎ (0602) 475215, fax: (0602) 475053
13 bedrooms
Credit cards 1 2 3

**★★★ 58% Holiday Inn Garden Court**
Castle Marina Park
☎ (0602) 500600, fax: (0602) 500433
100 bedrooms; double room £39.50-£57 (room only)
Credit cards 1 2 3 5

**★★★ 58% The Stage**
Gregory Boulevard
☎ (0602) 603261, fax: (0602) 691040
58 bedrooms.

**★★ 67% Hotel Windsor Lodge**
116 Radcliffe Rd, West Bridgford
☎ (0602) 813773, fax: (0602) 819405
49 bedrooms; double B&B £48-£50
Credit cards 1 2 3 5

**★★ 66% Westminster Hotel**
310-318 Mansfield Rd, Carrington
☎ (0602) 623023, fax: (0602) 691156
59 bedrooms
Credit cards 1 3

**★★ 65% Rufford**
52 Melton Road, West Bridgford,
☎ (0602) 814202, fax: (0602) 455801
35 bedrooms; double B&B £47-£54.05
Credit cards 1 2 3 5

**★★ 63% Priory**
Derby Rd, Wollaton Vale
☎ (0602) 221691
31 bedrooms
Credit cards 1 2 3 5

**★★ 62% Balmoral**
55-57 Loughborough Rd, West Bridgford
☎ (0602) 455020 & 818588, fax: (0602) 455683
31 bedrooms; double B&B £39.50-£48
Credit cards 1 3

**★★★ 56% Tudor Court**
Gypsy Ln, Draycott
☎ Derby (0332) 874581, fax: (0332) 873133
30 bedrooms; double B&B £45-£73
Credit cards 1 2 3 5

**★★ 66% Unicorn**
Gunthorpe Bridge, Gunthorpe
☎ (0602) 663612, fax: (0602) 664801
16 bedrooms
Credit cards 1 2 3 5

**★★★ 61% Yew Lodge**
33 Packington Hill, Kegworth
☎ (0509) 672518, telex: 341995, fax: (0509) 674730
54 bedrooms; double B&B £40-£65.50
Credit cards 1 2 3 5

**★★ ⊛ 72% Langar Hall**
Langar
☎ (0949) 60559, fax: (0949) 61045
10 bedrooms; double B&B £75-£100
Credit cards 1 2 3 5

**★★★ 62% Novotel Nottingham Derby**
Bostock Ln, Long Eaton
☎ (0602) 720106, telex: 377585
110 bedrooms
Credit cards 1 2 3 5

**★★ 67% Sleep Inn**
Bostock Ln, Long Eaton
☎ (0602) 460000, fax: (0602) 460726
101 bedrooms
Credit cards 1 2 3 5

**★★ 60% Europa**
20 Derby Rd, Long Eaton
☎ (0602) 728481
19 bedroom
Credit cards 1 2 3 5

**★★★ 61% Forte Posthouse Nottingham**
Bostocks Ln, Sandiacre
☎ (0602) 397800, fax: (0602) 490469
91 bedrooms; double room £39.50-£49.50 (room only)
Credit cards 1 2 3 5

**★★ 63% The Haven**
Grantham Rd, Whatton
☎ (0949) 50800, fax: (0949) 51454
33 bedrooms; double B&B £42-£48
Credit cards 1 2 3 5

### BED AND BREAKFAST

**Royston Hotel**
326 Mansfield Rd, Sherwood
☎ (0602) 622947
On the A60 out of the city; bedrooms individually furnished with care and attention.
8 bedrooms
Credit cards 1 3 4 5

**Crantock Hotel**
480 Mansfield Rd
☎ (0602) 623294
On the A60; bedrooms are equipped with modern amenities.
20 bedrooms; double B&B £30-£45
Credit cards 1 3

## WHERE TO STAY

### Grantham Commercial Hotel
24-26 Radcliffe Rd, West Bridgford
☎ (0602) 811373
Rooms are neat and well equipped.
22 bedrooms; double B&B £32-£38
Credit cards 1 3

### Park Hotel
7 Waverley St
☎ (0602) 786299 & 420010, fax: (0602) 424358
Period house close to city centre overlooking a park; well equipped bedrooms.
27 bedrooms
Credit cards 1 2 3

### P & J Hotel
277-279 Derby Rd, Lenton
☎ (0602) 783998
Small commercial hotel converted from a Victorian house.
19 bedrooms; double B&B from £40
Credit cards 1 2 3 5

### Around Nottingham

### Brackley House Hotel
31 Elm Av, Beeston
☎ (0602) 251787
A Continental atmosphere prevails at this well furnished guesthouse.
15 bedrooms
Credit cards 1 2 3

### Fairhaven Private Hotel
19 Meadow Rd, Beeston
☎ (0602) 227509
A clean modest hotel on the edge of town.
10 bedrooms; double b&B £28-£37.50

### Station Hotel
Station Rd, Hucknall
☎ (0602) 632588
Victorian public house, considerably modernised and with spacious bedrooms.
6 bedrooms; double B&B £40
Credit cards 1 3

### CAMPSITE

### ►►► Thornton's Holt Camping Park
Stragglethorpe, Radcliffe on Trent
☎ (0602) 332125
Five miles south of A52, 2 miles north of A46; pitch price from £5.50

## WHERE TO EAT

### RESTAURANTS

### ❀ Sonny's
3 Carlton St, Hockley
☎ (0602) 473041
Lunch: 12-2.30; from £9.50 and a la carte
Dinner: 7-10.30; from £12.50 and a la carte

### PUBS

### Ye Olde Trip to Jerusalem
Brewhouse Yard
☎ (0602) 473171
Originally the brewhouse for Nottingham Castle and a pub since 1189 (catering then for crusaders), this is certainly a place worth visiting, though it could be full of tourists. There are three real ales, an interesting range of whiskies and limited bar food. Children are not permitted inside the pub.
Open: 11am-3pm (4pm Saturday), 5.30-11pm; Sunday 12-3pm, 7-10.30pm
Bar food: 12-2pm

### Around Nottingham

### Bird in Hand
Main St, Blidworth
☎ (0623) 792356
There are lovely views across Sherwood Forest from this unpretentious village local. Some imaginative vegetarian dishes are included on the short, value-for-money menu. Beers include Mansfield Riding and Old Baily. There is a well kept garden with a play area and children are welcome inside the pub if eating.
Open: 11am-11pm; Sunday 12-3pm, 7-10.30pm
Bar food: Monday to Saturday 12-3pm, 5.30-8.30pm

### Waggon and Horses
Gypsy La, Bleasby, nr Southwell
☎ (0636) 830283
Good value pub fare, in an attractive and peacefully located village pub, consists of substantial, homely dishes. Theakston XB, Old Peculiar, Home Bitter and McEwans Export are on draught and morning coffee is available. Children are welcome anywhere and there is an outdoor play area.
Open: 11am-3pm, 6-11pm; Sunday 12-3pm, 7-10.30pm
Bar food: Tuesday to Sunday 12-2pm

### Cross Keys
Epperstone, nr Southwell
☎ (0602) 663033
A good village 'local' atmosphere prevails at this popular old inn. The food is home cooked and pies are particularly popular. Kimberley Classic Ale is dispensed from a handpump; there are also cask conditioned bitter and mild and a good range of single malt whiskies. Children are welcome in the family room and there is a spacious lawned garden.
Open: 11.45am-2.30pm, 6-11pm; Sunday 12-2.30pm, 7-10.30pm. Closed Monday lunchtime.
Bar food:

### Reindeer Inn
Main St, Hoveringham, nr Southwell
☎ (0602) 663629
Food and wine are taken seriously at this 17th-century inn overlooking the cricket pitch, with some excellent choices available to discerning evening diners. The lunchtime snack menu is imaginative too and, as well as Marstons Bitter, Pedigree and a guest beer, there are quality wines and unusual whiskies to enjoy. Children not permitted in public bar.
Open: 12-3pm, 5-11pm (opens 5.30pm on Monday); Sunday 12-3pm, 7-10.30pm. Closed Monday lunchtime except Bank Holidays
Bar food: Tuesday to Saturday 12-2pm; Sunday 12-3pm
Restaurant: Tuesday to Saturday 7-9.30pm

### Star Inn
Melton La, West Leake
☎ (0509) 852233
Choose between the traditionally furnished main bar, decorated with various rural implements, or the modernised and comfortable lounge bar. The pub is noted for its well kept draught Bass and Adnams ales and for a good-value cold table at lunchtime. A home-made hot dish is usually available. Children are welcome in eating areas and there are picnic tables outside.
Open: 12-2.30pm, 6-11pm; Sunday 12-3pm, 7-10.30pm
Bar food: Monday to Friday 12.30-2pm

# Perth Hunt

*For anyone seeking to combine a break in the countryside with some exciting National Hunt racing, Perth offers the perfect solution. This beautiful Tayside area has an abundance of alternative leisure activities with an ample choice of top-class golf courses and some superb salmon and trout fishing in the near vicinity.*

The fixture list has been carefully designed with the needs of holiday-makers in mind, so that all the meetings last for at least two days and are scheduled to avoid the depths of winter. Instead, they are run at the beginning of the jumps season (from August to October) and at the end (April and May). The pick of the bunch is the three-day Perth Festival Meeting in late April, a truly wonderful occasion.

The racecourse could hardly have been situated in a more alluring setting, hidden away among the picturesque woodland of Scone Park. Although the trees may occasionally obscure viewing, this is a very small price to pay considering the marvellous backdrop that they form and the intimate atmosphere that they help to create. There is always a tremendously warm welcome extended to any visitors and a trip to this delightful track, the most northerly in Britain, can not be too highly recommended.

### FURTHER INFORMATION

The Perth Hunt
Penrose Hill, Moffat, Dumfriesshire DG10 9BX
☎ (0683) 20131

### LOCATION AND HOW TO GET THERE

The course is situated in Scone Palace Park, Perth. Follow signposts from the A93 north of Perth. **Nearest Railway Station:** Perth; there is a bus service from Perth to the course on racedays.

---

### ADMISSION

All classes of day ticket give access to full betting facilities, including Tote.

**Day Tickets:**

CLUB £11 - access to bars, restaurant, private rooms

TATTERSALLS AND PADDOCK £6, senior citizens £3 - access to bars and snacks

COURSE £2 - access to mobile food trailer and picnic area. No bar.

**Annual membership:** £55 (requires a proposer and a seconder)

### COURSE FACILITIES

**Banks:**
there are no banks or cashpoint facilities on the course.

**For families:**
picnic area with refreshment kiosk and toilets.

---

## CALENDAR OF EVENTS

**April 20-22** – Spring Festival Meeting
**May 11-12** – evening meeting on Wednesday
**May 19** – evening meeting
**August 19-20**
**September 21-22**

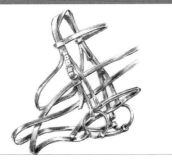

## WHERE TO STAY

### HOTELS

**★★★ ❀❀❀ 78% Murrayshall Country House Hotel & Golf Course**
New Scone
☎ (0738) 51171, telex: 76197, fax: (0738) 52595
19 bedrooms; double B&B £105-£125
Credit cards 1 2 3 5

**★★★ ❀❀ 73% Parklands**
St Leonards Bank
☎ (0738) 22451, fax: (0738) 22046
14 bedrooms; double B&B £75-£125
Credit cards 1 2 3

**★★★ ❀ 67% Huntingtower**
Crieff Rd, Almondbank
☎ (0738) 83771, fax: (0738) 83777
35 bedroom
Credit cards 1 2 3 5

**★★★ ❀ 63% Newton House**
Glencarse
☎ (0738) 86250, fax: (0738) 86717
10 bedrooms; double B&B £80
Credit cards 1 2 3 5

**★★★ 60% Queens Hotel**
Leonard St
☎ (0738) 25471, fax: (0738) 38496
50 bedrooms; double B&B from £78
Credit cards 1 2 3 5

**★★★ 59% Lovat**
90 Glasgow Rd
☎ (0738) 36555, telex: 76531, fax: (0738) 43123
30 bedrooms; double B&B from £64
Credit cards 1 2 3

**★★★ 59% The Royal George**
Tay St
☎ (0738) 24455, fax: (0738) 30345
42 bedrooms; double room £70-£95 (room only)
Credit cards 1 2 3 5

**★★★ 57% Isle of Skye Toby**
Queen's Bridge, Dundee Rd
☎ (0738) 24471, telex: 76185
56 bedrooms
Credit cards 1 2 3 5

**★★★ 57% Stakis City Mills**
West Mill St
☎ (0738) 28281, telex: 778704, fax: (0738) 43423
76 bedrooms; double room £69-£79 (room only)
Credit cards 1 2 3 5

### Around Perth

**★★★ ❀❀ 77% Ballathie House**
Kinclaven
☎ (0250) 883268, fax: (0250) 883396
27 bedrooms; double B&B £84-£149
Credit cards 1 2 3 5

**★★ 58% The Tayside**
Mill St, Stanley
☎ (0738) 828249, fax: (0738) 33449
17 bedrooms; double B&B £39-£65
Credit cards 1 3

### BED AND BREAKFAST

**Alpine**
7 Strathview Ter
☎ (0738) 37687
Spotless accommodation beside the A92.
6 bedrooms

**Ardfern House**
15 Pitcullen Crescent
☎ (0738) 22259
3 bedrooms; double B&B £32-£40

**Clark Kimberley**
57-59 Dunkeld Rd
☎ (0738) 37406
Friendly guesthouse offering high standard of accommodation.
8 bedrooms; double B&B £30-£32

**Clunie**
12 Pitcullen Crescent
☎ (0738) 23625
A short way from town centre; friendly with mainly modern bedrooms.
7 bedrooms; double B&B from £34

**Kinnaird**
5 Marshall Place
☎ (0738) 28021
Overlooking a park; attractively decorated bedrooms.
7 bedrooms; double B&B from £32

**Lochiel House**
13 Pitcullen Crescent
☎ 0738 33183
Delightful place to stay, with character and charm due largely to the proprietor, Rita Buchan.
3 bedrooms

**Park Lane**
17 Marshall Place
☎ (0738) 37218, fax: (0738) 43519
Comfortable, nicely appointed bedrooms; a few minutes' walk from the city centre.
6 bedrooms; double B&B £33-£37
Credit cards 1 3

### Around Perth

**Burrelton Park**
High St, Burrelton
☎ (08287) 206
Popular roadside hotel with reputation for hearty catering.
6 bedrooms; double B&B from £45
Credit cards 1 3

**Craighall Farm**
Forgandenny
☎ (0738) 812415
Modern bungalow admist peaceful countryside.
3 bedrooms

**Tophead Farm**
Tullybelton, Stanley
☎ (0738) 828259
Attractive farmhouse with glorious views from the garden, in peaceful position. Good bedrooms.
3 bedrooms; double B&B £32-£36

### CAMPSITE

**►►► Erigmore House Holiday Park**
Birnam
☎(03502), 236 due to change to (0350) 727236
Situated on B898 north of Perth; pitch price from £8 per night.

## WHERE TO EAT

### RESTAURANTS

**❀ Number Thirty Three**
33 Saint George St, Perth
☎ (0738) 33771
Small, popular restaurant offering fresh, carefully cooked seafood.
Lunch: 12-2.30
Dinner: 7-9.30
Credit cards 1 2 3

# Plumpton

*Set on the side of a steep hill, this undulating National Hunt track is one of the sharpest in the country. The oblong-shaped circuit has a circumference of just nine furlongs and the extremely tight bends require a handy type of horse as opposed to a long-striding galloper who will find it difficult to negotiate the turns.*

The fences in the back straight are all located on a downhill stretch and, when the ground is riding firm, as it generally does during the early and late season meetings, these are tackled at a breakneck pace. This inevitably leads to plenty of thrills and spills and the track has been rather unfairly nicknamed by jockeys as 'The Wall of Death'.

Even though the quality of racing may remain low, a good day out should be had by all thanks to the strenuous efforts that the management of the course have made to try and upgrade facilities. Over a million pounds was spent on the new stand alone and the restaurant and bar areas are now much more spacious following recent expansions. Another good point about this venue is its easy accessibility from London by rail. On race days, trains on the Victoria-Brighton line stop at Plumpton station which is just a short walk from the track.

## FURTHER INFORMATION

Pratt & Company
11 Boltro Road, Haywards Heath, Sussex
RG16 1BP
☎ (0444) 441111

## LOCATION AND HOW TO GET THERE

The course is between Lewes and Haywards Heath, about eight miles from Brighton. From the south coast approach via the A27 and the A273; from London take the M23 then either the A23, A273 or B2112.
**Nearest Railway Station:** Plumpton, adjacent to the racecourse.

## ADMISSION

All classes of day ticket give access to full betting facilities, including Tote.

**Day Tickets:**

CLUB £11 - access to bars, restaurant and hot food bar

TATTERSALLS AND PADDOCK £8 - access to bars, seafood bar, hot food bar, mobile catering, boxes and private rooms

CENTRE OF COURSE £3.50 - access to bar, mobile catering and picnic area

**Annual membership:** £90, plus £10 for car badge, if required

**Parking:** £1; picnic area parking in centre of course £3.50 per car plus £3.50 per occupant

## COURSE FACILITIES

**Banks:**
there are no banks or cashpoint facilities on the course.

**For families:**
picnic area with refreshment kiosk and toilets; children's play area on Bank Holidays and August Meeting only.

## CALENDAR OF EVENTS

| | |
|---|---|
| January 12 | August 29 |
| January 31 | September 12 |
| February 14 | October 18 |
| February 28 | October 31 |
| March 14 | November 14 |
| March 21 | December 6 |
| April 2 | December 28 |
| April 4 | |
| April 30 – evening meeting | |
| August 5 | |

## WHERE TO STAY

### HOTELS

**★★★ 63% Hickstead Resort**
Jobs Ln, Bolney
☎ (0444) 248023, telex: 877247, fax: (0444) 245280
50 bedrooms; double room from £72 (room only)
Credit cards 1 2 3 5

**★★★ 62% Norfolk Resort**
149 Kings Rd, Brighton
☎ ( 0273 738201, fax: 0273 821752
121 bedrooms; double room £66-£76 (room only)
Credit cards 1 2 3 5

**★★★ 61% Old Ship**
Kings Rd, Brighton
☎ (0273) 29001, telex: 877101, fax: 0273 820718
152 bedrooms; double B&B £75-£125
Credit cards 1 2 3 5

**★★★ 60% Excelsior**
205-209 Kingsway, Brighton
☎ (0273) 773991, fax: (0273) 746363
58 bedrooms
Credit cards 1 2 3 5

**★★★ 58% Imperial**
First Av, Brighton
☎ (0273) 777320, fax: (0273) 777310
76 bedrooms; double B&B £80
Credit cards 1 2 3 5

**★★★ 58% Sackville**
Kingsway, Brighton
☎ (0273) 736292, telex: 877830, fax: (0273) 205759
45 bedrooms

**★★★ 56% Courtlands**
19-27 The Drive, Brighton
☎ (0273) 731055, fax: (0273) 28295
53 bedrooms; double B&B £60-£78
Credit cards 1 2 3 5

**★★ ⚜⚜ 75% Topps**
17 Regency Square, Brighton
☎ (0273) 729334, fax: (0273) 203679
14 bedrooms; double B&B £64-£99
Credit cards 1 2 3 4 5

**★★ 58% St Catherines Lodge**
Seafront, Kingsway, Brighton
☎ (0273) 778181, fax: (0273) 774949
50 bedrooms; double B&B £50-£65
Credit cards 1 2 3 5

**★★★ ⚜⚜ 73% Ockenden Manor**
Ockenden Ln, Cuckfield
☎ (0444) 416111, fax: (0444) 415549
22 bedrooms; double B&B £95-£165
Credits cards 1 2 3 5

**★★★ 59% The Birch**
Lewes Rd, Haywards Heath
☎ (0444) 451565, fax: (0444) 440109
53 bedrooms
Credit cards 1 2 3 5

**★★ ⚜ 70% Tottington Manor**
Edburton, Henfield
☎ (0903) 815757, fax: (0903) 879331
6 bedrooms
Credit cards 1 2 3 5

**★★ 68% Sussex Pad**
Old Shoreham Rd, Lancing
☎ (0273) 454647, fax: (0273) 453010
19 bedrooms
Credit cards 1 2 3 4 5

**★★★ 54% Shelleys**
High St, Lewes
☎ (0273) 472361, fax: (0273) 483152
21 bedrooms; double room £99-£120 (room only)
Credit cards 1 2 3 5

**★★ 58% White Hart**
55 High St, Lewes
☎ (0273) 474676 & 476694, telex: 878468, fax: (0273) 476695
19 bedrooms
Credit cards 1 2 3 5

### BED AND BREAKFAST

**Adelaide Hotel**
51 Regency Square, Brighton
☎ (0273) 205286, fax: (0273) 220904
Freshly decorated and tastefully furnished bedrooms with welcoming proprietors.
12 bedrooms; double B&B £59-£75
Credit cards 1 2 3 5

**Allendal Hotel**
3 New Steine, Brighton
☎ (0273) 675436, fax: (0273) 602603
Charming proprietors and smart, modern bedrooms, exceptionally well equipped.
13 bedrooms; double B&B £54-£66
Credit cards 1 2 3 5

**Ambassador Hotel**
22 New Steine, Brighton
☎ (0273) 676869, fax: (0273) 689988
Family-run hotel offers of a range of neat, well equipped bedrooms.
9 bedrooms; double B&B £42-£57
Credit cards 1 2 3 5

**Arlanda Hotel**
20 New Steine, Brighton
☎ (0273) 699300, fax: (0273) 600930
Regency-style house offers a mixed style of accommodation. 12 bedrooms; double B&B £38-£66
Credit cards 1 2 3 5

**Ascott House Hotel**
21 New Steine, Marine Pde, Brighton
☎ (0273) 688085, fax: (0273) 623733
Small personally run hotel close to the seafront, offering bright, freshly decorated bedrooms.
12 bedrooms; double B&B £50-£70
Credit cards 1 2 3 5

**Bannings**
14 Upper Rock Gardens, Kemptown, Brighton
☎ (0273) 681403
Elegant town house with comfortable bedrooms and offering a hearty breakfast.
6 bedrooms; double B&B £36-£44
Credit cards 1 2 3 5

## WHERE TO STAY

### Claremont House
Second Av, Brighton
☎ (0273) 735161
Friendly and informal atmosphere,
bedrooms furnished to a high standard.
12 bedrooms
Credit cards 1 2 3 5

### George IV Hotel
34 Regency Square, Brighton
☎ (0273) 21196
Overlooking the gardens and sea, this hotel
provides smart bedrooms and every
conceivable convenience.
8 bedrooms; double B&B £45-£65
Credit cards 1 2 3 5

### Gullivers
10 New Steine, Brighton
☎ (0273) 695415, fax: (0252) 372774
Attractive bedrooms feature in this Regency
residence close to the seafront.
9 bedrooms; double B&B £42-£54
Credit cards 1 2 3 5

### New Steine Hotel
12a New Steine, Marine Pde, Brighton
☎ (0273) 681546
Smart, comfortable accommodation.
11 bedrooms; double B&B £39-£42

### Pier View Hotel
28 New Steine, Brighton
☎ (0273) 605310, fax: (0273) 688604
The King family create a warm welcome
here; freshly decorated rooms.
10 bedrooms; double B&B £39-£58

### Trouville Hotel
11 New Steine, Marine Pde, Brighton
☎ (0273) 697384
Seafront, family-run guesthouse offering
freshly decorated bedrooms.
9 bedrooms; double B&B £32-£46

### Twenty One
21 Charlotte St, Marine Pde, Brighton
☎ (0273) 686450
Exceptionally well equipped bedrooms,
each with its own charm.
6 bedrooms; double B&B £46-£68

### Harbour View
22 Mount Rd, Newhaven
☎ (0273) 512096
Situated on eastern edge of town with a
relaxed atmosphere
3 bedrooms

### Newhaven Marina Yacht Club Hotel
Fort Gate, Fort Rd, Newhaven
☎ (0273) 513976, fax: (0273) 517990
Fresh bedrooms with modern furniture
7 bedrooms; double B&B £42-£50
Credit cards 1 3

### Braemar House
Steyning Rd, Rottingdean
☎ (0273) 304263
Family run guesthouse offering simple but
well kept accommodation.
16 bedrooms; double B&B £28-£30

### Corner House
Steyning Rd, Rottingdean
☎ (0273) 304533
Friendly proprietor and simple, functional
bedrooms.
6 bedrooms; double B&B £29-£30

### Avondale Hotel
4-5 Avondale Rd, Seaford
☎ (0323) 890008
A family run hotel, close to town centre.
16 bedrooms; double B&B £30-£40
Credit cards 1 3

## CAMPSITES

### ►► Gallops Farm
Streat Ln, Streat, Plumpton
☎ (0273) 890387
Off the 2116 west of Plumpton village.

### ►►► Downsview Caravan Park
Bramlands Ln, Woodmancote, Henfield
☎ (0273) 492801
On the A281 east of Henfield; pitch price
from £8.25 per night

### Harwoods Farm
West End Lane, Henfield
☎ (0273) 492820.
Unspoilt site (tents only) down narrow lane;
pitch price from £3.50

## WHERE TO EAT

### RESTAURANTS

### Langan's Bistro
1 Paston Place, Brighton
☎ (0273) 606933
Down to earth and flavoursome cooking in a
relaxed friendly atosphere.
Lunch 12-2.15; from £15.70 and a la carte
Dinner 7-10.15; from £22 and a la carte

### Le Grandgousier
15 Western St, Brighton
☎ (0273) 772005
Small cosy restaurant serving simple, good
value bistro-style food.
Lunch: 12-1.30 £11.95
Dinner: 7-9.30 £11.95

### Whyte's
33 Western St, Brighton
☎ (0273) 776618
Cosy, small restaurant near the seafront,
serving sound, honest cooking in French
and English styles.
Lunch: from £13.95
Dinner: 7-10; from £13.95-£16.95

# Pontefract

*Despite its close proximity to the urbanisation around Leeds, Castleford and Featherstone, Pontefract remains very much a country setting and is therefore an ideal place to take a break from city life during the summer.*

Yet, at the same time, it could hardly be easier to reach as the course is situated within a stone's throw of the M62. This is an unpretentious venue which upholds the traditional values of its county in providing good, solid entertainment at a working man's price. To that end, facilities are compact and offer decent value for money. The track itself is a very stiff and unusually lengthy two-mile circuit with a tremendous emphasis being placed on stamina in long-distance contests. Indeed, of the courses that are devoted solely to Flat racing, it is probably the most testing in Britain. Early speed is still a vital ingredient for sprinters who run here, however, as there is a sharp bend in the track about two and a half furlongs from the finish and many lengths will be saved by gaining a good early position close to the rails. Consequently, a low draw on the inside is almost always a huge advantage.

## FURTHER INFORMATION

Pontefract Park Race Co Ltd
33 Ropergate, Pontefract WF8 1LE
☎ (0977) 703224

## LOCATION AND HOW TO GET THERE

The course is in the north of the town in Pontefract Park, adjoining the M62. Leave the motorway at junction 32 and take the A539 towards Pontefract. **Nearest Railway Station:** Pontefract Monkhill or Pontefract Baghill; there is no connecting bus service - Monkhill adjoins the park gates and Baghill is just half a mile away.

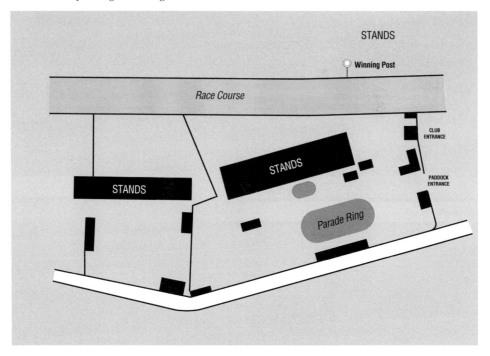

## ADMISSION

All classes of day ticket give access to full betting facilities, including Tote.

**Day tickets:**
Accompanied children under 16 are admitted free to all enclosures. No dogs allowed, except in car in Third Ring/Car park.

CLUB £12 - access to restaurant, bars, private rooms, seating in the stands

PADDOCK/TATTERSALLS £7 - access to self-service restaurant, bars, course betting office, betting ring, parade ring, unsaddling enclosure

SILVER RING/2ND ENCLOSURE £3 - access to cafeteria, bars, course betting office, betting ring

THIRD RING/CAR PARK £1.50, or £5 for car and up to four occupants - access to viewing stand (part of 2nd grandstand), cafeteria, bar, betting ring

**Annual membership:** £95, joint (husband and wife) £130, junior (under 21) £45

## COURSE FACILITIES

**Banks:**
there are no banks or cashpoint facilities on the course.

**For families:**
picnic area with refreshment kiosk and toilets; children's play area and creche (evenings and school holidays only) in Third Ring; lost children centre.

## CALENDAR OF EVENTS

April 13
April 19
April 25
May 27 – evening meeting
June 6-7
June 20
July 5

July 22 – evening meeting
August 3-4
August 23
September 19
October 3
October 20

## WHERE TO STAY

### HOTELS

**Around Pontefract**

**Granada Lodge**
Ferrybridge Service Area
☎ (0977) 670488, fax: (0977) 672945
35 bedrooms; double room £34.95 (room only)
Credit cards 1 2 3 5

**★★ 63% Owl**
Main Rd, Hambleton
☎ (0757) 228374, fax: (0757) 228125
9 bedrooms; double B&B £42-£47
Credit cards 1 2 3 5

**★★★★ 71% Holiday Inn**
Wellington St, Leeds
☎ (0532) 442200, telex: 557879, fax: (0532) 440460
125 bedrooms; double room £145 (room only)
Credit cards 1 2 3 4 5

**★★★★ 66% The Queen's**
City Square, Leeds
☎ (0532) 431323, telex: 55161, fax: (0532) 425154
188 bedrooms; double room £95 (room only)
Credit cards 1 2 3 5

**★★★ ❀❀ 79% Haley's Hotel & Restaurant**
Shire Oak Rd, Headingley
☎ (0532) 784446, fax: (0532) 753342
22 bedrooms; double B&B £112
Credit cards 1 2 3 5

**★★★ 64% Stakis Windmill**
King Rd, Seacroft, Leeds
☎ (0532) 732323, telex: 55452, fax: (0532) 323018
100 bedrooms; double room £79-£89 (room only)
Credit cards 1 2 3 4 5

**★★★ 50% Merrion**
Merrion Centre, Leeds
☎ (0532) 439191, telex: 55459, fax: (0532) 423527
120 bedrooms; double room from £85 (room only)
Credit cards 1 2 3 5

**★★★ 61% Forte Posthouse Leeds**
Lumby
☎ (0977) 682711, fax: (0977) 685462
105 bedrooms; double room £39.50-£49.50 (room only)
Credit cards 1 2 3 5

**★★★ 68% Monk Fryston Hall**
Monk Fryston
☎ (0977) 682369, fax: (0977) 683544
28 bedrooms; double B&B £92-£105
Credit cards 1 2 3

**★★★ 65% Wentbridge House**
Wentbridge
☎ (0977) 620444, fax: (0977) 620148
12 bedrooms
Credit cards 1 2 3 5

**Forte Travelodge**
Wentbridge
☎ (0977) 620711, Central Reservations: (0800) 850950, telex: 557457
56 bedrooms; double room £31.95 (room only)
Credit cards 1 2 3

## WHERE TO STAY

### Granada Lodge
M1, Wooley Edge Motorway Service Area
☎ (0924) 830569, fax: (0924) 830609
31 bedrooms
Credit cards 1 2 3 5

### BED AND BREAKFAST

### Ash Mount Hotel
22 Wetherby Road, Oakwood, Leeds
☎ (0532) 658164
Attractive stone-built house; smart rooms, comfortable and pleasantly furnished.
14 bedrooms; double B&B from £39.58
Credit cards 1 3

### Merevale Hotel
16 Wetherby Rd, Oakwood, Leeds
☎ (0532) 658933
Large detached house. Bedrooms of various sizes all coordinated with crisp duvets.
14 bedrooms
Credit cards 1 3

### Trafford House Hotel
18 Cardigan Road, Headingley, Leeds
☎ (0532) 752034, fax: (0532) 742422
Victorian house; accommodation is well furnished and comfortable.
18 bedrooms; double B&B £50-£53
Credit cards 1 3

### Holme Leigh
Pinfold Ln, Halton, Leeds
☎ (0532) 607889
A well-run family hotel on the eastern side of Leeds.
8 bedrooms

### CAMPSITES

### ►►► Camping & Caravanning Club Site
Roundhay Park, Elmette Ln, off Wetherby Rd, Leeds
☎ (0532) 652354 & (0203) 694995
Adjacent to Roundhay Park, 3.5 miles from the city centre; pitch price from £10.30 per night.

### ►►► Nostell Priory Holiday Homes
Top Park Wood, Nostell
☎ (0924) 863938
5 miles southeast of Wakefield off A638; pitch price from £6.50 per night.

## WHERE TO EAT

### RESTAURANTS

### 🏵 Brasserie Forty Four
42-44 The Calls
☎ (0532) 343232, fax: (0532) 343332
Fun place to eat with quality food at a reasonable price.
Lunch: 12-2.30; from £9.95 and a la carte
Dinner: 7-10.30; from £13 and a la carte
Credit cards 1 2 3

### PUBS

### Kings Arms
Heath Common, Kirkthorpe
☎ (0924) 377527
In a converted stables, this friendly and well kept pub includes some of its own brew among the range of draught beers. The food is impressive in quality and size. There is one room where children area allowed and there is a garden.
Open: 11am-3pm, 6-11pm; Sunday 12-3pm, 7-10.30pm
Bar food: 12-2pm, 7-9.30pm; Sunday 12-2
Restaurant: as bar food times

### The Chequers
Claypit La, Ledsham
☎ (0477) 683135
Ivy-clad pub dating from the 16th century with wood panelling and old beams inside. There is a good range of draught beers, a wine list and a simple range of bar food. There are two rooms where children are allowed.
Open: Monday to Friday 11am-3pm, 5.30-11pm; Saturday 11am-11pm; closed Sunday
Bar food: 12-2pm, 6-8.30pm
Restaurant: Tuesday to Saturday 7.30-9.45pm

# Redcar

*Set in the midst of the industrial heartland of the northeast of England, the racecourse at Redcar stands out like a green oasis. It is to be found just to the south of the town which is located a few miles away from Middlesbrough, close to the North Sea.*

In the old days, races were originally held on the nearby beaches, but now they take place on the narrow, left-handed track. The oval circuit has a long run-in of five furlongs which also forms part of the straight mile course where horses drawn high are greatly favoured.

This venue has really come to prominence in recent years thanks to the efforts of its owner, Lord Zetland, widely regarded as one of the Jockey Club's more radical thinkers. He introduced a completely new two-year-old event, the Racecall Gold Trophy, which is run at a televised Tuesday meeting in late October and carries over £100,000 in prize money. This huge sum explains why the contest regularly attracts many of the season's leading juveniles. Another feature race is the Zetland Gold Cup, a prestigious and valuable handicap that is held towards the end of May. The facilities here have also been dramatically improved of late and the standard of catering is now excellent.

### FURTHER INFORMATION

The Racecourse
Redcar, Cleveland TS10 2BY
☎ (0642) 484068

### LOCATION AND HOW TO GET THERE

Redcar is on the northeast coast, eight miles east of Middlesbrough. From the A1 take the A168, then the A19 and finally the A174 to Redcar. **Nearest Railway Station:** Redcar Central; the course is a five-minute walk from the station.

### ADMISSION

All classes of day ticket give access to full betting facilities, including Tote

**Day Tickets:**

CLUB £12 - access to bars, restaurant, snack areas, private rooms and boxes

TATTERSALLS £7, senior citizens £3.50 - access to bars, self-service restaurant, snack areas

COURSE £2.50, senior citizens £1.25 - access to bar and cafeteria

**Annual membership:** £92 single, £135 joint (husband and wife), £46 junior (under 21)

### COURSE FACILITIES

**Banks:**
there are no banks or cashpoint facilities on the course.

**For families:**
picnic area with refreshment kiosk and toilets; children's play area.

## CALENDAR OF EVENTS

| | |
|---|---|
| **May 9** | **August 24** |
| **May 30-31** – includes the Zetland Gold Cup | **September 23-24** |
| **June 17-18** | **October 4** |
| **July 6-7** – evening meeting on Wednesday | **October 13** |
| **July 20** – evening meeting | **October 25** – includes Racecall Gold Trophy |
| **August 2** | **November 1** |
| **August 5-6** | |

## WHERE TO STAY

### HOTELS

#### ★★★ 67% Park
Granville Ter, Redcar
☎ (0642) 490888, fax: (0642) 486147
26 bedrooms; double B&B £42–£72
Credit cards 1 2 3 5

#### Around Redcar

#### ★★★ ❀ 69% Grinkle Park
Easington
☎ (0287) 640515, fax: (0287) 641278
20 bedrooms
Credit cards 1 2 3 5

#### ★★★ 55% Marine
5/7 The Front, Seaton Carew, Hartlepool
☎ (0429) 266244, fax: (0429) 864144
25 bedrooms
Credit cards 1 2 3 5

#### ★★ 73% Ryedale Moor
3 Beaconsfield St, Headland, Hartlepool
☎ (0429) 231436, fax: (0429) 863787
13 bedrooms; double B&B £48–£54
Credit cards 1 2 3 5

#### ★★★ 50% Marton Way Toby
Marton Rd, Middlesbrough
☎ (0642) 817651, telex: 587783
53 bedrooms
Credit cards 1 2 3 5

#### ★★ 64% Highfield
358 Marton Rd, Middlesbrough
☎ (0642) 817638, fax: (0642) 821219
23 bedrooms; double B&B £50–£70
Credit cards 1 2 3 5

#### ★ 63% The Grey House
79 Cambridge Rd, Linthorpe,
Middlesborough
☎ (0642) 817485
9 bedrooms; double B&B £38–£49

### BED AND BREAKFAST

#### Claxton House Private Hotel
196 High St
☎ (0642) 486745
Well established hotel providing well
appointed accommodation.
17 bedrooms

#### Royal Oak Hotel
High Green, Great Ayton
☎ (0642) 722361, fax: (0642) 724047
An 18th-century coaching inn which has
historical associations with Captain Cook;
well furnished bedrooms.
5 bedrooms
Credit cards 1 3

### CAMPSITE

#### ►►► Tockett's Mill Caravan Park
Skelton Rd, Guisborough
☎ (0287) 610182
South of Redcar; pitch price from £6 per
night.

## WHERE TO EAT

### RESTAURANTS

#### ❀ Krimo's
8 The Front, Seaton Carew, Hartlepool
☎ (0429) 266120
Some of the best Mediterranean food on the
northeast coast.
Lunch: 12-1.30; from £5.50 and a la carte.
Dinner: 7-9.30; from £8.90 and a la carte.
Credit cards 1 3

### PUBS

#### The Ship
Saltburn
☎ (0287) 622361
Gloriously situated on the beach with high
cliffs beyond and views across the beautiful
bay, this very pretty Tetleys pub offers a
range of dishes to suit all tastes.
Open: 11am-3pm, 6-11pm; Sunday 12-
3pm, 7-10.30pm
Bar food: as opening times
Restaurant: evenings only

# Ripon

*This is one of the most aesthetically pleasing venues in Britain. Located among the beautiful Yorkshire Dales, it is a really lovely site to spend a day at the races. Great care has been taken to make the racecourse buildings look appealing to the eye and colourful flower-beds of many hues adorn the grounds.*

There is an extensive range of bars and restaurants while children are well catered for with a pair of playgrounds. This encourages lots of families to attend during the school holidays, creating a lively, happy atmosphere.

Flat racing is held throughout the spring and summer with a large number of the meetings being concentrated in August. The quality of competition is particularly good during this month and included among the races is the course's annual feature event, the Great St Wilfrid Handicap. This is a fiercely contested six-furlong sprint that draws runners from all over the country. The oval circuit has a large circumference of more than one and a half miles, but it is regarded as being a sharp track because of the slightly cramped bends. There are also minor surface undulations in the home straight, with a pronounced dip about a furlong from the finish.

## FURTHER INFORMATION

Ripon Race Company Ltd
P O Box 1, Ripon HG4 1DS
☎ (0765) 602156

## LOCATION AND HOW TO GET THERE

The course is two miles from the centre of Ripon on the B6265. The M1 ends in Leeds, to the south, from where you can continue north on the A61, through Harrogate to Ripon. To avoid the centre of Leeds, leave the M1 at junction 42, taking the M62 eastbound to junction 30, then take the A642 northwards to connect with the A1 beyond Garforth. Leave the A1 at the Baldersby intersection and take the A61. From the A1 southbound leave by the B6265 at Boroughbridge. **Nearest Railway Station:** Harrogate; there is a bus service from Harrogate to the centre of Ripon.

## ADMISSION

All classes of day ticket give access to full betting facilities, including Tote.

**Day tickets:**

CLUB £12 - access to restaurant, bar, boxes and private rooms

TATTERSALLS £7 - access to restaurants, bars, private rooms and fast food

SILVER RING £3 - access to restaurant, bar, ice cream

COURSE £2, or £7 for a car and up to four occupants - access to bar, snack bar and mobile refreshment outlets

**Annual membership:** £65 single, £100 joint (husband and wife), £45 junior (under 21)

## COURSE FACILITIES

**Banks:**
there are no banks or cashpoint facilities on the course

**For families:**
picnicking is permitted anywhere, but the Course enclosure is the only one where you can do so from your car; children's play areas in Silver Ring and Course enclosures; no lost children centre, but one of the ambulance rooms is used for this purpose.

## CALENDAR OF EVENTS

| | |
|---|---|
| April 6 | July 16 |
| April 14 | August 1 |
| April 23 | August 13 |
| May 25 | August 20 |
| June 15-16 | August 29-30 |
| July 4 | |

## WHERE TO STAY

### HOTELS

**★★★ 67% Ripon Spa**
Park St
☎ (0765) 602172, telex: 57780, fax: 0765 690770
40 bedrooms; double B&B £69.60-£90
Credit cards 1 2 3 5

**★★ 54% Unicorn**
Market Place
☎ (0765) 602202, telex: 57515, fax: 0765 600321
33 bedrooms; double B&B £50
Credit cards 1 2 3 5

### Around Ripon

**★★★ 74% Aldwark Manor**
Aldwark
☎ (03473) 8146, fax: (03473) 8867
17 bedrooms; double B&B £60-£80
Credit cards 1 2 3 5

**★★★ 66% Crown**
Horsefair, Boroughbridge
☎ (0423) 322328, fax: (0423) 324513
41 bedrooms; double B&B £49.95-£59.95
Credit cards 1 2 3 5

**★★★ 63% Rose Manor**
Horsefair, Boroughbridge
☎ (0423) 322245, fax: (0423) 324920
17 bedrooms; double room £68-£75 (room only)
Credit cards 1 2 3 5

**★★ 65% Bay Horse Inn & Motel**
Burnt Yates
☎ (0423) 770230
15 bedrooms
Credit cards 1 2 3

**★★★★ 67% Moat House International**
Kings Rd, Harrogate
☎ (0423) 500000, telex: 57575, fax: (0423) 524435
214 bedrooms; double B&B £119-£135
Credit cards 1 2 3 5

**★★★★ 64% Nidd Hall**
Nidd, Harrogate
☎ (0423) 771598, fax: (0423) 770931
38 bedrooms; double B&B £140-£230
Credit cards 1 2 3 5

**★★★★ 63% The Majestic**
Ripon Rd, Harrogate
☎ (0423) 568972, telex: 57918, fax: (0423) 502283
156 bedrooms; double room £90-£100 (room only)
Credit cards 1 2 3 5

**★★★ ❀❀ 74% Boar's Head**
Ripley, Harrogate
☎ (0423) 771888, fax: (0423) 771509
19 bedrooms; double B&B £98-£105
Credit cards 1 2 3

**★★★ ❀ 69% Balmoral Hotel & Restaurant**
Franklin Mount, Harrogate
☎ (0423) 508208, fax: (0423) 530652
20 bedrooms
Credit cards 1 2 3

**★★★ 68% Grants**
3-13 Swan Rd
☎ (0423) 560666, fax: (0423) 502550
41 bedrooms; double B&B £48-£128
Credit cards 1 2 3 5

**★★★ ❀ 67% White House**
10 Park Pde, Harrogate
☎ (0423) 501388
13 bedrooms
Credit cards 1 2 3 5

**★★★ 64% St George Swallow**
1 Ripon Rd, Harrogate
☎ (0423) 561431, telex: 57995, fax: (0423) 530037
93 bedrooms; double B&B £104
Credit cards 1 2 3 5

**★★★ 63% The Crown**
Crown Place, Harrogate
☎ (0423) 567755, telex: 57652, fax: (0423) 502284
121 bedrooms; double room £70-£85 (room only)
Credit cards 1 2 3 5

**★★★ 63% Studley**
Swan Rd, Harrogate
☎ (0423) 560425, telex: 57506, fax: (0423) 530967
36 bedrooms; double B&B £78-£95
Credit cards 1 2 3 5

**★★★ 61% Hospitality Inn**
Prospect Place, West Park, Harrogate
☎ (0423) 564601, telex: 57530, fax: (0423) 507508
71 bedrooms; double room £79-£89 (room only)
Credit cards 1 2 3 5

**★★ 72% Albany**
22-23 Harlow Moor Dr, Harrogate
☎ (0423) 565890
14 bedrooms
Credit cards 1 3 5

**★★ 70% Harrogate Brasserie Hotel & Bar**
28-30 Cheltenham Pde, Harrogate
☎ (0423) 505041, fax: (0423) 530920
14 bedrooms; double B&B £50-£65
Credit cards 1 3 5

**★★ 70% The Manor**
3 Clarence Dr, Harrogate
☎ (0423) 503916, fax: (0423) 568709
17 bedrooms; double B&B £52-£73
Credit cards 1 3

**★★ 68% Ascot House**
53 Kings Rd, Harrogate
☎ (0423) 531005, fax: (0423) 503523
22 bedrooms; double B&B £59-£69.50
Credit cards 1 2 3 5

**★★ 67% Abbey Lodge**
29-31 Ripon Rd, Harrogate
☎ (0423) 569712, fax: (0423) 530570
19 bedrooms; double B&B £42-£50.50
Credit cards 1 3

**★★ 67% Green Park**
Valley Dr, Harrogate
☎ (0423) 504681, telex: 57515, fax: (0423) 530811
43 bedrooms; double B&B £70
Credit cards 1 2 3 5

**★★ 64% Young's**
15 York Rd, off Swan Rd, Harrogate
☎ (0423) 567336 & 521231, fax: (0423) 500042
16 bedrooms; double B&B £50-£70
Credit cards 1 3

**★★ 63% Valley**
93-95 Valley Dr, Harrogate
☎ (0423) 504868, fax: (0423) 531940
14 bedrooms; double B&B £46-£56
Credit cards 1 3

**★★ 62% West Park**
West Park, Harrogate
☎ (0423) 524471
17 bedrooms
Credit cards 1 2 3 5

**★ 67% Britannia Lodge**
16 Swan Rd, Harrogate
☎ (0423) 508482
12 bedrooms; double B&B £40-£60
Credit cards 1 2 3

# WHERE TO STAY

**★ 70% Cavendish**
3 Valley Dr, Harrogate
☎ (0423) 509637, fax: (0423) 504429
9 bedrooms; double B&B £56-£65
Credit cards 1 3

**★ 70% Gables**
2 West Grove Rd, Harrogate
☎ (0423) 505625, fax: (0423) 561312
9 bedrooms; double B&B £52-£59
Credit cards 1 3

**★ 69 Grafton**
1-3 Franklin Mount, Harrogate
☎ (0423) 508491, fax: (0423) 523168
17 bedrooms; double B&B £50-£55
Credit cards 1 2 3 5

**★ 67% Alvera Court**
76 Kings Rd, Harrogate
☎ (0423) 505735, fax: (0423) 507996
12 bedrooms; double B&B £50-£67
Credit cards 1 3

**★ 67% Aston**
7-9 Franklin Mount, Harrogate
☎ (0432) 5624262 & 569534, fax: (0423)
505542
15 bedrooms; double B&B £46-£55
Credit cards 1 3

**★ 62% The Croft**
42-46 Franklin Rd, Harrogate
☎ (0423) 563326
13 bedrooms; double B&B £44-£56
Credit cards 1 3

**★★★ 69% Dower House**
Bond End, Knaresborough
☎ (0423) 863302, telex: 57202, fax: (0423)
867665
28 bedrooms; double B&B £70-£82.50
Credit cards 1 2 3 5

**★★★ ⊛ 76% Hob Green**
Markington
☎ (0423) 770031, telex: 57780, fax: (0423)
771589
12 bedrooms
Credit cards 1 2 3 5

**★★ 74% Jervaulx Hall**
Masham
☎ (0677) 60235, fax: (0969) 23206
10 bedrooms

**★★ 64% Nags Head Country Inn**
Pickhill
☎ (0845) 567391, fax: (0845) 567217
15 bedrooms
Credit cards 1 3

**★★ ⊛ 73% Sheppard's**
Church Farm, Front St, Sowerby, Thirsk
☎ (0845) 523655, fax: (0845) 524720
8 bedrooms
Credit cards 1 3

**★★ 62% Three Tuns Hotel**
Market Place, Thirsk
☎ (0845) 523124, fax: (0845) 526126
11 bedrooms; double room £55-£60 (room
only)
Credit cards 1 2 3 5

**★ 58% Old Red House**
Station Rd, Thirsk
☎ (0845) 524383
12 bedrooms; double B&B £30-£36
Credit cards 2 3 5

**★★ 65% The Angel Inn**
Long St, Topcliffe
☎ (0845) 577237, fax: (0845) 578000
15 bedrooms; double B&B £50-£60
Credit cards 1 3

## BED AND BREAKFAST

**The Crown**
Roecliffe, Boroughbridge
☎ (0423) 322578, fax: (0423) 324060
Delightful country inn with attractive
modern bedrooms that are furnished and
decorated to high standard.
12 bedrooms; double B&B £30-£55
Credit cards 1 3

**Alexa House & Stable Cottages**
26 Ripon Rd, Harrogate
☎ (0423) 501988, fax: (0423) 504086
Yorkshire hospitality in very congenial
surroundings; high standard throughout.
9 bedrooms; double B&B £46-£50
Credit cards 1 3

**Acacia Lodge**
21 Ripon Rd, Harrogate
☎ (0423) 560752
A few minutes walk from the town centre;
very attractively furnished and decorated
throughout.
5 bedrooms; double B&B from £44

**Ashley House Hotel**
36-40 Franklin Rd, Harrogate
☎ (0423) 5074747 & 560858
Attractive, friendly hotel with very well
equipped bedrooms.
16 bedrooms; double B&B £42-£56
Credit cards 1 3

**Ashwood House**
7 Spring Grove, Harrogate
☎ (0423) 560081
Bedrooms are mostly spacious and
comfortable.
10 bedrooms; double B&B £40-£46

**Delaine Hotel**
17 Ripon Rd, Harrogate
☎ (0423) 567974
Family-run Victorian house with tastefully
decorated bedrooms and attractive flower
gardens.
10 bedrooms; double B&B £47-£50
Credit cards 1 3

**Glenayr**
19 Franklin Mount, Harrogate
☎ (0423) 504259
Tastefully decorated and pleasantly
furnished with freshly prepared home-
cooked dinners.
6 bedrooms; double B&B £41-£45
Credit cards 1 2 3

**Knox Mill House**
Knox Mill Ln, Killinghall, Harrogate
☎ (0423) 560650
In a delightful peaceful location, a former
miller's house with attractive, comfortable
bedrooms.
3 bedrooms; double B&B from £32

**Scotia House Hotel**
66/68 Kings Rd, Harrogate
☎ (0423) 504361, fax: (0423) 526578
Well furnished private hotel with cosy
lounge.
14 bedrooms; double B&B £48-£52
Credit cards 1 3

**Stoney Lea**
13 Spring Grove, Harrogate
☎ (0423) 501524
Spacious and comfortable semi-detached
house with mixed facade of stone and
Tudor-style timbers.
7 bedrooms; double B&B £40

**Wharfedale House**
28 Harlow Moor Dr, Harrogate
☎ (0423) 522233
Immaculate hotel situated in pleasant
location and providing well appointed
bedrooms.
8 bedrooms; double B&B from £46

## WHERE TO STAY

### Wynnstay House
60 Franklin Rd, Harrogate
☎ (0423) 560476
Very comfortable, with particularly well appointed bedrooms.
5 bedrooms; double B&B £40
Credit cards 1 3

### Newton House Hotel
5/7 York Place, Knaresborough
☎ (0423) 863539, fax: (0423) 869614
Lovely Grade II listed house with individually decorated, spacious bedrooms.
12 bedrooms
Credit cards 1 3

### The Villa, The Villa Hotel
47 Kirkgate, Knaresborough
☎ (0423) 865370
Beautifully situated high above the River Nidd; bedrooms are furnished in period style.
6 bedrooms; double B&B £36-£40

### Bank Villa
Masham
☎ (0765) 689605
Well established, popular guesthouse offering personal service.
7 bedrooms; double B&B £33.50

### CAMPSITES

#### ▶▶▶ Ure Bank Caravan Park
Ure Bank Top
☎ (0765) 602964 & 607764
Near the town centre; pitch price from £4 per night.

#### ▶▶ North Sutton Farm
Sutton Grange
☎ (0765) 604037
Off unclassified road to Sutton Grange.

### Around Ripon

#### ▶▶▶ Allerton Park Caravan Site
Allerton Mauleverer, Allerton Park
☎ (0423) 330569
Quarter of a mile east of the A1, off the A59; pitch price from £8 per night.

#### ▶▶ Church Farm
Knaresborough Rd, Bishop Monkton
☎ (0765) 677405 & 677297
South of Ripon off the A61.

#### ▶▶ Shaws Trailer Park
Knaresborough Rd
☎ (0423) 884432 & 883622
On the A59 Harrogate-Knaresborough road; pitch price from £6.50 per night.

#### ▶▶▶ Sleningford Water Mill Caravan Site
North Stanley
☎ (0765) 635201
Adjacent to River Ure and A6108; pitch price from £7.50 per night.

#### ▶▶▶ Ripley Caravan Park
Knaresborough Rd, Ripley
☎ (0423) 770050
On B6165 south of Ripley; pitch price from £6.60 per night.

#### ▶▶ Hallgates Farm
Sawley
☎ (0765) 620275 & 620472
Southwest of Ripon; pitch price from £2 per night.

#### ▶▶▶ Sowerby Caravan Park
Sowerby, Thirsk
☎ (0845) 522753
Off A168 half a mile south; pitch price from £4.75 per night.

#### ▶▶▶ Woodhouse Farm Caravan & Camping Park
☎ (0765) 658309
Six miles west of Ripon off B6265; pitch price from £6.50 per night.

## WHERE TO EAT

### RESTAURANTS

#### ❀ Grundy's
21 Cheltenham Crescent, Harrogate
☎ (0423) 502610
Bright flavours, unusual combinations and an admirable wine list.
Lunch not served
Dinner: 7-10; from £11.95 and á la carte
Credit cards 1 2 3 5

#### ❀❀ Millers
1 Montpellier Mews, Harrogate
☎ (0423) 530708
Ambitious and accomplished cooking in a small mews restaurant.
Lunch: 12-2; from £9.50 and à la carte
Dinner: 7-10; from £16.50 à la carte
Credit cards 1 3

#### ❀ Four Park Place
4 Park Place, Knaresborough
☎ (0423) 868002
An intimate, smart dining room and a cheery bistro serving light, modern food with a touch of style.
Lunch: 12-2.30
Dinner from 7-9.30
Credit cards 1 3

### PUBS

#### Buck Inn
Thornton Watlass
☎ (0677) 422461
The original old stone bar dates from the 17th century and is very cosy. An interesting range of meals is offered and beers include Theakstons, Tetleys, Beamish and Carlton (LA) as well as a weekly guest beer. Whisky drinkers can choose between 45 single malts.
Open: 11am-2.30pm, 6-11pm; Sunday 12-3, 7-10.30pm
Bar food: 12-2pm, 6.45-9.30pm; Sunday 12-2, 7-9.30pm

# Royal Windsor

*A picturesque course which is situated in 165 acres of beautiful Berkshire countryside next to the banks of the River Thames. Loose horses have been known to go for a dip and one jockey even had to be saved from drowning after being carted into the water.*

On a more practical note, those wishing to arrive at the track in style can do so by taking the river bus during the summer.

Racing takes place all the year round, with the principal jumps fixtures being held on New Year's Day and in late February, the latter featuring the imortant Fairlawne Chase. Meetings are predominantly on the Flat, though, and particularly popular are the ones run on Monday evenings in mid-summer. These always attract large cosmopolitan crowds spanning the whole social spectrum. This creates the lively and entertaining atmosphere that makes Windsor such a unique and appealing venue. This is one of the two figure-of-eight tracks in Britain (the other is Fontwell) and an excellent close-up of the start of races over one and a half miles can be obtained by walking across to the centre of the course. Viewing is rather restricted from the main stands, however, especially in the Members Enclosure.

## FURTHER INFORMATION

The Racecourse Office
Windsor Racecourse, Maidenhead Road
Windsor, Berks SL4 5JJ
Telephone 0753 864726

## LOCATION AND HOW TO GET THERE

The course is by the River Thames, two miles from central Windsor on the A308. From the M4 junction 6 take the A355 to Windsor, cross the river, take slip road to A308 and follow signs.

**Nearest Railway Stations:** Windsor and Eton Riverside; there are frequent services from Waterloo; from both stations head for the Barry Avenue Promenade close to Windsor Bridge, from where there is a connecting riverboat service to and from the course on racedays.

Helicopter landing and take off facilities are available - telephone the secretary (0753) 865234 for advance permission.

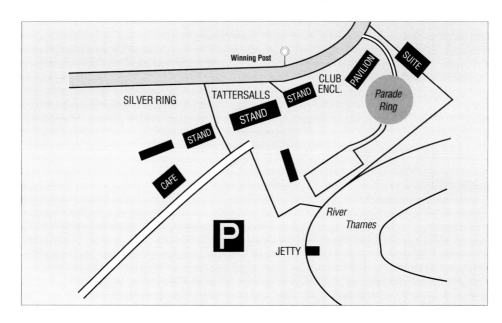

## ADMISSION

Children and wheelchair users are admitted free of charge to all enclosures.

**Day Tickets:**

CLUB ENCLOSURE £12 - access to paddock and parade ring, grandstand with some seating available, restaurant, bars, private boxes overlooking course and paddock, champagne bar, facilities for disabled; Tote, Tote bookmakers shop and credit only.

TATTERSALLS AND PADDOCK £8 - access to paddock and parade ring, viewing from terraces, bars, snack bars, facilities for disabled racegoers; Tote, Tote bookmakers shop and credit only

SILVER RING £4 - access to viewing from terraces, Tote, bars, cafeteria, snack bars, picnic area, facilities for disabled racegoers; Tote only

PICNIC AREA £12 per car, including all occupants

**Annual membership:** £100 includes 21 racedays and 6 reciprocal days at other courses

## COURSE FACILITIES

**Banks:**
there are no banks or cashpoint facilities on the course.

**For families:**
picnic area with refreshment kiosk and toilets in Silver Ring for all summer (flat) meetings and Saturdays and Bank Holidays in National Hunt season; children's play area; creche; baby changing facilities; lost children centre.

## CALENDAR OF EVENTS

**April 25** – evening meeting
**May 9** – evening meeting
**May 23** – evening meeting
**June 13** – evening meeting
**June 20** – evening meeting
**June 27** – evening meeting
**July 4** – evening meeting
**July 11** – evening meeting
**July 18** – evening meeting

**July 25** – evening meeting
**July 30** – evening meeting
**August 8**
**August 15**
**August 27** – evening meeting
**November 12** – jumping
**November 23** – jumping
**December 1** – jumping

## WHERE TO STAY

### HOTELS

**★★★★ 73% Oakley Court**
Windsor Rd, Water Oakley
☎ (0628) 74141, telex: 849958, fax: (0628) 37011
65 bedrooms; double room £145-£375 (room only)
Credit cards 1 2 3 5

**★★★ 68% The Castle**
High St
☎ (0753) 851011, telex: 849220, fax: (0753) 830244
104 bedrooms; double room £120-£140 (room only)
Credit cards 1 2 3 5

**★ 71% Aurora Garden**
14 Bolton Av
☎ (0753) 868686, fax: (0753) 831394
14 bedrooms
Credit cards 1 2 3 5

**★★ 58% Ye Harte & Garter**
High St
☎ (0753) 863426, fax: (0753) 830527
50 bedrooms; double B&B from £50
Credit Cards 1 2 3 5

**Around Windsor**

**★★★★ 57% Berystede**
Bagshot Rd, Sunninghill
☎ (0344) 23311, fax: (0344) 872301
91 bedrooms; double room £105-£112 (room only)
Credit cards 1 2 3 5

**★★ 67% Brockenhurst**
Brockenhurst Rd, Ascot
☎ (0344) 21912, fax: (0344) 873252
11 bedrooms; double B&B £75-£100.
Credit Cards 1 2 3 5

**★★ 65% Highclere**
19 Kings Rd, Sunninghill
☎ (0344) 25220, fax: (0344) 872528
12 bedrooms; double B&B £55-£80.
Credit Cards 1 2 3

**★★★★ 76% Pennyhill Park**
London Rd, Bagshot
☎ (0276) 71774, fax: (0276) 73217
22 bedrooms
Credit Cards 1 2 3 4 5

**★★★ 67% Bellhouse**
Oxford Rd, Beaconsfield
☎ (0753) 887121, telex: 848719, fax: (0753) 888231
136 bedrooms; double B&B £135-£145
Credit cards 1 2 3 4 5

**★★ 55% White Hart Toby**
Aylesbury End, Beaconsfield
☎ (0494) 671211, telex: 837882
34 bedrooms
Credit cards 1 2 3 5

## WHERE TO STAY

### ★★★ 65% Stirrups Country House
Maidens Green, Winkfield, Bracknell
☎ (0344) 882284, fax: (0344) 882300
24 bedrooms; double B&B £50-£85.
Credit Cards 1 2 3 5

### ★★★ 64% Burnham Beeches Moat House
Grove Road, Burnham
☎ (0628) 603333, fax: (0628) 603994
75 bedrooms; double B&B £98-£103
Credit Cards 1 2 3 4 5

### ★★ 54% The Manor
The Village Green, Datchet
☎ (0753) 543442, fax: (0753) 545292
30 bedrooms; double B&B £70-£90
Credit Cards 1 2 3 5

### ★★★★ 65% Runnymede
Windsor Rd, Egham
☎ (0784) 436171, telex: 934900, fax: (0784) 436340
172 bedrooms; double room £124-£137 (room only)
Credit Cards 1 2 3 5

### ★★ 61% Ethorpe
Packhorse Rd, Gerrards Cross
☎ (0753) 882039, fax: (0753) 887012
29 bedrooms; double B&B £50-£70
Credit cards 1 2 3 5

### ★★★★ 65% The Excelsior
Bath Rd, West Drayton
☎ 081-759 6611, telex: 24525, fax: 081-759 3421
839 bedrooms; double room £95-£120 (room only)
Credit cards 1 2 3 5

### ★★★★ 65% Heathrow Sterling
Terminal 4, Heathrow Airport
☎ 081-759 7755
400 bedrooms
Credit cards 1 2 3 5

### ★★★★ 62% Forte Crest
Sipson Road, West Drayton
☎ 081-759 2323, telex: 934280, fax: 081-897 8659
569 bedrooms; double room £80 (room only)
Credit cards 1 2 3 5

### ★★★★ 59% Holiday Inn Crowne Plaza
Stockley Rd, West Drayton
☎ (0895) 445555, telex: 934518, fax: (0895) 445122
300 bedrooms; double room £120-£150 (room only)
Credit cards 1 2 3 4 5

### ★★★★ 54% Heathrow Penta
Bath Rd, Heathrow Airport
☎ 081-897 6363, telex: 934660, fax: 081-897 1113
636 bedrooms; double room £127.50-£150 (room only)
Credit cards 1 2 3 5

### ★★★ 62% Forte Posthouse
Bath Rd, Heathrow Airport
☎ 081-759 2552, telex: 21777, fax: 081-564 9265
180 bedrooms; double room from £49.50 (room only)
Credit cards 1 2 3 5

### ★★ 50% Hotel Ibis Heathrow
112/114 Bath Rd, Heathrow Aiport
☎ 081-759 4888, telex: 929014, fax: 081-564 7894
354 bedrooms; double room £55 (room only)
Credit cards 1 2 3 5

### ★★★ ❀ 69% Ye Olde Bell
Hurley
☎ (0628) 825881, fax: (0628) 825939
36 bedrooms; double room £90-£100 (room only)
Credit cards 1 2 3 5

### ★★★★ 73% Fredrick's
Shoppenhangers Rd, Maidenhead
☎ (0628) 35934, telex: 849966, fax: (0628) 771054
37 bedrooms; double B&B £155-£165
Credit Cards 1 2 3 5

### ★★★ 63% Thames Riviera
At the Bridge, Maidenhead
☎ (0628) 74057, telex: 846687, fax: (0628) 776586
34 bedrooms; double B&B £60-£125
Credit Cards 1 2 3 4 5

### ★★★★ ❀ 70% The Compleat Angler
Marlow Bridge, Marlow
☎ (0628) 484444, telex: 848644, fax: (0628) 486388
64 bedrooms; double room £140-£155 (room only)
Credit cards 1 2 3 5

### ★★★ 60% The Thames Lodge
Thames St, Staines
☎ (0784) 464433, fax: (0784) 454858
44 bedrooms; double room £90-£105 (room only)
Credit cards 1 2 3 5

### ★★★★Y ❀❀ (RED) Cliveden
Taplow, signposted from all directions
☎ (0628) 668561, telex: 846562, fax: (0628) 661837
25 bedrooms
Credit cards 1 2 3 4 5

### ★★ ❀ 67% Chequers Inn
Kiln Ln, Woodburn Common
☎ (0628) 529575, fax: (0628) 850124
17 bedrooms; double B&B £77.50-£90
Credit cards 1 2 3

## WHERE TO STAY

### BED AND BREAKFAST

**Clarence Hotel**
9 Clarence Rd
☎ (0753) 864436, fax: (0753) 857060
Centrally placed historic hotel offering
attractive and well coordinated rooms.
21 bedroom; double B&B £49
Credit cards 1 2 3 5

**Melrose House**
53 Frances Rd
☎ (0753) 865328
Elegant Victorian house offering bright,
clean and very well equipped bedrooms.
9 bedrooms
Credit cards 1 3

### Around Windsor

**The Beeches**
19 The Avenue, Datchet
☎ (0753) 580722
Semi-detached, redbrick Victorian house
providing comfortable bed and breakfast
accommodation.
7 bedrooms; double B&B £45
Credit cards 1 3

**Bridgettine Convent**
Fulmer Common Rd, Iver Heath
☎ (0753) 662073, fax: (0753) 662645
Very attractive Tudor-style timbered house
where peace and tranquility are assured.
13 bedrooms.

**Holly Tree House**
Burford Close, Marlow Bottom, Marlow
☎ (0628) 891110, fax: (0628) 481278
Large modern detached property; tastefully
decorated bedrooms have every facility.
5 bedrooms; double B&B £62.50-£67.50
Credit cards 1 2 3

**Colnbrook Lodge**
Bath Rd, Colnbrook, Slough
☎ (0753) 685958
Comfortable and well equipped detached
house on the edge of the village.
8 bedrooms
Credit cards 1 3

### CAMPSITE

▶▶ **Laleham Park Camping Site**
Thameside. Signposted
☎ (09325) 64149
Southeast of Ascot; pitch price £7.80 per
night

## WHERE TO EAT

### RESTAURANTS

🏵🏵🏵🏵 **Waterside**
River Cottage, Ferry Rd, Bray
☎ (0628) 20691
Excellent French cuisine prepared by
Michael Roux in picturesque riverside
setting.
Lunch: 12-2 from £28 and à la carte
Dinner: 7-10 from £57.50 and à la carte
Credit cards 1 3 4 5

🏵🏵 **Cookham Tandoori**
High St, Cookham
☎ (06285) 22584
Smart, comfortable setting for fresh and
flavoursome Indian food.
Lunch: 12-2; from £12 à la carte
Dinner: 7-10.30; from £20 à la carte
Credit cards 1 2 3 5

🏵🏵 **La Bonne Franquette**
5 High St, Egham
☎ (0784) 439494, fax: (0784) 431473
Eclectic carte and overall good quality food
offered in this smart High Street restaurant.
Lunch: 12-2 from £14.50 and à la carte
Dinner: 7-9 from £27.50 and à la carte
Credit cards 1 2 3 5

🏵🏵 **Jade Fountain**
38 High St, Sunninghill
☎ (0344) 27070
Smart and friendly Chinese restaurant
offering high standard Chinese cuisine.
Lunch: 12-1.50 from £14.50 and à la carte
Dinner; 7-10.30 from £14.50 and à la carte
Credit cards 1 2 3 5

# Salisbury

*Salisbury may be better known for its awe-inspiring cathedral, but it is also home to an extremely attractive and popular racecourse. Around a dozen fixtures are scheduled here annually and a good standard of racing is maintained during the entire Flat season.*

July and August see the highest attendances, especially at the marvellous evening meetings. The faciliites are top-notch and this is one course where it is well worth paying a little extra for the added privileges of the Members enclosure - the restaurant and bar are particularly good in this section.

The wide track rises steadily throughout and there is a right-handed elbow in it, five furlongs from the finish. The course is used by many of the top trainers to introduce and educate their best two-year-olds so there is usually a smattering of potentially smart youngsters on view. It is appropriate, then, that the highlight of the year is a contest restricted to juveniles, the Veuve Clicquot Champagne Stakes, which is run towards the end of June. A man whose horses it usually pays to follow here is local handler Richard Hannon. He became champion trainer for the first time in 1992 and normally sends a strong raiding party down from his nearby base on the edge of Salisbury Plain.

## FURTHER INFORMATION

Salisbury Racecourse
Netherhampton, Salisbury, Wiltshire SP2 8PN
☎ (0722) 326461 / 327327

## LOCATION AND HOW TO GET THERE

The course is 3.5 miles southwest of Salisbury off the A3094 Netherhampton road. From the A303, take the A30 to Salisbury, continue on the A30 to the west of Salisbury, then take the A3094 to Netherhampton.
**Nearest Railway Station:** Salisbury; there is a connecting bus service to the course on racedays.

## ADMISSION

All classes of day ticket give access to full betting facilities, including Tote.

**Day Tickets:**

MEMBERS £12 - access to restaurant, bars, boxes, private rooms

TATTERSALLS £8 - access to bars and Tote betting shop
COURSE £3.50 - access to bar

**Annual membership:** £80

## COURSE FACILITIES

**Banks:**
there are no banks or cashpoint facilities on the course.

**For families:**
children's play area during July and August meetings only.

## CALENDAR OF EVENTS

April 28
May 5
May 27
June 7
June 22-23
July 9
July 28 – evening meeting
August 10-11
August 18 – evening meeting
September 1
September 28

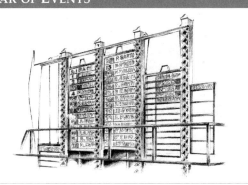

## WHERE TO STAY

### HOTELS

**★★★ 66% Rose & Crown**
Harnham Rd, Harnham
☎ (0722) 327908, telex: 47224, fax: (0722) 339816
28 bedrooms
Credit cards 1 2 3 5

**★★★ 65% Red Lion**
Milford St
☎ (0722) 323334, fax: (0722) 325756
56 bedrooms; double B&B £90–£100
Credit cards 1 2 3 5

**★★★ 63% The White Hart**
Saint John St
☎ (0722) 327476, fax: (0722) 412761
68 bedrooms; double room £54–£90 (room only)
Credit cards 1 2 3 5

**★★ 61% The Trafalgar**
33 Milford St
☎ (0722) 338686, fax: (0722) 414496
18 bedrooms; double B&B from £54
Credit cards 1 2 3 5

**★★ 60% County**
Bridge St
☎ (0722) 320229, fax: (0722) 414313
31 bedrooms; double B&B £50–£70
Credit cards 1 2 3 5

**★★ 60% King's Arms**
9-11 Saint John's St
☎ (0722) 327629, fax: (0722) 414246
15 bedrooms; double B&B £58–£80
Credit cards 1 2 3 5

### Around Salisbury

**Forte Travelodge**
Amesbury
☎ (0980) 624966 Central Reservations: (0800) 850950
32 bedrooms; double room £31.95 (room only)
Credit cards 1 2 3

**★★ 66% Ashburn Hotel & Restaurant**
Damerham Rd, Fordingbridge
☎ (0425) 652060
23 bedrooms; double B&B from £73
Credit cards 1 3

### BED AND BREAKFAST

**Byways House**
31 Fowlers Rd
☎ (0722) 328364, fax: (0722) 322146
Victorian house which is attractively decorated, comfortably furnished and has well equipped bedrooms.
23 bedrooms; double B&B from £35
Credit cards 1 3

**Cricket Field Cottage**
Skew Bridge, Wilton Rd
☎ (0722) 322595
Well appointed, en suite bedrooms are offered in this modernised gamekeeper's cottage.
5 bedrooms; double B&B £36–£38

**The Old House**
161 Wilton Rd
☎ (0722) 333433
Full of character with exposed beams and brick walls; furnished and decorated in country-cottage style.
6 bedrooms; double B&B from £32

**Glen Lyn**
6 Bellamy Ln, Milford Hill
☎ (0722) 327880
Substantial Victorian property a few minutes walk from the city centre.
9 bedrooms; double B&B £32–£36

**Hayburn Wyke**
72 Castle Rd
☎ (0722) 412627
Close to the cathedral; clean and bright accommodation.
6 bedrooms; double B&B £30–£38

**Leena's**
50 Castle Rd
☎ (0722) 335419
Small guesthouse with friendly, relaxed atmosphere.
6 bedrooms; double B&B £28–£31

**Old Bell**
2 Saint Ann St
☎ (0722) 327958, fax: (0722) 411485
Small 14th-century inn ideally situated close to the cathedral; low ceiling and beams.
7 bedrooms; double B&B £55–£60
Credit cards 1 2 3 5

**Holmhurst**
Downton Rd
☎ (0722) 323164
Detached red-brick family home; bedrooms are simply appointed and comfortable.
8 bedrooms; double B&B £30

**Swaynes Firs Farm**
Coombe Bissett
☎ (072589) 240
Friendly farmhouse seven miles from Salisbury on the A354 Blandford road.
3 bedrooms; double B&B £34–£36

**Warren**
15 High St, Downton
☎ (0725) 20263
A 15th-century house, lovingly furnished; bedrooms are clean and fresh flowers add colour.
6 bedrooms; double B&B £42

**The Swan**
Stoford, Wilton
☎ (0722) 790236
Popular roadside inn on the A36, 6 miles west of Salisbury. Comfortable bedrooms.
8 bedrooms; double B&B £40

## WHERE TO STAY

### CAMPSITES

**▶▶▶ Coombe Nurseries Touring Park**
Race Plain, Netherhampton, Salisbury
☎ (0722) 328451
Pitch price from £8 per night.

**▶▶▶▶ New Forest Country Holidays**
Sandy Balls Estate Ltd, Godshill
☎ (0425) 653042
Situated south of Salisbury near New Forest; pitch price from £12.50 per night.

**▶▶▶ Stonehenge Touring Park**
Orcheston, Shrewton
☎ (0980) 602304
Four miles from Stonehenge; pitch price from £6.50 per night.

## WHERE TO EAT

### RESTAURANTS

**⚜ Hour Glass**
Burgate, Fordingbridge
☎ (0425) 652348
Enjoyable, straightforward modern English dishes in cosy thatched cottage restaurant.
Lunch: 12-1.30; from £5.95 à la carte
Dinner: 7-9.30; from £17.95
Credit cards 1 3 5

**⚜⚜ The Three Lions**
Stuckton, Fordingbridge
☎ (0425) 652489
Variety and value from a spontaneous menu and exciting wine list.
Lunch: 12-1.30; from £12.85 à la carte
Dinner: 7-9; from £18.50 à la carte
Credit cards 1 3

**⚜⚜ Langley Wood**
Redlynch
☎ (0794) 390348
Straightforward French/English cooking in a relaxed rural setting.
Lunch by arrangement: Sunday lunch £12
Dinner: 7-11; from £15.50 à la carte
Credit cards 1 2 3 5

### PUBS

**Haunch of Venison**
14 Minster St
☎ (0722) 322024
Parts of this tiny pub date from 1320 when it was the church house, and one bar has a 600-year-old fireplace. Beers include Ringwood Best, Courage Best and Directors and there are 100 malt whiskies. Excellent value bar snacks are available, though space is rather limited.
Open: 11am-11pm; Sunday 12-3pm, 7-10.30pm
Bar food: 12-2.30pm, 7-9.30pm, except Sunday evening

**Around Salisbury**

**Horseshoe**
Ebbesbourne Wake
☎ (0722) 780474
Delightfully rustic and homely village pub with a pretty garden, beyond which are kept pot-bellied pigs, goats and a donkey. Adnams, Wadworth and Ringwood ales are drawn straight from the cask and hearty portions of reliable bar food are on offer.
Open: 11.30am-2.30pm, 6.30-11pm; Sunday 12-3pm, 7-10.30pm
Bar food: 12-2pm, 7-9.30pm, except Monday evening; Sunday 7-9pm
Restaurant: Tuesday to Saturday 7-9.30pm, Sunday 12-2pm

**Cuckoo Inn**
Hamptworth, Landford
☎ (0794) 390302
Tucked away down a series of country lanes this isolated thatched inn attracts lovers of real ale, with no less than 12 varieties on offer. Food is limited to rolls, ploughmans and pasties, but is always available. Children are allowed in the family room and garden bar.
Open: 11.30am-2.30pm, 6-11pm; Saturday 11am-11pm; Sunday 12-3pm, 7-10.30pm
Bar food: as opening times

**The Lamb Inn**
Hindon
☎ (074789) 573
Formerly a smuggling haunt and a posting inn, the Lamb has a charming long bar in which to enjoy dishes from an interesting bar menu. There are two real ales, an unusual Highland malt whisky and an extensive wine list. Children are allowed in the top bar only.
Open: 11am-11pm; Sunday 12-3pm, 7-10.3pm
Bar food: 12-2pm, 7-10pm
Restaurant: 12-2pm, 7-9.30pm
Accommodation: double B&B £55-£65

**Silver Plough**
Pitton
☎ (0722) 72266
Tucked away in a downland village, this welcoming 250-year-old converted farmhouse has won awards for the high quality of its food. There are four real ales and ten wines served by the glass from an excellent wine list. Children are allowed in the snug bar and the skittle alley, when not in use.
Open: 11am-3pm, 6-11pm
Bar food: 12-2pm, 7-9.30pm
Restaurant: 12-2pm, 7-10pm (closed Sunday and Monday evenings)

# Sandown Park

*In 1992, Sandown was voted 'Racecourse of the Year', an accolade it richly deserved, It was in fact the tenth time in the last 15 years that this Surrey venue has been awarded the title, which give a pretty good indication of its justifiable popularity.*

Located a mere 15 miles from the centre of London in leafy Esher, this course is the nearest thing to a racing Utopia. The track is set in a spectacular amphitheatre with the grandstand ideally situated to give a superb view of the action. The facilities are exemplary and the atmosphere is second to none.

The quality of racing does justice to the fantastic surroundings and stirring finishes can nearly always be guaranteed on the stiff uphill climb to the winning post. There is a full programme of events under both codes with nearly thirty fixtures staged here annually. The evening meetings are a delight during summer and the jumps fixtures can not be matched for excitement in winter. One of the major attractions of the equine calendar is the Whitbread Gold Cup Day at the end of April. The famous handicap chase of that name is the feature race of an outstanding mixed card which also includes an important Derby trial on the Flat. Crowds are huge at this meeting and it is sensible to purchase tickets in advance as numbers may be restricted for safety reasons. Another highlight is the Coral-Eclipse Stakes in early June, an extremely valuable Group One event that attracts Europe's top middle-distance performers.

## FURTHER INFORMATION

Club Secretary
Sandown Park Racecourse, Esher,
Surrey KT10 9AJ
☎ (0372) 463072/464348

## LOCATION AND HOW TO GET THERE

Sandown Park is 13 miles from central London via the A3 and four miles southwest of Kingston on the A307. Leave the M3 at junction 1 and take the A308 towards Kingston, passing Kempton Park on the left; turn right onto the A309, then right again onto the A307. From the M25, leave at junction 10, and approach via the A3.

**Nearest Railway Station:** Esher; the station is within easy walking distance of the course.

## ADMISSION

**Day Tickets:**

Accompanied children under 16 are admitted free to all enclosures.

CLUB feature days £22, £14 junior (16-25 years); premium days £15, £11 junior; normal days £13, £10 junior - access to restaurants, bars, snacks, private rooms, boxes and facilities for disabled racegoers

GRANDSTAND feature days £13; premium days £10; normal days £9 - access to self-service restaurant, bars, snacks, facilities for disabled racegoers, creche due to open in April 1993

PARK feature days £4; premium and normal days £3 - access to bar, snacks and mobile catering; good view of steeplechase fences and flat sprint course

**Parking:** Members car park £2; Portsmouth Road car park free.

**Annual membership:** £180, junior £75, includes free members' car park label, exclusive use of Club Bar with balcony, free admission for a guest to one meeting. Joint Jumping Membership (Sandown Park and Kempton Park): £140, includes 20 days of jumping and one day's racing at Cheltenham.

## COURSE FACILITIES

**Banks:**
there are no banks or cashpoint facilities on the course, but cheques can be cashed at the Secretary's office during the hours between gates opening and the last race.

**For families:**
picnic area; children's play area; creche due to open April 1993; lost children taken to secretary's office

## CALENDAR OF EVENTS

**April 22-23** – flat; includes Gardner Merchant Mile on Friday.
Whitbread Gold Cup and Thresher Classic Trial on Saturday
**May 30-31** – includes Temple Stakes and Brigadier Gerard Stakes
**June 10-11** – flat
**July 1-2** – Hong Kong Day on Friday. Coral-Eclipse Day on Saturday
**July 13-14** – includes Harpers and Queen Evening on Wednesday.
Milcars Stakes on Thursday
**July 20** – evening meeting

**August 10** – evening meeting
**August 19-20** – includes Solario Stakes on Friday. Variety Club Day
on Saturday
**September 13-14** – flat
**November 5** – National Hunt
**December 2-3** – includes Crowngap Winter Hurdle on Friday.
William Hill Handicap Hurdle on Saturday

## WHERE TO STAY

### HOTELS

**Around Sandown Park**

**★★ 62% Heathside**
Brighton Rd, Burgh Heath
☎ (0737) 353355, fax: (0737) 370857
73 bedrooms; double B&B £75-£85
Credit cards 1 2 3 5

**★★★ ⊛ 61% Thatchers Resort**
Epsom Rd, East Horsley
☎ (04865) 4291, fax: (04865) 4222
36 bedrooms; double room £80-£90 (room
only)
Credit cards 1 2 3 5

**★★★★ 65% The Excelsior**
Bath Rd, West Drayton
☎ 081-759 6611, telex: 24525, fax: 081-
759 3421
839 bedrooms; double room £95-£120
(room only)
Credit cards 1 2 3 5

**★★★★ 65% Heathrow Sterling**
Terminal 4, Heathrow Airport
☎ 081-759 7755
400 bedrooms
Credit cards 1 2 3 5

**★★★★ 62% Forte Crest**
Sipson Road, West Drayton
☎ (0895) 445555, telex: 934518, fax:
(0895) 445122
380 bedroom; double room £120-£150
(room only)
Credit cards 1 2 3 4 5

**★★★★ 54% Heathrow Penta**
Bath Rd, Heathrow Airport
☎ 081-897 6363, telex: 934660, fax: 081-
897 1113
636 bedrooms; double room £127.50-£150
(room only)
Credit cards 1 2 3 5

**★★★ 62% Forte Posthouse**
Bath Rd, Heathrow Airport
☎ 081-759 2552, telex: 21777, fax: 081-
564 9265
180 bedrooms; double room from £49.50
(room only)
Credit cards 1 2 3 5

**★★ 50% Hotel Ibis Heathrow**
112/114 Bath Rd, Heathrow Airport
☎ 081-759 4888, telex: 929014, fax: 081-
564 7894
354 bedrooms; double room £55 (room
only)
Credit cards 1 2 3 5

**★★★★Y ⊛ 65% Cannizaro House**
West Side, Wimbledon Common, London
SW19
☎ 081-879 1464, telex: 9413837, fax: 081-
879 7338
46 bedrooms; double room from £118
(room only)
Credit cards 1 2 3 4 5

**★★★ ⊛ 67% Carnarvon**
Ealing Common, London W5
☎ 081-992 5399, telex: 935114, fax: 081-
992 7082
145 bedrooms; double room from £104
(room only)
Credit cards 1 2 3 5

**★★★ ⊛ 72% Woodlands Park**
Woodlands Ln, Stoke D'Abernon
☎ (037284) 3933, telex: 919246
59 bedrooms
Credit cards 1 2 3 5

### BED AND BREAKFAST

**Around Sandown Park**

**Epsom Downs Hotel**
9 Longdown Rd, Epsom
☎ (0372) 740643, fax: (0372) 723259
Charming hotel located in peaceful
residential area; modern, well equipped
accommodation.
14 bedrooms; double B&B £43.45-£71.50
Credit cards 1 2 3 5

**The White House**
Downs Hill Rd, Epsom
☎ (0372) 722472, fax: (0372) 744447
15 bedrooms
Credit cards 1 3

**Kings Lodge**
5 Kings Rd, London SW19
☎ 081-545 0191, fax: 081-545 0381
Bedrooms furnished to very high standard.
7 bedrooms;
Credit cards 1 2 3 5

**Trochee Hotel**
21 Malcolm Rd, London SW19
☎ 081-946 1579 & 3924, fax: 081-785
4058
Old-fashioned but soundly maintained
guesthouse.
17 bedrooms; double B&B £49
Credit cards 1 3

**Wimbledon Hotel**
78 Worple Rd, London SW19
☎ 081-946 9265, fax: 081-946 1581
Detached Victorian house offering a choice
to suit everyone.
Credit cards 1 3 5

**Worcester House**
38 Alwyne Rd, London SW19
☎ 081-946 1300, fax: 081-785 4058
Choice of brightly decorated bedrooms, all
equipped with modern amenities.
9 bedrooms; double B&B £59.50
Credit cards 1 3 5

## WHERE TO STAY

### Chiswick Hotel
73 Chiswick High Rd, London W4
☎ 081-994 1712, fax: 081-742 2585
Well equipped accommodation, furnished in modern style.
33 bedrooms; double B&B from £82.50
Credit cards 1 2 3 5

### Wellmeadow Lodge
24 Wellmeadow Rd, Hanwell, London W7
☎ 81-567 7294, fax: 081-556 3468
Charming little guesthouse quietly situated and personally supervised.
5 bedrooms; double B&B £61-£70
Credit cards 1 2 3

### Glen Court
St Johns Hill Rd, Woking
☎ (0483) 764154
Attractive Edwardian house; spacious comfortable bedrooms, traditionally furnished.
12 bedrooms
Credit cards 1 3

## CAMPSITES

### ►► Laleham Park Camping Site
Laleham
☎ (09325) 64149]
Northwest of Epsom beside the Thames; pitch price from £7.80 per night

## WHERE TO EAT

### RESTAURANTS

### Around Sandown Park

### ❀❀ Le Raj
211 Firtree Rd, Epsom
☎ (0737) 371371
Excellent Indian cuisine in stylish air-conditioned restaurant.
Lunch 12-2.30
Dinner: 7-11

### ❀ Khamwan
5 White Hart Ln, Barnes, London SW13
☎ 081-876 3335
Mainly modern cuisine; daily changing menu and informal attentive service.
Lunch: 12-3; from £6.95
Dinner: 7-11.45
Credit cards 1 2 3

### ❀ Riva 169 Church Rd, Barnes, London
SW13,
☎ 081-748 0434
Regional Italian cooking in small attractive urban restaurant.
Lunch: 12-2.30
Dinner: 7-11
Credit cards 1 3

### ❀❀ Sonny's
94 Church Rd, Barnes, London SW13
☎ 081-748 0393, fax: 081-748 2698
Reliable imaginative modern cooking in stylish
informal brasserie-type restaurant.
Lunch: 12-2.30; from £11.95
Dinner: 7-11.30; from £11.95 and à la carte
Credit cards 1 3

### ❀❀ Crowthers
481 Upper Richmond Rd West, East Sheen, London SW14
☎ 081-876 6372
Popular local restaurant with good modern cooking and a warm welcome.
Lunch: 12-1.45
Dinner: 7-10.45
Credit cards 1 2 3

### ❀❀ Maxim
153-155 Northfield Av, Ealing, London W13
☎ 081-567 1719 & 081-840 1086
Popular local Chinese restaurant with Peking specialities and consistent standards.
Lunch: 12-2.30; from £8 and à la carte
Dinner: 7-12pm; from £8
Credit cards 1 2 3 5

### ❀❀ Michels
13 High St, Ripley
☎ (0483) 224777 & 222940
Stylish town house where the cooking shows more than a dash of flair.
Lunch: 12-1.45; from £17 and à la carte
Dinner: 7-9; from £20 and à la carte
Credit cards 1 2 3

# Sedgefield

*With its relaxed, warm and welcoming atmosphere, Sedgefield has rightly gained a reputation for being a friendly racecourse. Recent redevelopment has included a brand new pavilion and the upgrading of the existing facilities, all with the needs of disabled racegoers in mind.*

These changes were very necessary as the stands had begun to look antiquated and the amenities were definitely on the limited side. The situation is much improved now and the course has still managed to retain its old-fashioned charm and individual character that makes it such an enticing venue. It is also good to see that admission prices remain amongst the lowest in the land.

The track is in beautiful, rolling countryside and is a peaceful and tranquil setting for the 21 National Hunt meetings staged here every year, usually on Tuesdays. The standard of racing is only average and the most valuable event in the calendar is, appropriately enough, a selling hurdle which is run in early May. The oval circuit is undulating and essentially sharp in character, though the run-in rises fairly steeply and long-distance chases provide a thorough test of stamina when the ground is riding soft.

## FURTHER INFORMATION

Dennis Riley, Racecourse Manager, 23a The Green Billingham, Cleveland TS23 1ES
☎ (0642) 559050

## LOCATION AND HOW TO GET THERE

The racecourse is situated just outside the southwestern edge of Sedgefield, which is just 10 miles from Teesside and Darlington on the A689; it is three miles east of the A1(M) and seven miles west of the A19, via the A689.

## ADMISSION

All classes of day ticket give access to full betting facilities, including Tote.

**Day Tickets:**

Accompanied children under 16 are admitted free. Parking is free, though there is parking in the paddock enclosure for £2 per day.

PADDOCK £7, senior citizens £3.50 - access to bars, restaurants, private boxes and rooms

COURSE £2 - access to bar and snack bar

## COURSE FACILITIES

**Banks:**
there are no banks or cashpoint facilities on the course.

**For families:**
lost children's centre in Secretary's office.

## CALENDAR OF EVENTS

| | |
|---|---|
| January 5 | May 18 |
| January 26 | September 2 |
| February 1 | September 13 |
| February 16 | September 28 |
| February 22 | October 11 |
| March 8 | October 27 |
| March 15 | November 8 |
| March 26 | November 18 |
| April 29 – evening meeting | December 6 |
| May 5 – evening meeting | December 26 |

## WHERE TO STAY

### HOTELS

**★★★ 67% Hardwick Hall**
☎ (0740) 20253, telex: 537681, fax: (0740) 22771
17 bedrooms
Credit cards 1 2 3 5

**★★ 66% Crosshill**
1 The Square
☎ (0740) 20153 & 21206
8 bedrooms; double B&B £56-£62
Credit cards 1 2 3

### Around Sedgefield

**★★★ 70% Park Head**
New Coundon, Bishop Coundon, Bishop Auckland
☎ (0388) 661727
15 bedrooms
Credit cards 1 2 3 4 5

**★★ 61% The Postchaise**
36 Market, Bishop Auckland
☎ (0388) 661296
12 bedrooms
Credit cards 1 3 5

**★★★ 71% Hallgarth Country House**
Coatham Mundeville, Darlington
☎ (0325) 300400, fax: (0325) 310083
40 bedrooms; double B&B £85-£90
Credit cards 1 2 3 5

**★★★ 67% Headlam Hall**
Headlam, Gainford, Darlington
☎ (0325) 730238, fax: (0325) 730790
17 bedrooms; double B&B £65-£80
Credit cards 1 2 3

**★★★ 62% White Horse**
Darlington
☎ (0325) 382121, telex: 778704, fax: (0325) 355953
40 bedrooms; double room £49.50 (room only)
Credit cards 1 2 3 5

**★★★ 61% Swallow King's Head**
Priestgate, Darlington
☎ (0325) 380222, telex: 587112, fax: (0325) 382006
86 bedrooms; double B&B £85-£100
Credit cards 1 2 3 5

**★★★★ 68% Royal Country**
Old Elvet, Durham
☎ 091-386 6821, telex: 538238, fax: 091-386 0704
150 bedrooms; double B&B £45-£102
Credit cards 1 2 3 4 5

**★★★ 69% Ramside Hall**
Carrville, Durham
☎ 091-386 5282, telex: 537681, fax: 091-386 0399
82 bedrooms; double B&B from £90
Credit cards 1 2 3 5

**★★★ 68% Three Tuns**
New Elvet, Durham
☎ 091-386 4326, telex: 583238, fax: 091-386 1406
47 bedrooms; double B&B £69-£87.50
Credit cards 1 2 3 5

**★★★ 61% Bowburn Hall**
Bowburn, Durham
☎ 091-377 0311, telex: 537681, fax: 091-377 3459
19 bedrooms; double B&B £60-£65
Credit cards 1 2 3 5

**★★ 65% Bridge Toby**
Croxdale, Durham
☎ 091-378 0524, telex: 538156, fax: 091-378 9981
46 bedrooms
Credit cards 1 2 3 5

**★★ 63% Newton Grange**
Finchale Rd, Brasside, Newton Hall, Durham
☎ 091-386 0872
13 bedrooms
Credit cards 1 3 5

**★★ 58% Rainton Lodge**
West Rainton, Durham
☎ 091-5120540 & 5120534, fax: 091-584 1221
25 bedrooms; double B&B £35-£45
Credit cards 1 3

**★ 67% Redhills**
Redhills Ln, Crossgate Moor, Durham
☎ 091-386 4331, telex: 537681
6 bedrooms
Credit cards 1 2 3 5

**★★ 69% Hardwicke Hall Manor**
Hesleden
☎ (0429) 836326, fax: 091-587 2334
11 bedrooms; double B&B £50-£60
Credit cards 1 2 3 5

**★★★★ 66% Redworth Hall Hotel & Country Club**
Redworth
☎ (0388) 772442, fax: (0388) 775112
100 bedrooms; double B&B £110-£145
Credit cards 1 2 3 5

**★★★ 59% Eden Arms Swallow Hotel**
Rushyford
☎ (0388) 720541, fax: (0388) 721871
46 bedrooms; double B&B £50-£90
Credit cards 1 2 3 5

**★★★★ 55% Swallow**
10 John Walker Square, Stockton-on-Tees
☎ (0642) 679721, telex: 587895, fax: (0642) 601714
124 bedrooms; double B&B from £94
Credit cards 1 2 3 4 5

**★★★ ✿ 70% Parkmore**
636 Yarm Rd, Eaglescliffe, Stockton-on-Tees
☎ (0642) 786815, telex: 58298, fax: (0642) 790485
55 bedrooms; double B&B £50-£78
Credit cards 1 2 3 5

**★★★ 60% Forte Posthouse Teeside**
Low Ln, Thornaby-on-Tees
☎ (0642) 591213, fax: (0642) 594989
135 bedrooms; double room £39.50-£69.50 (room only)
Credit cards 1 2 3 5

**★★★ 55% Billingham Arms**
The Causeway, Billingham
☎ (0642) 553661 & 360880, telex: 587746, fax: (0642) 552104
69 bedrooms; double room £23-£62 (room only)
Credit cards 1 2 3 4 5

**★★ 62% Claireville**
519 Yarm Rd, Eaglescliffe
☎ (0642) 780378, fax: (0642) 784109
19 bedrooms; double B&B £42-£49
Credit cards 1 3 5

**★★★ 64% St George**
Middleton St George
☎ (0325) 332631, telex: 587623, fax: (0325) 333851
59 bedrooms; double B&B from £79
Credit cards 1 2 3 5

**★★ 64% Crossways**
Dunelm Rd, Thornley
☎ (0429) 821248, fax: (0429) 820034
23 bedrooms; double B&B £90
Credit cards 1 2 3 5

**★★ ✿ 64% Kensington Hall**
Kensington Ter, Willington
☎ (0388) 745071
10 bedrooms; double B&B £45-£48
Credit cards 1 3 5

## WHERE TO STAY

### BED AND BREAKFAST

**Dun Cow**
High St
☎ (0740) 20894
Charming old inn situated near the racecourse; unusual bedrooms and excellent cuisine.
6 bedrooms; double B&B from £45
Credit cards 1 2 3 5

**Around Sedgefield**

**Woodland**
63 Woodland Rd, Darlington
☎ (0325) 461908
Victorian terraced house situated on the A68, with well maintained bedrooms.
8 bedrooms; double B&B from £38

**Lothlorien**
48/49 Front St, Witton Gilbert, Durham
☎ 091-371 0067
Quaint roadside cottage; charming proprietoress.
3 bedrooms; double B&B £30-£34

**Bay Horse**
Brandon, Durham
☎ 091-378 0498
Attractive stone-built inn; comfortable, well equipped bedrooms. Good value bar meals.
4 bedrooms; double B&B £35
Credit cards 1

**The Edwardian Hotel**
72 Yarm Rd, Stockton-on-Tees
☎ (0642) 615655
Bright, very well equipped cosy bedrooms.
6 bedrooms
Credit cards 1

## WHERE TO EAT

### RESTAURANTS

**❀ Victor's**
84 Victoria Rd, Darlington
☎ (0325) 480818
Imaginative cooking at bargain prices in a friendly town-centre restaurant.
Lunch: 12-2; from £7.50
Dinner: 7-10.30; from £18
Credit cards 1 2 3 5

### PUBS

See **Dun Cow** and **Bay Horse**, under Bed and Breakfast above.

# Southwell

*This Midlands course is one of only two in Britain where racing is held both on a turf and an all weather track, the other being Lingfield. There are, not surprisingly, many striking similarities between the two venues.*

They both stage huge numbers of fixtures annually (around 70), the quality of racing is not the highest and attendances on weekdays are often pitiful. To be fair to Southwell, though, the atmosphere here is more animated than at Lingfield and spectators are more numerous, particularly at the Saturday meetings which can be quite lively. The best card is over the jumps in mid-March when all the races carry decent prize money.

This Nottinghamshire course may be somewhat lacking in beauty, but the facilities are substantial. A *Sporting Life* is provided free upon entry in place of a racecard and there is a profusion of bars and restaurants fom which to choose. Particularly recommended is the friendly little eating-house called 'Flo's', which serves some terrific home-made food at very reasonable prices. The parade ring is attractively laid out while the copious stands provide excellent viewing of the track. An interesting recent initiative here is that some trainers are now actually based at the racecourse stables. This system is prevalent throughout America and has the potential for further development in this country.

## FURTHER INFORMATION

R A M Racecourses Ltd
Southwell Racecourse, Rolleston, Near Newark
Notts NG25 0TS
☎ (0636) 814481

## LOCATION AND HOW TO GET THERE

The course is seven miles west of Newark, midway between the A1 and the M1. Leave the M1 at junction 28, take the A38 to Mansfield, then the A617 towards Newark on Trent.
**Nearest Railway Station:** Rolleston; there is no connecting bus service to the course.

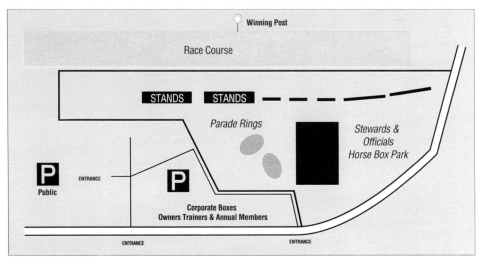

## ADMISSION

All classes of day ticket give access to full betting facilities, including Tote.

MEMBERS £10 - access to restaurant, bar and private boxes

TATTERSALLS £5 - access to restaurant, bars and marquee

## COURSE FACILITIES

**Banks:**
there are no banks or cashpoint facilities on the course.

**For families:**
picnic area; children's play area; baby-changing facilities; lost children centre

## CALENDAR OF EVENTS

**April 25** – flat
**May 2** – jumping
**May 9** – flat
**May 11** – jumping
**May 14** – flat
**May 21** – jumping; evening meeting
**May 24** – flat
**June 3** – flat
**June 10** – flat
**June 18** – flat; evening meeting
**July 9** – flat; evening meeting
**July 13** – flat
**July 16** – flat; evening meeting
**July 23** – flat
**July 28** – flat

**August 5** – flat
**August 12** – flat
**August 29** – jumping
**September 1** – jumping
**September 5** – flat
**September 26** – flat
**November 8** – jumping
**November 16** – flat
**November 22** – jumping
**November 25** – jumping
**November 30** – flat
**December 13** – jumping
**December 15** – flat
**December 21** – jumping
**December 27** – flat

## WHERE TO STAY

### HOTELS

**★★★ 65% Saracen's Head**
Market Place
☎ (0636) 812701, fax: (0636) 815408
27 bedrooms; double room £75–£90 (room only)
Credit cards 1 2 3 5

### Around Southwell

**★★ 66% Unicorn**
Gunthorpe Bridge, Gunthorpe
☎ (0602) 663612, fax: (0602) 664801
16 bedrooms
Credit cards 1 2 3 5

**★★ 66% Grange**
73 London Rd, Newark-on-Trent
☎ (0636) 703399, fax: (0636) 702328
15 bedrooms; double B&B £52.50–£59.50
Credit cards 1 3

**★★ 60% South Parade**
117-119 Baldertongate, Newark-on-Trent
☎ (0636) 703008, fax: (0522) 510182
16 bedrooms; double B&B £50–£59.50
Credit cards 1 2 3

**★★ 55% Midland**
Muskam Rd, Newark-on-Trent
☎ (0636) 73788
10 bedrooms
Credit cards 1 2 5

**Forte Travelodge**
North Muskham, Newark-on-Trent
☎ (0636) 703635, Central Reservations: (0800) 850950
30 bedrooms; double room £31.95 (room only)
Credit cards 1 2 3

**★★ 63% The Haven**
Grantham Rd, Whatton
☎ (0949) 50800, fax: (0949) 51454
33 bedrooms; double B&B £42–£48
Credit cards 1 2 3 5

### BED AND BREAKFAST

**Old Rectory**
Main St, Kirton
☎ (0623) 861540, telex: 378505
Attractive detached Georgian house offering pleasant accommodation.
10 bedrooms
Credit cards 1 3

### CAMPSITES

**►►► Thornton's Holt Camping Park**
Stragglethorpe, Radcliffe on Trent
☎ (0602 332125
Half a mile south of the A52 and 2 miles north of the A46.

## WHERE TO EAT

### RESTAURANTS

#### ✿✿ Black Swan
Hillside, Beckingham
☎ (0636) 626474
Highly competent modern English cooking
and efficient service in a village inn.
Lunch: 12-2; from £14.50 and à la carte
Dinner: 7-9; from £14.50 and à la carte
Credit cards 1 3

### PUBS

#### Bird in Hand
Main St, Blidworth
☎ (0623) 792356
There are lovely views across Sherwood
Forest from this unpretentious village local
which offers some imaginative vegetarian
dishes are included on the short, value-for-
money menu. Beers include Mansfield
Riding and Old Baily. There is a well kept
garden with a play area and children are
welcome inside the pub if eating.
Open: 11am-11pm; Sunday 12-3pm, 7-
10.30pm
Bar food: Monday to Saturday 12-3pm,
5.30-8.30pm

#### Waggon and Horses
Gypsy La, Bleasby, nr Southwell
☎ (0602) 830283
Good value pub fare, in an attractive and
peacefully located village pub, consists of
substantial, homely dishes. Theakston ►B,
Old Peculiar, Home Bitter and McEwans
Export are on draught and morning coffee is
available. Children are welcome anywhere
and there is an outdoor play area.
Open: 11am-3pm, 6-11pm; Sunday 12-
3pm, 7-10.30pm
Bar food: Tuesday to Sunday 12-2pm

#### Cross Keys
Epperstone, nr Southwell
☎ (0602) 663033
A good village 'local' atmosphere prevails at
this popular old inn. The food is home
cooked and pies are particularly popular.
Kimberley Classic Ale is dispensed from a
handpump; there are also cask conditioned
bitter and mild and a good range of single
malt whiskies. Children are welcome in the
family room and there is a spacious lawned
garden.
Open: 11.45am-2.30pm, 6-11pm; Sunday
12-2.30pm, 7-10.30pm. Closed Monday
lunchtime.
Bar food:

#### Reindeer Inn
Main St, Hoveringham, nr Southwell
☎ (0602) 663629
Food and wine are taken seriously at this
17th-century inn overlooking the cricket
pitch with some excellent choices available
to discerning evening diners. The lunchtime
snack menu is imaginative too and, as well
as Marstons Bitter, Pedigree and a guest
beer, there are quality wines and unusual
whiskies to enjoy. Children not permitted in
public bar.
Open: 12-3pm, 5-11pm (opens 5.30pm on
Monday); Sunday 12-3pm, 7-10.30pm.
Closed Monday lunchtime except Bank
Holidays
Bar food: Tuesday to Saturday 12-2pm;
Sunday 12-3pm
Restaurant: Tuesday to Saturday 7-9.30pm

#### Cross Keys
Upton
☎ (0636) 813269
Heavily beamed ceilings, a winter log fire
and tasteful furnishings characterise this
agreeable old pub. There is an extensive list
of wines by the bottle and glass, and beers
include Marstons Pedigree, Boddingtons
Bitter, Batemans ►►►B and Brakspears
Bitter. An interesting selection of home-
made dishes is available. Children are
welcome in the family room and restaurant
and there is an outdoor play area.
Open: 11.30am-2.30pm, 5-11pm; Sunday
12-2.30, 7-10.30pm
Bar food: 11.30-2.30pm, 6-10pm; Sunday
12-2pm, 7-10pm
Restaurant: Wednesday to Saturday 7-
10pm, Sunday 12-2pm

# Stratford-upon-Avon

*The name of Stratford-upon-Avon is, of course, recognised the world over as the birthplace of William Shakespeare. As a result, this charming town, with its splendid theatrical tradition, is one of the major tourist attractions in Britain.*

Indeed, its popularity is second only to London in terms of the number of visitors it receives each year. Anyone planning a trip here should definitely try to fit in a day at the races. National Hunt meetings are held from September to June, with the spring and autumn fixtures particularly recommended.

There is always a lovely atmosphere at this delightful little racecourse. Crowds are really enthusiastic about their sport and horses return to a loud ovation in the winner's enclosure. The facilities are good and this is an ideal place to pack a picnic and drive into the centre of the course where there is also a large indoor bar that serves snacks. A good level of competition is maintained throughout the year with the highlight being the two-day meeting which draws the jumps season to a close in early June. There is a terrific end of term feel with a real party mood prevailing. The feature race on the Saturday is the Horse and Hound Cup, a prestigious hunter chase for which runners will travel from far and wide to compete.

## FURTHER INFORMATION

Stratford-on-Avon Racecourse Co Ltd
Luddington Road, Stratford-upon-Avon
Warwicks CV37 9SE
☎ (0789) 267949

## LOCATION AND HOW TO GET THERE

The course is approximately one mile from the town centre via the A439 Evesham road. From the M5 southbound, leave at junction 6 and take the A4538 southwards before turning left onto the A422 for Stratford; from the M5 northbound, leave at junction 7, and head towards Worcester for a short distance before turning right onto the A422 for Stratford; from the M42 south of Birmingham, leave at junction 4 and take the A44 southwards to Stratford.

**Nearest Railway Station:** Stratford upon Avon; there is no connecting bus service to the course on racedays.

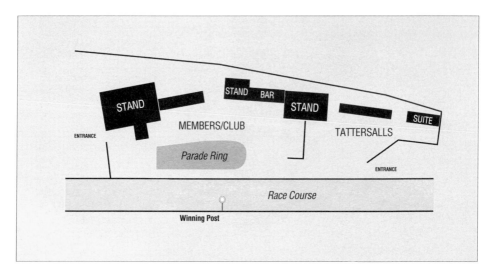

## ADMISSION

All classes of day ticket give access to full betting facilities, including Tote.

**Day Tickets:**

CLUB/MEMBERS ENCLOSURE £11 (£12 for Horse & Hound 2 days) - access to several bars, champagne bar, Annual Members' tea room, snack bars

TATTERSALLS £7.50 (£8 Horse and Hound 2 days) - access to Paddock Suite with restaurant and bars, viewing stand, private boxes

CENTRE COURSE £3.50 - access to bar, snack bar

**Annual membership:** £75, Car label £5

## COURSE FACILITIES

**Banks:**
there are no banks or cashpoint facilities on the course.

**For families:**
picnic area with refreshment kiosk and toilets; children's play area.

---

## CALENDAR OF EVENTS

**February 5**
**March 5**
**March 24**
**April 16**
**May 13** – evening meeting
**May 20** – evening meeting
**June 3-4** – Horse and Hound Meeting; evening meeting on Friday; includes Horse and Hound Cup (final Champion Hunters' Steeplechase)

**August 13**
**September 3** – Coventry Day
**October 15**
**October 27**
**November 22**
**December 28**

*169*

## WHERE TO STAY

### HOTELS

**★★★★ 64% Welcombe**
Warwick Rd
☎ (0789) 295252, telex: 31347, fax: (0789) 414666
76 bedrooms; double B&B from £135
Credit cards 1 2 3 5

**★★★★ 62% Moat House International**
Bridgefoot
☎ (0789) 414411, telex: 311127, fax: (0789) 298589
247 bedrooms; double B&B £120
Credit cards 1 2 3 5

**★★★★ 61% The Shakespeare**
Chapel St
☎ (0789) 294771, fax: (0789) 415411
63 bedrooms; double room £100-£130 (room only)
Credit cards 1 2 3 5

**★★★ 74% Windmill Park Hotel & Country Club**
Warwick Rd
☎ (0789) 731173, fax: (0789) 731131
100 bedrooms; double B&B £97-£115
Credit cards 1 2 3 5

**★★★ 64% Grosvenor House**
Warwick Rd
☎ (0789) 266087
40 bedrooms
Credit cards 1 2 3 5

**★★★ 59% Alveston Manor**
Clopton Bridge
☎ (0789) 204581, telex: 31324, fax: (0789) 414095
108 bedrooms; double room £95-£105 (room only)
Credit cards 1 2 3 5

**★★★ 59% Dukes**
Payton St
☎ (0789) 269300, telex: 31430, fax: (0789) 414700
22 bedrooms; double B&B £69.50-£105
Credit cards 1 2 3 5

**★★★ 59% Forte Posthouse**
Bridgefoot
☎ (0789) 266761, fax: (0789) 414547
60 bedrooms; double room £39.50-£49.50 (room only)
Credit cards 1 2 3 5

**★★★ 56% The White Swan**
Rother St
☎ (0789) 297022, fax: (0789) 268773
37 bedrooms; double room £85 (room only)
Credit cards 1 2 3 5

**★★★ 54% Falcon**
Chapel St
☎ (0789) 205777, telex: 312522, fax: (0789) 414260
73 bedrooms; double B&B £70-£99
Credit cards 1 2 3 4 5

**★★ 71% Stratford House**
Sheep St
☎ (0789) 268288, fax: (0789) 295580
11 bedrooms; double B&B £55-£82
Credit cards 1 2 3 5

**★★ 65% The Coach House Hotel**
16-17 Warwick Rd
☎ (0789) 204109 & 299468, fax: (0789) 415916
10 bedrooms
Credit cards 1 2 3

### Around Stratford-upon-Avon

**★★★ ❀ 75% Salford Hall**
Abbot's Salford
☎ (0386) 871300, fax: (0386) 871301
33 bedrooms; double B&B £95-£120
Credit cards 1 2 3 5

**★★★ 64% Kings Court**
Kings Coughton, Alcester
☎ (0789) 763111, fax: (0789) 400242
19 bedrooms; double B&B £58
Credit cards 1 2 3

**★★ 56% Cherrytrees**
Stratford Rd, Alcester
☎ (0789) 762505
24 bedrooms; double B&B £39.50-£50
Credit cards 1 2 3

**★★★★ 75% Ettington Park**,
Alderminster
☎ (0789) 450123, fax: (0789) 450472
48 bedrooms; double B&B £145-£185
Credit cards 1 2 3 5

**★★★ 67% The Glebe at Barford**
Church St, Barford
☎ (0926) 624218, fax: (0926) 624625
41 bedrooms; double B&B £80-£105
Credit cards 1 2 3 5

**★★★ ❀❀❀ 78% Billesley Manor**
Billesley
☎ (0789) 400888, fax: (0789) 764145
41 bedrooms; double B&B £128-£160
Credit cards 1 2 3 5

**★★★ ❀❀ 79% Charingworth Manor**
Charingworth
☎ (0386) 78555, telex: 333444, fax: (0386) 78353
24 bedrooms; double B&B £110-£210
Credit cards 1 2 3 5

## WHERE TO STAY

### ★★★ 58% Charlecote Pheasant Country
Charlecote
☎ (0789) 470333, fax: (0789) 470222
67 bedrooms; double B&B £85-£125
Credit cards 1 2 3 5

### ★★★ 77% Cotswold House
The Square, Chipping Campden
☎ (0386) 840330, fax: (0386) 840310
15 bedrooms; double B&B £90-£144
Credit cards 1 2 3

### ★★★ ✪ 70% Seymour House
High St, Chipping Campden
☎ (0386) 840429, telex: 31626, fax: (0386) 804369
15 bedrooms; double room £51-£117.50 (room only)
Credit cards 1 2 3

### ★★ 69% Noel Arms
High St, Chipping Campden
☎ (0386) 840317, fax: (0386) 841136
26 bedrooms; double B&B £78-£88
Credit cards 1 2 3

### ★★★ 60% Three Ways
Mickleton
☎ (0386) 438429, fax: (0386) 438118
40 bedrooms; double B&B £68-£72
Credit cards 1 2 3 5

### ★★ 66% Warwick Arms
High St, Warwick
☎ (0926) 492759, fax: (0926) 410587
35 bedrooms; double B&B £60-£80
Credit cards 1 2 3 5

### ★★ 58% Lord Leycester
Jury St, Warwick
☎ (0926) 491481, telex: 41363, fax: (0926) 491561
52 bedrooms; double B&B £69
Credit cards 1 2 3 5

### ★ 63% Penderrick
36 Coten End, Warwick
☎ (0926) 499399 & 497252
7 bedrooms
Credit cards 1 2 3 5

### ★★ 60% Swan House
The Green, Wilmcote
☎ (0789) 267030, fax: (0789) 204875
8 bedrooms; double B&B £50-£60
Credit cards 1 2 3

## BED AND BREAKFAST

### Brook Lodge
192 Alcester Rd
☎ (0789) 295988
Nicely decorated, well kept guesthouse.
7 bedrooms; double B&B £34-£38
Credit cards 1 2 3 5

### Craig Cleeve House
67-69 Shipston Rd
☎ (0789) 296573, fax: (0789) 299452
On the A34 south of Clopton Bridge; bright fresh accommodation and friendly hosts.
15 bedrooms; double B&B £51
Credit cards 1 2 3 5

### Eastnor House Hotel
Shipston Rd
☎ (0789) 268115
On the A34, just 300 metres from the theatre; bright, fresh accommodation.
9 bedrooms; double B&B £39-£52
Credit cards 1 3

### Graveside Barn
Binton
☎ (0789) 750502 & 297000, fax: (0789) 298056
3 bedrooms; double B&B £40-£60
Credit cards 1 2 3

### Highcroft
Banbury Rd
☎ (0789) 296293
Spacious attractive rooms with antique or pine furniture; well equipped.
2 bedrooms; double B&B £30-£35

### Hollies
'The Hollies', 16 Evesham Place
☎ (0789) 266857
Close to the town centre; a popular guesthouse offering a warm welcome.
6 bedrooms.

### Kawartha House
39 Grove Rd
☎ (0789) 204469
Cosy, friendly guesthouse on the Evesham road.
6 bedrooms

### Melita Private Hotel
37 Shipston Rd
☎ (0789) 292432
A friendly family run gueshouse on the A34, close to the river and major attractions.
12 bedrooms; double B&B £45-£58
Credit cards 1 2 3

### Moonraker House
40 Alcester Rd
☎ (0789) 299346, fax: (0789) 295504
Unusual guesthouse, spread over four properties, with attractive bedrooms.
15 bedrooms; double B&B £37-£55
Credit cards 1 2 3

### The Payton Hotel
6 John St
☎ (0789) 266442
Bedrooms are attractively decorated and furnished; friendly, welcoming proprietors.
5 bedrooms; double B&B £48
Credit cards 1 2 3

### Sequoia House Private Hotel
51-53 Shipston Rd
☎ (0789) 268852
Opposite the Royal Shakespeare Theatre; several types of room available, from the cosy cottage annexe to the exceptionally well furnished, luxury no-smoking rooms.
25 bedrooms; double B&B £35-£72
Credit cards 1 2 3 5

### Twelfth Night
Evesham Place
☎ (0789) 414595
Delightfully refurbished Victorian villa; pretty rooms with welcome extra touches.
7 bedrooms; double B&B £38-£52
Credit cards 1 3

### Victoria Spa Lodge
Bishopton Ln
☎ (0789) 267985 & 204728
Victorian Spa Lodge, enjoying peaceful, leafy setting at the side of the Stratford Canal.
7 bedrooms; double B&B from £45
Credit cards 1 3

### Virginia Lodge
12 Evesham Place
☎ (0789) 292157
Well kept, friendly guesthouse close to the centre of Stratford.
7 bedrooms; double B&B £34-£40

### Oxstalls Farm
Warwick Rd
☎ (0789) 205277
This farmhouse provides bright, fresh bedrooms. It is also a thoroughbred stud farm.
18 bedrooms

## WHERE TO STAY

### Around Stratford

**Coughton Cross**
The Old Post House, Alcester Rd, Coughton
☎ (0789) 400166
Generally spacious accommodation.
8 bedrooms

**The Malt House**
Broad Campden, Chipping Campden
☎ (0386) 840295, fax: (0386) 841334
Unique bedrooms with period furniture; set in picturesque village.
3 bedrooms; double B&B £55–£75
Credit cards 1 3

**Woodside Country House**
Langley Rd, Claverdon
☎ (0926) 842446
3 bedrooms; double B&B £28–£34

**Church Farm**
Dorsington
☎ (0789) 720471 & (0831) 504194
An 18th-century house offering comfortable, well equipped bedrooms.
7 bedrooms; double B&B £27–£34

**Whitfield Farm**
Ettington
☎ (0789) 740260
Spacious farmhouse on the A429; comfortable, attractive accommodation.
3 bedrooms; double B&B £26–£32

**Halford Bridge**
Fosse Way, Halford
☎ (0789) 740382
Spacious Cotswold stone road-house, situated on the A429, offering pretty, well equipped bedrooms.
6 bedrooms; double B&B £35–£46
Credit cards 1 3

**Croft**
Haseley Knob
☎ (0926) 484447
Five miles northwest of Warwick.
5 bedrooms; double B&B £33–£42

**Northleigh House**
Five Ways Rd, Hatton
☎ (0926) 484203
Bedrooms have thoughtful extras and high standards are maintained throughout by the friendly proprietress.
6 bedrooms; double B&B £42–£54

**Redlands Farm**
Banbury Rd, Lighthorne
☎ (0926) 651241
Open-air swimming pool is available to guests; Mrs Stanton provides wholesome dishes.
3 bedrooms; double B&B £30–£32

**Newbold Nurseries**
Newbold on Stour
☎ (0789) 450285
Spacious, simply appointed bed and breakfast accommodation.
2 bedrooms; double B&B from £28

**Nolands Farm & Country Restaurant**
Oxhill
☎ (0926) 640309
Set in a tranquil valley, with comfortable bedrooms. Clay pigeon shooting and riding can be arranged nearby.
9 bedrooms; double B&B £30–£44
Credit cards 1 3

**Red Lion Hotel**
Main St, Long Compton
☎ (060884) 221
5 bedrooms; double B&B from £50
Credit cards 1 3

**Shrewley House**
Shrewley
☎ (092684) 2549, fax: (092684) 2216
Charming listed Grade II Georgian farmhouse. Exceptionally wide range of facilities.
9 bedrooms; double B&B £52–£58
Credit cards 1 3

**Bug in the Blanket**
Castle Farm, Studley
☎ (0527) 854275, fax: (0527) 854897
Quirky but pleasing farmhouse with good range of facilities.
2 bedrooms; double B&B from £35

**The Old Rectory**
Vicarage Ln, Sherbourne
☎ (0926) 624562
Tastefully restored house offering very comfortable accommodation and home-cooked food.
14 bedrooms; double B&B £39–£50
Credit cards 1 2 3

**Austin House**
96 Emscote Rd, Warwick
☎ (0926) 493583
Guesthouse offering modest accommodation.
6 bedrooms; double B&B £27–£33
Credit cards 1 2 3 5

**Avon**
7 Emscote Rd, Warwick
☎ (0926) 491367
Clean, simply appointed bed and breakfast accommodation.
7 bedrooms; double B&B £30

**Cambridge Villa Private Hotel**
20A Emscote Rd, Warwick
☎ (0926) 491169
Simply appointed bedrooms; enthusiastic Italian owner.
16 bedrooms
Credit cards 1 3

**Tudor House**
West St, Warwick
☎ (0926) 495447, fax: (0926) 492948
Tudor house retaining much wattle and daub and timbers; cosy bedrooms.
11 bedrooms; double B&B from £54
Credit cards 1 2 3

**Swan Cottage**
The Green, Wilmcote
☎ (0789) 266480
Original beams, flagstone floors; warm welcome given to guests from the proprietors.
3 bedrooms; double B&B £28–£37

**Whitchurch Farm**
Whitchurch, Wimpstone
☎ (0789) 450275
Lovely Georgian farmhouse part of a working farm; bedrooms recently improved with good en suite facilities.
3 bedrooms; double B&B £28–£34

### CAMPSITES

▶ **Island Meadow Caravan Park**
The Mill House, Aston Cantlow
☎ (0789) 488273
Quarter of a mile west of Aston Cantlow; pitch price from £5 per night.

▶▶▶ **Ranch Caravan Park**
Honeybourne
☎ (0386) 830744
In the Vale of Evesham 2m from B4035; pitch price from £4.50 per night.

## WHERE TO EAT

### RESTAURANTS

### ❋ Hunter's Lodge
High St, Broadway
☎ (0386) 853247
Oak beams, open fires, a splendid summer garden, an informal atmosphere and simple, tasty food.
Lunch: 12-2; from £12.85
Dinner: 7-9.45; from £15
Credit cards 1 2 3 5

### PUBS

### Bell
Alderminster
☎ (0789) 450414
An adventurous menu, a high standard of cooking and a wine list to match are the main attractions of the 17th-century pub. Beers include Marston Pedigree and Flowers Best and Original. Children are welcome.
Open: 12-2.30pm, 7-11pm; Sunday 12-2.30pm, 7-10.30pm
Bar food: 12-2pm, 7-9.30pm; Sunday 12-1.45pm, 7-9pm
Restaurant: times as bar food

### Ferry
Alveston
☎ (0789) 269883
Friendly village-centre pub offering well prepared and promptly served food at a range of prices, all good value for money. Theakston Best, Bass, Wadworth 6X and Flowers Original are on sale, along with a selection of wines. Children over 5 years old are welcome.
Open: 11am-2.30pm, 6-11pm; Sunday 12-2.30pm, 7-10.30
Bar food: 11.45am-2pm, 6.30-9pm; Sunday 12-2pm

### Kings Head
Aston Cantlow
☎ (0789) 488242
This is an attractive and unspoilt half-timbered pub with a small, well tended garden. Beers include Marston Pedigree, Flowers IPA, Boddingtons Bitter and Mild and Murphy's Stout; there is a reasonable selection of wines and a tasty range of bar meals. No children under 14 in the bar.
Open: 12-2.30pm, 7-11pm; Sunday 12-2.30pm, 7-10.30pm
Bar food: as opening hours, except Sunday and Monday evenings

### Broom Tavern
High St, Broom, nr Bidford-on-Avon
☎ (0789) 773656
This busy village pub is popular for its wide choice of well prepared food, served promptly in unstinting portions. Beers include Bass, Flowers Best and Murphy's Stout and there is an extensive wine list. Children are welcome and the small lawned area outside has a bouncy castle.
Open: 11am-3pm, 6.30-11pm (opens at 6pm on Saturday); Sunday 11am-3pm, 7-10.30pm
Bar food: 12-2pm, 7-10pm
Restaurant: as bar food

### Chequers
91 Main Rd, Ettington
☎ (0789) 740387
This vine-clad village pub is a friendly meeting place offering skilfully prepared food and a choice of beers which includes Adnams Bitter, Marston Pedigree, Everard Tiger and Beacon and guest ales. Children are welcome and there is a play area.
Open: 10.30am-2.30pm, 6-11pm; Sunday 12-2.30pm, 7-10.30pm
Bar food: 12-1.45pm, 6.30-9.30pm (until 9.45 on Friday and Saturday); Sunday 12-1.45pm, 7-9.30pm

### Howard Arms
Lower Green, Ilmington
☎ (0608) 82226
Inviting stone-built pub overlooking the village green with old beams, stone floor and open fires. Good home-cooked food is on offer in generous portions and there is an extensive wine list. Beers include Marston Pedigree, Flowers Best and guest ales. Children are welcome.
Open: 11am-2.30pm, 7-11pm (opens 6.30pm in summer); Sunday 12-3pm, 7-10.30pm
Bar food: 12-2pm, 7-9pm (9.30pm on Friday and Saturday); Sunday 12-2pm
Restaurant: Tuesday to Saturday 7-9pm; Sunday 12-2pm
Accommodation: double B&B £40

### Navigation
Old Warwick Rd, Lapworth
☎ (0564) 783337
With a well-tended garden beside the Grand Union Canal, this is a popular pub providing good, substantial bar meals and barbecues on summer Sunday lunchtimes. Beers include Mitchells & Butlers Mild and Brew XI, Bass and a guest beer.
Open: 11am-2.30pm, 5.30-11pm; Saturday 11am-3pm, 6-11pm; Sunday 12-3pm, 7-10.30pm
Bar food: 12-2pm, 6-9pm; Sunday 12-2pm, 7-9pm

### Fleur de Lys
Lapworth St, Lowsonford, nr Henley-in-Arden
☎ (0564) 782431
This long, cottage-like pub has a pleasant waterside garden with access to the Stratford-upon-Avon canal. Visitors with young children will feel particularly welcome as there is a family room with toys and high chairs, and there is a play area in the garden. Good value food is expertly cooked and served promptly and, in addition to the real ales, there is a wide selection of wines.
Open: 11am-11pm; Sunday 12-3pm, 7-10.30pm
Bar food: 12-9.30pm; Sunday 12-2pm, 7-9.30pm

### White Bear
High St, Shipston-on-Stour
☎ (0608) 661558
Comfortable old pub in the centre of this small market town, offering a high standard of cooking and some unusual choices from the menu. Beers include Bass, Mitchells & Butlers Mild and Brew XI and some guest beers; there is a wide choice of malt whiskies. Children are welcome.
Open: 11am-3pm, 6-11pm; Sunday 12-3pm, 7-10.30pm
Bar food: 12-2pm, 6.30-9.30pm (until 10pm on Friday and Saturday); no food on Sunday
Restaurant: times as bar food
Accommodation: double B&B £47

### Royal Oak
Whatcote, nr Shipston-on-Stour
☎ (0295) 680319
Thick stone walls and tiny windows testify to this interesting pub's great age, parts of which date back to 1168. The three alternating real ales are Castle Eden Ale, Marstons Pedigree and Boddingtons Bitter, and Murphy's Stout is also available; there is also an extensive wine list to accompany the good bar meals. Children are only allowed into the pub if they are eating, but there is an outdoor play area.
Open: 10.30am-2.30pm, 6-11pm; Sunday 12-3pm, 7-10.30pm
Bar food: 12-2pm, 6-10pm; Sunday 12-2pm, 7-10pm

# Taunton

*This small West Country course has done much to restore its somewhat tarnished reputation in the past few years. As is the case at most venues in this area, there has always been an extremely friendly atmosphere, with plenty of jolly local farmers in attendance.*

It is only recently, however, that facilities have been upgraded to a decent standard. The substantial amount of money that was designated for refurbishments has thankfully been well spent. The range of bars and hospitality suites has been extended and the Tattersalls Enclosure boasts a new restaurant whose glass front overlooks the track, similar to the design found at many greyhound stadiums.

The course is itself not unlike an elongated version of a greyhound track. There are two long straights, each with four fences in them, and a pair of extremely tight bends. Their sharp nature caused so many complaints that they are now banked, the camber helping runners to negotiate the turns safely. Even so, this is not a favourite circuit of many of the top National Hunt trainers, with the notable exception of Martin Pipe. He trains nearby, just outside Wellington, and it is very rare for him to leave any of the dozen meetings here empty-handed. The best fixtures are in late November and mid-March with the latter card featuring a valuable handicap hurdle and long-distance chase.

## FURTHER INFORMATION

Taunton Racecourse
Orchard Portman, Taunton TA3 7BL
☎ (0823) 337172

## LOCATION AND HOW TO GET THERE

The course is two miles south of Taunton on the B3170 Honiton-Corfe road. Leave the M5 at junction 25 if travelling from north or east, junction 26 if travelling from the south. Take A38 into Taunton and continue, avoiding the town centre. At traffic lights opposite Sainsbury's take the B3170 Honiton/Corfe road, crossing the motorway to reach the course. From the A303 take the A358 at Ilminster and continue to Taunton, then follow directions above.

**Nearest Railway Station:** Taunton; there is no connecting bus service to the course.

## ADMISSION

Bookmakers and Tote available to all classes of ticket holders; NARBOL shop situated in paddock area not available to Centre Course.

**Day Tickets:**

1993 prices not available at time of going to press, those quoted below were in operation during 1992.

CLUB £10 - access to Members' bars, buffet

PADDOCK £7.50 - access to bars, restaurant, buffet, hospitality suites

CENTRE COURSE £4 - access to Centre Course bar and buffet

**Annual membership:** £60 single £98 double

## COURSE FACILITIES

**Banks:**
there are no banks or cashpoint facilities on the course.

**For families:**
picnic area with refreshment kiosk and toilets

## CALENDAR OF EVENTS

**April 15** – evening meeting
**April 22** – evening meeting
**May 7** – Arab Horse Racing
**September 22**
**October 13**

**November 10**
**November 24**
**December 8**
**December 29**

## WHERE TO STAY

### HOTELS

**★★★ (RED) ❀❀❀ Castle**
Castle Green
☎ (0823) 271671, fax: (0823) 336066
33 bedrooms; double B&B £99-£180
Credit cards 1 2 3 5

**★★★ 66% Rumwell Manor**
Rumwell
☎ (0823) 461902, fax: (0823) 254861
20 bedrooms; double B&B £70-£85
Credit cards 1 2 3

**★★★ 63% Forte Posthouse**
Deane Gate Av
☎ (0823) 332222, fax: (0823) 332266
97 bedrooms; double room £39.50-£49.50
(room only)
Credit cards 1 2 3 5

**★★★ 59% The County**
East St
☎ (0823) 337651, fax: (0823) 334517
66 bedrooms; double room £75-£90 (room only)
Credit cards 1 2 3 5

**★★ 65% Corner House**
Park St
☎ (0823) 284683 & 272665, fax: (0823) 323464
33 bedrooms
Credit cards 1 3

**★★ 64% Falcon**
Henlade
☎ (0823) 442502, fax: (0823) 442670
11 bedrooms; double B&B £45-£55
Credit cards 1 2 3

### Around Taunton

**★★★ 70% Walnut Tree Inn**
North Petherton, Bridgwater
☎ (0278) 662255, telex: 46529, fax: (0278) 663946
28 bedrooms; double B&B £66-£92
Credit cards 1 2 3 5

**★★ 64% Friarn Court**
37 St Mary, Bridgwater
☎ (0278) 452859, fax: (0278) 452988
12 bedrooms; double B&B £40-£69.90
Credit cards 1 2 3 5

**★★ 62% Shrubbery**
Ilminster
☎ (0460) 52108, telex: 46379, fax: (0460) 53660
13 bedrooms; double B&B £40-£80
Credit cards 1 2 3 4 5

**Forte Travelodge**
Ilminster
☎ (0460) 53748, Central Reservations: (0800) 850950
32 bedrooms; double room £31.95 (room only)
Credit cards 1 2 3

**Roadchef Lodge**
Tauton Deane Motorway Service Area, Trull
☎ (0823) 332228, fax: (0823) 338131
39 bedrooms; double room from £35 (room only)
Credit cards 1 2 3 4 5

**★★ 59% Beambridge**
Sampford Arundel, Wellington
☎ (0823) 672223
18 bedrooms; double B&B from £41.50
Credit cards 1 3

**★★ 69% The Belfry Country Hotel**
Yarcombe
☎ (040486) 234 & 588, fax: (040486) 579
6 bedrooms; double B&B £59-£63
Credit cards 1 3 4

### BED AND BREAKFAST

**Meryan House Hotel**
Bishop's Hull
☎ (0823) 337445
Charming period residence; graceful, attractive decoration; early booking strongly recommended.
12 bedrooms; double B&B £45-£49
Credit cards 1 3

**Higher Dipford Farm**
Trull
☎ (0823) 275770 & 257916
Grade II listed farmhouse; friendly proprietors and lots of character.
3 bedrooms; double B&B from £50
Credit cards 2

**Brookfield**
16 Wellington Rd
☎ (0823) 272786
Comfortable warm relaxed guesthouse.
8 bedrooms; double B&B £25-£30

### Around Taunton

**Frog Street Farm**
Beercrocombe
☎ (0823) 480430
Still a working farm; attractive Somerset longhouse, clad in wisteria; friendly, cosy atmosphere.
3 bedrooms; double B&B from £50

**Whittles Farm**
Beercrocombe
☎ (0823) 480301
Ivey clad period house with welcoming hosts and attractive en suite bedrooms.
3 bedrooms; double B&B £40-£42

**The Old Bakery**
Burrowbridge
☎ (082369) 234
Bedrooms are simple, clean and comfortable; warm welcoming family.
6 bedrooms
Credit cards 1 3

**Watermead**
83 High St, Chard
☎ (0460) 62834
Warm welcome; simply furnished bedrooms.
9 bedrooms; double B&B £30-£32

## WHERE TO STAY

### Old Manor Farmhouse
Norton Fitzwarren
☎ (0823) 289801
Warm and welcoming, relaxed atmosphere;
very well equipped bedrooms.
7 bedrooms; double B&B £42-£46
Credit cards 1 2 3 5

### Gamlins Farm
Greenham, Wellington
☎ (0823) 672596
Well presented farmhouse offering good
value for money.
3 bedrooms; double B&B £30-£36

### Pinksmoor Mill House
Pinksmoor, Wellington
☎ (0823) 672361
An old mill dating back to 13th century;
now a working farm; warm and welcoming.
3 bedrooms; double B&B from £32

### Higher House
West Bagborough
☎ (0823) 432996
Superb views; comfortable bedrooms, a
charming place to stay.
6 bedrooms; double B&B £38-£53
Credit cards 1 3

## CAMPSITES

### ►► Toulton Farm
Cothelstone
☎ (082345) 458
North of Taunton

### ►►► Holly Bush Park
Culmhead
☎ (082342) 515
South of Taunton; pitch price from £4.50
per night.

### ►►►► Camping & Caravanning Club Site
The Turnpike, Howley
☎ (0460) 66036 & (0203) 694995
South of Taunton between the A303 and
A30; pitch priced from £10.30 per night.

### ►►► Gamlins Farm Caravan Park
Gamlins Farm, Greenham, Wellington
☎ (0823) 672596
Situated off the A38 on the Greenham road;
pitch price from £6.50

## WHERE TO EAT

### RESTAURANT

### Around Taunton

### ✿ Nightingales
Bath House Farm, Lower West Hatch
☎ (0823) 480806 & 480392
Imaginative dishes, relaxed unpretentious
service, in a simply decorated former cider
house.
Dinner only: 7-9.30 from £19
Credit cards 1 3

### PUBS

### Around Taunton

### Rising Sun
Knapp, North Curry
☎ (0823) 490436
This whitewashed Somerset longhouse,
dating from 1480, is tucked away in a
remote village near the Somerset Levels.
Exmoor Ale, Boddingtons and Bass are on
tap and there is a good wine list to
complement the constantly changing menu,
which specialises in fresh fish dishes and
represents good value for money. There is a
room where children are allowed and there
are gardens at the front and rear of the pub.
Open: 11.30am-2.30pm, 6.30-11pm;
Sunday 12-3pm, 7-10.30pm
Bar food: 12-2pm, 7.30-9.30pm. Only
ploughmans' are available on Sundays.
Restaurant: 12-2pm, 7-9.30pm. Only a
traditional roast on Sunday

### Greyhound
Staple Fitzpaine
☎ (0823) 480227
A good choice of beers is available in this
former hunting lodge dating from 1640, and
a good variety of food is on offer in both the
bar and the restaurant. Children are
welcome anywhere and there is a play area
outside.
Open: 11am-3pm, 5-11pm
Bar food: 12-2pm, 7-10pm
Restaurant: as bar food

### Rose & Crown
Wood Hill, Stoke St Gregory
☎ (0823) 490296
This 300-year-old pub (said to be haunted)
offers interesting home-cooked bar meals,
with an emphasis on fresh fish. Beers
include Eldridge Pope Royal Oak and
Thomas Hardy Country Bitter, Exmoor Ale
and Toby Bitter. Children are only allowed in
the restaurant, where half-portions are
available.
Open: 11am-2.30pm, 7-11pm
Bar food: 12-2pm, 7-10pm
Restaurant: as bar food
Accommodation: double room £34

# Thirsk

*A North Yorkshire track which is probably unrivalled in the attractiveness of its setting. The picturesque Hambleton Hills form a gorgeous backdrop to this pretty little course which is situated in real James Herriot country.*

Given the natural beauty of the surroundings and the wonderfully relaxed atmosphere that pervades the air here, it is a pity that racing is restricted to just 13 fixtures on the Flat. The most popular of these meetings are in May and August when the sun is usually guaranteed to be shining.

The track is a left-handed oval circuit of a mile and a quarter. There is a slightly undulating run in of half a mile with an additional spur to provide a straight six-furlong course (horses drawn high have a big advantage in sprints). The track is deceptively sharp and a good jockey can sometimes steal a race by establishing a big early lead - top northern rider Mark Birch is a past master at this art round here. The standard of competition is fair and there are a couple of significant contests, the Classic Trial in mid-April and the Thirsk Hunt Cup, a competitive handicap that is run at the start of May.

### FURTHER INFORMATION

Thirsk Racecourse Ltd
Station Road, Thirsk, North Yorkshire YO7 1QL
☎ (0845) 522276

### LOCATION AND HOW TO GET THERE

The course is to the west of Thirsk on the A61, which links directly with the A1 in the west and the A19 in the east.
**Nearest Railway Station:** Thirsk; there is no connecting bus service, but the course is just ten minutes walk from the station.

---

## ADMISSION

All classes of day ticket give access to full betting facilities, including Tote.

**Day tickets:**
Accompanied children under 16 are admitted free

MEMBERS £12 – access to restaurants, bars, boxes, private rooms

TATTERSALLS £7, senior citizens £3.50 – access to bars and self-service restaurant

SILVER RING £3, senior citizens £1.50 – access to bars and self-service buffet

NUMBER 3 RING/COURSE £2, £6 for car with up to four adults and all children

**Annual membership:** £65, Associate (man/woman and one other member of family) £110, junior (17-21) £35 – includes exchange days with other northern racecourses, 10 days free entry to Yorkshire county cricket matches and free entry to the Arab Horse Society Meeting on September 18.

## COURSE FACILITIES

**Banks:**
there are no banks or cashpoint facilities on the course.

**For families:**
picnic area in Number 3 Ring with refreshment kiosk and toilets; supervised creche; baby changing facilities

---

## CALENDAR OF EVENTS

| | |
|---|---|
| April 15-16 | July 29-30 |
| April 30 | August 8 – evening meeting |
| May 13-14 | August 26 |
| June 14 | September 3 |
| July 15 | September 17 – Arab Horse Society Meeting |

## WHERE TO STAY

### HOTELS

**★★ 62% Three Tuns Hotel**
Market Place
☎ (0845) 523124, fax: (0845) 526126
11 bedrooms; double B&B £55-£60
Credit cards 1 2 3 5

**★ 58% Old Red House**
Station Rd
☎ (0845) 524383
6 bedrooms; double B&B £30-£36
Credit cards 2 3 5

### Around Thirsk

**★★ 62% Motel Leeming**
Great North Rd, Bedale
☎ (0677) 422122, fax: (0677) 424507
40 bedrooms; double B&B £49
Credit cards 1 2 3 5

**★★ 70% Hawnby**
Hawnby
☎ (04396) 202, fax: (04396) 417
6 bedrooms; double B&B from £70
Credit cards 1 3

**★★ 61% White Rose**
Leeming Bar
☎ (0677) 422707 & 424941, fax: (0677) 425123
18 bedrooms; double B&B from £42
Credit cards 1 2 3 5

**★★★ 72% Solberge Hall**
Newby Wiske, Northallerton
☎ (0609) 779191, telex: 61686, fax: (0609) 780472
25 bedrooms; double B&B £75-£100
Credit cards 1 2 3 5

**★★★ 66% Sundial**
Darlington Rd, Northallerton
☎ (0609) 780525, fax: (0609) 780491
28 bedrooms; double room £45-£69
Credit cards 1 2 3 5

**★★ 69% The Golden Lion**
Market Place, Northallerton
☎ (0609) 777411, fax: (0609) 773250
26 bedrooms; double room from £75 (room only)
Credit cards 1 2 3 5

**★★ 64% Nags Head Country Inn**
Pickhill
☎ (0845) 567391, fax: (0845) 567217
15 bedrooms
Credit cards 1 3

**★★★ 67% Ripon Spa**
Park St, Ripon
☎ (0765) 602172, telex: 57780, fax: (0765) 690770
40 bedrooms; double B&B £69.60-£90
Credit cards 1 2 3 5

**Market Place, Ripon**
☎ (0765) 602202, telex: 57515, fax: (0765) 600321
33 bedrooms; double B&B £50
Credit cards 1 2 3 5

**★★ ✿ 73% Sheppard's**
Church Farm, Front St, Sowerby
☎ (0845) 523655, fax: (0845) 524720
8 bedrooms
Credit cards 1 3

**★★ 65% The Angel Inn**
Long St, Topcliffe
☎ (0845) 577237, fax: (0845) 578000
15 bedrooms; double B&B £50-£60
Credit cards 1 3

### BED AND BREAKFAST

**Blairgowrie Country House**
Crakehall, Bedale
☎ (0748) 811377
Charming farmhouse with friendly welcoming atmosphere; bedrooms are comfortable, pretty and tastefully decorated.
2 bedrooms; double B&B from £30

**Forresters Arms Hotel**
Kilburn
☎ (03476) 386
Attractive inn, dating from the 12th-century, with particularly well furnished bedrooms.
8 bedrooms
Credit cards 1 3

**Alverton**
26 South Pde, Northallerton
☎ (0609) 776207
Attractive and comfortable Victorian terraced house.
5 bedrooms; double B&B £33.50-£37

**Porch House**
68 High St, Northallerton
☎ (0609) 779831
Historic house, with beams and other original features.
5 bedrooms; double B&B £42
Credit cards 1 3

**Windsor**
56 South Pde, Northallerton
☎ (0609) 774100
Thoughtfully furnished and equipped bedrooms.
6 bedrooms; double B&B £36
Credit cards 1 3

**Old Farmhouse Country Hotel**
Raskelf
☎ (0347) 21971
Delightful cottage-style hotel retaining much of its original character; renowned for its hospitality and delicious food.
10 bedrooms; double B&B £67-£80

### CAMPSITES

**►►► Sowerby Caravan Park**
Sowerby
☎ (0845) 522753
One mile from Thirsk on the Sowerby Road; pitch price from £4.75

**► Hutton Bonville Caravan Park**
Church Ln, Hutton Bonville, Northallerton
☎ (060981) 416
On the A167; pitch price from £5.50 per night.

**►►► Sleningford Water Mill Caravan Site**
North Stainley
☎ (0765) 635201
Adajacent to A6108; pitch price from £7.50 per night.

**►► Cotel Ghyll Caravan Park**
Osmotherley
☎ (060983) 425
Situated off A19; pitch price from £5 per night.

## WHERE TO EAT

### RESTAURANTS

### Around Thirsk

#### ⚜⚜ McCoys (Tontine Inn)
Staddle Bridge
☎ (060982) 671
Stylish cooking in a relaxed, oriental setting of palms and parasols.
Lunch: 12-2
Dinner: 7-11
Credit cards 1 2 3 5

### PUBS

### Around Thirsk

#### Crab and Lobster
Asenby
☎ (0845) 577286
This white, thatched cottage with vines and shuttered windows is just outside Asenby on a fairly busy road. The food is of excellent quality and there is an extensive wine list. Draught ales include Youngers and Theakstons and scrumpy is also available. Children are welcome, with the 'snug' area available for families.
Open: 11.30am-3pm, 6.30-11pm; Sunday 12-3
Bar food: 12-2pm, 7-9.30 or 10pm
Restaurant: 11.30am-3pm, 6.30-11pm; Sunday 12-3 (book six weeks in advance for weekends)

#### Abbey Inn
Coxwold
☎ (03476) 204
An attractive old Yorkshire stone pub near to Byland Abbey, offering very tasty, good value meals. Draught beers include EP Traditional, Theakstons and Guinness and there is a good wine list. Children are welcome in the pub and there is a large garden.
Open: 10am-2.30pm, 6.30-11pm, but closed Sunday evening and all day Monday.
Bar food: as opening times

#### Fauconberg Arms
Coxwold
☎ (03476) 214
Pretty Yorkshire stone pub in the centre of the village, with a relaxed and friendly atmosphere. The fresh, home-made food is above average and includes some interesting choices. Draught beers include John Smiths, Theakstons, Tetley and Guinness and there is a large wine list. Children are welcome.
Open: 11am-3pm, 6.30-11pm; Sunday 12-3pm, 7-10.30pm
Bar food: 12-2pm, 7-9.45pm
Accommodation: double B&B £40

#### Three Tuns
Osmotherley
☎ (0609) 83301
The front of this very pretty 17th-century stone pub is covered with vines and flowers and there is a lovely walled garden. Beers on draught include Youngers No3 and Scotch, Theakstons Best, Old Peculiar and XB, and Beamish, and there is a good range of wines on offer. The food is of a high standard and represents good value. Children are welcome and the 'snug' is designated a family room.
Open: 12-2.30pm, 7-11pm; Sunday 12-3pm, 7-10.30pm
Bar food: 12-2.30pm, 7-9.30pm; Sunday 12-2 only.
Restaurant: as bar food
Accommodation: double B&B £50

#### Nags Head
Pickhill
☎ (0845) 567391
Generous portions of high quality food are on offer here as well as a list of 106 wines and draught beers which include Youngers, Theakstons Old Peculiar, XB and Best, and Hambleton (a local brew). Children are welcome and there is an outdoor play area.
Open: 11am-11pm; Sunday 12-3pm, 7-10.30pm
Bar food: 12-2pm, 6-10pm; Sunday 12-2pm, 7-9.30pm
Restaurant: Monday to Saturday 7-9.30pm; Sunday 12-2pm
Accommodation: double B&B £42

#### Buck Inn
Thornton Watlass
☎ (0677) 422461
The original old stone bar dates from the 17th century and is very cosy. An interesting range of meals is offered and beers include Theakstons, Tetleys, Beamish and Carlton (LA) as well as a weekly guest beer. Whisky drinkers can choose between 45 single malts.
Open: 11am-2.30pm, 6-11pm; Sunday 12-3, 7-10.30pm
Bar food: 12-2pm, 6.45-9.30pm; Sunday 12-2, 7-9.30pm

#### Wombwell Arms
Wass
☎ (03476) 280
Dating from the 17th century, this whitewashed stone pub in the village centre offers good value, substantial meals and a good range of quality wines. Draught beers include Camerons Traditional Bitter, Everards Old Original and Guinness. Children are welcome and there is a separate family room, though children under 8 years are not accommodated overnight.
Open: 12-2.30pm, 7-11pm; Sunday 12-3, 7-10.30pm
Bar food: 12-2pm, 7-10pm
Accommodation: double B&B from £43

# Towcester

*This is, without any shadow of a doubt, the stiffest National Hunt course in Britain. The track is a mile and three quarters in circumference with the last mile providing a punishing test of stamina.*

There is a steep climb before the turn into the home straight which then rises steadily all the way to the winning post. On heavy ground, long-distance contests can become a gruelling slog with the runners almost appearing to be moving in slow motion in the closing stages. A jockey even commented once that he was travelling so slowly that he could have finished quicker by jumping off his horse and dragging it to the line.

This is not said to put anyone off making a visit to this charming rural track. Quite the contrary, in fact, as there is no better venue at which to witness the total embodiment of the spirit of National Hunt racing. Winners, both equine and human, have to show real courage and determination in order to triumph here and that is why this course ranks as a firm favourite among jumping enthusiasts. The facilities are perfectly adequate, if somewhat cramped, and a fantastic view of the action can be obtained from the upper reaches of the quaint old grandstand.

## FURTHER INFORMATION

Towcester Race Club
Easton Neston, Towcester, Northants NN12 7HS
☎ (0327) 53414 on racedays; 50672 at other times

## LOCATION AND HOW TO GET THERE

The course is half a mile south of Towcester on the old Watling Street. Leave the M1 at junction 15A and take the A5.
**Nearest Railway Stations:** Northampton (9 miles) or Milton Keynes (12 miles); there are no connecting bus services to the course, but there are services from both towns' bus stations to Towcester town centre.

## ADMISSION

All classes of day ticket give access to full betting facilities, including Tote.

**Day tickets:**
CLUB £10 – access to bar, restaurant, snack bar, boxes

TATTERSALLS £7 – access to bar and buffet

COURSE £3, or £12 for a car and occupants – access to bar and snacks

**Annual Membership:** £60

## COURSE FACILITIES

**Banks:**
there are no banks or cashpoint facilites on the course.

**For families:**
picnic area with refreshment kiosk and toilets; children's play area.

## CALENDAR OF EVENTS

| | | |
|---|---|---|
| January 7 | May 2 | November 10 |
| February 3 | May 9 – evening meeting | November 19 |
| February 15 | May 27 – evening meeting | December 3 |
| March 10 | July 2 – Arab Horse Racing | December 15 |
| April 2 | July 16 – Arab Horse Racing | |
| April 4 | October 5 | |

## WHERE TO STAY

### HOTELS

**★★★ 64% Saracens Head**
219 Watling St
☎ (0327) 50414, fax: (0327) 359879
21 bedrooms

**Forte Travelodge**
☎ (0327) 359105, Central Reservations:
(0800) 850950
33 bedrooms; double room £31.95 (room only)
Credit cards 1 2 3

### Around Towcester

**★★★ 66% Buckingham Lodge**
Ring Rd South, Buckingham
☎ (0280) 822622, fax: (0280) 823074
70 bedrooms; double B&B £56-£79
Credit cards 1 2 3

**★★★ 64% Heyford Manor**
The High St, Flore
☎ (0327) 349022, telex: 312437, fax:
(0327) 349017
54 bedrooms; double B&B £50-£78
Credit cards 1 2 3 5

**★★★ 65% Hatton Court**
Bullington End, Hanslope
☎ (0908) 510044, fax: (0908) 510945
20 bedrooms
Credit cards 1 2 3 5

**★★★★ 65% Stakis Country Court**
100 Watering Ln, Collingtree, Northampton
☎ (0604) 700666, telex: 312523, fax:
(0604) 702850
144 bedrooms; double room £94 (room only)
Credit cards 1 2 3 4 5

**★★★★ 59% Swallow**
Eagle Dr, Northampton
☎ (0604) 768700, telex: 31562, fax:
(0604) 769011
122 bedrooms; double B&B from £99
Credit cards 1 2 3 5

**★★★ 66% Northampton Moat House**
Silver Street, Town Centre, Northampton
☎ (0604) 22441, fax: (0604) 230614
142 bedrooms; double B&B £70-£93
Credit cards 1 2 3 4 5

**★★★ 63% Westone Moat House**
Ashley Way, Weston Favell
☎ (0604) 406262, telex: 312587, fax:
(0604) 415023
66 bedrooms; double B&B £76.50
Credit cards 1 2 3 5

**★★ 69% Lime Trees**
8 Langham Place, Barrack Rd, Northampton
☎ (0604) 32188, fax: (0604) 233012
21 bedrooms
Credit cards 1 2 3 5

**★★ 65% Thorplands Toby**
Talavera Way, Round Spinney, Northampton
☎ (0604) 494241
30 bedrooms
Credit cards 1 2 3 5

**★★ 60% Grand**
Gold St, Northampton
☎ (0604) 250511
62 bedrooms; double B&B £60
Credit cards 1 2 3 5

**★★★ 69% Crossroads**
Weedon
☎ (0327) 40354, fax: (0327) 40849
50 bedrooms; double B&B £59.50-£69.50
Credit cards 1 2 3 5

**★★ 66% Heart Of England**
Daventry Rd, Weedon
☎ (0327) 40335
12 bedrooms
Credit cards 1 2 3 5

**★★ 61% Globe**
High St, Weedon
☎ (0327) 40336, fax: (0327) 349058
17 bedrooms; double B&B £38-£42
Credit cards 1 2 3 5

### BED AND BREAKFAST

**Mill Farm**
Gayhurst
☎ (0908) 611489
Attractive 17th-century farmhouse with warm, comfortable bedrooms.
3 bedrooms; double B&B £30-£35

**Poplars Hotel**
Cross Street, Moulton
☎ (0604) 643983
Quiet village location; comfortable bedrooms and personal service are provided.
21 bedrooms; double B&B £45
Credit cards 1 3

**Hollington**
22 Abington Grove, Northampton
☎ (0604) 32584
Predominantly commercial guesthouse; modest accommodation, and friendly owners.
7 bedrooms; double B&B £25-£30

### CAMPSITES

**►► Barnstones Caravan & Camping Site**
Great Bourton, Banbury
☎ (0295) 750289
North of Banbury; about 25 miles west of Towcester via the A43, A422 and A423.
pitch price from £5 per night.

## WHERE TO EAT

### RESTAURANTS

### Around Towcester

**Vine House**
100 High St, Paulerspury
☎ (032733) 267, fax: (032733) 309
Skilful, reliable cooking in a small cottage-style hotel restaurant.
Lunch: 12-2.30; from £13.95
Dinner: 7-10; from £19.50
Credit cards 1 3

**French Partridge**
Horton
☎ (0604) 870033
Superb modern cooking which offers good value for money in an old-established village restaurant.
Dinner: 7-9; from £21

**Roadhouse**
16 High St, Roade
☎ (0604) 863372
Unassuming enjoyable food in a smart, cottage-style restaurant.
Lunch: 12-1.45; from £17.50 and à la carte
Dinner: 7-9.30; from £17 à la carte
Credit cards 1 2 3

### PUBS

### Around Towcester

**Bartholomew Arms**
30 High St, Blakesley
☎ (0327) 860292
The cosy beamed bars of this welcoming 18th-century pub are full of interesting collections. There are three well kept real ales – Websters Yorkshire Bitter, Ruddles County and Marstons Pedigree – and an excellent range of 70 malt whiskies. The homely pub fare represents good value for money, with half-portions available for children (welcome in the back room only).
Open: 11am-2.30pm, 5.30-11pm; Sunday 12-3pm, 7-10.30pm
Bar food: 12-2pm, 6-9.30pm, Sunday 12-2pm, 7-9.30pm
Accommodation: double B&B £36-£40

# Uttoxeter

*This is widely regarded as the most go-ahead track in the British Isles. Under the inspired leadership of its owner, Stan Clarke, the course's management have, in a remarkably short period of time, transformed this Midlands venue from a second-rate site into a major centre of equine excellence.*

The numbers of runners and spectators have continued to grow, despite its out of the way location and the recession. This bears testimony to its universal appeal among owners, trainers and punters alike. There is to be no resting on any laurels, however, as plans for further enlargement are already afoot in order to cope with the ever increasing demand.

If ever the phrase 'user-friendly' could be legitimately applied to a racecourse, then Uttoxeter fits the bill. Bands frequently play, there are fun-fairs on big days and senior citizens often benefit from generous discount schemes. The staff are genuinely considerate and amongst the most friendly ever encountered on a racecourse. The standard of catering is superb and corporate entertainment is another area that is booming here - there can be few better places to hire a box. Finally, a word about the racing, which is restricted solely to the jumps. Once again, there has been a significant recent improvement in this sphere, with the levels of prize money and the standard of competition rising steadily all the time. The richest race in the calendar is the Midlands Grand National, run in mid-March.

## FURTHER INFORMATION

Uttoxeter Leisure & Development Co Ltd
The Racecourse, Wood Lane, Uttoxeter, Staffordshire ST14 8BD
☎ (0889) 562561

## LOCATION AND HOW TO GET THERE

The course is half a mile southeast of Uttoxeter town centre off the B5017. From the M6 southbound leave at junction 15 and take the A50 eastwards; from the northbound direction, leave at junction 13, go into Stafford and take the A518 to Uttoxeter. Alternatively, to avoid the busy M6 around Birmingham, take the M42 to junction 10, then west on the A5. At Tamworth, take the A51 through Lichfield and on to Rugeley. Here turn right onto the B5013 for Uttoxeter. From the M1, leave at junction 22 and take the A50 through Ashby-de-la-Zouch and Burton to Uttoxeter. **Nearest Railway Station:** Uttoxeter; the station adjoins the course. From the inter-city network, it is necessary to change at Derby or Stoke for Uttoxeter; there is also a service from Crewe.

## ADMISSION

The SP Betting Shop is in Members and Tattersalls only; there is also a mobile facility in the Silver Ring on Saturdays and Bank Holidays.

**Day tickets:**
MEMBERS £12, £15 for Midlands National (20 March in 1993) – access to Members' stand, bars, restaurant, champagne and seafood bar, boxes and private rooms

TATTERSALLS £8, £10 for Midlands National (see above) – access to bars, restaurant and champagne and seafood bar

SILVER RING £5 – access to bars and snacks

CENTRE COURSE £3 – access to bars and snacks

**Annual membership:** £100, couple £150; senior citizen £90, couple £130; junior (under 21) £50 – includes free racecard at all home fixtures and reciprocal meetings at certain other courses.

## COURSE FACILITIES

**Banks:**
there are no banks or cashpoint facilities on the course.

**For families:**
picnic area with refreshment kiosk and toilets; children's play area on Bank Holidays only; lost children centre.

## CALENDAR OF EVENTS

**April 2** – jumping
**April 4** – jumping
**April 30** – jumping
**May 4** – jumping; evening meeting
**May 19** – jumping; evening meeting
**May 30** – jumping
**June 2** – jumping
**June 4** – Arab Horse Society Racing (flat)

**August 18** – jumping; evening meeting
**August 20** – Arab Horse Society Racing (flat)
**September 7** – jumping
**October 1** – jumping
**October 12** – jumping
**November 2-3** – jumping
**December 1** – jumping
**December 16-17** – jumping

## WHERE TO STAY

### HOTELS

**★★ 63% Bank House**
Church St
☎ (0889) 566922, fax: (0889) 567565
16 bedrooms; double B&B £46.50-£66.50
Credit cards 1 2 3 5

**Forte Travelodge**
Ashbourne Rd
☎ (0889) 562043, Central Reservations: (0800) 850950
32 bedrooms; double room £31.95
Credit cards 1 2 3

**Around Uttoxeter**

**★★ 61% Bull's Head Inn**
High St, Alton
☎ (0538) 702307
6 bedrooms
Credit cards 1 3

**★★★ 69% Ashbourne Oaks Lodge**
Derby Rd, Ashbourne
☎ (0335) 46666, fax: (0335) 46549
50 bedrooms
Credit cards 1 3

**★★ ❀ 75% Callow Hall**
Mappleton Rd, Ashbourne
☎ (0335) 43403 & 42412, fax: (0335) 43624
12 bedrooms; double B&B £90-£120
Credit cards 1 2 3 5

**★★ 64% Olivers**
Wolseley Bridge, Little Haywood
☎ (0889) 881325
4 bedrooms

**★★ 59% Cedar Tree**
Main Road, Brereton, Rugeley
☎ (0889) 584241
14 bedrooms; double B&B £40-£48
Credit cards 1 2 3 5

**Forte Travelodge**
Western Springs Rd, Rugeley
☎ (0889) 570096, Central Reservations: (0800) 850950
32 bedrooms; double room £31.95
Credit cards 1 2 3

### BED AND BREAKFAST

**Hillcrest**
3 Leighton Rd, Uttoxeter
☎ (0889) 564627
Family-run guesthouse in elevated position.
7 bedrooms
Credit cards 1 2 3

**Marsh Farm**
Abbots Bromley
☎ (0283) 840323
In pleasant village famed for its ancient annual tradition, the Horn Dance; the farm has been modernised but retains its exposed beams.
2 bedrooms; double B&B £27-£30

**Dairy House Farm**
Alkmonton
☎ (0335) 330359
Friendly hosts welcome guests to this comfortably modernised 16th-century house.
7 bedrooms; double B&B £32-£38

## WHERE TO STAY

### Queen's Arms
Mayfield
☎ (0335) 42271
Standing close to a busy junction; lively inn
providing darts, pool and live entertainment
at weekends.
4 bedrooms

### Bank House
Farley Ln, Oakamoor
☎ (0538) 702810
High quality accommodation is offered in
this welcoming family home; lovely big old
rooms with antique furniture.
3 bedrooms; double B&B £46-£60

### Admiral Jervis Country Hotel
Mill Rd, Oakamoor
☎ (0538) 702187
An 18th-century inn overlooking River
Churnet in a picturesque village.
6 bedrooms; double B&B from £39
Credit cards 1 3

### CAMPSITES

### ►► Caravan Club Site
Uttoxeter Racecourse
☎ (0889) 564172 & 562561
Off the B5017; pitch price from £3 per night.

### ►► Sandybrook Hall Holiday Park
Buxton Rd, Ashbourne
☎ (0335) 42679
One mile north of Ashbourne on A515; pitch
price from £5.50 per night.

### ►► Star Caravan & Camping Park
Cotton, Oakamoor
☎ (0538) 702256 & 702219
One and a quarter miles northeast off
B5417; pitch price from £4.50 per night.

### ►►► Silver Trees Caravan Park
Stafford Brook Rd, Penkridge Bank, Rugeley
☎ (0889) 582185
Off the Penkridge-Rugeley road 2 miles
from Rugeley; pitch price from £7 per night.

## WHERE TO EAT

### RESTAURANT

### Around Uttoxeter

### ✿✿ Old Beams Restaurant
Leek Rd, Waterhouses
☎ (0538) 308254, fax: (0538) 308157
Cottage-style restaurant serving simple but
tasty modern English/French food.
Lunch: 12-2; from £16.50
Dinner: 7-10; from £30
Credit cards 1 2 3 5

### PUBS

### Around Uttoxeter

### Horseshoe Inn
Main St, Tatenhill, nr Burton upon Trent
☎ (0283) 64913
This charming old building in the village
centre has an attractive garden for summer
days and a wood-burning stove for wintry
nights. It specialises in wines from the
Beaujolais and Macon regions of France
and there is a good selection of malt
whiskies; draught beers on offer are
Marston's and Guinness. The bar food is
well presented and reasonably priced. There
is a family room and an outdoor play area
for children.
Open: 11 or 11.30am-3pm, 5.30-11pm;
Sunday 12-3pm, 7-10.30pm
Bar food: Monday 12-2pm; Tuesday to
Saturday 12-2pm, 6-9.15pm; Sunday 12-
1.30pm
Restaurant: times as bar food

# Warwick

*Races were first held at Warwick during the 18th century, when crowds of 50,000 watched the renowned 'King's Plates'. Steeplechases were staged here from the beginning of the 19th century and, in the 1900s, this course was several times host to the National Hunt Chase, a contest now permanently based at Cheltenham.*

Another interesting historical fact about this venue is that the longest ever recorded leap by a racehorse took place here in 1836 when The Chandler cleared a distance of 36 feet.

It would probably be fair to say that Warwick's past is more illustrious than its present. It is now very much a bread and butter type track, offering a fair standard of racing in a pleasant laid-back atmosphere. Some two dozen meetings are split almost evenly between the Flat and National Hunt, with the jumps fixtures holding a slight edge in quality. The most prestigious contest of the year is the Warwick National at the end of January, while there is also an excellent card in late February which features several important trials for the Cheltenham Festival. Facilities have been generally upgraded, with the addition of new bars and private boxes, but the viewing areas are rather cramped and the big hill in the middle of the course obscures some of the action in the back straight.

## FURTHER INFORMATION

Warwick Racecourse Company Ltd
Hampton Street, Warwick CV34 6HN
☎ (0926) 491553

## LOCATION AND HOW TO GET THERE

The racecourse is within half a mile of the centre of Warwick, 20 miles southeast of Birmingham and two miles from Royal Leamington Spa. Leave the M40 at junction 15 and take the A429 into the centre of Warwick, from where the course is signposted.

**Nearest Railway Station:** Warwick; there are no connecting bus services to the course

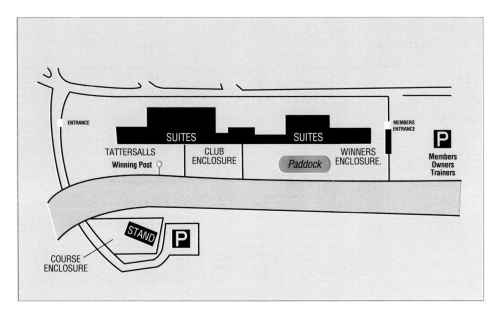

## ADMISSION

All classes of day ticket give access to full betting facilities, including Tote.

**Day tickets:**
Accompanied children under 16 are admitted free to all enclosures.

CLUB £12 – access to members bar, all grandstands, hospitality suites

TATTERSALLS (GRANDSTAND & PADDOCK) £8 – access to paddock, winners enclosure, betting shop, bar and restaurant

COURSE £5 – access to bar, snack bar, betting shop (Saturdays and Bank Holidays), picnic area, parking

**Annual Membership:** £110 full, £65 National Hunt, £50 junior – includes vouchers for new members, redeemable against racecards and refreshments; reciprocal arrangements at certain other courses on certain days; two days of polo at the local club. Members may bring a guest racing on two occasions during the year. National Hunt members enjoy these benefits on National Hunt Racedays only.

## COURSE FACILITIES

**Banks:**
there are no banks or cashpoint facilities on the course.

**For families:**
picnic area with refreshment kiosk and toilets, children's play area

## CALENDAR OF EVENTS

**April 4** – flat
**April 15** – flat; evening meeting
**May 2** – flat
**May 7** – National Hunt; evening meeting
**May 21** – National Hunt; evening meeting
**May 28** – flat; evening meeting

**June 18** – flat; evening meeting
**June 20** – flat; evening meeting
**June 29** – flat
**July 8** – flat;
**July 23** – flat; evening meeting
**August 29** – flat

**October 3-4** – flat
**October 29** – National Hunt
**November 15** – National Hunt
**November 26** – National Hunt
**December 12** – National Hunt
**December 29** – National Hunt

## WHERE TO STAY

### HOTELS

**★★ 66% Warwick Arms**
High St
☎ (0926) 492759, fax: (0926) 410587
35 bedrooms; double B&B £60-£80
Credit cards 1 2 3 5

**★★ 58% Lord Leycester**
Jury St
☎ (0926) 491481, telex: 41363, fax: (0926) 491561
52 bedrooms; double B&B £69
Credit cards 1 2 3 5

**★ 63% Penderrick**
36 Coten End
☎ (0926) 499399 & 497252
7 bedrooms
Credit cards 1 2 3 5

### Around Warwick

**★★ 66% Old Mill**
Mill Hill, Baginton
☎ (0203) 303588, fax: (0203) 307070
20 bedrooms; double B&B £50-£70
Credit cards 1 2 3 5

**★★★ 67% The Glebe at Barford**
Church St, Barford
☎ (0926) 624218, fax: (0926) 624625
41 bedrooms; double B&B £80-£105
Credit cards 1 2 3 5

**★★★ ⊛ 74% Nailcote Hall**
Nailcote Ln, Berkswell, Balsall Common
☎ (0203) 466174, fax: (0203) 470720
20 bedrooms
Credit cards 1 2 3

**★★★ 60% Brandon Hall**
Main St, Brandon
☎ (0203) 542571, fax: (0203) 544909
60 bedrooms; double room £80-£105
(room only)
Credit cards 1 2 3 5

**★★★ 58% Charlecote Pheasant Country Hotel**
Charlecote
☎ (0789) 470333, fax: (0789 470222
67 bedrooms; double B&B £85-£125
Credit cards 1 2 3 5

**★★★★ 57% De Vere**
Cathedral Square, Coventry
☎ (0203) 633733, fax: (0203) 225299
190 bedrooms; double B&B £40-£105
Credit cards 1 2 3 4 5

**★★★ ⊛ 68% Brooklands Grange Hotel & Restaurant**
Holyhead Rd, Coventry
☎ (0203) 601601, fax: (0203) 601277
30 bedrooms; double B&B £90-£95
Credit cards 1 2 3 5

**★★★ 66% Coventry Knight**
Ryton on Dunsmore, Coventry
☎ (0203) 301585
49 bedrooms; double B&B £42-£84
Credit cards 1 2 3 4 5

**★★★ 64% Leofric**
Broadgate, Coventry
☎ (0203) 221371, telex: 311193, fax: (0203) 551352
94 bedrooms; double room £94.50-£135
(room only)
Credit cards 1 2 3 5

**★★★ 63% Forte Crest**
Hinckley Rd, Walsgrave, Coventry
☎ (0203) 613261, telex: 311292, fax: (0203) 621736
147 bedrooms; double room £49.50-£80
(room only)
Credit cards 1 2 3 5

## WHERE TO STAY

**★★★ 61% The Chace**
London Rd, Willenhall, Coventry
☎ (0203) 303398, fax: (0203) 301816
67 bedrooms; double room £85 (room
only)
Credit cards 1 2 3 5

**★★★ 61% Hylands**
Warwick Rd, Coventry
☎ (0203) 501600, fax: (0203) 501027
55 bedrooms; double B&B £70-£85
Credit cards 1 2 3 5

**★★★ 58% Novotel Coventry**
Wilsons Ln, Coventry
☎ (0203) 365000, telex: 31545, fax:
(0203) 362422
100 bedrooms
Credit cards 1 2 3 4 5

**★★★ 56% Forte Posthouse**
Rye Hill, Allesley, Coventry
☎ (0203) 402151, fax: (0203) 402235
184 bedrooms; double room £39.50-
£49.50 (room only)
Credit cards 1 2 3 5

**★★ 62% Beechwood**
Standpits Ln, Keresley, Coventry
☎ (0203 338662, fax: (0203 337080
24 bedrooms; double B&B from £56.50
Credit cards 1 3 5

**Campanile**
4 Wigston Rd, Walsgrave, Coventry
☎ (0203) 622311, telex: 317454, fax:
(0203) 602362
50 bedrooms
Credit cards 1 2 3

**Campanile**
Abbey Rd, Whitley, Coventry
☎ (0203) 639922
51 bedrooms

**★★ 56% Eathorpe Park**
Fosse Way, Eathorpe
☎ (0926) 632245 & 632632, fax: (0926)
632481
14 bedrooms
Credit cards 1 2 3 5

**★★★ 66% Honiley Court**
Honiley
☎ (0926) 484234, fax: (0926) 484474
62 bedrooms; double B&B £74
Credit cards 1 2 3 5

**★★★ 63% De Montfort**
The Square, Kenilworth
☎ (0926) 55944, fax: (0926) 57830
96 bedrooms
Credit cards 1 2 3 5

**★★★ 58% Perquito Chesford Grange**
Chesford Bridge, Kenilworth
☎ (0926) 59331, fax: (0926) 59075
130 bedrooms
Credit cards 1 2 3 5

**★★ 64% Clarendon House**
Old High St, Kenilworth
☎ (0926) 57668, telex: 311240, fax:
(0926) 50669
31 bedrooms; double B&B £80-£85
Credit cards 1 3

**★★★ (RED) ❀❀❀ Mallory Court**
Harbury Ln, Bishop's, Tachbrook,
Leamington Spa tel: (0926) 330214, fax:
(0926) 451714
10 bedrooms; double B&B £108-£220
Credit cards 1 3

**★★★ 70% Regent**
77 The Parade, Leamington Spa
☎ (0926) 427231, telex: 311715, fax:
(0926) 450728
80 bedrooms
Credit cards 1 2 3 5

**★★★ 61% Falstaff**
16-20 Warwick New Rd, Leamington Spa
☎ (0926) 312044, fax: (0926) 450574
65 bedrooms
Credit cards 1 2 3 4 5

**★★★ 59% Manor House**
Avenue Rd, Leamington Spa
☎ (0926) 423251, fax: (0926) 425933
53 bedrooms
Credit cards 1 2 3 4 5

**★★ 71% Tuscany**
Warwick Place, Leamington Spa
☎ (0926) 332233, fax: (0926) 332232
10 bedrooms
Credit cards 1 2 3 5

**★★ 69% Adams**
22 Avenue Rd, Leamington Spa
☎ (0926) 450742 & 422758, fax: (0926)
313110
14 bedrooms; double B&B £49.50-£58
Credit cards 1 2 3 5

**★★ 61% Beech Lodge**
Warwick New Rd, Leamington Spa
☎ (0926) 422227
13 bedrooms; double B&B £45-£60
Credit cards 1 2 3

**★★ 58% Angel**
143 Regent St, Leamington Spa
☎ (0926) 881296
36 bedrooms; double B&B £39-£59
Credit cards 1 2 3

**★★ 57% Abbacourt**
40 Kenilworth Rd, Leamington Spa
☎ (0926) 451755, fax: (0926) 450330
24 bedrooms
Credit cards 1 2 3 4 5

**★ (RED) ❀ Lansdowne**
87 Clarendon St, Leamington Spa
☎ (0926) 450505, fax: (0926) 420604
15 bedrooms; double B&B £49.90-£57.90
Credit cards 1 3

**★★★ 60% Three Ways**
Mickleton
☎ (0386) 438429, fax: (0386) 438118
40 bedrooms; double B&B £68-£72
Credit cards 1 2 3 5

**★★ 66% Woodhouse**
Leamington Rd, Princethorpe
☎ (0926) 632131 & 632303, fax: (0926)
632131
17 bedrooms
Credit cards 1 2 3 5

**★★★★ 64% Welcombe**
Warwick Rd, Stratford-upon-Avon
☎ (0789) 295252, telex: 31347, fax:
(0789) 414666
76 bedrooms; double B&B from £135
Credit cards 1 2 3 5

## WHERE TO STAY

**★★★★ 62% Moat House International**
Bridgefoot, Stratford-upon-Avon
☎ (0789) 414411, telex: 311127,
fax: (0789) 298589
247 bedrooms; double B&B £120
Credit cards 1 2 3 5

**★★★★ 61% The Shakespeare**
Chapel St, Stratford-upon-Avon
☎ (0789) 294771, fax: (0789) 415411
63 bedrooms; double room £100-£130
(room only)
Credit cards 1 2 3 5

**★★★ 74% Windmill Park Hotel & Country Club**
Warwick Rd, Stratford-upon-Avon
☎ (0789) 731173, fax: (0789) 731131
100 bedrooms; double B&B £97-£115
Credit cards 1 2 3 5

**★★★ 64% Grosvenor House**
Warwick Rd, Stratford-upon-Avon
☎ (0789 266087
40 bedrooms
Credit cards 1 2 3 5

**★★★ 59% Alveston Manor**
Clopton Bridge, Stratford-upon-Avon
☎ (0789) 204581, telex: 31324, fax:
(0789) 414095
108 bedrooms; double £95-£105
(room only)
Credit cards 1 2 3 5

**★★★ 59% Dukes**
Payton St, Stratford-upon-Avon
☎ (0789) 269300, telex: 31430, fax:
(0789) 414700
22 bedrooms; double B&B £69.50-£105
Credit cards 1 2 3 5

**★★★ 59% Forte Posthouse**
Bridgefoot, Stratford-upon-Avon
☎ (0789) 266761, fax: (0789) 414547
60 bedrooms; double room £39.50-£49.50
(room only)
Credit cards 1 2 3 5

**★★★ 56% The White Swan**
Rother St, Stratford-upon-Avon
☎ (0789) 297022, fax: (0789) 268773
37 bedrooms; double room £85 (room only)
Credit cards 1 2 3 5

**★★★ 54% Falcon**
Chapel St, Stratford-upon-Avon
☎ (0789) 205777, telex: 312522, fax:
(0789) 414260
73 bedrooms; double B&B £70-£99
Credit cards 1 2 3 4 5

**★★ 71% Stratford House**
Sheep St, Stratford-upon-Avon
☎ (0789) 268288, fax: (0789) 295580
11 bedrooms; double B&B £55-£82
Credit cards 1 2 3 5

**★★ 65% The Coach House Hotel**
16-17 Warwick Rd, Stratford-upon-Avon
☎ (0789) 204109 & 299468, fax: (0789) 415916
10 bedrooms
Credit cards 1 2 3

**★★ 60% Swan House**
The Green, Wilmcote
☎ (0789) 267030, fax: (0789) 204875
8 bedrooms; double B&B £50-£60
Credit cards 1 2 3

## BED AND BREAKFAST

**The Old Rectory**
Vicarage Ln, Sherbourne,
☎ (0926) 624562
Tastefully restored house offering very
comfortable accommodation and home-
cooked food.
14 bedrooms; double B&B £39-£50
Credit cards 1 2 3

**Austin House**
96 Emscote Rd,
☎ (0926) 493583
Guesthouse offering modest
accommodation.
6 bedrooms; double B&B £27-£33
Credit cards 1 2 3 5

**Avon**
7 Emscote Rd
☎ (0926) 491367
Clean, simply appointed bed and breakfast
accommodation.
7 bedrooms; double B&B £30

**Cambridge Villa Private Hotel**
20A Emscote Rd
☎ (0926) 491169
Simple accommodation in hotel run by an
enthusiastic Italian owner.
16 bedrooms
Credit cards 1 3

**Tudor House**
West St
☎ (0926) 495447, fax: (0926) 492948
Tudor house retaining much wattle and
daub and timbers; cosy bedrooms.
11 bedrooms; double B&B from £54
Credit cards 1 2 3

**Around Warwick**

**Woodside Country House**
Langley Rd, Claverdon
☎ (0926) 842446
3 bedrooms; double B&B £28-£34

**Hearsall Lodge Hotel**
1 Broad Ln, Coventry
☎ (0203) 674543
Professionally run guesthouse situated
close to the A45
13 bedrooms
Credit cards 1 3

**Three Spires**
62 Grosvenor Rd, Coventry
☎ (0203) 632596
Just off the Kenilworth road; bright, fresh
bedrooms.
2 bedrooms; double B&B from £26
Credit cards 1 3

**Ashleigh House**
17 Park Rd, Coventry
☎ (0203) 223804
Compact rooms with modest furnishings.
10 bedrooms; double B&B £28-£32

**Croft Hotel**
23 Stoke Green, Off Binley Rd, Coventry
☎ (0203) 457846
Pleasant guesthouse with friendly owners.
12 bedrooms; double B&B from £42
Credit cards 1 3

## WHERE TO STAY

### Fairlight
14 Regent St, Coventry
☎ (0203) 224215
Close to city centre, providing simple,
value-for-money accommodation.
12 bedrooms; double B&B from £28

### Croft
Haseley Knob
☎ (0926) 484447
Five miles northwest of Warwick.
5 bedrooms; double B&B £33-£42

### Northleigh House
Five Ways Rd, Hatton
☎ (Warwick 0926 484203
Bedrooms have many thoughtful extras in
this charming guesthouse, with high
standards throughout ensured by friendly
hostess.
6 bedrooms; double B&B £42-£54

### Abbey
41 Station Rd, Kenilworth
☎ (0926) 512707
A warm welcome is assured at this
guesthouse, set in a residential area.
7 bedrooms; double B&B £32-£38

### Castle Laurels Hotel
22 Castle Rd, Kenilworth
☎ (0926) 56179, fax: (0926) 54954
Attractive, spacious Victorian house
opposite the castle and Abbey Fields.
12 bedrooms; double B&B £43-£47
Credit cards 1 3

### Ferndale
45 Priory Rd, Kenilworth
☎ (0926) 53214
Attractive, comfortable accommodation.
8 bedrooms; double B&B £30-£32

### Hollyhurst
47 Priory Rd, Kenilworth
☎ (0926) 53882
Friendly and welcoming guesthouse, with
bright fresh bedrooms providing a good
range of facilities.
8 bedrooms; double B&B £32-£36

### Victoria Lodge Hotel
180 Warwick Rd, Kenilworth
☎ (0926) 512020, fax: (0926) 58703
Charming hosts and excellent standards of
cleanliness and maintenance throughout.
5 bedrooms; double B&B £44-£46
Credit cards 1 2 3

### Coverdale Private Hotel
8 Portland St, Leamington Spa
☎ (0926) 330400, fax: (0926) 833388
Attractive well situated Georgian house,
offering a high level of comfort.
8 bedrooms; double B&B from £42
Credit cards 1 3

### Flowerdale House
58 Warwick New Rd, Leamington Spa
☎ (0926) 426002, fax: (0926) 883699
Delightful Victorian property offering
attractive accommodation.
6 bedrooms; double B&B £34-£42

### Milverton House Hotel
1 Milverton Terrace, Leamington Spa
☎ (0926) 428335
Friendly proprietors; attractive bedrooms.
10 bedrooms; double B&B £34-£48
Credit cards 1 2 3

### Hill Farm
Lewis Rd, Radford, Leamington Spa
☎ (0926) 337571
This popular farmhouse is just off the A45.
6 bedrooms; double B&B £26-£34

### Buckland Lodge Hotel
35 Avenue Rd, Leamington Spa
☎ (0926)423843
Victorian Villa situated on a wide tree-lined
avenue.
10 bedrooms; double B&B £36-£46
Credit cards 1 2 3 5

### Charnwood
47 Avenue Rd, Leamington Spa
☎ (0926)831074
Close to town centre, providing attractive,
well equipped accommodation.
6 bedrooms; double B&B £27-£36
Credit cards 1 3 5

### Glendower
8 Warwick Place, Leamington Spa
☎ (0926) 422784
Situated on the main road into Leamington
Spa; offering generally spacious
accommodation.
9 bedrooms; double B&B £28-£42

### Redlands Farm
Banbury Rd, Lighthorne
☎ (0926) 651241
Open-air swimming pool is available to
guests; Mrs Stanton provides wholesome
dishes.
3 bedrooms; double B&B £30-£32

### Marton Fields
Marton
☎ (0926) 632410
Attractive red-brick period farmhouse set in
delightful gardens; charming host.
3 bedrooms

### Shrewley House
Shrewley
☎ (Claverdon 092684 2549, faax 092684
2216
Charming listed Grade II Georgian
farmhouse with an exceptionally wide range
of facilities and high standards throughout.
9 bedrooms; double B&B £52-£58
Credit cards 1 3

### Brook Lodge
192 Alcester Rd, Stratford-upon-Avon
☎ (0789) 295988
Nicely decorated, well kept guesthouse.
7 bedrooms; double B&B £34-£38
Credit cards 1 2 3 5

### Craig Cleeve House
67-69 Shipston Rd, Stratford-upon-Avon
☎ (0789) 296573, fax: (0789) 299452
On the A34 south of Clopton Bridge; bright
fresh accommodation; friendly hosts.
15 bedrooms; double B&B £51
Credit cards 1 2 3 5

### Eastnor House Hotel
Shipston Rd, Stratford-upon-Avon
☎ (0789) 268115
On the A34, just 300m from the theatre;
bright, fresh accommodation.
9 bedrooms; double B&B £39-£52
Credit cards 1 3

## WHERE TO STAY

### Gravelside Barn
Binton, Stratford-upon-Avon
☎ (0789) 750502 & 297000, fax: (0789) 298056
3 bedrooms; double B&B £40-£60
Credit cards 1 2 3

### Highcroft
Banbury Rd, Stratford-upon-Avon
☎ (07890 296293
Spacious attractive rooms which are well equipped and have antique or pine furniture.
2 bedrooms; double B&B £30-£35

### Hollies 'The Hollies'
16 Evesham Place, Stratford-upon-Avon
☎ (0789) 266857
Close to the town centre; popular hostess who gives a warm welcome.
6 bedrooms.

### Kawartha House
39 Grove Rd,Stratford-upon-Avon
☎ (0789) 204469
Cosy, friendly guesthouse on the Evesham road.
6 bedrooms

### Melita Private Hotel
37 Shipston Rd, Stratford-upon-Avon
☎ (0789) 292432
A friendly family run gueshouse on the A34 close to the river and major attractions.
12 bedrooms; double B&B £45-£58
Credit cards 1 2 3

### Moonraker House
40 Alcester Rd, Stratford-upon-Avon
☎ (0789) 299346, fax: (0789) 295504
Unusual guesthouse, spread over four properties, with attractive bedrooms.
15 bedrooms; double B&B £37-£55
Credit cards 1 2 3

### They Payton Hotel
6 John St, Stratford-upon-Avon
☎ (0789) 266442
Bedrooms are attractively decorated and furnished; friendly, welcoming proprietors.
5 bedrooms; double B&B £48
Credit cards 1 2 3

### Sequoia House Private Hotel
51-53 Shipston Rd, Stratford-upon-Avon
☎ (0789) 268852
Opposite the Royal Shakespeare Theatre; several types of room are available, from the cosy cottage annexe to the exceptionally well furnished, luxury no-smoking rooms.
25 bedrooms; double B&B £35-£72
Credit cards 1 2 3 5

### Twelfth Night
Evesham Place, Stratford-upon-Avon
☎ (0789) 414595
Delightfully refurbished Victorian villa; pretty rooms with welcome extra touches.
7 bedrooms; double B&B £38-£52
Credit cards 1 3

### Victoria Spa Lodge
Bishopton Ln, Stratford-upon-Avon
☎ (0789) 267985 & 204728
Victorian Lodge in a peaceful, leafy setting at the side of the Stratford Canal.
7 bedrooms; double B&B from £45
Credit cards 1 3

### Virginia Lodge
12 Evesham Place, Stratford-upon-Avon
☎ (0789) 292157
Well kept, friendly guesthouse close to the centre of Stratford.
7 bedrooms; double B&B £34-£40

### Oxstalls Farm
Warwick Rd, Stratford-upon-Avon
☎ (0789) 205277
This farmhouse, providing bright fresh accommodation, is also a thoroughbred stud farm.
18 bedrooms

### Swan Cottage
The Green, Wilmcote
☎ (0789) 266480
A warm welcome is assured at this guesthouse with original beams and flagstone floors.
3 bedrooms; double B&B £28-£37

### CAMPSITES

▶ Island Meadow Caravan Park
The Mill House, Aston Cantlow
☎ (0789) 488273
Quarter of a mile west of Aston Cantlow; pitch price from £5 per night.

## WHERE TO EAT

### RESTAURANTS

#### Around Warwick

#### ✸✸ Restaurant Bosquet
97A Warwick Rd, Kenilworth
☎ (0926) 52463
Generous portions of honest-to-goodness provincial French cooking and friendly, helpful service.
Lunch by reservation only; from £19
Dinner: 7-9.30; from £19 and à la carte.
Credit cards 1 2 3

### PUBS

#### Around Warwick

#### Bell
Alderminster
☎ (0789) 450414
An adventurous menu, a high standard of cooking and a wine list to match are the main attractions of the 17th-century pub. Beers include Marston Pedigree and Flowers Best and Original. Children are welcome.
Open: 12-2.30pm, 7-11pm; Sunday 12-2.30pm, 7-10.30pm
Bar food: 12-2pm, 7-9.30pm; Sunday 12-1.45pm, 7-9pm
Restaurant: times as bar food

#### Ferry
Alveston
☎ (0789) 269883
Friendly village-centre pub offering well prepared and promptly served food at a range of prices, all good value for money. Theakston Best, Bass, Wadworth 6▶ and Flowers Original are on sale, along with a selection of wines. Children over 5 years old are welcome.
Open: 11am-2.30pm, 6-11pm; Sunday 12-2.30pm, 7-10.30
Bar food: 11.45am-2pm, 6.30-9pm; Sunday 12-2pm

#### Kings Head
Aston Cantlow
☎ (0789) 488242
This is an attractive and unspoilt half-timbered pub with a small, well tended garden. Beers include Marston Pedigree, Flowers IPA, Boddingtons Bitter and Mild and Murphy's Stout; there is a reasonable selection of wines and a tasty range of bar meals. No children under 14 in the bar.
Open: 12-2.30pm, 7-11pm; Sunday 12-2.30pm, 7-10.30pm
Bar food: as opening hours, except Sunday and Monday evenings

#### Malt Shovel
Lower End, Bubbenhall, nr Coventry
☎ (0203) 301141
With an Italian licensee, it is not surprising that some Italian dishes appear on the good-value menu, nor that Italian wines are a speciality. However, beer drinkers will not be disappointed, with Ansells Bitter and Mild, Bass and Tetley Bitter on tap. Dating from the 16th century, the brick and timber pub has a small patio at the front and a garden adjoining a bowling green. Children welcome anywhere at lunchtime and early evening.
Open: 11.30am-2.30pm, 6-11pm; Sunday 12-2.30pm, 7-10.30pm
Bar food: 12-2pm, 6.30-9.30pm. No food Sunday evening.

#### Chequers
91 Main Rd, Ettington
☎ (0789) 740387
This vine-clad village pub is a friendly meeting place offering skilfully prepared food and a choice of beers which includes Adnams Bitter, Marston Pedigree, Everard Tiger and Beacon and guest ales. Children are welcome and there is a play area in the garden.
Open: 10.30am-2.30pm, 6-11pm; Sunday 12-2.30pm, 7-10.30pm
Bar food: 12-1.45pm, 6.30-9.30pm (until 9.45 on Friday and Saturday); Sunday 12-1.45pm, 7-9.30pm

#### Navigation
Old Warwick Rd, Lapworth
☎ (0564) 783337
With a well-tended garden beside the Grand Union Canal, this is a popular pub providing good, substantial bar meals and barbecues on summer Sunday lunchtimes. Beers include Mitchells & Butlers Mild and Brew XI, Bass and a guest beer. Children are welcome only in a room beyond the bar and in the garden.
Open: 11am-2.30pm, 5.30-11pm; Saturday 11am-3pm, 6-11pm; Sunday 12-3pm, 7-10.30pm
Bar food: 12-2pm, 6-9pm; Sunday 12-2pm, 7-9pm

#### Fleur de Lys
Lapworth St, Lowsonford, nr Henley-in-Arden
☎ (0564) 782431
This long, cottage-like pub has a pleasant waterside garden with access to the Stratford-upon-Avon canal. Visitors with young children will feel particularly welcome as there is a family room with toys and high chairs, and there is a play area in the garden. Good value food is expertly cooked and served promptly and, in addition to the real ales, there is a wide selection of wines.
Open: 11am-11pm; Sunday 12-3pm, 7-10.30pm
Bar food: 12-9.30pm; Sunday 12-2pm, 7-9.30pm

#### Old Mint
Coventry St, Southam
☎ (0926) 812339
This stone pub was already three centuries old when Cromwell used it as a mint during the Civil War (the collection of antique swords, pikes and guns in the main bar is an apropriate reminder). An unusually wide range of beers is on offer, including Wadworth 6X, Whitbread Original and Best Bitter, Bass, Marston Pedigree, Hook Norton Bitter, Boddingtons Bitter, Taylor Landlord and Murphy's Stout – as well as a guest beer or two. Also to accompany the bar meals is an extensive wine list. Children are welcome in the small bar and restaurant and the garden has a pool with miniature watermill and (usually) a bouncy castle.
Open: Monday to Friday 11am-3pm, 6.30-11pm; Saturday 11am-11pm; Sunday 12-3pm, 7-10.30pm
Bar food: Monday to Friday 12-2, 7-10pm; Saturday 12-3pm, 6-10pm; Sunday 12-2.30pm, 7-9.30pm

# Wetherby

*Yorkshire is blessed with an abundance of racecourses, of which Wetherby is undoubtedly the premier jumping venue. This popular National Hunt track offers first class facilities to racegoers and provides superb all-round visibility of the course from the stands.*

It is conveniently located just off the A1, making access exceptionally easy, and has a large catchment area, the major cities of Harrogate, Leeds and York all being within a close radius. As a consequence, crowds are always large, creating a cracking atmosphere.

There are 14 meetings held here annually and the quality of the runners is usually high. Part of the reason for this is that the track is regarded as one of the fairest in Britain. The mile and a half oval circuit has wide straights and easy bends, suiting the long-striding horse, and the stiff fences are a good test of an animal's jumping ability. Trainers, therefore, find it more difficult than usual to come up with excuses for beaten horses here.

The best fixtures are on Boxing Day and at the end of October, when an outstanding Saturday televised card includes three top events, the Charlie Hall Chase, the West Yorkshire Hurdle and the Wensleydale Juvenile Hurdle.

This National Hunt course offers first class facilities to racegoers and provides superb all-round visibility of the course from the stands.

### LOCATION AND HOW TO GET THERE

The course is on the B1224 Wetherby-York road, adjacent to, and visible from, the A1.
**Nearest Railway Stations:** Leeds or York; there are no connecting bus services to the course.

---

### ADMISSION

All classes of day ticket give access to full betting facilities, including Tote

**Day tickets:**
Accompanied children under 16 are admitted free.

MEMBERS/CLUB £12 – access to bar, restaurant

GRANDSTAND/TATTERSALLS £7 – access to bar, self-service restaurant

COURSE £2, or £6 for car and up to four adults – access to bar, self-service restaurant

### COURSE FACILITIES

**Banks:**
there are no banks or cashpoint facilities on the course.

**For families:**
picnic area with refreshment kiosk and toilets; children's play area

---

## CALENDAR OF EVENTS

| | |
|---|---|
| April 4-5 | November 15 |
| May 4 – evening meeting | December 3 |
| May 30 | December 26-27 |
| October 12 | |
| October 28-29 | |

## WHERE TO STAY

### HOTELS

**★★★ (RED) ❀ Wood Hall**
Trip Ln, Linton
☎ (0937) 587271, fax: (0937) 584353
22 bedrooms
Credit cards 1 2 3 4 5

**★★★ 76% Linton Spring Country House**
Sickling Hall Rd
☎ (0937) 585353, fax: (0937) 67579
12 bedrooms
Credit cards 1 2 3 5

**★★★ 57% Wetherby Resort**
Leeds Rd
☎ (0937) 583881, fax: (0937) 580062
72 bedrooms; double room £80 (room only)
Credit cards 1 2 3 5

**Around Wetherby**

**★★★ 74% Aldwark Manor**
Aldwark
☎ (03473) 8146, fax: (03473) 8867
17 bedrooms; double B&B £60-£80
Credit cards 1 2 3 5

**★★★ (RED) ❀❀ Bilbrough Manor Country House**
Bilbrough
☎ (0937) 834002, fax: (0937) 834724
12 bedrooms
Credit cards 1 2 3 5

**Forte Travelodge**
Bilbrough
☎ (0973) 531823, Central Reservations: (0800) 850950
36 bedrooms; double room £31.95 (room only)
Credit cards 1 2 3

**★★★ 66% Harewood Arms**
Harrogate Rd, Harewood
☎ (0532) 886566
24 bedrooms; double B&B £63-£78
Credit cards 1 2 3 4 5

**★★★★ 67% Moat House International**
Kings Rd, Harrogate
☎ (0423) 500000, telex: 57575, fax: (0423) 524435
214 bedrooms; double B&B £119-£135
Credit cards 1 2 3 5

**★★★★ 64% Nidd Hall**
Nidd, Harrogate
☎ (0423) 771598, fax: (0423) 770931
38 bedrooms; double B&B £140-£230
Credit cards 1 2 3 5

**★★★★ 63% The Majestic**
Ripon Rd, Harrogate
☎ (0423) 568972, telex: 57918, fax: (0423) 502283
156 bedrooms; double room £90-£100 (room only)
Credit cards 1 2 3 5

**★★★ ❀❀ 74% Boar's Head**
Ripley, Harrogate
☎ (0423) 771888, fax: (0423) 771509
19 bedrooms; double B&B £98-£105
Credit cards 1 2 3

**★★★ ❀ 69% Balmoral Hotel & Restaurant**
Franklin Mount, Harrogate
☎ (0423) 508208, fax: (0423) 530652
20 bedrooms
Credit cards 1 2 3

**★★★ 68% Grants**
3-13 Swan Rd, Harrogate
☎ (0423) 560666, fax: (0423) 502550
41 bedrooms; double B&B £48-£128
Credit cards 1 2 3 5

**★★★ ❀ 67% White House**
10 Park Pde, Harrogate
☎ (0423) 501388
13 bedrooms
Credit cards 1 2 3 5

**★★★ 64% St George Swallow**
1 Ripon Rd, Harrogate
☎ (0423) 561431, telex: 57995, fax: (0423) 530037
93 bedrooms; double B&B £104
Credit cards 1 2 3 5

**★★★ 63% The Crown**
Crown Place, Harrogate
☎ (0423) 567755, telex: 57652, fax: (0423) 502284
121 bedrooms; double room £70-£85
Credit cards 1 2 3 5

**★★★ 63% Studley**
Swan Rd, Harrogate
☎ (0423) 560425, telex: 57506, fax: (0423) 530967
36 bedrooms; double B&B £78-£95
Credit cards 1 2 3 5

**★★★ 61% Hospitality Inn**
Prospect Place, West Park
☎ (0423) 564601, telex: 57530, fax: (0423) 507508
71 bedrooms; double room £79-£89 (room only)
Credit cards 1 2 3 5

**★★ 72% Albany**
22-23 Harlow Moor Dr, Harrogate
☎ (0423) 565890
14 bedrooms
Credit cards 1 3 5

**★★ 70% Harrogate Brasserie Hotel & Bar**
28-30 Cheltenham Pde, Harrogate
☎ (0423) 505041, fax: (0423) 530920
14 bedrooms; double B&B £50-£65
Credit cards 1 3 5

**★★ 70% The Manor**
3 Clarence Dr, Harrogate
☎ (0423) 503916, fax: (0423) 568709
17 bedrooms; double B&B £52-£73
Credit cards 1 3

**★★ 68% Ascot House**
53 Kings Rd, Harrogate
☎ (0423) 531005, fax: (0423) 503523
22 bedrooms; double B&B £59-£69.50
Credit cards 1 2 3 5

**★★ 67% Abbey Lodge**
29-31 Ripon Rd, Harrogate
☎ (0423) 569712, fax: (0423) 530570
19 bedrooms; double B&B £42-£50.50
Credit cards 1 3

**★★ 67% Green Park**
Valley Dr, Harrogate
☎ (0423) 504681, telex: 57515, fax: (0423) 530811
43 bedrooms; double B&B £70
Credit cards 1 2 3 5

**★★ 64% Young's**
15 York Rd, off Swan Rd, Harrogate
☎ (0423) 567336 & 521231, fax: (0423) 500042
16 bedrooms; double B&B £50-£70
Credit cards 1 3

**★★ 63% Valley**
93-95 Valley Dr, Harrogate
☎ (0423) 504868, fax: (0423) 531940
14 bedrooms; double B&B £46-£56
Credit cards 1 3

## WHERE TO STAY

**★★ 62% West Park**
West Park, Harrogate
☎ (0423) 524471
17 bedrooms
Credit cards 1 2 3 5

**★ 67% Britannia Lodge**
16 Swan Rd, Harrogate
☎ (0423) 508482
12 bedrooms; double B&B £40-£60
Credit cards 1 2 3

**★ 70% Cavendish**
3 Valley Dr, Harrogate
☎ (0423) 509637, fax: (0423) 504429
9 bedrooms; double B&B £56-£65
Credit cards 1 3

**★ 70% Gables**
2 West Grove Rd, Harrogate
☎ (0423) 505625, fax: (0423) 561312
9 bedrooms; double B&B £52-£59
Credit cards 1 3

**★ 69 Grafton**
1-3 Franklin Mount, Harrogate
☎ (0423) 508491, fax: (0423) 523168
17 bedrooms; double B&B £50-£55
Credit cards 1 2 3 5

**★ 67% Alvera Court**
76 Kings Rd, Harrogate
☎ (0423) 505735, fax: (0423) 507996
12 bedrooms; double B&B £50-£67
Credit cards 1 3

**★ 67% Aston**
7-9 Franklin Mount, Harrogate
☎ (0432) 5624262 & 569534, fax: (0423) 505542
15 bedrooms; double B&B £46-£55
Credit cards 1 3

**★ 62% The Croft**
42-46 Franklin Rd, Harrogate
☎ (0423) 563326
13 bedrooms; double B&B £44-£56
Credit cards 1 3

**★★★ 69% Dower House**
Bond End, Knaresborough
☎ (0423) 863302, telex: 57202, fax: (0423) 867665
28 bedrooms; double B&B £70-£82.50
Credit cards 1 2 3 5

**★★★ 64% Stakis Windmill**
Ring Rd, Seacroft, Leeds
☎ (0532) 732323, telex: 55452, fax: (0532) 323018
100 bedrooms; double room £79-£89 (room only)
Credit cards 1 2 3 4 5

## BED AND BREAKFAST

**Prospect House**
8 Caxton St
☎ (0937) 582428
Close to town centre, offering clean, simple bedrooms.
6 bedrooms; double B&B £30-£31

## Around Wetherby

**The Royal Hotel**
182 High St, Boston Spa
☎ (0937) 842142, fax: (0937) 541036
An 18th-century village inn offering comfortable bedrooms.
13 bedrooms; double B&B £50-£70
Credit cards 1 2 3 5

**Duke of Connaught Hotel**
Copmanthorpe Grange
☎ (090484) 318
Cosy beamed bar; en suite accommodation.
14 bedrooms; double B&B £45
Credit cards 1 3

**Alexa House & Stable Cottages**
26 Ripon Rd, Harrogate
☎ (0423) 501988, fax: (0423) 504086
Yorkshire hospitality in very congenial surroundings, with high standards throughout.
9 bedrooms; double B&B £46-£50
Credit cards 1 3

**Acacia Lodge**
21 Ripon Rd, Harrogate
☎ (0423) 560752
A few minutes walk from the town centre; very attractively furnished and decorated throughout.
5 bedrooms; double B&B from £44

**Ashley House Hotel**
36-40 Franklin Rd, Harrogate
☎ (0423) 5074747 & 560858
Attractive, friendly hotel with very well equipped bedrooms.
16 bedrooms; double B&B £42-£56
Credit cards 1 3

**Ashwood House**
7 Spring Grove, Harrogate
☎ (0423) 560081
Bedrooms are mostly spacious and comfortable.
10 bedrooms; double B&B £40-£46

**Delaine Hotel**
17 Ripon Rd, Harrogate
☎ (0423) 567974
Family-run Victorian house with attractive flower gardens and tastefully decorated bedrooms.
10 bedrooms; double B&B £47-£50
Credit cards 1 3

**Glenayr**
19 Franklin Mount, Harrogate
☎ (0423) 504259
Tastefully decorated and pleasantly furnished, with freshly prepared home-cooked dinners.
6 bedrooms; double B&B £41-£45
Credit cards 1 2 3

**Knox Mill House**
Knox Mill Ln, Killinghall, Harrogate
☎ (0423) 560650
A former miller's house in a delightful peaceful location, with attractive, comfortable bedrooms.
3 b3edrooms; double B&B from £32

**Scotia House Hotel**
66/68 Kings Rd, Harrogate
☎ (0423) 504361, fax: (0423) 526578
Well furnished private hotel with cosy lounge.
14 bedrooms; double B&B £48-£52
Credit cards 1 3

**Stoney Lea**
13 Spring Grove, Harrogate
☎ (0423) 501524
Spacious and comfortable semi-detached house with mixed facade of stone and Tudor-style timbers.
7 bedrooms; double B&B £40

**Wharfedale House**
28 Harlow Moor Dr, Harrogate
☎ (0423) 522233
Immaculate hotel situated in pleasant location; exceedingly well appointed bedrooms.
8 bedrooms; double B&B from £46

## WHERE TO STAY

### Wynnstay House
60 Franklin Rd, Harrogate
☎ (0423) 560476
Very comfortable guesthouse, with
particularly well appointed bedrooms.
5 bedrooms; double B&B £40
Credit cards 1 3

### Newton House Hotel
5/7 York Place, Knaresborough
☎ (0423) 863539, fax: (0423) 869614
Lovely Grade II listed house with
individually decorated, spacious bedrooms.
12 bedrooms
Credit cards 1 3

### The Villa, The Villa Hotel
47 Kirkgate, Knaresborough
☎ (0423) 865370
Situated high above the River Nidd;
bedrooms furnished in period style.
6 bedrooms; double B&B £36-£40

### Wellgarth House
Wetherby Rd, Rufforth
☎ (090483) 592 & 595
A large well appointed modern house on the
edge of the village.
8 bedrooms; double B&B £28-£36
Credit cards 1 3

### Shann House
47 Kirkgate, Tadcaster
☎ (0937) 833931
Georgian town house with spacious
bedrooms.
8 bedrooms; double B&B from £36
Credit cards 1 3

## CAMPSITES

### ►►► Allerton Park Caravan Site
Allerton Mauleverer, Allerton Park
☎ (0423) 330569
Quarter of a mile east of the A1, off the A59:
pitch price from £8 per night.

### ►►► Moor Lodge Park
Blackmoor Ln, Harewood
☎ (0937) 572424
West of Wetherby; pitch price from £6 per
night.

### ►► Shaws Trailer Park
Knaresborough Rd, Harrogate
☎ (0423) 884432 & 883622
On the A59 Harrogate-Knaresborough road;
pitch price from £6.50 per night.

## WHERE TO EAT

### RESTAURANTS

#### Around Wetherby

#### ❀❀❀ La Jardinière
174 High St, Boston Spa
☎ (0937) 845625
Sound, mainly French cooking and a
hospitable atmosphere in a cottage setting.
Lunch: Sundays only; from £14.50 à la carte
Dinner: 7-10; from £18.95 à la carte
Credit cards 1 3

#### ❀ Grundy's
21 Cheltenham Crescent, Harrogate
☎ (0423) 502610
Bright flavours, unusual combinations and
an admirable wine list.
Lunch not served
Dinner: 7-10; from £11.95 and á la carte
Credit cards 1 2 3 5

#### ❀❀ Millers
1 Montpellier Mews, Harrogate
☎ (0423) 530708
Ambitious and accomplished cooking in a
small mews restaurant.
Lunch: 12-2; from £9.50 and à la carte
Dinner: 7-10; from £16.50 à la carte
Credit cards 1 3

#### ❀ Four Park Place
4 Park Place, Knaresborough
☎ (0423) 868002
An intimate, smart dining room and a
cheery bistro serving light, modern food
with a touch of style.
Lunch: 12-2.30
Dinner from 7-9.30
Credit cards 1 3

### PUBS

#### Around Wetherby

#### Bingley Arms
37 Church Lane, Bardsley
☎ (0937) 572462
This ancient ivy-clad pub is in the centre of
a pretty village, its two bars quiet and roomy
with old beams and panelling. Tetley Bitter
and Mild are on draught and bar meals are
good value. Children are welcome and there
is a lovely terraced garden, full of flowers.
Open: Monday to Thursday 11am-3pm, 6-
11pm; Friday and Saturday 11am-11pm;
Sunday 12-3pm, 7-10.30pm
Bar food: 12-2pm, 6-8pm; Sunday 12-2pm.
Restaurant: Wednesday to Saturday 6-9pm;
Sunday 12-2pm

#### White Swan
Wighill
☎ (0937) 832217
This is a very pretty and unspoilt old pub,
scheduled as a location for filming 'The
Darling Buds of May' in the near future. Lots
of pictures of horses adorn the interior
where a fairly standard selection of good bar
meals is on offer. Beers include Tetley's,
Stones and Theakstons and there is an
above average wine list. Children are
welcome in the pub and there are two
grassed gardens.
Open: 12-3pm, 6-11pm; Sunday 12-3pm,
7-10.30pm
Bar food: 12-2pm, 6-9.30pm; Sunday 12-
2pm.
Restaurant: 6-9.30pm.

# Wincanton

*This small and very charming West Country course is the ideal place ot visit for anyone wanting to get a real feel for the jumping game. The crowds here are made up of professionals and genuine enthusiasts who know and love their sport.*

They will be only too pleased to answer questions and make newcomers feel part of the occasion. Facilities are good and the catering deserves a special mention.

Top-class National Hunt horses can be seen in action on most race days throughout the winter months at this popular venue. One of the highlights of the early part of the jumps season is the Desert Orchid South Western Pattern Chase in late October. This famous grey, in whose honour the race is named, was a tremendous course specialist in his day, thrilling the public with his spectacular front running displays. Now in happy retirement, he still usually attends this meeting, leading the pre-race parade in front of the stands. Other notable contests are the Jim Ford Challenge Cup and Kingwell Pattern Hurdle, both run on the same Thursday at the end of Feburary. These are well established trials for the Gold Cup and Triumph Hurdle at Cheltenham in March and a big turnout is always in evidence, as is the case at the Boxing Day fixture.

## FURTHER INFORMATION

Mrs Jenny Michell
Racecourse Secretary, Wincanton Racecourse, Wincanton, Somerset BA9 8BJ
Telephone: (0963) 32344

## LOCATION AND HOW TO GET THERE

The course is north of Wincanton, off the B3081. From the M3, leave at junction 8 and take the A303 to Wincanton; from the M4, leave at junction 17 and take the A429 south through Chippenham, then the A350. Keep on the A350 until it joins the A303, then turn right for Wincanton. From the M5, leave at junction 25 and take the A358 eastwards towards Ilminster. Join the A303 and continue eastwards to Wincanton.

**Nearest Railway Stations:** Gillingham (Dorset) or Castle Cary; there are no connecting bus services to the course.

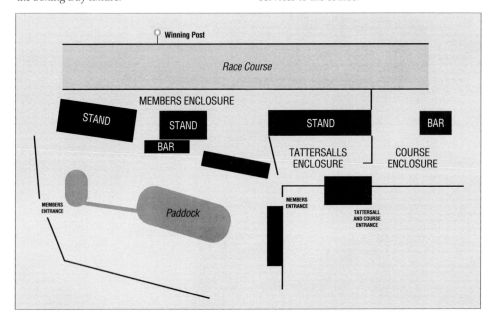

## ADMISSION

All classes of day ticket give access to full betting facilities.

**Day tickets:**
MEMBERS/CLUB £11.50 – access to members' stand, and Hatherleigh stand, paddock and parade ring, bars, restaurant, boxes and private rooms

TATTERSALLS £8 – access to grandstand, paddock and winners enclosure, bars, hot and cold snacks

COURSE £3.50, car £3.50 – access to stand, bar with hot and cold snacks

**Annual Membership:** £90 – includes reciprocal racing days at several other courses

## COURSE FACILITIES

**Banks:**
there are no banks or cashpoint facilities on the course.

**For families:**
picnic area with refreshment kiosk and toilets, lost children centre at raceday office and police hut.

## CALENDAR OF EVENTS

**April 4**
**May 7** – evening meeting
**October 6**
**October 20** – includes The Desert Orchid S W Pattern Steeplechase
**November 3** – includes The Badger Beer Steeplechase and The Silver Buck Steeplechase

**December 26** – includes The Mid Season Steeplechase and The Lord Stalbridge Memorial Gold Cup

## WHERE TO STAY

### HOTELS

**Around Wincanton**

**★★ 57% Pecking Mill Inn & Hotel**
Evercreech
☎ (0749) 830336
6 bedrooms
Credit cards 1 2 3 5

**★★ (RED) ❀❀ Stock Hill House**
Stock Hill, Gillingham
☎ (0747) 823626, fax: (0747) 825628
8 bedrooms; double B&B £160–£210
Credit cards 1 3

**★★ 59% Holbrook House**
Holbrook
☎ (0963) 32377
20 bedrooms; double B&B £60–£72
Credit cards 1 2 3

**★★★ ❀ 67% Royal Chase**
Royal Chase Roundabout, Shaftesbury
☎ (0747) 53355, telex: 418414, fax: (0747) 51969
35 bedrooms; double B&B from £77
Credit cards 1 2 3 5

**★★★ 58% The Grosvenor**
The Commons, Shaftesbury
☎ (0747) 52282, fax: (0747) 54755
41 bedrooms; double room £70 (room only)
Credit cards 1 2 3 5

**★★★ ❀ 70% Eastbury**
Long St, Sherborne
☎ (0935) 813131, telex: 46644, fax: (0935) 817296
15 bedrooms; double B&B £98–£108
Credit cards 1 3

**★★★ 64% Antelope**
Greenhill, Sherborne
☎ (0935) 812077, fax: (0935) 816473
19 bedrooms; double B&B £57–£65
Credit cards 1 2 3 5

**★★★ 60% Forte Posthouse**
Horsecastle Ln, Sherborne
☎ (0935) 813191, fax: (0935) 816493
59 bedrooms; double room £39.50–£49.50 (room only)
Credit cards 1 2 3 5

**★★ 60% Half Moon Toby**
Half Moon St, Sherborne
☎ (0935) 812017
15 bedrooms
Credit cards 1 2 3

### BED AND BREAKFAST

**Around Wincanton**

**The George Hotel**
Market Place, Castle Cary
☎ (0963) 50761
A 15th-century former coaching inn, with all the comfort and charm of such an old-world establishment.
15 bedrooms; double B&B £50–£60
Credit cards 1 3

**Lower Church Farm**
Rectory Ln, Charlton Musgrove
☎ (0963) 32307
Small, very welcoming farmhouse with old beams, exposed brickwork and fireplaces.
3 bedrooms; double B&B £25–£30

**Toomer Farm**
Henstridge
☎ (0963) 250237
Old farmhouse providing pleasant accommodation.
3 bedrooms; double B&B from £30

## WHERE TO STAY

### Stalls Farm
Longleat
☎ (0985) 844323
A warm and friendly welcome is assured at this comfortable farmhouse.
3 bedrooms; double B&B from £30

### Stuford Mead Farm
Longleat
☎ (0373) 832213
Comfortable, spacious and very well kept accommodation; friendly owners.
4 bedrooms; double B&B £32-£36

### Chetacombe House Hotel
Chetcombe Rd, Mere
☎ (0747) 860219
Elegant and comfortable detached property on the edge of the village.
5 bedrooms; double B&B from £48
Credit cards 1 2 3

### Talbot Hotel
The Square, Mere
☎ (0747) 860427
Comfortable accommodation; public bars have character and charm.
7 bedrooms
Credit cards 1 2 3

### George at Nunney
Church St, Nunney
☎ (0373) 836458 & 836565
Very hospitable establishment near the well known medieval castle.
11 bedrooms; double B&B £40-£52
Credit cards 1 3

### Kings Arms
Leq Square, Shepton Mallet
☎ (0749) 343781
A well managed and very popular inn, dating back to 1660.
3 bedrooms; double B&B £33-£40
Credit card 1

### Venn Farm
Sherborne
☎ (0963) 250598
Located on the A30, this farm offers a warm and friendly atmosphere.
3 bedrooms

### The Ship
West Stour
☎ (074785) 640 due to change to (0747) 838640
Fine views of Blackmore Vale; cosy bars.
6 bedroom; double B&B £38-£42
Credit cards 1 3

## CAMPSITE

### ►► Wincanton Racecourse Caravan Club Site
☎ (0963) 34276
One mile from the town centre off the A3081.

### ►► Batcombe Vale Caravan Park
Batcombe, Bruton
☎ (0749) 830246
North of Wincanton; pitch price from £7 per night.

## WHERE TO EAT

### RESTAURANTS

**Around Wincanton**

### ❀ Truffles
95 High St, Bruton
☎ (0749) 812255
Skilful modern interpretation of classic French traditions in a pleasant cottage setting.
Lunch: 12-2; from £12.95
Dinner: 7-10.30; from £19.50

### ❀❀ La Fleur de Lys
25 Salisbury St, Shaftesbury
☎ (0747) 53717
Enjoyable modern French/English cooking in pretty and comfortable surroundings.
Lunch: 12-2.30; from £8 à la carte
Dinner: 7-10.30; from £17.95 and à la carte
Credit cards 1 3

### ❀❀ Pheasants
24 Greenhill, Sherborne
☎ (0935) 815252
An attractive stone house offering modern English cooking with the emphasis on game.
Lunch: 12-2; from £11.50 and à la carte
Dinner: 7-10.30; from £20
Credit cards 1 3

# Wolverhampton

*This Midlands venue has recently undergone a major facelift. It was granted a £2 million loan from the Levy Board to become the third course to lay down an all weather track, with the intention of introducing both floodlit and trotting races into this country.*

Such ventures have proved incredibly successful elsewhere in the world, most notably Australia and Hong Kong, and it will be fascinating to see how they fare in Britain.

This ambitious redevelopment plan, which includes both a hotel and a conference centre and cost a staggering total of £15 million, was about to be completed at the time of going to press. It is due to be officially opened by Her Majesty The Queen in June 1994.

Clearly, then, the future looks very exciting for Wolverhampton. Meetings are run under both codes, many of them on Mondays with the Boxing Day and evening fixtures attracting healthy attendances. Visitors are afforded a genuinely warm welcome and the massive programme of improvements has provided many new facilities. A new tiered restaurant offers excellent views of the track which is triangular in shape and extremely sharp in nature, greatly favouring front-runners.

## FURTHER INFORMATION

Wolverhampton Racecourse
Gorsebrook Road, Wolverhampton BV6 0PE
☎ (0902) 24481

## LOCATION AND HOW TO GET THERE

The course is in Gorsebrook Road, Wolverhampton. From M6 junction 10a, turn onto the M54, leaving at junction 2 to drive south on the A449. At the fifth roundabout turn right and the racecourse is on the right-hand side.

**Nearest Railway Station:** Wolverhampton; there is a connecting bus service to the course on racedays.

## ADMISSION

All classes of day ticket give access to full betting facilities, including Tote.

**Day tickets:**
MEMBERS/CLUB £10 – access to bars, boxes, banqueting suite.

COURSE £5 – access to bars

**Annual Membership:** £120

## COURSE FACILITIES

**Banks:**
there are no banks or cashpoint facilities on the course.

**For families:**
picnic area with refreshment kiosk and toilets.

## CALENDAR OF EVENTS

| | |
|---|---|
| **April 2** – flat; evening meeting | **August 6** – flat; evening meeting |
| **April 16** – flat; evening meeting | **August 20** – flat; evening meeting |
| **May 14** – flat; evening meeting | **August 29** – flat |
| **May 28** – flat; evening meeting | **September 3** – flat; evening meeting |
| **June 11** – flat; evening meeting | **September 17** – flat; evening meeting |
| **June 23** – flat | **October 1** – flat; evening meeting |
| **June 25** – flat; evening meeting | **October 15** – flat; evening meeting |
| **June 27** – flat | **October 29** – flat; evening meeting |
| **July 1** – flat | **November 12** – flat; evening meeting |
| **July 9** – flat; evening meeting | **November 26** – flat; evening meeting |
| **July 11** – flat | **December 10** – flat; evening meeting |
| **July 15** – flat | **December 27** – jumping |
| **July 23** – flat | **December 31** – flat; evening meeting |

## WHERE TO STAY

### HOTELS

**★★★ 60% Goldthorn**
Penn Rd
☎ (0902) 29216, fax: (0902) 710419
93 bedrooms; double room £55-£95 (room only)
Credit cards 1 2 3 5

**★★★ 60% Park Hall**
Park Drive, Goldthorn Park
☎ (0902) 331121, telex: 333546, fax: (0902) 344760
57 bedrooms; double room from £74.50 (room only)
Credit cards 1 2 3 4 5

**★★ 68% Ely House**
53 Tettenhall Rd
☎ (0902) 311311, fax: (0902) 21098
18 bedrooms; double B&B £40-£68
Credit cards 1 2 3 5

**★★ 62% York**
138-140 Tettenhall Rd
☎ (0902) 758211, fax: (0902) 758212
16 bedrooms; double B&B £35-£55
Credit cards 1 2 3 5

### Around Wolverhampton

**★★★ 68% Roman Way**
Watling St, Hatherton, Cannock
☎ (0543) 572121, fax: (0543) 502749
56 bedrooms; double B&B from £71.95
Credit cards 1 2 3

**Longford House Travel Inn**
Watling St, Longford, Cannock
☎ (0543) 572721, fax: (0543) 466130
38 bedrooms

**★★★ 61% Ward Arms**
Birmingham Rd, Dudley
☎ (0384) 458070, telex: 335464, fax: (0384) 457502
72 bedrooms; double B&B £75
Credit cards 1 2 3

**★★ 60% Station**
Birmingham Rd, Dudley
☎ (0384) 253418, telex: 335464, fax: (0384) 457503
38 bedrooms; double B&B £59.50-£71.50
Credit cards 1 2 3

**Forte Travelodge**
Dudley Rd, Dudley
☎ (0384) 481579, Central Reservations: (0800) 850950
32 bedrooms; double room £31.50 (room only)
Credit cards 1 2 3

**★★★ 62% Forte Posthouse Birmingham**
Chapel Ln, Great Barr
☎ 021-357 7444, fax: 021-357 7503
192 bedrooms; double room £39.50-£49.50 (room only)
Credit cards 1 2 3 5

**★★★ 58% Great Barr Hotel & Conference Centre**
Pear Tree Dr, off Newton Rd, Great Barr
☎ 021-357 1141, fax: 021-357 7557
114 bedrooms; double room £40-£72 (room only)
Credit cards 1 2 3 4 5

**★★★ 58% The Kingfisher Hotel & Country Club**
Kidderminster Rd, Wall Heath, Kingswinford
☎ (0384) 273763 & 401145, fax: (0384) 277094
23 bedrooms; double B&B £58
Credit cards 1 2 3

**★★ 63% Talbot**
High St, Stourbridge
☎ (0384) 394350, telex: 335464, fax: (0384) 371318
25 bedrooms; double B&B £65-£78
Credit cards 1 2 3

**★★★ ❀ 66% Fairlawns**
178 Little Aston Road, Aldridge, Walsall
☎ (0922) 55122, fax: (0922) 743210
35 bedrooms; double B&B £50-£79.50
Credit cards 1 2 3 4 5

**★★★ 66% Friendly Hotel**
20 Wolverhampton Rd West, Bentley
☎ (0922) 724444, telex: 334854, fax: (0922) 723148
155 bedrooms; double room £66-£76.50 (room only)
Credit cards 1 2 3 5

**★★★ 62% Forte Posthouse**
Birmingham Rd, Walsall
☎ (0922) 33555, fax: (0922) 612034
98 bedrooms; double room £39.50-£49.50 (room only)
Credit cards 1 2 3 5

**★★★ 60% Beverley**
58 Lichfield Rd, Walsall
☎ (0922) 614967 & 22999, fax: (0922) 724187
30 bedrooms; double B&B £40-£50
Credit cards 1 3

**★★★ 58% Barons Court**
Walsall Rd, Walsall Wood, Walsall
☎ (0543) 452020, fax: (0543) 361276
100 bedrooms; double B&B from £55
Credit cards 1 2 3 4 5

**★★ 65% Abberley**
Bescot Rd, Wallsall
☎ (0922) 22447, fax: (0922) 30256
13 bedrooms
Credit cards 1 2 3 5

**★★★ 61% West Bromwich Moat House**
Birmingham Rd, West Bromwich
☎ 021-553 6111, telex: 336232, fax: 021-525 7403
180 bedrooms; double room £69.50 (room only)
Credit cards 1 2 3 5

**★★★ ❀❀ 72% Old Vicarage**
Worfield
☎ (07464) 497, telex: 35438, fax: (07464) 552
10 bedrooms; double B&B £85.50-£100
Credit cards 1 2 3 5

## WHERE TO STAY

### BED AND BREAKFAST

#### Around Wolverhampton

#### Highfield House Hotel
Holly Rd, Rowley Regis, Blackheath
☎ 021-559 1066
Commercial guesthouse with friendly
proprietors.
14 bedrooms; double B&B £40-£55
Credit cards 1 3

#### Moors Farm & Country Restaurant
Chillington Ln, Codsall
☎ (0902) 842330
A busy working farm, well known in the area
for both its accommodation and restaurant.
6 bedrooms; double B&B £36-£46

#### Limes Hotel
260 Hagley Rd, Pedmore, Stourbridge
☎ (0562) 882689
A predominantly commercial guesthouse in
a pleasant residential area.
11 bedrooms; double B&B £32-£42
Credit cards 1 2 3

## WHERE TO EAT

### RESTAURANTS

#### ✿✿✿ Sloan's
27-29 Chad Square, Hawthorne Rd,
Edgbaston, Birmingham
☎ 021-455 6697, fax: 021-454 4335
Well balanced dishes, skilfully prepared and
attractively presented.
Lunch: 12-2; from £14.50 and à la carte
Dinner: 7-10; from £23 and à la carte
Credit cards 1 2 3 5

#### ✿ Henry's
27 St Pauls Square, Birmingham
☎ 021-200 1136
Very popular Chinese restaurant with polite,
unobtrusive service.
Lunch: 12-1.45; from £15 and à la carte
Dinner: 7-10.45; from £15 and à la carte
Credit cards 1 2 3 5

### PUBS

#### Around Wolverhampton

#### The Crooked House
Coppice Mill, nr Himley
☎ (0384) 238583
This is a local curiosity – a 19th-century
building affected by subsidence to the point
where its floors, walls and doors all slope
noticeably! Three bars in Victorian style
serve draught Banks's Bitter and Mild, Harp,
Kronenberg 1664 and Grolsch lager and
Woodpecker cider. Bar menus offer snacks
and salads alongside a range of traditional
hot dishes. Only children having meals are
permitted in the bars.
Open: 11am-11pm; Sunday 12-3pm, 7-
10.30pm
Bar food: 12-2pm, Sunday lunch.

#### The Little Dry Dock
Windmill End, Netherton, nr Dudley
☎ (0384) 235369
The front door wings of this canalide
Victorian pub are narrowboat rudders and
the bar itself is an authentic narrowboat.
With its floor covered with lino and
sawdust, this is an effective reminder of
another era. The value-for-money menu of
good, home-cooked food may be
accompanied by a pint of 'Mad' O'Rourke's
Little Lumphammer or Holts Mild or Entire.
Children are welcome.
Open: 11am-3pm, 7-11pm; Sunday 12-
3pm, 7-10.30pm
Bar food: 11am-2.30pm, 6-10pm; Sunday
12-3pm, 7-9.30pm

#### Church Tavern
High St, Quarry Bank, nr Brierley Hill
☎ (0384) 68757
The ample portions of plain but tasty bar
food served in this early Victorian 'local' in
the town's High Street represents excellent
value for money. Holts Entire, Bitter and
Mild are available on draught and the
atmosphere is quiet and pleasant. No
children under 14 in the bar, but there is
outside seating.
Open: 11am-3pm, 5-11pm; Friday and
Saturday 11am-11pm; Sunday 12-3pm, 7-
10.30pm
Bar food: 12-2pm for main meals; snacks at
other times.

#### The Manor House
Hall Green Rd, Stone Cross, nr West
Bromwich
☎ 021-588 2035
Many original features are preserved in this
timbered 13th-century manor house, set in
extensive grounds and entered through a
gatehouse over the moat. The five bars
retain much of the character of the manorial
hall with beams, exposed timbers, shields
and banners; there is also a small museum
of artefacts found in the moat. Well known
locally for its cask-conditioned ales, the
Manor House has Banks's Mild and Bitter as
well as Harp, Grolsch and Kronenberg
1664. Fresh home-cooked bar food is
available in the bar or the separate
restaurant.
Open: 11.30am-2.30pm, 7-11pm; Sunday
12-2.30pm, 7-10.30pm
Bar food: 12-2pm, 7-10pm.
Restaurant: 12-1.45pm, 7-9.30pm, but
closed Monday, Saturday lunch and Sunday
evening. Booking advisable.

#### Mad O'Rourke's Pie Factory
Hurst Lane, Tipton
☎ 021-557 1402
Brightly painted and typically O'Rourke in
style, with life-sized model pigs and cows
on roof and walls, this town pub-with-a-
difference offers superb value in well
cooked and generously served bar food.
Little Pub Company wines are served
alongside draught beers that include Mad
O'Rourke's Little Lumphammer, Holts Entire
and Ansells Mild. Children are welcome.
Open: 11am-3pm, 6-11pm; Sunday 12-
3pm, 7-10.30pm
Bar food: during opening hours until one
hour before closing

# Worcester

*Worcester is the favourite racetrack of many National Hunt trainers. The long oval circuit of 13 furlongs has easy bends and very fair fences. There is always plenty of room for jockeys to manoevre, making this a perfect venue to introduce novices, both over hurdles and fences. As a result, fields are large, creating an open betting market that proves a boon to punters.*

The emphasis is usually on quantity rather than quality, although there are a couple of valuable Grade Two events, the Aga Worcester Novice's Chase in mid-November and the Cavalier Chase at the beginning of March.

Meetings are held during ten months of the jumps season, from August through to May. The vast majority of fixtures are run on Wednesdays and Saturdays, with the evening cards a particular delight in summer. There are some fine facilities available to racegoers and these are being improved all the time. One slight disadvantage of this beautiful course is that it is situated right on the banks of the River Severn, which makes it prone to flooding during the depths of winter. On rare occasions, the whole track has even become submerged, with only the grandstand remaining above water, causing the site to look more like a marina than a racecourse.

## FURTHER INFORMATION

Mr J H A Bennett
Ryall Cottage, Upton on Severn,
Worcester WR8 0PN
☎ (0905) 25364

## LOCATION AND HOW TO GET THERE

The course is on the eastern bank of the River Severn, five minutes' walk from the city centre. From the north, leave the M5 at junction 6, from the south leave the M5 at junction 7.
**Nearest Railway Station:** Worcester (Foregate Street); there is no connecting bus service, but the course is within easy walking distance.

## ADMISSION

All classes of day ticket give access to full betting facilities, including Tote.

**Day tickets:**
MEMBERS/CLUB £12 – access to bar, restaurant, boxes and private rooms

TATTERSALLS £9 – access to bar and boxes

CENTRE COURSE £4, senior citizens £2 – access to bar, picnic parking and children's play area

## COURSE FACILITIES

**Banks:**
there are no banks or cashpoint facilities on the course.

**For families:**
picnic area with refreshment kiosk and toilets, children's play area, lost children centre

## CALENDAR OF EVENTS

| | |
|---|---|
| **April 13** – jumping | **September 9-10** – jumping |
| **April 23** – jumping; evening meeting | **September 24** – jumping |
| **May 7** – jumping | **October 8** – jumping |
| **May 18** – jumping | **October 22** – jumping |
| **August 6** – jumping; evening meeting | **November 9** – jumping |
| **August 8** – jumping | **November 28** – jumping |
| **August 25** – jumping | **December 7** – jumping |

## WHERE TO STAY

### HOTELS

**★★★ ❀ 69% Fownes Resort**
City Walls Rd
☎ (0905) 613151, telex: 335021, fax:
(0905) 23742
61 bedrooms; double room from £81 (room
only)
Credit cards 1 2 3 5

**★★★ 63% Star**
Foregate St
☎ (0905) 24308, fax: (0905) 23440
46 bedrooms; double B&B £67-£69.30
Credit cards 1 2 3

**★★★ 59% The Giffard**
High St
☎ (0905) 726262, fax: (0905) 723458
103 bedrooms; double room £75 (room
only)
Credit cards 1 2 3 5

**★★ 62% Loch Ryan Hotel**
119 Sidbury Rd
☎ (0905) 351143
10 bedrooms; double B&B £45-£60
Credit cards 1 2 3 5

**★★ 62% Ye Olde Talbot**
Friar St
☎ (0905) 23573, telex: 333315, fax:
(0905) 612760
29 bedrooms; double B&B £50-£67
Credit cards 1 2 3 5

**★★ 55% Diglis Hotel**
Riverside, Severn St
☎ (0905) 353518, fax: (0905) 776177
14 bedrooms; double B&B £62.50
Credit cards 1 3

**★ 59% Park House**
12 Droitwich Rd
tel (0905) 21816, fax: (0905) 612178
7 bedrooms; double B&B £36-£40

### Around Worcester

**★★★ 64% Bank House Hotel Golf &
Country Club**
Hereford Rd, Bransford
☎ (0886) 833551, fax: (0886) 832461
83 bedrooms; double B&B £65-£100
Credit cards 1 2 3 5

**★★★ 64% Colwall Park**
Colwall
☎ (0684) 40206, fax: (0684) 40847
20 bedrooms; double B&B £76.50-£86.50
Credit cards 1 2 3

**★★★★ 70% Chateau Impney**
Droitwich
☎ (0905) 774411, fax: (0905) 772371
67 bedrooms; double room £59.95-£119.95
(room only)
Credit cards 1 2 3 5

**★★★★ 56% Raven**
Droitwich
☎ (0905) 772224, fax: (0905) 772371
72 bedrooms; double room £59.95-£119.95
(room only)
Credit cards 1 2 3 5

**Forte Travelodge**
Rashwood Hill, Droitwich
☎ (052786) 545, Central Reservations:
(0800) 850950
32 bedrooms; double room £31.95 (room
only)
Credit cards 1 2 3

**★★ 58% The Chequers Inn**
Chequers Lane, Fladbury
☎ (0386) 860276 & 860527
8 bedrooms; double B&B £61
Credit cards 1 2 3

**★ 62% Talbot**
Knightwick
☎ (0886) 21235, fax: (0886) 21060
10 bedrooms; double B&B £39-£52.50
Credit cards 1 3

**★★★ 64% Abbey**
Abbey Rd, Malvern
☎ (0684) 892332, telex: 335008, fax:
(0684) 892662
105 bedrooms
Credit cards 1 2 3 5

**★★★ 58% Foley Arms**
Worcester Rd, Malvern
☎ (0684) 573397, fax: (0684) 569665
26 bedrooms; double B&B £85-£95
Credit cards 1 2 3 5

**★★ 66% Great Malvern**
Graham Rd, Malvern
☎ (0684) 563411, fax: (0684) 560514
14 bedrooms; double B&B £42-£60
Credit cards 1 2 3 5

**★★ 63% Mount Pleasant**
Belle Vue Terrace, Malvern
☎ (0684) 561837, fax: (0684) 569968
15 bedrooms; double B&B £59-£73
Credit cards 1 2 3 5

**★★ 61% Cotford**
51 Graham Rd, Malvern
☎ (0684) 572427
16 bedrooms; double B&B £58-£60
Credit cards 1 3

**★★ 58% Montrose**
23 Graham Rd, Malvern
☎ (0684) 572335
14 bedrooms
Credit cards 1 2 3

**★ 63% Deacons**
34 Worcester Rd, Malvern
☎ (0684) 566990
9 bedrooms; double B&B £38-£45
Credit cards 1 3

**★★★ ❀ 65% Cottage in the Wood**
Holywell Rd, Malvern Wells
☎ (0684) 573487, fax: (0684) 560662
8 bedrooms; double B&B £89-£125
Credit cards 1 2 3

## WHERE TO STAY

### ★★ 63% Essington
Holywell Rd, Malvern Wells
☎ (0684) 561177
9 bedrooms
Credit cards 1 3

### ★★★ 58% White Lion
High St, Upton upon Severn
☎ (0684) 592551, fax: (0684) 592251
10 bedrooms; double B&B from £67.75
Credit cards 1 2 3 5

### ★★ 63% Star
High St, Upton upon Severn
☎ (0684) 592300, telex: 877247, fax:
(0684) 592929
17 bedrooms; double B&B £44-£54
Credit cards 1 2 3 5

### ★★ 72% Holdfast Cottage
Welland
☎ (0684) 310288
8 bedrooms; double B&B £68-£72
Credit cards 1 3

### BED AND BREAKFAST

### 40 Britannia Square
☎ (0905) 611920, fax: (0905) 27152
Attractive 18th-century town house in
famous square which reflects the owner's
interior design background.
3 bedrooms

### Wyatt
40 Barbourne Rd
☎ (0905) 26311
Well maintained guesthouse with spacious
lounge and pretty dining room.
8 bedrooms; double B&B £30-£32
Credit cards 1 3

### Around Worcester

### Nightingale Hotel
Bishampton
☎ (0386) 82521 & 82384
Mock-Tudor farmhouse in 200 acres of land
offering warm hospitality, a high standard of
accommodation and excellent food.
4 bedrooms; double B&B £45
Credit cards 1 3

### The Lion
Clifton upon Teme
☎ (08865) 617 & 235
Cheerful old inn, dating back to 1207, with
modern facilities in the bedrooms.
2 bedrooms; double B&B £55
Credit cards 1 3

### The Larches
46 Worcester Rd, Droitwich
☎ (0905) 773441
A warm welcome and cosy bedrooms are on
offer in this 18th-century house near the
famous Brine Bath.
4 bedrooms; double B&B £34

### Old Parsonage Farm
Hanley Castle
☎ (0684) 310124
A fine old house with views of the castle and
Malvern Hills, offering a high standard of
accommodation in spacious, well furnished
rooms, good food and over 100 wines
available.
3 bedrooms; double B&B £42-£47
Credit card 2

### Phepson Farm
Himbleton
☎ (090569) 205
Rambling 17th-century farmhouse with
cosy bedrooms and comfortable lounge,
just 5 miles from the M5.
5 bedrooms; double B&B from £30

### Leigh Court
Leigh
☎ (0886) 32275
Large, very interesting early 17th-century
farmhouse with spacious accommodation,
furnished in period style, and full size
billiard table for guests' use.
3 bedrooms

### Sidney House Hotel
40 Worcester Rd, Malvern
☎ (0684) 574994
Grade II listed house with views over the
Severn Valley. Bedrooms are particularly
well equipped and hosts are hospitable.
8 bedrooms; double B&B £44-£49
Credit cards 1 2 3

### Pool House
Upton upon Severn
☎ (0684) 592151
Lovely Queen Anne house in attractive
grounds on the banks of the Severn;
spacious, comfortable bedrooms.
9 bedrooms; double B&B £35-£50
Credit cards 1 3

### CAMPSITES

### Around Worcester

### ► Three Counties Exhibition Centre
The Showground, Malvern
☎ (0684) 892751
3m south of Malvern off B4209; pitch price
from £4.50-£6.20

### ►► Lenchford Caravan Park
Shrawley
☎ (0905) 620246
7 miles north of Worcester on B4196
Stourport road, 1 mile south of Shrawley;
close to River Severn; pitch price £5-£7.50

## WHERE TO EAT

### RESTAURANTS

**🏵️🏵️ Brown's**
The Old Cornmill, South Quay
☎ (0905) 26263
Spacious and attractive restaurant serving
interesting English and French food.
Last lunch 1.45pm; £15
Last dinner 9.45pm; £30
Credit cards 1 2 3 5

### Around Worcester

**🏵️ The Gables**
Great Witley (northwest of Worcester on
A443)
☎ (0299) 896944
Last lunch 2pm
Last dinner 9.30pm; dinner not served
Sunday
Credit cards 1 2 3 5

### PUBS

### Around Worcester

**Bluebell**
4 Charlford Rd, Barnard's Green, Great
Malvern
☎ (0684) 575031
The combination of sensibly priced, well
cooked food and an appealing setting
guarantees this pub's popularity. Marston
Pedigree and Banks's Mild are among the
beers on draught, along with half a dozen
lagers. Children are only permitted in the
eating areas, but there is an outdoor play
area and seating in the patio garden.
Open: 11.30am-3pm, 6-11pm; Sunday 12-
3pm, 7-10.30pm
Bar food: 12-2pm, 6.30-10pm; Sunday 12-
2.3opm, 7-9.30pm

**Three Kings**
Hanley Castle
☎ (0684) 592686
This brick and timber village centre pub has
remained largely unspoilt since it was built
around 500 years ago. Butcombe and
Thwaites Bitters are served, along with
guest beers from the likes of Bunces,
Shepherd Neame and Smiles. A range of
reasonably priced bar meals and snacks are
available. Children are welcome in the room
without a bar.
Open: 11am-2.30pm, 7-11pm, but flexible,
depending on trade; Sunday 12-3pm, 7-
10.30pm
Bar food: As opening hours within reason,
but not Sunday evening
Accommodation: double B&B £40

**Talbot**
Knightwick, nr Bromyard
☎ (0886) 21235
This substantial, white-painted building in
an attractive hamlet dates from the late 15th
century, but with modern additions. Bass,
Banks's Bitter, Marston Pedigree and
Boddingtons are among the beers on sale,
while the extensive wine list matches the
menu for cosmopolitan variety. The pub
hosts regular displays of morris dancing
and occasional folk music. Children are
welcome anywhere at the landlord's
discretion.
Open: 11am-11pm; Sunday 12-3pm, 7-
10.30pm
Bar food: 12-2pm, 6.30-9.30pm; Sunday
12-2pm, 7.30-9pm
Restaurant: times as bar food
Accommodation: double B&B £52.50

**Kings Arms**
Ombersley
☎ (0905) 620315
Five chefs are employed here to provide the
interesting and varied menu of value-for-
money dishes. Bass and Boddingtons Mild
are on sale, along with a wide selection of
malt whiskies. Some 600 years old, the pub
is an impressive black and white building
with a courtyard in front and garden at the
back. Children over 8 years are welcome if
eating.
Open: 11am-2.45pm, 5.30-11pm; Sunday
12-3pm, 7-10.30pm (possibly extending
opening hours for the dining area in the
afternoon)
Bar food: 12-2.15pm, 6-10pm; Sunday as
opening times, until 10pm

**Anchor**
Wyre Piddle
☎ (0386) 552799
The landlord of this popular riverside pub is
a chef, and his imaginative special dishes,
served in addition to the brief daily menu,
give him the chance to show off his skills.
There is an excellent, well-balanced wine
list, and beer drinkers are not overlooked,
with Flowers, Boddingtons and Banks's on
tap. The low, white-painted building dates
back to the 17th century and at the back a
terraced garden drops steeply down to the
River Avon.
Open: 11am-2.30pm, 6-11pm; Sunday 12-
3pm, 7-10.30pm
Bar food: 12-2.30pm, 7-9.30pm; Sunday
12-2pm, 7-9pm
Restaurant: times as bar food, but closed
Sunday evening

# Yarmouth

*This popular Norfolk coastal resort, 20 miles east of Norwich, offers the perfect opportunity to combine a break at the seaside with some exciting Flat racing. Meetings are always well attended by holiday-makers, many of whom take advantage of the buses that are laid on to take them to the track from various points in the town, including the sea front.*

The course also goes out of its way to cater for families. A supervised adventure playground has been specially designed to keep the children happy and there are plenty of outlets selling fast food and snacks.

This is one of the nearest venues to the major equine centre of Newmarket and many of the top trainers there like to frequent this course. the quality of racing is therefore usually well above average, particularly in the contests for two-year-olds. The track is a narrow oval circuit with a long run-in of five furlongs which also forms part of the straight mile course. It is very level and galloping in nature, suiting big, long-striding horses. Fixtures are held throughout the summer, with the three-day meeting in mid-September and the evening card in July the main highlights of the year.

## FURTHER INFORMATION

The Racecourse
Jellicoe Road, Great Yarmouth, Norfolk NR30 4AU
☎ (0493) 843254

## LOCATION AND HOW TO GET THERE

The racecourse is on the A1064 Caister road, one and a half miles north of Great Yarmouth and is signposted from the roundabout at the end of the A47.
**Nearest Railway Station:** Great Yarmouth; there is a connecting bus service to the course on racedays.

## ADMISSION

All classes of day ticket give access to full betting facilities, including Tote.

**Day tickets:**
Children under 16 are admitted free.

MEMBERS £12 – access to bar, law, tea room

TATTERSALLS £8.50 – access to seafood restaurant, carvery & à la carte restaurant, bars, seafood counters and fast food

SILVER RING/FAMILY £4.50 or £15 for car and up to four adults – access to bars, snacks and ice cream

**Annual Membership:** £90, first guest £70, second guest £60

## COURSE FACILITIES

**Banks:**
there are no banks or cashpoint facilities on the course.

**For families:**
picnic area with refreshment kiosk and toilets; children's play area with train, pony rides, bouncy castle and fair in Silver Ring/Family enclosure; baby changing facilities; lost children centre.

## CALENDAR OF EVENTS

**June 1** – flat
**June 8** – flat
**June 21** – flat
**June 29-30** – flat; evening meeting on Wednesday
**July 13** – flat; evening meeting
**July 20-21** – flat
**July 28** – flat

**August 9** – flat
**August 17-18** – flat
**August 29** – Arab Horse Society Raceday
**September 13-15** – flat
**October 19** – flat
**October 26** – flat

## WHERE TO STAY

### HOTELS

**★★★ 70% Cliff**
Gorleston
☎ (0493) 662179, telex: 975608, fax: (0493) 653617
30 bedrooms
Credit cards 1 2 3 5

**★★★ 66% Carlton**
Marine Pde
☎ (0493) 855234, telex: 975642, fax: (0493) 852220
95 bedrooms; double B&B £78.50-£88.50
Credit cards 1 2 3 4 5

**★★★ ✿ 62% Imperial**
North Dr
☎ (0493) 851113, fax: (0493) 852229
39 bedrooms; double B&B £65-£68
Credit cards 1 2 3 4 5

**★★★ 60% Meridian Dolphin**
Albert Square
☎ (0493) 855070, telex: 975037, fax: (0493) 853798
49 bedrooms
Credit cards 1 2 3 5

**★★ 64% Burlington**
11 North Dr
☎ (0493) 844568 & 842095, fax: (0493) 331848
27 bedrooms; double B&B £39-£70
Credit cards 1 2 3 5

**★★ 64% Regency**
5 North Dr
☎ (0493) 843759, fax: (0493) 330411
13 bedrooms; double B&B £46-£54
Credit cards 1 2 3 5

### Around Great Yarmouth

**Forte Travelodge**
Acle
☎ (0493) 751970, Central Reservations: (0800) 850950
40 bedrooms; double room £31.95 (room only)
Credit cards 1 2 3

**★★ 63% Broadlands**
Bridge Rd, Oulton Broad, Lowestoft
☎ (0502) 516031, fax: (0502) 501454
52 bedrooms; double B&B £63-£70
Credit cards 1 2 3 5

**★★ 61% Victoria**
Kirkley Cliff Rd, Lowestoft
☎ (0502) 574433, fax: (0502) 501529
36 bedrooms
Credit cards 1 2 3 5

**★ 61% Denes**
Corton Rd, Lowestoft
☎ (0502) 564616 & 500679
12 bedrooms
Credit cards 1 2 3 5

**★★★ 63% South Walsham Hall**
The Street, South Walsham
☎ (060549) 378 & 591, fax: (060549) 519
17 bedrooms
Credit cards 1 2 3 5

### BED AND BREAKFAST

**Balmoral Private Hotel**
65 Avondale Rd
☎ (0493) 662538
Cheerful, modest guesthouse maintaining a consistent standard.
7 bedrooms; double B&B £30-£50

**Georgian House**
☎ (0493) 842623
Popular, good value establishment.
19 bedrooms; double B&B £35-£45

**Helm House**
2 Trafalgar Rd
☎ (0493) 843385
Cheerful, energetic hostess runs this guesthouse with care and attention to detail.
11 bedrooms.

**Spindrift**
36 Wellesley Rd
☎ (0493) 858674
Victorian building on a tree-lined avenue parallel with the seafront.
8 bedrooms; double B&B £28-£40
Credit cards 1 3

**Squirrels Nest**
71 Avondale Rd
☎ (0493)) 662746, fax: (0493 662746
A few steps from the beach in a quiet area of Gorlestone; friendly proprietor.
9 bedrooms; double B&B £32-£64
Credit cards 1 2 3

**Frandor**
120 Lowestoft Rd
☎ (0493) 662112
Situated close to town centre; simply furnished guesthouse with relaxed atmosphere.
6 bedrooms
Credit cards 1 3

**Jennis Lodge**
63 Avondale Rd
☎ (0493) 662840
A well located guesthouse a few steps from the seafront.
11 bedrooms; double B&B £28-£36

### Around Yarmouth

**Albany Hotel**
400 London Rd South, Lowestoft
☎ (0502) 574394
Comfortable and well run establishment on the A12 south of the town.
7 bedrooms
Credit cards 1 3

**Amity**
396 London Rd South, Lowestoft
☎ (0502) 572586
Clean and tidy accommodation behind a red painted facade.
12 rooms; double B&B from £32
Credit cards 1 2 3

**Fairways**
398 London Rd South, Lowestoft
☎ (0502) 572659
Friendly, carefully maintained guesthouse.
7 bedrooms; double B&B from £32
Credit cards 1 2 3

**Kingsleigh**
44 Marine Pde, Lowestoft
☎ (0502) 572513
Nicely kept guesthouse with some sea views.
6 bedrooms; double B&B£30-£36

**Rockville House**
6 Pakefield Rd, Lowestoft
☎ (0502) 581011 & 574891
A professional approach and genuine consideration for guests is evident at this popular guesthouse.
8 bedrooms; double B&B from £34
Credit cards 1 3

## WHERE TO STAY

### Somerton House
7 Kirkley Cliff, Lowestoft
☎ (0502) 565665
Comfortable and attractive guesthouse on the seafront, with high standards maintained by enthusiastic and friendly proprietors. 8 bedrooms; double B&B from £34
Credit cards 1 2 3 5

### CAMPSITES

►►► Rose Farm Touring & Camping Park
Stepshort, Belton
☎ (0493) 780896
Off A143 south of Great Yarmouth.

►►► **Wild Duck Caravan & Chalet Park**
Belton
☎ (0493) 780268
South of Great Yarmouth; pitch price from £5 per night.

►►► **Grasmere Caravan Park**
9 Bultitude's Loke, Yarmouth Rd, Caister-on-Sea
☎ (0493) 720382
Off A149; pitch price from £5.85 per night.

►►► **Old Hall Leisure Park**
High St, Caiser-on-Sea
☎ (0493) 720400
Close to the A149; pitch price from £5.85 per night.

►►► **Clippesby Holidays**
Clippesby
☎ (0493) 369367
Southwest of Great Yarmouth; pitch price from £6.60 per night.

►►► **Scratby Hall Caravan Park**
Scratby
☎ (0493) 730283
North of Great Yarmouth, close to the beach and Norfolk Broads.

## WHERE TO EAT

### PUBS

### Around Yarmouth

### Fisherman's Return
The Lane, Winterton-on-Sea
☎ (0493) 393305
The fact that it is just ten minutes' walk from the beach and has a garden filled with play equipment in summer makes this pub very popular with families. Very good, sensibly priced meals include seasonal daily specials and Adnams Best Bitter and Courage Directors are available on draught. There is also a choice of 20 to 25 malt whiskies and a guest wine. Children under are 14 not permitted in the bar, but there is a family room and a garden room in summer.
Open: summer every day 11am-2.30pm, 6-11pm; winter Monday to Saturday 11-2.30pm, 7-11pm; Sunday 11-3pm, 7-10.30pm
Bar food: summer 11am-2pm, 6-9.30pm; winter 11am-2pm, 7-9.30pm
Accommodation: double B&B up to £40

### Sutton Staithe Hotel
Sutton Staithe
☎ (0692) 580244
This 18th-century red brick inn, halfway between a pub and an hotel, enjoys a rural setting right beside Sutton Broad. A good range of draught beers includes Adnams, Ruddles and Websters Bitters, with Adnams on cask, while a decent wine list accompanies a menu of fairly priced but unadventurous bar food. Children are welcome in the eating area.
Open: summer all day; winter 11am-2.30pm, 6-11pm; Sunday 12-3pm, 7-10.30pm
Bar food: 12-2pm, 7-9pm daily
Restaurant: 7-9.30pm (booking necessary)
Accommodation: double room £49

### The Lodge
Vicarage Rd, Salhouse
☎ (0603) 782828
Originally a Georgian rectory, this large and comfortable red brick pub is set in its own extensive grounds on the edge of the village. The range of beverages on offer includes over 80 malt whiskies as well as a good choice of draught beers (Woodfordes, Stones, Greene King IPA and Murphy's Stout). The selection of bar meals is very ordinary by comparison, but it is advisable to book a table in the carvery at popular times. Children are welcome if eating and there is an outdoor play area.
Open: 10.30am-3pm, 5.30-11pm; Sunday 12-3pm, 7-10.30pm
Bar food: 12-2pm, 7.30-9.30pm (except Sunday evenings in winter)

### The Reedham Ferry Inn
Reedham
☎ (0493) 700429
A marvellous place to moor – or, if you are land based, to sit and watch passing boats or the ferry plying back and forth across the Yare, this white-painted, grey-roofed inn dating from the late 17th century stands right on the waterfront with tables on its jetty. The modern sun room running across the front of the bar and restaurant provides a suitable area for children (welcome anywhere except in the bar and until 9pm in the restaurant). Beverages range from Scrumpy Jack to continental lagers and local wines, with Adnams and Woodfordes beer on draught. Good-value bar food is available.
Open: 11am-3pm, 6.30-11pm (7-11pm in winter); Sunday 12-3pm, 7-10.30pm
Bar food: 12-2pm, 7-10pm
Restaurant: as bar food; booking preferred

### The Swan
Ingham, nr Stalham
☎ (0692) 581099
A good choice of bottled beers supplements those on draught (Woodfordes Wherry, Adnams Bitter and Mild, Murphy's, Double Dragon and guest beers) at this lovely 14th-century thatched inn, and a decent wine list is also available. Set next to the church in the centre of the village, the Swan offers reasonably priced excellent home-cooked food. Children are welcome and there is a family room as well as an outdoor play area.
Open: 11am-3pm, 6-11pm; Sunday 12-3pm, 7-10.30pm
Bar food: Tuesday to Saturday 12-2pm, 6.30-9pm; Sunday 12-2.30pm
Accommodation: double B&B £52-£62

# York

*This beautiful cathedral city is steeped in history, as indeed is the racecourse.
Top-class Flat racing has been held since 1731 on the turf of The Knavesmire, renowned
as the place where Dick Turpin was hanged.*

Fifteen fixtures are now schedule here each year, with more than two million pounds in prize money attracting some of the finest bloodstock to compete. The highlights are the three-day midweek meetings in May and August.

The former includes two significant Classic trials, the Dante and Musidora Stakes while the latter is regarded as one of the most influential meetings in the racing calendar. It is known as the Ebor Festival, named after the famous handicap of that title, and features a plethora of important races. Best of these are the Juddmonte International, Yorkshire Oaks and Nunthorpe Stakes, all prestigious Group One contests.

These meetings have also become important social events and York is often described as the Royal Ascot of the north, although locals prefer to think of Royal Ascot as the York of the south. Entrance fees are suitably steep for the Members Enclosure on the big occasions, but the champagne is considerably cheaper than at most southern tracks and the atmosphere is unsurpassed anywhere. The facilities are first class in all sections of the course, with a superb selection of restaurants from which to choose. There is also an Information Service to help all racegoers get the best from their day out, from giving directions to showing beginners how to place a bet. No praise is too high for this marvellous venue.

## York Racing Museum

Permanently on display on the fourth floor of the grandstand is a fine collection of old prints and racing memorabilia. The museum has a close affiliation with the National Racing Museum at Newmarket, who participate in an exchange of exhibits throughout the year.

Open: from 11.30am on each raceday; by appointment at other times.

## FURTHER INFORMATION

York Race Committee
The Racecourse, York YO2 1EX
☎ (0904) 620911

## LOCATION AND HOW TO GET THERE

The racecourse is to the south of the city centre on Knavesmire Road. From the south or west take the A64; from the northeast take the northern bypass linking the A19 to the A64; from the north on the A1, take the A59 turning to York, just south of Boroughbridge, and join the northern bypass.

**Nearest Railway Station:** York, one mile from the course; there are connecting bus services on racedays. The journey from London Kings Cross to York station is around two hours.

There are landing facilities for light aircraft close to the course – contact the racecourse office for details.

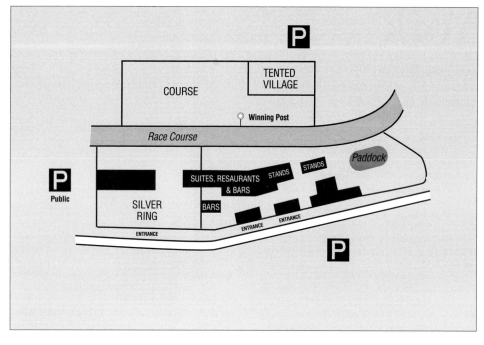

---

## ADMISSION

All classes of day ticket give access to full betting facilities, including Tote.

**Day tickets:**
Tickets may be purchased in advance for all enclosures. Three-day passes may be purchased for all enclosures at the May and August Meetings at a reduced price. Accompanied children under 16 are admitted free to all enclosures, but children under 12 are not admitted to the County Stand during the May and August meetings.

COUNTY STAND £16, £18 in May, £28 in August – access to Members dining room, champagne bar, seafood bar, bars and snacks

TATTERSALLS £9, £10 in May, £12 in August – access to bar and self-service restaurant

SILVER RING £4 – access to self-service restaurant and fish and chip shop

COURSE £2.50

## COURSE FACILITIES

**Banks:**
Barclays Bank is available on the course, open 12noon to 4pm; there are no cashpoint facilities.

**For families:**
picnic area with refreshment kiosk and toilets; children's play area at some meetings; baby changing facilities; lost children centre.

---

## CALENDAR OF EVENTS

**May 10-12** – includes Tattersalls Musidora Stakes, The Homeowners Dante Stakes, The Yorkshire Cup and Duke of York Stakes

**June 10-11** – includes Innovative Marketing Sprint and William Hill Trophy; Timeform Charity Day on Saturday

**July 8-9** – includes Ralph Country Homes Handicap and John Smith's Magnet Cup

**August 16-18** – includes The Juddmonte International Stakes, Great Voltigeur, Tote Ebor, Scottish Equitable Gimcrack, Aston Upthorpe Yorkshire Oaks, Keeneland Nunthorpe Stakes, Bradford and Bingley Handicap and Lowther Stakes

**August 31-September 1** – includes Batleys Cash and Carry Day on Wednesday. Sun Life of Canada Garrowby Stakes and Strensall Stakes on Thursday

**October 5-6** – includes The Ousegate Handicap and Allied Dunbar Handicap

**October 8** – includes The Coral Sprint Trophy and The Rockingham Stakes

## WHERE TO STAY

### HOTELS

**★★★★ 64% Swallow**
Tadcaster Rd
☎ (0904) 701000, telex: 57582, fax: (0904) 702308
113 bedrooms; double B&B £99-£105
Credit cards 1 2 3 5

**★★★★ 62% Holiday Inn**
Tower St
☎ (0904) 648111, telex: 57566, fax: (0904) 610317
128 bedrooms; double room £114-£120 (room only)
Credit cards 1 2 3 4 5

**★★★★ 59% Royal York**
Station Rd
☎ (0904) 653681, telex: 657912, fax: (0904) 623503
123 bedrooms; double B&B £100
Credit cards 1 2 3 4 5

**★★★★ 50% Viking**
North St
☎ (0904) 659822, telex: 57937, fax: (0904) 641793
188 bedrooms; double B&B £105-£112
Credit cards 1 2 3 5

**★★★ (RED) ❀ The Grange**
Clifton
☎ (0904) 644744, fax: (0904) 612453
29 bedrooms; double B&B £98-£135
Credit cards 1 2 3 5

**★★★ (RED) ❀❀ Middlethorpe Hall**
Bishopthorpe Rd
☎ (0904) 641241, telex: 837108, fax: (0904) 620176
29 bedrooms; double room £115-£189 (room only)
Credit cards 1 2 3 5

**★★★ 72% Dean Court**
Duncombe Place
☎ (0904) 625082, telex: 57584, fax: (0904) 620305
40 bedrooms
Credit cards 1 2 3 4 5

**★★★ 71% Ambassador**
125 The Mount
☎ (0904) 641316, fax: (0904) 640259
19 bedrooms; double B&B from £99
Credit cards 1 3

**★★★ ❀ 70% Mount Royal**
The Mount
☎ (0904) 628856, telex: 57414, fax: (0904) 611171
23 bedrooms; double B&B £70-£110
Credit cards 1 2 3 5

**★★★ ❀ 68% York Pavilion**
45 Main St, Fulford
☎ (0904) 622099, telex: 57305, fax: (0904) 626939
21 bedrooms; double B&B £60-£90
Credit cards 1 2 3 5

**★★★ 64% Forte Posthouse**
Tadcaster Rd
☎ (0904) 707921, telex: 57798, fax: (0904) 702804
139 bedrooms; double room £39.50-£69.50 (room only)
Credit cards 1 2 3 5

**★★★ 63% Novotel**
Fishergate
☎ (0904) 611660, telex: 57556, fax: (0904) 610925
124 bedrooms
Credit cards 1 2 3 5

**★★★ 62% Monkbar**
Monkbar
☎ (0904) 638086, fax: (0904) 629195
47 bedrooms; double B&B £85-£95
Credit cards 1 2 3 5

**★★ 74% Kilima**
129 Holgate Rd
☎ (0904) 658844 & 625787, telex: 57928, fax: (0904) 612083
15 bedrooms; double B&B from £68
Credit cards 1 2 3 5

**★★ 70% Heworth Court**
76-78 Heworth Green
☎ (0904) 425156 & 425126, fax: (0904) 415290
27 bedrooms; double B&B from £64
Credit cards 1 2 3 5

**★★ 69% Beechwood Close**
19 Shipton Rd, Clifton
☎ (0904) 658378, fax: (0904) 647124
14 bedrooms; double B&B £50-£62.50
Credit cards 1 2 3

**★★ 68% Town House**
98-104 Holgate Rd
☎ (0904) 636171, fax: (0904) 623044
23 bedrooms; double B&B from £44
Credit cards 1 3

**★★ 65% Hudsons**
60 Bootham
☎ (0904) 621267, fax: (0904) 654719
30 bedrooms; double B&B £69-£75
Credit cards 1 2 3 5

**★★ 64% Cottage**
3 Clifton Green
☎ (0904) 643711, fax: (0904) 611230
20 bedrooms; double B&B £45-£60
Credit cards 1 2 3 5

**★★ 64% Disraelis**
140 Acomb Rd
☎ (0904) 781181, fax: (0904) 788044
12 bedrooms; double B&B £60-£78
Credit cards 1 2 3

**★★ 64% Holgate Bridge**
106-108 Holgate Rd
☎ (0904) 635971, fax: (0904) 670049
14 bedrooms; double B&B £35-£52
Credit cards 1 2 3

**★★ 63% Clifton Bridge**
Water End, Clifton
☎ (0904) 610510, fax: (0904) 640208
14 bedrooms; double B&B £50-£60
Credit cards 1 2 3

**★★ ❀ 63% Elliotts**
Sycamore Place, Bootham
☎ (0904) 623333
18 bedrooms
Credit cards 1 3 4 5

**★★ 63% Savages**
15 St Peters Grove
☎ (0904) 610818, fax: (0904) 627729
18 bedrooms; double B&B £40-£68
Credit cards 1 2 3 5

**★★ 62% Alhambra Court**
31 St Mary's, Bootham
☎ (0904) 628474
25 bedrooms; double B&B £49.50-£58
Credit cards 1 3

**★★ 62% Ashcroft**
294 Bishopthorpe Rd
☎ (0904) 659286, fax: (0904) 640107
15 bedrooms; double B&B from £66
Credit cards 1 2 3 5

**★★ 62% Knavesmire Manor**
302 Tadcaster Rd
☎ (0904) 702941, fax: (0904) 709274
13 bedrooms; double B&B £45-£69
Credit cards 1 2 3 5

## WHERE TO STAY

### ★★ 61% Abbot's Mews
6 Marygate Ln, Bootham
☎ (0904) 634866, telex: 57777, fax:
(0904) 612848
53 bedrooms; double B&B £63-£110
Credit cards 1 2 3 5

### ★★ 61% Lady Anne Middletons Hotel
Skeldergate
☎ (0904) 632257 & 630456, fax: (0904) 613043
55 bedrooms; double B&B £70-£75
Credit cards 1 2 3

### ★★ 60% Newington
147 Mount Vale
☎ (0904) 625173, fax: (0904) 679937
40 bedrooms; double B&B £54-£62
Credit cards 1 2 3

### ★ 66% Fairmount
230 Tadcaster Rd, Mount Vale
☎ (0904) 638298, fax: (0904) 627626
12 bedrooms; double B&B £40-£62
Credit cards 1 3

### ★★★ (RED) Bilbrough Manor Country House
Bilbrough
☎ (0937) 834002, fax: (0937) 834724
12 bedrooms
Credit cards 1 2 3 5

### Forte Travelodge
Bilbrough
☎ (0973) 531823, Central Reservations: (0800) 850950
36 bedrooms; double room £31.95 (room only)
Credit cards 1 2 3

### ★★★ 69% Parsonage Country House
Main St, Escrick
☎ (0904) 878111, due to change to 728111, telex: 556505, fax: (0904) 878151, due to change to 728151
13 bedrooms; double B&B £87.50
Credit cards 1 2 3 5

### ★★ 63% Old Rectory
Sutton upon Derwent
☎ (0904) 608548
6 bedrooms
Credit cards 1

### BED AND BREAKFAST

### Arndale Hotel
290 Tadcaster Rd
☎ (0904) 702424
Beautifully furnished Victorian residence with delightful character.
10 bedrooms; double B&B £44-£60

### Grasmead House Hotel
1 Scarcroft Hill, The Mount
☎ (0904) 629996
Charming small, family-run hotel furnished with antiques and run by friendly owners.
6 bedrooms; double B&B £54
Credit cards 1 3

### Acer Hotel
52 Scarcroft Hill, The Mount
☎ (0904) 653839 & 628046, fax: (0904) 640421
This friendly hotel has well appointed bedrooms and a good value dinner menu.
6 bedrooms; double B&B £41-£51
Credit cards 1 3

### Alfreda
61 Heslington Ln, Fulford
☎ (0904) 631698
Surrounded by spacious gardens in quiet location.
10 bedrooms; double B&B £28-£48
Credit cards 1 3

### Ashbourne House
139 Fulford Rd
☎ (0904) 639912
In quiet area on the fringe of the city; friendly service.
6 bedrooms
Credit cards 1 3

### Bedford
108/110 Bootham
☎ (0904) 624412
Nicely decorated, neatly maintained Victorian property.
14 bedrooms; double B&B £40-£50
Credit cards 1 3

### Beech House
6-7 Longfield Terrace, Bootham
☎ (0904) 634581 & 630951
Family-run guesthouse situated in a quiet street near the town centre.
9 bedrooms; double B&B £34-£46

### Bootham Bar Hotel
4 High Petergate
☎ (0904) 658516
Delightful 18th-century house just inside one of the fortified gateways to the city.
9 bedrooms; double B&B £48-£64
Credit cards 1 3

### Byron House Hotel
7 Driffield Ter, The Mount
☎ (0904) 632525
Elegant late Regency-style house with particularly lofty and spacious bedrooms.
10 bedrooms; double B&B £60-£70
Credit cards 1 2 3 5

### Cavalier Private Hotel
39 Monkgate
☎ (0904) 636615 & 640769
Early Georgian listed building close to the town centre.
10 bedrooms; double B&B £36-£44

### Coach House Hotel
Marygate
☎ (0904) 652780
A few minutes walk from the city centre, this old hotel has beams and exposed brickwork.
13 bedrooms
Credit cards 1 3

### Collingwood Hotel
63 Holgate Rd
☎ (0904) 783333
Listed Georgian house on the A59. Well equipped bedrooms, one with four-poster.
10 bedrooms; double B&B £46-£54
Credit cards 1 2 3 5

### Curzon Lodge and Stable Cottages
23 Tadcaster Rd, Dringhouses
☎ (0904) 703157
Attractive whitewashed listed building close to the racecourse.
5 bedrooms; double B&B £42-£56
Credit cards 1 3

### Dray Lodge Hotel
Murton
☎ (0904) 489591, fax: (0904) 488587
Small hotel off the A166; once a carriage or rulley works; retains many original features.
8 bedrooms; double B&B £36-£44
Credit cards 1 2 3

## WHERE TO STAY

### Field House Hotel
2 St George's Place
☎ (0904) 639572
Conveniently situated for both the
racecourse and town centre.
17 bedrooms
Credit cards 1 2 3

### Four Poster Lodge
68-70 Heslington Rd, off Barbican Rd
☎ (0904) 651170
Victorian villa, near city-centre, with
attractive bedrooms.
10 bedrooms
Credit cards 1 3

### Midway House Hotel
145 Fulford Rd
☎ (0904) 659272
Tastefully modernised detached Victorian
house, with well appointed, comfortable
accommodation.
12 bedrooms; double B&B £34-£50
Credit cards 1 2 3 5

### Orchard Court Hotel
4 St Peters Grove
☎ (0904) 653964
Close to city centre; bedrooms are well
appointed.
11 bedrooms; double B&B £44-£58
Credit cards 1 3

### Le Petit Hotel & Restaurant Francais
103 Mount Rd
☎ (0904) 647339
Conveniently situated between town centre
and racecourse; warm welcome and neat
accommodation.
6 bedrooms
Credit cards 1 2 3

### St Denys Hotel
St Denys Rd
☎ (0904) 622207
Former vicarage offering comfortable
spacious accommodation.
10 bedrooms; double B&B £40-£50
Credit cards 1 3

### Scarcroft Hotel
61 Wentworth Rd, The Mount
☎ (0904) 633386
Friendly, helpful owners; attractive
individually decorated bedrooms.
7 bedrooms

### Around York

### Ship
Acaster Malbis
☎ (0904) 705609 & 703888
Once frequented by Cromwell's soldiers,
this is an attractive building and most
rooms have views of the river.
8 bedrooms; double B&B from £40
Credit cards 1 3

### Duke of Connaught Hotel
Compmanthorpe Grange, Copmanthorpe
☎ (090484) 318
Five miles from York; en suite
accommodation and cosy beamed lounge
bar.
14 bedrooms; double B&B £45
Credit cards 1 3

### High Catton Grange
High Catton
☎ (0759) 71374
Attractive farmhouse with its own working
farm; tastefully decorated bedrooms.
3 bedrooms

### Ivy House
Kexby
☎ (0904) 489368
Situated on the A1079 York-Hull road, this
farmhouse offers neat bedrooms and cosy
public rooms, all run by a friendly owner.
3 bedrooms

### Derwent Lodge
Low Catton
☎ (0759) 71468
Eight miles south of York; owned and run by
a charming family and offering high level of
comfort.
6 bedrooms; double B&B from £37

### Hall Farm
North Duffield
☎ (0757) 288301
Brick-built Yorkshire farmhouse, offering a
sound standard of accommodation.
3 bedrooms

### Wellgarth House
Wetherby Rd, Rufforth
☎ (090483) 592 & 595
A large well appointed modern house on the
edge of the village.
8 bedrooms; double B&B £28-£36
Credit cards 1 3

### Shann House
47 Kirkgate, Tadcaster
☎ (0937 833931
A Georgian town house with en suite
bedrooms.
8 bedrooms; double B&B from £36
Credit cards 1 3

### Cuckoo Nest Farm
Wilberfoss
☎ (07595) 365
Small traditional farmhouse on the A1079;
simple, well maintained accommodation.
2 bedrooms

## CAMPSITES

### ▶▶▶ Rawcliffe Caravan Site
Manor Lane, Shipton Rd
☎ (0904) 624422
Situated on an ex-RAF bomber airfield;
pitch price from £9.70 per night.

### Around York

### ▶▶▶ Chestnut Farm Caravan Park
Acaster Malbis
☎ (0904) 704676
South of York; pitch price from £6.75 per
night.

### ▶▶ Moor End Farm
Acaster Malbis
☎ (0904) 706727
South of York; pitch price from £7 per night.

### ▶▶▶▶ Cawood Holiday Park
Ryther Rd, Cawood
☎ (0757) 268450
Half a mile northwest of Cawood on B1233;
pitch price from £7.50 per night.

### ▶▶ Swallow Hall Caravan Park
Crockey Hill
☎ (0904) 448219
Near the A19 south of York; pitch price from
£6.50 per night.

### ▶▶▶ Fangfoss Old Station Caravan Park
Old Station House, Fangfoss
☎ (07595) 491
East of York; pitch price from £5.50 per
night.

## WHERE TO STAY

### ►► Naburn Locks Caravan & Camping Park
Naburn
☎ (0904) 87697
Two miles south of the York bypass; pitch price from £7 per night.

### ►►► Weir Caravan Park
Stamford Bridge
☎ (0759) 71377
Off A166; pitch price from £8.50 per night.

### ►►► Goosewood Caravan Park
Sutton-on-the-Forest
☎ (0347) 810829
North of York

## WHERE TO EAT

### RESTAURANTS

### ❀❀ 19 Grape Lane
19 Grape Ln
☎ (0904) 636366
Atmospheric little restaurant with sound modern English cooking.
Lunch: 12-1.45; from £7.50 à la carte
Dinner: 7-10.30; from £18.95 and à la carte
Credit cards 1 3

### ❀❀ Melton's
7 Scarcroft Rd
☎ (0904) 634341, fax: (0904) 629233
Careful, accurate cooking at reasonable prices in a simple, stylish restaurant.
Lunch: 12-2; from £10.50 à la carte
Dinner: 7-10; from £14.60 à la carte
Credit cards 1 3

### PUBS

### Around York

### Abbey Inn
Coxwold
☎ (03476) 204
An attractive old Yorkshire stone pub near to Byland Abbey, offering very tasty, good value meals. Draught beers include EP Traditional, Theakstons and Guinness and there is a good wine list. Children are welcome in the pub and there is a large garden.
Open: 10am-2.30pm, 6.30-11pm, but closed Sunday evening and all day Monday.
Bar food: as opening times

### Fauconberg Arms
Coxwold
☎ (03476) 214
Pretty Yorkshire stone pub in the centre of the village, with a relaxed and friendly atmosphere. The fresh, home-made food is above average and includes some interesting choices. Draught beers include John Smiths, Theakstons, Tetley and Guinness and there is a large wine list. Children are welcome.
Open:11am-3pm, 6.30-11pm; Sunday 12-3pm, 7-10.30pm
Bar food: 12-2pm, 7-9.45pm
Accommodation: double B&B £40

### Wombwell Arms
Wass
☎ (03476) 280
Dating from the 17th century, this whitewashed stone pub in the village centre offers good value, substantial meals and a good range of quality wines. Draught beers include Camerons Traditional Bitter, Everards Old Original and Guinness. Children are welcome and there is a separate family room, though children under 8 years are not accommodated overnight.
Open: 12-2.30pm, 7-11pm; Sunday 12-3, 7-10.30pm
Bar food: 12-2pm, 7-10pm
Accommodation: double B&B from £43

### White Swan
Wighill
☎ (0937) 832217
This is a very pretty and unspoilt old pub, scheduled as a location for filming 'The Darling Buds of May' in the near future. Lots of pictures of horses adorn the interior where a fairly standard selection of good bar meals is on offer. Beers include Tetley's, Stones and Theakstons and there is an above average wine list. Children are welcome in the pub and there are two grassed gardens.
Open: 12-3pm, 6-11pm; Sunday 12-3pm, 7-10.30pm
Bar food: 12-2pm, 6-9.30pm; Sunday 12-2pm.
Restaurant: 6-9.30pm.

# The Curragh

*The Curragh is the premier Flat course in Ireland. It is situated in the beautiful rolling countryside of County Kildare and the facilities are some of the best to be found anywhere in the country.*

This venue is regarded as the home of Irish Flat racing and it plays host to all five Irish Classics.

The 2000 and 1000 Guineas are held on successive Saturdays in mid-May and then the highlight of the Turf calendar comes on a Sunday in late June, in the shape of the Budweiser Irish Derby. This is an immensely valuable contest, both in terms of prestige and prize money, and it often attracts both the Epsom and French Derby winners. A huge attendance is guaranteed, as is the case two weeks later at the Kildangan Stud Irish Oaks. Mid-September sees the final Classic, the Jefferson Smurfit Irish St Leger, the feature event of an outstanding card which also includes the National Stakes, an important Group One contest for two-year-olds.

## FURTHER INFORMATION

The Curragh Racecourse
Co Kildare, Republic of Ireland
☎ (045) 41205

## LOCATION AND HOW TO GET THERE

The course is about 27 miles southwest of Dublin on the N7, one mile past Newbridge (Droichead Nua).

**Nearest Railway Station:** Curragh; special train services run to most meetings from the principal stations in the south and west as well as from Dublin. For full details contact Iarnrod Eireann (01) 366222.

Bus Eireann run a special Race Bus from Dublin's Central Bus Station (Busarus) on racedays. For full details contact Bus Eireann (01) 366111.

## ADMISSION

There is no reserved enclosure at the Curragh, except during the Budweiser Irish Derby Meeting in June, and apart from this meeting, all facilities – bars, restaurant, self-service restaurant etc – are available to all racegoers. Boxes, reserved seats on the upper levels of the Stands and private suites are let on a yearly basis – contact The Manager for details.

**Day tickets:**
Accompanied children under 14 are admitted free to all meetings except the Irish Derby (see below); there is a 50% reduction for senior citizens and students showing evidence of age.

Regular Meetings: IR£6
Classic and Group 1 Meetings: IR£7.50
Irish Derby Meeting: West End Enclosure IR£8, children under 14 IR£2; Reserved enclosure IR£22, children under 14 IR£6; reserved seats IR£28

**transfers:** available from West End to Reserved Enclosure on Derby Day on payment of the appropriate difference in admission charges, as long as it is not sold out in advance.

**Annual Membership:** IR95, senior citizens and students IR£45 – includes free parking, access to the Members, Owners and Trainers Bar and a reserved portion of the Stand at the West End.

## COURSE FACILITIES

**Banks:**
The Bank of Ireland is available at some, but not all meetings. As dates and times vary, it is advisable to check with the racecourse in advance. There are no cashpoint facilities on the course.

**For families:**
A Tiny Tots Centre is provided at the west end of the Stand and there is an outdoor children's playground in the same area, both under qualified supervision. Neither facility is available on Irish Derby Day. There are also baby-changing facilities and a lost children centre.

## CALENDAR OF EVENTS

**April 2** – Open Meeting
**April 10** – includes Lincolnshire Handicap Gladness Stakes
**April 23** – includes Victor McCalmont Tetrarch Stakes
**May 15** – includes Irish 2000 Guineas
**May 21** – includes Irish 1000 Guineas
**June 1** – evening charity meeting
**June 4** – includes Gallinule Stakes
**June 25-26** – includes Independent Newspapers Pretty Polly Stakes. Budweiser Irish Derby on Sunday
**July 9** – includes Kildangan Stud Irish Oaks

**July 23** – includes Meld Stakes and Rockingham Handicap
**August 13** – includes Royal Whip and Desmond Stakes
**August 27** – includes Tattersalls Breeders Stakes
**September 11** – includes Moyglare Stud Stakes
**September 17** – includes Jefferson Smurfit Memorial Irish St Ledger
**September 25** – includes Irish Cesarewitch
**October 15** – includes Juddmonte EBF Beresford Stakes and Blandford Stakes
**November 2** – includes Eyrefield EBF Flat Race

## WHERE TO STAY

**HOTELS**

**Around The Curragh**

**★★★ 56% Downshire House**
Blessington
☎ (045) 65199, fax: (045) 65335
14 bedrooms
Credit cards 1 3

**★★ 56% Curryhills House**
Prosperous
☎ (045) 68150, fax: (045) 68805
10 bedrooms; double B&B from IR£58
Credit cards 1 3

**The following hotels are within about 20 miles or so:**

**★★★ 56% Green Isle**
Clondalkin (northeast of The Curragh on the outskirts of Dublin)
☎ (01) 593406, telex: 90280, fax: (01) 592178
48 bedrooms
Credit cards 1 2 3 5

**★★★ 57% Finnstown Country House Hotel & Golf Course**
Newcastle Rd, Lucan (northeast of The Curragh)
☎ (01) 6280644, fax: (01) 6281088
25 bedrooms; double B&B IR£98
Credit cards 1 2 3 5

**★★★ 54% Lucan Spa**
Lucan (northeast of The Curragh)
☎ (01) 6280494, fax: (01) 6280841
50 bedrooms
Credit cards 1 2 3 4 5

**★★★★★ 82% The Kildare Hotel & Country Club**
Straffan (northeast of The Curragh)
☎ (01) 6273333, fax: (01) 6273312
36 bedrooms; double room IR£230-IR£265 (room only)
Credit cards 1 2 3 5

**Dublin Hotels**
Dublin is about 27 miles from The Curragh. The following hotels are in the central or southern part of the city with easy access to the N7.

**★★★★ 🌸🌸 68% Conrad**
Earlsfort Terrace
☎ (01) 765555, telex: 91827, fax: (01) 765424
190 bedrooms; double room IR£165 (room only)
Credit cards 1 2 3 5

**★★★★ 🌸🌸 64% Jurys**
Ballsbridge
☎ (01) 605000, telex: 93723, fax: (01) 605540
284 bedrooms; double room IR£129.37-IR£196.88 (room only)
Credit cards 1 2 3 5

**★★★★ 62% Burlington**
Leeson St
☎ (01) 605222, telex: 93815, fax: (01) 608496
500 bedrooms; double room from IR£90 (room only)
Credit cards 1 2 3 4 5

**★★★ 67% Stephen's Hall**
14-17 Lower Leeson St
☎ (01) 610585, fax: (01) 610606
37 bedrooms; double room IR£130 (room only)
Credit cards 1 2 3 5

**★★★ 63% Central**
1-5 Exchequer St
☎ (01) 6797302, fax: (01) 6797303
70 bedrooms
Credit cards 1 2 3 5

**★★★ 59% Hotel Montrose**
Stillorgan Rd
☎ (01) 2693311, telex: 91207, fax: (01) 2691164
190 bedrooms; double room from IR£75 (room only)
Credit cards 1 2 3 4 5

**★★★ 58% Tara Tower**
Merrion Rd
☎ (01) 2694666, telex: 90790, fax: (01) 2691027
100 bedrooms; double room from IR£75 (room only)
Credit cards 1 2 3 4 5

**★★ 🌸🌸 73% Longfield's**
Fitzwilliam St
☎ (01) 761367, fax: (01) 761542
28 bedrooms; double B&B IR£104

## WHERE TO STAY

### BED AND BREAKFAST

#### Around The Curragh

**Setanta Farm**
Castlekeely, Carragh, nr Naas
☎ (045) 76481
Modern farm bungalow in peaceful area,
about six miles north of The Curragh.
5 bedrooms; double B&B IR£28

**Kingswood Country House,**
Old Kingswood, Naas Rd, Clondalkin
☎ (01) 592428 & 592207
On the southwestern outskirts of the city on
the N7.
7 bedrooms; double B&B IR£55-IR£70
Credit cards 1 2 3

**Silverspring House**
Firmount, nr Prosperous
☎ (045) 68481
Modern house in peaceful location, with
well kept gardens.
4 bedrooms

**Westown Farm**
Johnstown
☎ (045) 97006
Modern house half a mile off the N7 north of
Naas.
5 bedrooms

**Chapel View Farm**
Gormanstown, Kilcullen
☎ (045) 81325
About two miles east of the racecourse.
6 bedrooms
Credit cards 1 3

**Dublin Bed and Breakfast**
(See note under Dublin Hotels)

**Aberdeen Lodge**
53-55 Park Av
☎ (01) 2838155, fax: (01) 2837877
Edwardian house, tastefully refurbished to
the highest standards with excellent
bedrooms.
16 bedrooms
Credit cards 1 2 3 5

**Ariel House**
52 Lansdowne Rd
☎ (01) 685512, fax: (01) 685845
Luxurious Victorian mansion with antique-
furnished rooms and charming proprietors.
28 bedrooms; double B&B IR£60-IR£100
Credit cards 1 3

**Beddington**
181 Rathgar Rd
☎ (01) 978047, fax: (01) 978275
14 bedrooms; double B&B IR£45-IR£50
Credit cards 1 3

**The Fitzwilliam**
41 Upper Fitzwilliam St
☎ (01) 600199, fax: (01) 767488
Newly renovated to a very high standard,
this house is in the heart of Georgian
Dublin.
12 bedrooms;
Credit cards 1 2 3 5

**Georgian House**
20 Baggot St Lower
☎ (01) 618832, fax: (01) 618834
Large Georgian house close to the city
centre.
34 bedrooms; double B&B IR£53.68-
IR£79.20
Credit cards 1 2 3 5

**The Grey Door**
22-23 Upper Pembroke St
☎ (01) 763286, fax: (01) 76387
Elegant, tastefully restored Georgian house
in the heart of the City – the AA's Best
Newcomer for the Republic of Ireland for
1992-3 – with a choice of two restaurants.
7 bedrooms; double B&B IR£101.95-
IR£111.95
Credit cards 1 2 3 5

**Marelle**
92 Rathfarnham Rd, Terenure
☎ (01) 904590
Attractive house, recently refurbished, set
back from the N81 road, south of the city.
6 bedrooms; double B&B from IR£40
Credit cards 1 3

**Morehampton Lodge**
113 Morehampton Rd, Donnybrook
☎ (01) 2837499, fax: (01) 2837595
Beautifully restored to a high standard, this
Victorian house to the south of the city
centre, has excellent bedrooms and
particularly charming proprietors. Breakfasts
are highly recommended.
5 bedrooms: double B&B IR£50-IR£57
Credit cards 1 3

**St Aiden's**
32 Brighton Rd, Rathgar
☎ (01) 902011 & 906178, fax: (01) 92034
10 bedrooms; double B&B IR£45-IR£50
Credit cards 1 2 3

### CAMPSITES

#### Around The Curragh

**►►►► Kirwans Caravan &
Camping Park**
Mountrath Rd, Portlaoise
☎ (0502) 21688
About 26 miles southwest of The Curragh
off the N7; 3 miles southeast of Portlaoise;
pitch price IR£6-IR£7 per night

**►►► Shankill Caravan Park**
Sherrington Park, Shankill
☎ (01) 2820011
On the east coast, just south of Dublin;
about 30 miles drive from The Curragh.

# Down Royal

*This is one of only two racecourses in Northern Ireland, the other being Downpatrick, and visitors from the mainland can be assured of a tremendously warm welcome from the knowledgeable locals - all of whom will be only too willing to pass on a few hot tips.*

In past years, the facilities could best be described as rudimentary, but the course is being greatly modernised in 1993 with the construction of a new covered grandstand with boxes, a restaurant and several fast-food outlets.

The Down Royal Corporation was originally launched by James II in 1685 and racing has been held at this venue for over 200 years. Eleven meetings now take place here annually under both codes, the cards often including a mixture of both Flat and National Hunt contests. The standard of competition may not be top flight, but the bookmakers are fair and offer a wide variety of interesting bets. The highlight of the year is the Ulster Harp Derby meeting, run on a Tuesday in mid-July. This attracts runners from all over Ireland and there is a real carnival atmosphere.

## FURTHER INFORMATION

Down Royal Corporation of Horse Breeders
Maze, Lisburn, Co Antrim BT7 5RW
Northern Ireland

## LOCATION AND HOW TO GET THERE

The course is at Maze, near Lisburn, about 12 miles southwest of the centre of Belfast on the A1 then the A3. It is signposted from the Sprucefield Roundabout in Lisburn.
**Nearest Railway Station:** Lisburn; there is no connecting bus service to the course.

## ADMISSION

There are no separate enclosures at Down Royal; all racegoers have access to all the facilities.

**Day tickets:** £6 – access to bar, restaurant, boxes, private rooms

**Annual Membership:** £50

## COURSE FACILITIES

**Banks:**
there are no banks or cashpoint facilities on the course.

**For families:**
picnic area

## CALENDAR OF EVENTS

| | |
|---|---|
| March 17 | July 14 – evening meeting |
| April 13 | September 17 |
| May 2 | October 8 |
| May 30 – evening meeting | October 22 |
| July 13 | December 26 |

## WHERE TO STAY

### HOTELS

**Around Down Royal**

**★★★ 67% Ballynahinch Castle**
Ballynahinch
☎ (095) 31006 & 31086, fax: (095) 31085
28 bedrooms
Credit cards 1 2 3 5

**★★★ 66% Stormont**
587 Upper Newtonards Rd, Belfast
☎ (0232) 658621, telex: 748198 Storm G,
fax: (0232) 480240
106 bedrooms; double B&B £110
Credit cards 1 2 3 5

**★★★ 57% Plaza**
15 Brunswick St, Belfast
☎ (0232) 333555, fax: (0232) 232999
80 bedrooms; double B&B £55-£75
Credit cards 1 2 3 5

**★★ 63% Renshaws**
75 University St, Belfast
☎ (0232) 333366, fax: (0232) 333399
19 bedrooms; double B&B from £68.03
Credit cards 1 2 3 5

### BED AND BREAKFAST

**Around Down Royal**

**Brook Lodge**
Old Ballynahinch Rd, Cargacroy, Lisburn
☎ (0846) 638454
A high standard of accommodation and
good home-cooked food are offered at this
modern farmhouse just off the A49.
5 bedrooms; double B&B £32

**Malone**
79 Malone Rd, Belfast
☎ (0232) 669565
Spacious, comfortable accommodation in
detached Victorian villa to the south of the
city centre, close to the University.
8 bedrooms; double B&B £37-£43

**Camera**
44 Wellington Park, Belfast
☎ (0232) 660026 & 667856
In a quiet residential road between the
Lisburn and Malone roads, close to the
University. Simple accommodation with a
relaxed, friendly atmosphere.
11 bedrooms; double B&B from £34
Credit cards 1 3

## WHERE TO EAT

### RESTAURANTS

**Around Down Royal**

**❀ Grange**
Main St, Waringstown
☎ (0762) 881989
Charming restaurant in 17th century former
planter's home, offering good, honest
cooking based on fresh local produce.
Last lunch: 1.45pm; £8.90-£16.50 a la carte
Last dinner: 9.30pm; £14.80-£19.20 a la
carte

**❀❀❀ Roscoff**
2 Lesley House, Shaftesbury Sq, Belfast
☎ (0232) 331532
Vibrant, friendly and relaxing restaurant
providing high standards of French food in
smart surroundings. Good quality local
produce, including fresh fish, meat, game
and organic vegetables, are used and an
excellent value lunch menu is available.
Last lunch: 2.15pm; £11.95 & a la carte.
Lunch not served Saturday.
Last dinner: 10.30pm; £17.50 & a la carte

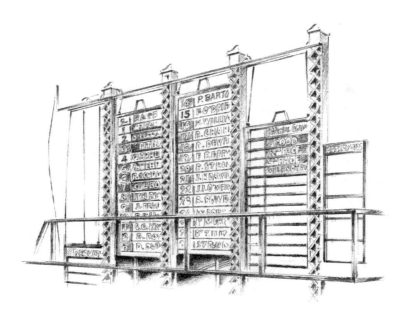

# Fairyhouse

*This glorious country venue became the first official steeplechase course in Ireland when it was inaugurated in 1851. In keeping with its proud tradition, the quality of the jumping events is still high, although racing here is mixed now, with fixtures being staged throughout the year.*

One of the major high spots of the Irish equestrian calendar is the three-day Easter Festival meeting. This begins on Easter Monday with the Jameson Irish Grand National, a handicap chase which carries nearly IR£60,000 in prize money and attracts plenty of British competitors - Desert Orchid was a past winner of this race.

There are many other valuable contests spread over the three days and this is a marvellous place to take a break over the Easter period. The hospitality of the Irish is legendary and newcomers to the sport will be welcomed with open arms - after all, racing is part of the national heritage. The facilities at the course are reasonable and the almost square-shaped track has stiff fences, which certainly catch out any dodgy jumpers.

## FURTHER INFORMATION

Fairyhouse Racecourse
Ratoath, Co Meath, Republic of Ireland

## LOCATION AND HOW TO GET THERE

The course is about 12 miles northwest of the centre of Dublin, between the N2 and the N3. It is clearly signposted on each side of Ashbourne on the N2, and between Clonee and Dunshaughlin on the N3.
**Nearest Railway Station:** Dublin; there is a direct bus service from Dublin to the racecourse. For full details contact Bus Eireann (01) 366111.

## ADMISSION

All classes of day ticket give access to full betting facilities, including Tote.

**Day tickets:**
RESERVED IR£7-IR£10 – access to bars, restaurants, members' room, boxes, private rooms, indoor Tote facilities

GENERAL IR£5-IR£7 – access to bars, restaurants, parade ring, Owners & Trainers' bar and stand

**Annual membership:** IR£75

## COURSE FACILITIES

**Banks:**
there is a mobile office of the Allied Irish Bank on the course, open throughout racing, as well as cashpoint facilities.

**For families:**
picnicking is allowed outside the enclosures; there is a children's play area, baby changing facilities and a lost children centre.

## CALENDAR OF EVENTS

**April 4-6** – Easter Festival; including Irish Grand National on Easter Monday
**May 28**
**August 3**
**September 3**

**October 1**
**November 16**
**Decmber 3-4**

## WHERE TO STAY

### HOTELS

**Around Fairyhouse**

★★★★ ❀❀ **68% Conrad**
Earlsfort Terrace, Dublin
☎ (01) 765555, telex: 91827, fax: (01) 765424
190 bedrooms; double room IR£165 (room only)
Credit cards 1 2 3 5

★★★★ ❀❀ **64% Jurys**
Ballsbridge, Dublin
☎ (01) 605000, telex: 93723, fax: (01) 605540
284 bedrooms; double room IR£129.37-IR£196.88 (room only)
Credit cards 1 2 3 5

★★★★ **62% Burlington**
Leeson St, Dublin
☎ (01) 605222, telex: 93815, fax: (01) 608496
500 bedrooms; double room from IR£90 (room only)
Credit cards 1 2 3 4 5

★★★ **67% Stephen's Hall**
14-17 Lower Leeson St, Dublin
☎ (01) 610585, fax: (01) 610606
37 bedrooms; double room IR£130 (room only)
Credit cards 1 2 3 5

★★★ **63% Central**
1-5 Exchequer St, Dublin
☎ (01) 6797302, fax: (01) 6797303
70 bedrooms
Credit cards 1 2 3 5

★★★ ❀❀ **61% Marine**
Sutton, Dublin
☎ (01) 322613, fax: (01) 390442
27 bedrooms; double B&B IR£76-IR£90
Credit cards 1 2 3 5

★★★ **61% Skylon**
Drumcondra Rd, Dublin
☎ (01) 379121, telex: 90790, fax: (01) 372778
82 bedrooms
Credit cards 1 2 3 4 5

★★★ **59% Hotel Montrose**
Stillorgan Rd, Dublin
☎ (01) 2693311, telex: 91207, fax: (01) 2691164
190 bedrooms; double room from IR£75 (room only)
Credit cards 1 2 3 4 5

★★★ **58% Tara Tower**
Merrion Rd, Dublin
☎ (01) 2694666, telex: 90790, fax: (01) 2691027
100 bedrooms; double room from IR£75 (room only)
Credit cards 1 2 3 4 5

★★ ❀❀❀ **73% Longfield's**
Fitzwilliam St, Dublin
☎ (01) 761367, fax: (01) 761542
28 bedrooms; double B&B IR£104

★★★ **53% Howth Lodge**
Howth
☎ (01) 321010, fax: (01) 322268
46 bedrooms; double room IR£54-IR£64 (room only)
Credit cards 1 2 3 4 5

★★★ **57% Finnstown Country House Hotel & Golf Course**
Newcastle Rd, Lucan
☎ (01) 6280644, fax: (01) 6281088
25 bedrooms; double B&B IR£98
Credit cards 1 2 3 5

★★★ **54% Lucan Spa**
Lucan
☎ (01) 6280494, fax: (01) 6280841
50 bedrooms
Credit cards 1 2 3 4 5

★★★ **60% Grand**
Malahide
☎ (01) 8450633, telex: 31446, fax: (01) 8450987
100 bedrooms; double B&B IR£90-IR£103.50
Credit cards 1 2 3 5

### BED AND BREAKFAST

**Around Fairyhouse**

**Cherryfield Farm**
Summerhill
☎ (0405) 57034
Impressive, large house with nice frontage on working dairy farm.
4 bedrooms

**Aberdeen Lodge**
53-55 Park Av, Dublin
☎ (01) 2838155, fax: (01) 2837877
Edwardian house, tastefully refurbished to the highest standards with excellent bedrooms.
16 bedrooms
Credit cards 1 2 3 5

**Ariel House**
52 Lansdowne Rd, Dublin
☎ (01) 685512, fax: (01) 685845
Luxurious Victorian mansion with antique-furnished rooms and charming proprietors.
28 bedrooms; double B&B IR£60-IR£100
Credit cards 1 3

**Charleville Guest Inn**
268-272 North Circular Rd, Dublin
☎ (01) 386633, fax: (01) 385854
In an elegant terrace of renovated Victorian houses close to the city centre.
18 bedrooms; double B&B IR£44
Credit cards 1 2 3 5

**Egan's**
7-9 Iona Park, Glasnevin, Dublin
☎ (01) 303611 & 303818, fax: (01) 303312
Comfortable Victorian house in a quiet suburb in the northern part of the city; renowned for its friendly and cheerful atmosphere.
25 bedrooms; double B&B IR£44-IR£55
Credit cards 1 3

## WHERE TO STAY

### The Fitzwilliam
41 Upper Fitzwilliam St, Dublin
☎ (01) 600199, fax: (01) 767488
Newly renovated to a very high standard, this house is in the heart of Georgian Dublin.
12 bedrooms;
Credit cards 1 2 3 5

### Georgian House
20 Baggot St Lower, Dublin
☎ (01) 618832, fax: (01) 618834
Large Georgian house close to the city centre.
34 bedrooms; double B&B IR£53.68-IR£79.20
Credit cards 1 2 3 5

### The Grey Door
22-23 Upper Pembroke St, Dublin
☎ (01) 763286, fax: (01) 76387
Elegant, tastefully restored Georgian house in the heart of the City – the AA's Best Newcomer for the Republic of Ireland for 1992-3 – with a choice of two restaurants.
7 bedrooms; double B&B IR£101.95-IR£111.95
Credit cards 1 2 3 5

### Iona House
5 Iona Park, Dublin
☎ (01) 306217 & 306855, fax: (01) 306732
Family-run Victorian house in quiet residential area to the north of the city; large modern bedrooms, comfortable lounge and small garden.
14 bedrooms; double B&B from IR£46

### Marelle
92 Rathfarnham Rd, Terenure
☎ (01) 904590
Attractive house, recently refurbished, set back from the N81 road, south of the city.
6 bedrooms; double B&B from IR£40
Credit cards 1 3

### Morehampton Lodge
113 Morehampton Rd, Donnybrook
☎ (01) 2837499, fax: (01) 2837595
Beautifully restored to a high standard, this Victorian house to the south of the city centre, has excellent bedrooms and particularly charming proprietors. Breakfasts are highly recommended.
5 bedrooms: double B&B IR£50-IR£57
Credit cards 1 3

### CAMPSITE

### North Beach Caravan & Camping Park
North Beach, off Skerries Rd, Rush
☎ (01) 8437131
East of Fairyhouse, on the coast north of Dublin; pitch price IR£10

# Leopardstown

*There are a total of 26 racecourses in Ireland, of which Leopardstown is the most likely to top any popularity poll. This picturesque track has many virtues, including its superb location just five miles from the centre of Dublin.*

Admission charges are low and the facilities outstanding. There are three main restaurants all offering a good standard of catering and an even wider choice of bars. The stands provide excellent viewing of the action.

Another great advantage of this galloping, left-handed track is that the turf drains very well, so that meetings rarely have to be abandoned because of waterlogging (a common problem in Ireland). This is particularly beneficial during the early months of the year, when some high class National Hunt contests are staged here. The second Saturday in January sees the Ladbroke, a fiercely contested handicap hurdle which always produces a close finish. At the end of this same month comes the AIG Europe Champion Hurdle and then mid-February witnesses the valuable and prestigious Hennessy Cognac Gold Cup Chase. These last two events take place on Sundays and are acknowledged as extremely important trials for the Cheltenham Festival. A consistently high level of competition is also maintained on the Flat.

The highlights are the Heinz 57 Phoenix Stakes in early August and the Kerry Group Champion Stakes in mid-September, both Group One events that draw runners from all over Europe.

## FURTHER INFORMATION

Leopardstown Racecourse
Stillorgan, Dublin, Republic of Ireland
☎ (01) 2893607

## LOCATION AND HOW TO GET THERE

The course is five miles south of Dublin City centre at Stillorgan. Take the N11 Wexford road and follow signs.
**Nearest Railway Station:** Blackrock (DART services); there is a connecting bus service to the course on racedays, except Sundays. There is also a direct bus service from Dublin's Central Bus Station (Busarus). For full details contact Bus Eireann (01) 302222.

## ADMISSION

All classes of day ticket give access to full betting facilities, including Tote.

**Day tickets:**
BOX LEVEL IR£20 – access to bars, boxes, private rooms

RESERVED IR£8-IR£10 – access to bars, restaurant and snack bar

GRANDSTAND IR£6-IR£8 – access to bars and snack bar

**Annual Membership:** IR£90

## COURSE FACILITIES

**Banks:**
There is a Bank of Ireland facility in the Reserved Enclosure, open half an hour before the first race until the start of the second last race; there are no cashpoint facilities on the course.

**For families:**
Children's play area; baby changing facilities; lost children centre.

## CALENDAR OF EVENTS

**April 16** – includes Guineas Trial
**May 7** – includes Derrinstown Stud Derby Trial
**May 18**
**June 6** – includes Ballyogan Stakes
**June 8**
**July 16** – includes Golden Pages Handicap
**August 1** – includes Joe McGrath Sprint

**August 7** – includes Waterford Foods Sprint
**August 20** – includes Heinz 57 Phoenix Sprint
**September 10** – includes Guinness Champion Stakes
**October 29** – Intervarsity Race Day
**November 13** – includes Leopardstown November Handicap
**December 26-29** – includes Denny Chase, Findus Chase, Ericsson Chase and Bookmakers Hurdle

## WHERE TO STAY

### HOTELS

**★★ 63% Royal**
Main St, Bray
☎ (01) 2862935, telex: 33502, fax: (01) 2867373
67 bedrooms
Credit cards 1 2 3 5

**★★★ 70% Fitzpatrick Castle**
Killiney
☎ (01) 2840700, telex: 30353, fax: (01) 2850207
85 bedrooms
Credit cards 1 2 3 4 5

**★★★ 59% Court**
Killiney
☎ (01) 2851622, telex: 33244, fax: (01) 2852085
86 bedrooms
Credit cards 1 2 3 5

**Around Leopardstown**

**★★★★ ❀❀ 68% Conrad**
Earlsfort Terrace, Dublin
☎ (01) 765555, telex: 91827, fax: (01) 765424
190 bedrooms; double room IR£165 (room only)
Credit cards 1 2 3 5

**★★★★ ❀❀ 64% Jurys**
Ballsbridge, Dublin
☎ (01) 605000, telex: 93723, fax: (01) 605540
284 bedrooms; double room IR£129.37-IR£196.88 (room only)
Credit cards 1 2 3 5

**★★★★ 62% Burlington**
Leeson St, Dublin
☎ (01) 605222, telex: 93815, fax: (01) 608496
500 bedrooms; double room from IR£90 (room only)
Credit cards 1 2 3 4 5

**★★★ 67% Stephen's Hall**
14-17 Lower Leeson St, Dublin
☎ (01) 610585, fax: (01) 610606
37 bedrooms; double room IR£130 (room only)
Credit cards 1 2 3 5

**★★★ 63% Central**
1-5 Exchequer St, Dublin
☎ (01) 6797302, fax: (01) 6797303
70 bedrooms
Credit cards 1 2 3 5

**★★★ 59% Hotel Montrose**
Stillorgan Rd, Dublin
☎ (01) 2693311, telex: 91207, fax: (01) 2691164
190 bedrooms; double room from IR£75 (room only)
Credit cards 1 2 3 4 5

**★★★ 58% Tara Tower**
Merrion Rd, Dublin
☎ (01) 2694666, telex: 90790, fax: (01) 2691027
100 bedrooms; double room from IR£75 (room only)
Credit cards 1 2 3 4 5

**★★★ 56% Green Isle**
Clondalkin, Dublin
☎ (01) 593406, telex: 90280, fax: (01) 592178
48 bedrooms
Credit cards 1 2 3 5

**★★ ❀❀ 73% Longfield's**
Fitzwilliam St, Dublin
☎ (01) 761367, fax: (01) 761542
28 bedrooms; double B&B IR£104

**★★★ 59% Hotel Victor**
Rochestown Av, Dun Laoghaire
☎ (01) 2853555 & 2853102, telex: 93366, fax: (01) 2853914
64 bedrooms
Credit cards 1 2 3 4 5

**★★ 60% Pierre**
Victoria Terrace, Seafront, Dun Laoghaire
☎ (01) 2800291, fax: (01) 2843332
40 bedrooms
Credit cards 1 2 3

### BED AND BREAKFAST

**Around Leopardstown**

**Aberdeen Lodge**
53-55 Park Av Dublin
☎ (01) 2838155, fax: (01) 2837877
Edwardian house, tastefully refurbished to the highest standards with excellent bedrooms.
16 bedrooms
Credit cards 1 2 3 5

**Ariel House**
52 Lansdowne Rd, Dublin
☎ (01) 685512, fax: (01) 685845
Luxurious Victorian mansion with antique-furnished rooms and charming proprietors.
28 bedrooms; double B&B IR£60-IR£100
Credit cards 1 3

**Beddington**
181 Rathgar Rd, Dublin
☎ (01) 978047, fax: (01) 978275
14 bedrooms; double B&B IR£45-IR£50
Credit cards 1 3

**The Fitzwilliam**
41 Upper Fitzwilliam St, Dublin
☎ (01) 600199, fax: (01) 767488
Newly renovated to a very high standard, this house is in the heart of Georgian Dublin.
12 bedrooms;
Credit cards 1 2 3 5

**Georgian House**
20 Baggot St Lower, Dublin
☎ (01) 618832, fax: (01) 618834
Large Georgian house close to the city centre.
34 bedrooms; double B&B IR£53.68-IR£79.20
Credit cards 1 2 3 5

## WHERE TO STAY

### The Grey Door
22-23 Upper Pembroke St, Dublin
☎ (01) 763286, fax: (01) 76387
Elegant, tastefully restored Georgian house
in the heart of the City – the AA's Best
Newcomer for the Republic of Ireland for
1992-3 – with a choice of two restaurants.
7 bedrooms; double B&B IR£101.95-
IR£111.95
Credit cards 1 2 3 5

### Kingswood Country House,
Old Kingswood, Naas Rd, Clondalkin,
Dublin
☎ (01) 592428 & 592207
On the southwestern outskirts of the city on
the N7.
7 bedrooms; double B&B IR£55-IR£70
Credit cards 1 2 3

### Marelle
92 Rathfarnham Rd, Terenure, Dublin
☎ (01) 904590
Attractive house, recently refurbished, set
back from the N81 road, south of the city.
6 bedrooms; double B&B from IR£40
Credit cards 1 3

### Morehampton Lodge
113 Morehampton Rd, Donnybrook, Dublin
☎ (01) 2837499, fax: (01) 2837595
Beautifully restored to a high standard, this
Victorian house to the south of the city
centre, has excellent bedrooms and
particularly charming proprietors.
Breakfasts are highly recommended.
5 bedrooms; double B&B IR£50-IR£57
Credit cards 1 3

### St Aiden's
32 Brighton Rd, Rathgar, Dublin
☎ (01) 902011 & 906178, fax: (01) 92034
10 bedrooms; double B&B IR£45-IR£50
Credit cards 1 2 3

### Ferry
15 Clarinda Park North, Dun Laoghaire
☎ (01) 2808301
Large Victorian house overlooking People's
Park.
6 bedrooms; double B&B IR£35-IR£37
Credit cards 1 3

### Tara Hall
24 Sandycove Rd, Sandycove, Dun
Laoghaire
☎ (01) 2805120
Large Victorian house on main road
catering for tourist and commercial
business.
6 bedrooms
Credit cards 1 3

### CAMPSITES

**Around Leopardstown**

►►► **Shankill Caravan Park**
Sherrington Park, Shankill
☎ (01) 2820011
On the east coast, just south of Dublin

►►►► **Roundwood Caravan Park**
Roundwood
☎ (01) 2818163
About 17 miles south, on the R755 between
Enniskerry and Laragh, in the Wicklow
Mountains; pitch price IR£8-IR£9 per night.

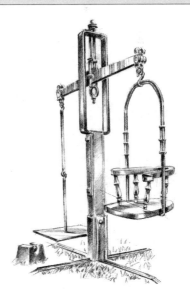

# Punchestown

*The Emerald Isle is renowned for its luscious verdancy and there is certainly plenty in evidence at this jewel of a racecourse. With the scenic Wicklow Mountains in the background and the sweeping countryside of County Kildare in the foreground, this is an idyllic site at which to enjoy the spectacle of some of Ireland's finest thoroughbreds in action.*

One of the biggest meetings of the entire year is held at this course towards the end of April. This three-day mid-week National Hunt Festival is growing in importance every season, with the levels of sponsorship and prize money increasing all the time. 1992 saw a record number of British horses travelling across to participate and the standard of competition now almost rivals that at the Cheltenham and Aintree Festivals. A wide variety of contests are run over the undulating track, which provides a stiff test of stamina. Among the most interesting is a novel four-mile 'bank race', where runners have to negotiate a series of natural obstacles, including walls ditches and Irish banks.

## FURTHER INFORMATION

Punchestown Racecourse
Naas, Co Kildare, Republic of Ireland
E (045) 97704

## LOCATION AND HOW TO GET THERE

The course is twenty miles south of Dublin or the N7, two miles outside Naas.
**Nearest Railway Station:** Newbridge; there are no connecting bus services to the course.

## ADMISSION

All classes of day ticket give access to full betting facilities, including Tote.

**Day tickets**
GRANDSTAND IR£5 weekdays, IR£6 Sunday, IR£8 Festival Meeting – access to bars, restaurant and Children's adventure playground.
RESERVED Free on weekdays, IR£2 Saturday, IR£3 Sunday, IR£5 Festival Meeting – access to bar, Champagne bar, restaurant, seafood restaurant and Festival hospitality pavilions.

## COURSE FACILITIES

**Banks:**
A mobile facilities and cashpoint is available during the Festival Meeting, open throughout racing

**For families:**
Picknicking is possible, though there is no formal area; there is a children play area and a lost children centre.

## CALENDAR OF EVENTS

**April 26-28** – Festival Meeting
**October 6**
**October 20**
**November 6**
**November 26**
**December 10**
**December 31**

## WHERE TO STAY

### HOTELS

**Around Punchestown**

**★★★ 56% Downshire House**
Blessington
☎ (045) 65199, fax: (045) 65335
14 bedrooms
Credit cards 1 3

**★★ 56% Curryhills House**
Prosperous
☎ (045) 68150, fax: (045) 68805
10 bedrooms; double B&B from IR£58
Credit cards 1 3

**★★★★★ 82% The Kildare Hotel & Country Club**
Straffan
☎ (01) 6273333, fax: (01) 6273312
36 bedrooms; double room IR£230-IR£265
(room only)
Credit cards 1 2 3 5

**The following hotels are within about 20 miles:**

**★★★ 56% Green Isle**
Clondalkin (about 18 miles northeast on the outskirts of Dublin)
☎ (01) 593406, telex: 90280, fax: (01) 592178
48 bedrooms
Credit cards 1 2 3 5

**★★★ 57% Finnstown Country House Hotel & Golf Course**
Newcastle Rd, Lucan (about 15 miles northeast)
☎ (01) 6280644, fax: (01) 6281088
25 bedrooms; double B&B IR£98
Credit cards 1 2 3 5

**★★★ 54% Lucan Spa**
Lucan (about 15 miles northeast)
☎ (01) 6280494, fax: (01) 6280841
50 bedrooms
Credit cards 1 2 3 4 5

**Dublin Hotels**
Dublin is about 20 miles from Punchestown. The following hotels are in the central or southern part of the city with easy access to the N7.

**★★★★ ❀❀ 68% Conrad**
Earlsfort Terrace
☎ (01) 765555, telex: 91827, fax: (01) 765424
190 bedrooms; double room IR£165 (room only)
Credit cards 1 2 3 5

**★★★★ ❀❀ 64% Jurys**
Ballsbridge
☎ (01) 605000, telex: 93723, fax: (01) 605540
284 bedrooms; double room IR£129.37-IR£196.88 (room only)
Credit cards 1 2 3 5

**★★★★ 62% Burlington**
Leeson St
☎ (01) 605222, telex: 93815, fax: (01) 608496
500 bedrooms; double room from IR£90
(room only)
Credit cards 1 2 3 4 5

**★★★ 67% Stephen's Hall**
14-17 Lower Leeson St
☎ (01) 610585, fax: (01) 610606
37 bedrooms; double room IR£130 (room only)
Credit cards 1 2 3 5

**★★★ 63% Central**
1-5 Exchequer St
☎ (01) 6797302, fax: (01) 6797303
70 bedrooms
Credit cards 1 2 3 5

**★★★ 59% Hotel Montrose**
Stillorgan Rd
☎ (01) 2693311, telex: 91207, fax: (01) 2691164
190 bedrooms; double room from IR£75
(room only)
Credit cards 1 2 3 4 5

**★★★ 58% Tara Tower**
Merrion Rd
☎ (01) 2694666, telex: 90790, fax: (01) 2691027
100 bedrooms; double room from IR£75
(room only)
Credit cards 1 2 3 4 5

**★★ ❀❀ 73% Longfield's**
Fitzwilliam St
☎ (01) 761367, fax: (01) 761542
28 bedrooms; double B&B IR£104

### BED AND BREAKFAST

**Around Punchestown**

**Chapel View Farm**
Gormanstown, Kilcullen
☎ (045) 81325
About five miles southwest of the racecourse via the N9.
6 bedrooms
Credit cards 1 3

**Setanta Farm**
Castlekeely, Carragh, nr Naas
☎ (045) 76481
Modern farm bungalow in peaceful area close to the racecourse.
5 bedrooms; double B&B IR£28

**Westown Farm**
Johnstown
☎ (045) 97006
Modern house half a mile off the N7 north of Naas.
5 bedrooms

**Silverspring House**
Firmount, nr Prosperous
☎ (045) 68481
Modern house in peaceful location, with well kept gardens.
4 bedrooms

**Dublin Bed and Breakfast**
(See note under Dublin Hotels)

**Aberdeen Lodge**
53-55 Park Av
☎ (01) 2838155, fax: (01) 2837877
Edwardian house, tastefully refurbished to the highest standards with excellent bedrooms.
16 bedrooms
Credit cards 1 2 3 5

**Ariel House**
52 Lansdowne Rd
☎ (01) 685512, fax: (01) 685845
Luxurious Victorian mansion with antique-furnished rooms and charming proprietors.
28 bedrooms; double B&B IR£60-IR£100
Credit cards 1 3

## WHERE TO STAY

### Beddington
181 Rathgar Rd
☎ (01) 978047, fax: (01) 978275
14 bedrooms; double B&B IR£45-IR£50
Credit cards 1 3

### The Fitzwilliam
41 Upper Fitzwilliam St
☎ (01) 600199, fax: (01) 767488
Newly renovated to a very high standard, this house is in the heart of Georgian Dublin.
12 bedrooms;
Credit cards 1 2 3 5

### Georgian House
20 Baggot St Lower
☎ (01) 618832, fax: (01) 618834
Large Georgian house close to the city centre.
34 bedrooms; double B&B IR£53.68-IR£79.20
Credit cards 1 2 3 5

### The Grey Door
22-23 Upper Pembroke St
☎ (01) 763286, fax: (01) 76387
Elegant, tastefully restored Georgian house in the heart of the City – the AA's Best Newcomer for the Republic of Ireland for 1992-3 – with a choice of two restaurants.
7 bedrooms; double B&B IR£101.95-IR£111.95
Credit cards 1 2 3 5

### Kingswood Country House,
Old Kingswood, Naas Rd, Clondalkin
☎ (01) 592428 & 592207
On the southwestern outskirts of the city on the N7.
7 bedrooms; double B&B IR£55-IR£70
Credit cards 1 2 3

### Marelle
92 Rathfarnham Rd, Terenure
☎ (01) 904590
Attractive house, recently refurbished, set back from the N81 road, south of the city.
6 bedrooms; double B&B from IR£40
Credit cards 1 3

### Morehampton Lodge
113 Morehampton Rd, Donnybrook
☎ (01) 2837499, fax: (01) 2837595
Beautifully restored to a high standard, this Victorian house to the south of the city centre, has excellent bedrooms and particularly charming proprietors. Breakfasts are highly recommended.
5 bedrooms: double B&B IR£50-IR£57
Credit cards 1 3

### St Aiden's
32 Brighton Rd, Rathgar
☎ (01) 902011 & 906178, fax: (01) 92034
10 bedrooms; double B&B IR£45-IR£50
Credit cards 1 2 3

### CAMPSITES

**Around Punchestown**

►►► **Shankill Caravan Park**
Sherrington Park, Shankill
☎ (01) 2820011
On the east coast, just south of Dublin.

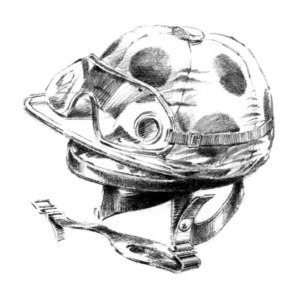

# Other Irish Racecourses

**Ballinrobe Racecourse**
Ballinrobe
Co Mayo
Republic of Ireland
☎ (092) 41448

**Bellewstown Racecourse**
Bellewstown
Drogheda
Co Louth
Republic of Ireland
☎ (041) 38368

**Clonmel Racecourse**
Powerstown Park
Clonmel
Co Tipperary
Republic of Ireland
☎ (052 22611 & 22852

**Downpatrick Racecourse**
Downpatrick
Co Down
Northern Ireland
☎ (0396) 612054

**Dundalk Racecourse**
Dowdaliehill
Dundalk
Co Louth
Republic of Ireland
☎ (042) 71271

**Galway Racecourse**
Ballybrit
Galway
Co Galway
Republic of Ireland
☎ (091) 53870

**Gowran Park Racecourse**
Gowran
Co Kilkenny
Republic of Ireland
☎ (056) 26110, 26126 or 26173

**Greenpark Racecourse**
Limerick
Co Limerick
Republic of Ireland
☎ (061) 29377

**Kilbeggan Racecourse**
Kilbeggan
Co Westmeath
Republic of Ireland
☎ (0506) 32176

**Killarney Racecourse**
Killarney
Co Kerry
Republic of Ireland
☎ (064) 31125

**Laytown Racecourse**
Laytown
Co Meath
Republic of Ireland
☎ (041) 23425

**Listowel Racecourse**
Listowel
Co Kerry
Republic of Ireland
☎ (068) 21144

**Mallow Racecourse**
Mount Ruby
Mallow
Co Cork
Republic of Ireland
☎ (022) 21565 & 22017

**Naas Racecourse**
Kingsfurze
Tipper Road
Naas
Co Kildare
Republic of Ireland
☎ (045) 97391

**Navan Racecourse**
Proudstown
Navan
Co Meath
Republic of Ireland
☎ (046) 21350

**Roscommon Racecourse**
Lenabane
Roscommon
Co Roscommon
Republic of Ireland
☎ (0903) 26231

**Sligo (Cleveragh) Racecourse**
Cleveragh
Sligo
Co Sligo
Republic of Ireland
☎ (071) 62484

**Thurles Racecourse**
Tipperary
Co Tipperary
Republic of Ireland
☎ (0504) 22253

**Tipperary Racecourse**
Limerick Junction
Co Tipperary
Republic of Ireland
☎ (062) 51357

**Tralee Racecourse**
Ballybeggan Park
Tralee
Co Kerry
Republic of Ireland
☎ (066) 26188 or 26139

**Waterford & Tramore Racecourse**
Tramore
Co Waterford
Republic of Ireland
☎ (051) 81425

**Wexford Racecourse**
Bettyville
Newtown Road
Wexford
Co Wexford
Republic of Ireland
☎ (051) 21681

# Racing Fixtures 1994

*UNDER THE ORDERS OF THE BRITISH HORSERACING BOARD*
*The fixtures have been divided into three areas – North, Midlands and South – as defined by*
*The Racecourse Association. Flat race meetings are in capital letters, evening meetings are*
*marked \*, (AWT) following the name of a meeting indicates an All Weather Track fixture*

| | | **JANUARY** | |
|---|---|---|---|
| | **NORTH** | **MIDLANDS** | **SOUTH** |
| 1 Saturday | Catterick Bridge | Nottingham | LINGFIELD PARK (AWT) |
| | | SOUTHWELL (AWT) | Newbury |
| 3 Monday | Ayr | Cheltenham | Exeter |
| (Bank Hol) | | Leicester | Windsor |
| | | WOLVERHAMPTON (AWT) | |
| 4 Tuesday | | | LINGFIELD PARK (AWT) |
| | | | Newton Abbot |
| 5 Wednesday | Sedgefield | Southwell (AWT) | Lingfield Park |
| 6 Thursday | | Market Rasen | Lingfield Park (AWT) |
| | | Worcester | |
| 7 Friday | Edinburgh | SOUTHWELL (AWT) | |
| | | Towcester | |
| 8 Saturday | Haydock Park | Warwick | LINGFIELD PARK (AWT) |
| | | *WOLVERHAMPTON (AWT) | Sandown Park |
| 10 Monday | | WOLVERHAMPTON (AWT) | Lingfield Park |
| 11 Tuesday | | Leicester | Chepstow |
| | | | LINGFIELD PARK (AWT) |
| 12 Wednesday | Kelso | Southwell (AWT) | Plumpton |
| 13 Thursday | Wetherby | | Lingfield Park (AWT) |
| | | | Wincanton |
| 14 Friday | Edinburgh | SOUTHWELL (AWT) | Ascot |
| 15 Saturday | Newcastle | Warwick | Ascot |
| | | | LINGFIELD PARK (AWT) |
| 17 Monday | Carlisle | WOLVERHAMPTON (AWT) | Fontwell Park |
| 18 Tuesday | | | Folkestone |
| | | | LINGFIELD PARK (AWT) |
| 19 Wednesday | | Ludlow | Windsor |
| | | Southwell (AWT) | |
| 20 Thursday | Ayr | | Lingfield Park (AWT) |
| | | | Taunton |
| 21 Friday | Catterick Bridge | SOUTHWELL (AWT) | Kempton Park |
| 22 Saturday | Catterick Bridge | Market Rasen | Kempton Park |
| | Haydock Park | *WOLVERHAMPTON (AWT) | LINGFILED PARK (AWT) |
| 24 Monday | | Leicester | |
| | | WOLVERHAMPTON (AWT) | |
| 25 Tuesday | | Nottingham | Chepstow |
| | | | LINGFIELD PARK (AWT) |
| 26 Wednesday | Sedgefield | Southwell (AWT) | Lingfield Park |
| 27 Thursday | | Huntingdon | Lingfield Park (AWT) |
| | | | Newton Abbot |
| 28 Friday | Doncaster | SOUTHWELL (AWT) | Wincanton |
| | | Uttoxeter | |
| 29 Saturday | Ayr | Cheltenham | LINGFIELD PARK (AWT) |
| | Doncaster | | |
| 31 Monday | | WOLVERHAMPTON (AWT) | Plumpton |

## FEBRUARY

| | | NORTH | MIDLANDS | SOUTH |
|---|---|---|---|---|
| 1 | Tuesday | Sedgefield | Nottingham | LINGFIELD PARK (AWT) |
| 2 | Wednesday | | Leicester | Windsor |
| | | | Southwell (AWT) | |
| 3 | Thursday | Edinburgh | Towcester | Lingfield Park (AWT) |
| 4 | Friday | Kelso | SOUTHWELL (AWT) | Lingfield Park |
| 5 | Saturday | Wetherby | Stratford-on-Avon | Chepstow |
| | | | *WOLVERHAMPTON (AWT) | LINGFIELD PARK (AWT) |
| | | | | Sandown Park |
| 7 | Monday | | WOLVERHAMPTON (AWT) | Fontwell Park |
| 8 | Tuesday | Carlisle | Warwick | LINGFIELD PARK (AWT) |
| 9 | Wednesday | | Ludlow | Ascot |
| | | | Southwell (AWT) | |
| 10 | Thursday | | Huntingdon | Lingfield Park (AWT) |
| | | | | Wincanton |
| 11 | Friday | | Bangor-on-Dee | Newbury |
| | | | SOUTHWELL (AWT) | |
| 12 | Saturday | Ayr | Uttoxeter | LINGFIELD PARK (AWT) |
| | | Catterick Bridge | | Newbury |
| 14 | Monday | | Hereford | Plumpton |
| | | | WOLVERHAMPTON (AWT) | |
| 15 | Tuesday | | Towcester | LINGFIELD PARK (AWT) |
| | | | | Newton Abbot |
| 16 | Wednesday | Sedgefield | Southwell (AWT) | Folkestone |
| | | | Worcester | |
| 17 | Thursday | | Leicester | Lingfield Park (AWT) |
| | | | | Sandown Park |
| | | | | Taunton |
| 18 | Friday | Edinburgh | Fakenham | Sandown Park |
| | | | SOUTHWELL (AWT) | |
| 19 | Saturday | Newcastle | Nottingham | Chepstow |
| | | | *WOLVERHAMPTON (AWT) | LINGFIELD PARK (AWT) |
| | | | | Windsor |
| 21 | Monday | | WOLVERHAMPTON (AWT) | Fontwell Park |
| 22 | Tuesday | Sedgefield | Huntingdon | LINGFIELD PARK (AWT) |
| 23 | Wednesday | Doncaster | Southwell (AWT) | Folkestone |
| | | | Warwick | |
| 24 | Thursday | Catterick Bridge | | Lingfield Park (AWT) |
| | | | | Wincanton |
| 25 | Friday | Haydock Park | SOUTHWELL (AWT) | Kempton Park |
| 26 | Saturday | Edinburgh | Market Rasen | Kempton Park |
| | | Haydock Park | | LINGFIELD PARK (AWT) |
| 28 | Monday | | Leicester | Plumpton |
| | | | WOLVERHAMPTON (AWT) | |

## MARCH

| | | NORTH | MIDLANDS | SOUTH |
|---|---|---|---|---|
| 1 | Tuesday | | Nottingham | LINGFIELD PARK (AWT) |
| 2 | Wednesday | Wetherby | Southwell (AWT) | |
| | | | Worcester | |
| 3 | Thursday | | Ludlow | Lingfield Park (AWT) |
| | | | Warwick | Taunton |
| 4 | Friday | Kelso | SOUTHWELL (AWT) | Newbury |
| 5 | Saturday | Doncaster | Hereford | LINGFIELD PARK (AWT) |
| | | | Stratford-on-Avon | Newbury |
| | | | *WOLVERHAMPTON (AWT) | |
| 7 | Monday | Doncaster | WOLVERHAMPTON (AWT) | Windsor |
| 8 | Tuesday | Sedgefield | Leicester | Lingfield Patk (AWT) |
| 9 | Wednesday | Catterick Bridge | Bangor-on-Dee | Folkestone |
| | | | Southwell (AWT) | |
| 10 | Thursday | Carlisle | Towcester | Wincanton |
| 11 | Friday | Ayr | Market Rasen | Grand Military M (Sandown Park) |
| 12 | Saturday | Ayr | Southwell | Chepstow |
| | | | | Grand Military M (Sandown Park) |
| 14 | Monday | | | Plumpton |
| | | | | Taunton |
| 15 | Tuesday | Sedgefield | N H Meeting (Cheltenham) | |
| 16 | Wednesday | | N H Meeting (Cheltenham) | Newton Abbot |
| | | | Huntingdon | |
| 17 | Thursday | Hexham | N H Meeting (Cheltenham) | LINGFIELD PARK (AWT) |
| 18 | Friday | | Fakenham | Lingfield Park |
| | | | Southwell | |
| 19 | Saturday | Newcastle | Uttoxeter | Chepstow |
| | | | *WOLVERHAMPTON (AWT) | Lingfield Park |
| 21 | Monday | Newcastle | | Plumpton |
| 22 | Tuesday | Newcastle | Nottingham | Fontwell Park |
| 23 | Wednesday | Kelso | Worcester | Exeter |
| 24 | Thursday | DONCASTER | Stratford-on-Avon | Wincanton |
| 25 | Friday | DONCASTER | Ludlow | Newbury |
| 26 | Saturday | DONCASTER | Bangor-on-Dee | LINGFIELD PARK (AWT) |
| | | Sedgefield | WARWICK | Newbury |
| 28 | Monday | Hexham | | FOLKESTONE |
| 29 | Tuesday | NEWCASTLE | | Royal Artillery M (Sandown Park) |
| 30 | Wednesday | CATTERICK BRIDGE | Worcester | Ascot |
| 31 | Thursday | HAMILTON PARK | LEICESTER | BRIGHTON |

| | | **APRIL** | | |
|---|---|---|---|---|
| | **NORTH** | **MIDLANDS** | | **SOUTH** |
| 2 | Saturday | Carlisle<br>HAYDOCK PARK | Towcester<br>Uttoxeter<br>*WOLVERHAMPTON (AWT) | KEMPTON PARK<br>Newton Abbot<br>Plumpton |
| 4 | Monday<br>(Bank Hol) | Carlisle<br>NEWCASTLE<br>Wetherby | Fakenham<br>Hereford<br>Huntingdon<br>Market Rasen<br>NOTTINGHAM<br>Towcester<br>Uttoxeter<br>WARWICK | Chepstow<br>KEMPTON PARK<br>Newton Abbot<br>Plumpton<br>Wincanton |
| 5 | Tuesday | NEWCASTLE<br>Wetherby | | Chepstow |
| 6 | Wednesday | RIPON | Ludlow | Ascot |
| 7 | Thursday | Aintree | LEICESTER | BRIGHTON |
| 8 | Friday | BEVERLEY<br>Aintree | | LINGFIELD PARK (AWT) |
| 9 | Saturday | BEVERLEY<br>Aintree | Hereford | |
| 11 | Monday | Kelso | | FOLKESTONE |
| 12 | Tuesday | Sedgefield | NEWMARKET CRAVEN | |
| 13 | Wednesday | PONTEFRACT | NEWMARKET CRAVEN<br>Worcester | |
| 14 | Thursday | Ayr<br>RIPON | NEWMARKET CRAVEN | |
| 15 | Friday | Ayr<br>THIRSK | *WARWICK | NEWBURY<br>*Taunton |
| 16 | Saturday | Ayr<br>THIRSK | Bangor-on-Dee<br>Stratford-on-Avon<br>*WOLVERHAMPTON (AWT) | NEWBURY |
| 18 | Monday | EDINBURGH | NOTTINGHAM | BRIGHTON |
| 19 | Tuesday | PONTEFRACT | | FOLKESTONE |
| 20 | Wednesday | CATTERICK BRIDGE<br>Perth | Cheltenham | *KEMPTON PARK<br>*Newton Abbot |
| 21 | Thursday | BEVERLEY<br>Perth | | Fontwell Park |
| 22 | Friday | CARLISLE<br>Perth | *Ludlow | SANDOWN PARK<br>*Taunton |
| 23 | Saturday | *Hexham<br>RIPON | LEICESTER<br>Market Rasen<br>*Worcester | SANDOWN PARK (Mixed) |
| 25 | Monday | *Hexham<br>PONTEFRACT | SOUTHWELL (AWT) | *WINDSOR |
| 26 | Tuesday | | NOTTINGHAM | *Ascot<br>BATH |
| 27 | Wednesday | Kelso | *Cheltenham<br>*Huntingdon | ASCOT<br>Exeter |
| 28 | Thursday | HAMILTON PARK | NEWMARKET SPRING | SALISBURY |
| 29 | Friday | HAMILTON PARK<br>*Sedgefield | *Bangor-on-Dee<br>NEWMARKET SPRING | Newton Abbot |
| 30 | Saturday | HAYDOCK PARK<br>*Hexham<br>THIRSK | Hereford<br>NEWMARKET SPRING<br>Uttoxeter | *Plumpton |

## MAY

| | | NORTH | MIDLANDS | SOUTH |
|---|---|---|---|---|
| 2 | Monday (Bank Hol) | DONCASTER<br>Haydock Park<br>NEWCASTLE | Ludlow<br>Southwell<br>Towcester<br>WARWICK | Exeter<br>Fontwell Park<br>KEMPTON PARK |
| 3 | Tuesday | | CHESTER | Newton Abbot |
| 4 | Wednesday | EDINBURGH<br>*Wetherby | CHESTER<br>*Uttoxeter | BRIGHTON |
| 5 | Thursday | CARLISLE<br>*HAMILTON PARK<br>*Sedgefield | CHESTER | SALISBURY |
| 6 | Friday | BEVERLEY<br>CARLISLE | *Market Rasen | LINGFIELD PARK<br>*Wincanton |
| 7 | Saturday | BEVERLEY<br>*Newcastle | *Warwick<br>Worcester | BATH<br>LINGFIELD PARK |
| 9 | Monday | REDCAR | SOUTHWELL (AWT)<br>*Towcester | *WINDSOR |
| 10 | Tuesday | YORK | | Chepstow<br>*United Hunts M (Folkestone) |
| 11 | Wednesday | *Perth<br>YORK | Hereford<br>*Huntingdon<br>Southwell | |
| 12 | Thursday | Perth<br>YORK | | BRIGHTON |
| 13 | Friday | THIRSK | NOTTINGHAM<br>*Stratford-on-Avon | NEWBURY<br>*Newton Abbot |
| 14 | Saturday | *HAMILTON PARK<br>THIRSK | Bangor-on-Dee<br>SOUTHWELL (AWT)<br>*WOLVERHAMPTON (AWT) | *LINGFIELD PARK<br>NEWBURY |
| 16 | Monday | EDINBURGH | | BATH |
| 17 | Tuesday | BEVERLEY | *Cheltenham | GOODWOOD |
| 18 | Wednesday | Sedgefield | Worcester | GOODWOOD |
| 19 | Thursday | NEWCASTLE<br>*Perth | *Uttoxeter | Exeter<br>GOODWOOD |
| 20 | Friday | CATTERICK BRIDGE<br>HAMILTON PARK | *Fakenham<br>NEWMARKET<br>*Stratford-on-Avon | |
| 21 | Saturday | AYR<br>CATTERICK BRIDGE | NEWMARKET<br>*Southwell<br>*Warwick | *KEMPTON PARK<br>LINGFIELD PARK |
| 23 | Monday | AYR | LEICESTER | *WINDSOR |
| 24 | Tuesday | | *SOUTHWELL (AWT) | FOLKESTONE |
| 25 | Wednesday | Cartmel<br>HAMILTON PARK<br>*RIPON | | BRIGHTON<br>*NEWBURY |
| 26 | Thursday | CARLISLE | Hereford | BRIGHTON |
| 27 | Friday | HAYDOCK PARK<br>*PONTEFRACT | NOTTINGHAM<br>*Towcester | SALISBURY |
| 28 | Saturday | Cartmel<br>DONCASTER<br>HAYDOCK PARK<br>Hexham | *WARWICK<br>*WOLVERHAMPTON (AWT) | KEMPTON PARK<br>LINGFIELD PARK |
| 30 | Monday (Bank Hol) | Cartmel<br>DONCASTER<br>REDCAR<br>Wetherby | Hereford<br>Huntingdon<br>LEICESTER<br>Uttoxeter | CHEPSTOW<br>Fontwell Park<br>SANDOWN PARK |
| 31 | Tuesday | *Hexham<br>REDCAR | LEICESTER | *SANDOWN PARK |

| | | JUNE | | |
| | NORTH | MIDLANDS | SOUTH |
|---|---|---|---|
| 1 | Wednesday | *BEVERLEY | YARMOUTH | EPSOM DOWNS |
| 2 | Thursday | BEVERLEY | Uttoxeter | EPSOM DOWNS |
| 3 | Friday | CATTERICK BRIDGE | SOUTHWELL (AWT) | EPSOM DOWNS |
| | | *HAYDOCK PARK | *Stratford-on-Avon | *GOODWOOD |
| 4 | Saturday | DONCASTER | *Market Rasen | *CHEPSTOW |
| | | HAYDOCK PARK | Stratford-on-Avon | EPSOM DOWNS |
| | | | | |
| 6 | Monday | PONTEFRACT | NOTTINGHAM | |
| 7 | Tuesday | PONTEFRACT | | SALISBURY |
| 8 | Wednesday | BEVERLEY | YARMOUTH | *KEMPTON PARK |
| | | *HAMILTON PARK | | |
| 9 | Thursday | HAMILTON PARK | | NEWBURY |
| 10 | Friday | *EDINBURGH | SOUTHWELL (AWT) | *GOODWOOD |
| | | YORK | | SANDOWN PARK |
| 11 | Saturday | YORK | *LEICESTER | BATH |
| | | | *WOLVERHAMPTON (AWT) | *LINGFIELD PARK |
| | | | | SANDOWN PARK |
| | | | | |
| 13 | Monday | EDINBURGH | *NOTTINGHAM | BRIGHTON |
| | | | | *WINDSOR |
| 14 | Tuesday | THIRSK | | ROYAL ASCOT |
| 15 | Wednesday | RIPON | | ROYAL ASCOT |
| 16 | Thursday | RIPON | | ROYAL ASCOT |
| 17 | Friday | AYR | *NEWMARKET | ROYAL ASCOT |
| | | REDCAR | | *GOODWOOD |
| 18 | Saturday | AYR | *SOUTHWELL (AWT) | ASCOT |
| | | REDCAR | *WARWICK | *LINGFIELD PARK |
| | | | | |
| 20 | Monday | EDINBURGH | *WARWICK | *WINDSOR |
| | | PONTEFRACT | | |
| 21 | Tuesday | | | BRIGHTON |
| | | | YARMOUTH | *NEWBURY |
| 22 | Wednesday | CARLISLE | *CHESTER | *KEMPTON PARK |
| | | | | SALISBURY |
| 23 | Thursday | CARLISLE | WOLVERHAMPTON (AWT) | SALISBURY |
| 24 | Friday | DONCASTER | NEWMARKET | *BATH |
| | | *NEWCASTLE | | *GOODWOOD |
| | | | | LINGFIELD PARK |
| 25 | Saturday | *DONCASTER | NEWMARKET | CHEPSTOW |
| | | NEWCASTLE | *WOLVERHAMPTON (AWT) | *LINGFIELD PARK |
| | | | | |
| 27 | Monday | *HAMILTON PARK | NOTTINGHAM | *WINDSOR |
| | | | WOLVERHAMPTON (AWT) | |
| 28 | Tuesday | | | CHEPSTOW |
| | | | | FOLKESTONE |
| 29 | Wednesday | CATTERICK BRIDGE | WARWICK | *EPSOM DOWNS |
| | | | *YARMOUTH | |
| 30 | Thursday | CATTERICK BRIDGE | YARMOUTH | BRIGHTON |
| | | *HAYDOCK PARK | | |

## JULY

| | | NORTH | MIDLANDS | SOUTH |
|---|---|---|---|---|
| 1 | Friday | *BEVERLEY<br>HAYDOCK PARK | *NOTTINGHAM<br>WOLVERHAMPTON (AWT) | SANDOWN PARK |
| 2 | Saturday | BEVERLEY<br>HAYDOCK PARK | | BATH<br>SANDOWN PARK |
| 4 | Monday | EDINBURGH<br>*RIPON | LEICESTER | *WINDSOR |
| 5 | Tuesday | PONTEFRACT | NEWMARKET JULY | |
| 6 | Wednesday | *REDCAR | NEWMARKET JULY | BATH<br>*KEMPTON PARK |
| 7 | Thursday | REDCAR | NEWMARKET JULY | *CHEPSTOW |
| 8 | Friday | *AYR<br>YORK | *CHESTER<br>WARWICK | *LINGFIELD PARK |
| 9 | Saturday | *CARLISLE<br>YORK | CHESTER<br>*SOUTHWELL (AWT)<br>*WOLVERHAMPTON (AWT) | LINGFIELD PARK<br>SALISBURY |
| 11 | Monday | EDINBURGH | *LEICESTER<br>WOLVERHAMPTON (AWT) | *WINDSOR |
| 12 | Tuesday | EDINBURGH | | FOLKESTONE |
| 13 | Wednesday | CATTERICK BRIDGE | SOUTHWELL (AWT)<br>*YARMOUTH | *SANDOWN PARK |
| 14 | Thursday | CATTERICK BRIDGE<br>*HAMILTON PARK | | *CHEPSTOW<br>SANDOWN PARK |
| 15 | Friday | *HAMILTON PARK<br>THIRSK | *NEWMARKET<br>WOLVERHAMPTON (AWT) | NEWBURY |
| 16 | Saturday | *AYR<br>RIPON | NEWMARKET<br>*SOUTHWELL (AWT) | *LINGFIELD PARK<br>NEWBURY |
| 18 | Monday | AYR<br>*BEVERLEY | | BATH<br>*WINDSOR |
| 19 | Tuesday | BEVERLEY | | FOLKESTONE |
| 20 | Wednesday | DONCASTER<br>*REDCAR | YARMOUTH | *SANDOWN PARK |
| 21 | Thursday | *DONCASTER<br>HAMILTON PARK | YARMOUTH | BRIGHTON |
| 22 | Friday | CARLISLE<br>*PONTEFRACT | CHESTER | ASCOT |
| 23 | Saturday | AYR<br>NEWCASTLE | SOUTHWELL (AWT)<br>*WARWICK<br>*WOLVERHAMPTON (AWT) | ASCOT |
| 25 | Monday | NEWCASTLE | *NOTTINGHAM | LINGFIELD PARK<br>*WINDSOR |
| 26 | Tuesday | BEVERLEY | | GOODWOOD |
| 27 | Wednesday | CATTERICK BRIDGE | *LEICESTER | *EPSOM DOWNS<br>GOODWOOD |
| 28 | Thursday | *HAMILTON PARK | SOUTHWELL (AWT)<br>YARMOUTH | GOODWOOD<br>*SALISBURY |
| 29 | Friday | *EDINBURGH<br>THIRSK | Bangor-on-Dee<br>*NEWMARKET | GOODWOOD |
| 30 | Saturday | THIRSK | *Market Rasen<br>NEWMARKET | GOODWOOD<br>Newton Abbot<br>*WINDSOR |

| | | **AUGUST** | |
|---|---|---|---|
| | **NORTH** | **MIDLANDS** | **SOUTH** |
| 1 Monday | RIPON | | Newton Abbot |
| 2 Tuesday | REDCAR | | BRIGHTON |
| 3 Wednesday | PONTEFRACT | *NOTTINGHAM | BRIGHTON |
| | | | Exeter |
| | | | *KEMPTON PARK |
| 4 Thursday | PONTEFRACT | | BATH |
| | | | BRIGHTON |
| 5 Friday | *HAYDOCK PARK | *NEWMARKET | Plumpton |
| | REDCAR | SOUTHWELL (AWT) | |
| 6 Saturday | AYR | NEWMARKET | *LINGFIELD PARK |
| | HAYDOCK PARK | *WOLVERHAMPTON (AWT) | |
| | REDCAR | *Worcester | |
| 8 Monday | *THIRSK | *LEICESTER | WINDSOR |
| | | Worcester | |
| 9 Tuesday | | YARMOUTH | BATH |
| 10 Wednesday | BEVERLEY | | Fontwell Park |
| | | | SALISBURY |
| | | | *SANDOWN PARK |
| 11 Thursday | BEVERLEY | | Newton Abbot |
| | | | SALISBURY |
| 12 Friday | *CATTERICK BRIDGE | SOUTHWELL (AWT) | FOLKESTONE |
| | *HAYDOCK PARK | | NEWBURY |
| 13 Saturday | RIPON | Bangor-on-Dee | *LINGFIELD PARK |
| | | *NOTTINGHAM | NEWBURY |
| | | Stratford-on-Avon | |
| 15 Monday | HAMILTON PARK | | WINDSOR |
| 16 Tuesday | YORK | | FOLKESTONE |
| 17 Wednesday | CARLISLE | *Hereford | *KEMPTON PARK |
| | YORK | YARMOUTH | |
| 18 Thursday | AYR | *Uttoxeter | SALISBURY |
| | YORK | YARMOUTH | |
| 19 Friday | Perth | CHESTER | SANDOWN PARK |
| 20 Saturday | Perth | CHESTER | SANDOWN PARK |
| | RIPON | *Market Rasen | |
| | | *WOLVERHAMPTON (AWT) | |
| 22 Monday | Hexham | NOTTINGHAM | |
| 23 Tuesday | PONTEFRACT | | BRIGHTON |
| 24 Wednesday | REDCAR | | BRIGHTON |
| | | | Exeter |
| 25 Thursday | EDINBURGH | Worcester | LINGFIELD PARK |
| 26 Friday | THIRSK | NEWMARKET AUGUST | GOODWOOD |
| 27 Saturday | Cartmel | *Hereford | GOODWOOD |
| | NEWCASTLE | NEWMARKET AUGUST | *WINDSOR |
| 29 Monday (Bank Hol) | Cartmel | Huntingdon | CHEPSTOW |
| | NEWCASTLE | Southwell | EPSOM DOWNS |
| | RIPON | WARWICK | Newton Abbot |
| | | WOLVERHAMPTON (AWT) | Plumpton |
| 30 Tuesday | RIPON | | EPSOM DOWNS |
| 31 Wednesday | YORK | | Fontwell Park |
| | | | Newton Abbot |

## SEPTEMBER

| | | NORTH | MIDLANDS | SOUTH |
|---|---|---|---|---|
| 1 | Thursday | YORK | Southwell | SALISBURY |
| 2 | Friday | HAYDOCK PARK | | KEMPTON PARK |
| | | Sedgefield | | |
| 3 | Saturday | HAYDOCK PARK | Stratford-on-Avon | KEMPTON PARK |
| | | THIRSK | *WOLVERHAMPTON (AWT) | |
| 5 | Monday | HAMILTON PARK | SOUTHWELL(AWT) | |
| 6 | Tuesday | | LEICESTER | LINGFIELD PARK |
| 7 | Wednesday | DONCASTER | Uttoxeter | Exeter |
| 8 | Thursday | DONCASTER | | FOLKESTONE |
| | | | | Newton Abbot |
| 9 | Friday | DONCASTER | Worcester | GOODWOOD |
| 10 | Saturday | DONCASTER | Bangor-on-Dee | CHEPSTOW |
| | | | Worcester | GOODWOOD |
| 12 | Monday | | LEICESTER | BATH |
| | | | | Plumpton |
| 13 | Tuesday | Sedgefield | YARMOUTH | SANDOWN PARK |
| 14 | Wednesday | BEVERLEY | YARMOUTH | Exeter |
| | | | | SANDOWN PARK |
| 15 | Thursday | WESTERN M (AYR) | YARMOUTH | LINGFIELD PARK |
| | | BEVERLEY | | |
| 16 | Friday | WESTERN M (AYR) | Huntingdon | NEWBURY |
| 17 | Saturday | WESTERN M (AYR) | Market Rasen | NEWBURY |
| | | CATTERICK BRIDGE | *WOLVERHAMPTON (AWT) | |
| 19 | Monday | EDINBURGH | NOTTINGHAM | FOLKESTONE |
| | | PONTEFRACT | | |
| 20 | Tuesday | | NOTTINGHAM | KEMPTON PARK |
| 21 | Wednesday | Perth | CHESTER | BRIGHTON |
| 22 | Thursday | Perth | | ASCOT |
| | | | | Taunton |
| 23 | Friday | HAYDOCK PARK | | ASCOT |
| | | REDCAR | | |
| 24 | Saturday | Carlisle | Market Rasen | ASCOT |
| | | HAYDOCK PARK | Worcester | |
| | | REDCAR | | |
| 26 | Monday | HAMILTON PARK | SOUTHWELL (AWT) | BATH |
| | | | | Fontwell Park |
| 27 | Tuesday | NEWCASTLE | | BRIGHTON |
| | | | | Exeter |
| 28 | Wednesday | Sedgefield | NEWMARKET OCTOBER | FOLKESTONE |
| | | | | SALISBURY |
| 29 | Thursday | | Cheltenham | LINGFIELD PARK |
| | | | NEWMARKET OCTOBER | |
| 30 | Friday | Hexham | NEWMARKET OCTOBER | GOODWOOD |

| | | NORTH | OCTOBER<br>MIDLANDS | SOUTH |
|---|---|---|---|---|
| 1 | Saturday | Kelso | NEWMARKET OCTOBER<br>Uttoxeter<br>*WOLVERHAMPTON (AWT) | Chepstow<br>GOODWOOD |
| 3 | Monday | PONTEFRACT | WARWICK | |
| 4 | Tuesday | REDCAR | WARWICK | Newton Abbot |
| 5 | Wednesday | HAYDOCK PARK<br>YORK | Market Rasen<br>Towcester | |
| 6 | Thursday | HAYDOCK PARK<br>YORK | Ludlow | Wincanton |
| 7 | Friday | Carlisle | Cheltenham | ASCOT |
| 8 | Saturday | Ayr<br>YORK | Bangor-on-Dee<br>Worcester | ASCOT |
| 10 | Monday | Carlisle | LEICESTER | Fontwell Park |
| 11 | Tuesday | Sedgefield | LEICESTER | CHEPSTOW |
| 12 | Wednesday | Wetherby | Uttoxeter | Exeter |
| 13 | Thursday | Hexham<br>REDCAR | NEWMARKET HOUGHTON | Taunton |
| 14 | Friday | CATTERICK BRIDGE | Ludlow<br>NEWMARKET HOUGHTON | |
| 15 | Saturday | CATTERICK BRIDGE<br>Kelso | NEWMARKET HOUGHTON<br>Stratford-on-Avon<br>*WOLVERHAMPTON (AWT) | Kempton Park |
| 17 | Monday | | NOTTINGHAM<br>Hereford | FOLKESTONE |
| 18 | Tuesday | | | CHEPSTOW<br>Plumpton |
| 19 | Wednesday | Newcastle | YARMOUTH | Exeter |
| 20 | Thursday | PONTEFRACT | | NEWBURY<br>Wincanton |
| 21 | Friday | DONCASTER | Fakenham | Newbury |
| 22 | Saturday | DONCASTER | Huntingdon<br>Worcester | NEWBURY |
| 24 | Monday | | LEICESTER | LINGFIELD PARK |
| 25 | Tuesday | REDCAR | LEICESTER | Newton Abbot |
| 26 | Wednesday | | Cheltenham<br>YARMOUTH | Fontwell Park |
| 27 | Thursday | Sedgefield | NOTTINGHAM<br>Stratford-on-Avon | |
| 28 | Friday | Wetherby | Bangor-on-Dee<br>NEWMARKET | |
| 29 | Saturday | Wetherby | NEWMARKET<br>Warwick<br>*WOLVERHAMPTON (AWT) | Ascot |
| 31 | Monday | NEWCASTLE | | Plumpton |

| | | NOVEMBER | |
|---|---|---|---|
| | **NORTH** | **MIDLANDS** | **SOUTH** |
| 1 Tuesday | REDCAR | | Exeter |
| 2 Wednesday | Haydock Park | Uttoxeter | Kempton Park |
| | Kelso | | |
| 3 Thursday | EDINBURGH | Uttoxeter | LINGFIELD PARK (AWT) |
| | | | Wincanton |
| 4 Friday | DONCASTER | Market Rasen | |
| | Hexham | | |
| 5 Saturday | DONCASTER | | Chepstow |
| | Newcastle | | Sandown Park |
| 7 Monday | Carlisle | | FOLKESTONE |
| 8 Tuesday | Sedgefield | Southwell | Fontwell Park |
| 9 Wednesday | | Worcester | LINGFIELD PARK (AWT) |
| | | | Newbury |
| 10 Thursday | Kelso | Towcester | Taunton |
| 11 Friday | Ayr | Cheltenham | LINGFIELD PARK (AWT) |
| | | Huntingdon | |
| 12 Saturday | Ayr | Cheltenham | Windsor |
| | | Nottingham | |
| | | *WOLVERHAMPTON (AWT) | |
| 14 Monday | | Leicester | Plumpton |
| 15 Tuesday | Wetherby | Warwick | Newton Abbot |
| 16 Wednesday | Haydock Park | Hereford | Kempton Park |
| | | SOUTHWELL (AWT) | |
| 17 Thursday | Haydock Park | Ludlow | |
| 18 Friday | Sedgefield | Leicester | Ascot |
| 19 Saturday | Catterick Bridge | Market Rasen | Ascot |
| | Aintree | Towcester | |
| 21 Monday | Catterick Bridge | | Folkestone |
| 22 Tuesday | | Huntingdon | |
| | | SOUTHWELL (AWT) | |
| | | Stratford-on-Avon | |
| 23 Wednsday | Hexham | Cheltenham | Windsor |
| 24 Thursday | Carlisle | Nottingham | Taunton |
| 25 Friday | | Bangor-on-Dee | Newbury |
| | | Southwell | |
| 26 Saturday | Newcastle | Warwick | LINGFIELD PARK (AWT) |
| | | *WOLVERHAMPTON (AWT) | Newbury |
| 28 Monday | Kelso | Worcester | LINGFIELD PARK (AWT) |
| 29 Tuesday | Newcastle | Leicester | Fontwell Park |
| 30 Wednesday | Catterick Bridge | Huntingdon | |
| | | SOUTHWELL (AWT) | |

| | | **DECEMBER** | | |
|---|---|---|---|---|
| | **NORTH** | **MIDLANDS** | **SOUTH** | |
| 1 | Thursday | | Uttoxeter | LINGFIELD PARK (AWT) |
| | | | | Windsor |
| 2 | Friday | | Hereford | Exeter |
| | | | | Sandown Park |
| 3 | Saturday | Wetherby | Towcester | Chepstow |
| | | | | Sandown Park |
| 5 | Monday | Edinburgh | Ludlow | |
| 6 | Tuesday | Sedgefield | | Plumpton |
| 7 | Wednesday | Haydock Park | Worcester | LINGFIELD PARK (AWT) |
| 8 | Thursday | Haydock Park | Fakenham | Taunton |
| 9 | Friday | Doncaster | Cheltenham | |
| | | Hexham | | |
| 10 | Saturday | Doncaster | Cheltenham | Lingfield Park |
| | | | *WOLVERHAMPTON (AWT) | |
| 12 | Monday | | Warwick | Newton Abbot |
| 13 | Tuesday | | Southwell | Folkestone |
| 14 | Wednesday | | Bangor-on-Dee | Exeter |
| | | | | LINGFIELD PARK (AWT) |
| 15 | Thursday | Kelso | SOUTHWELL (AWT) | |
| | | | Towcester | |
| 16 | Friday | Catterick Bridge | Market Rasen | |
| | | | Uttoxeter | |
| 17 | Saturday | Catterick Bridge | Nottingham | Ascot |
| | | | Uttoxeter | LINGFIELD PARK (AWT) |
| 19 | Monday | Edinburgh | | Lingfield Park |
| 20 | Tuesday | | Hereford | LINGFIELD PARK (AWT) |
| 21 | Wednesday | Hexham | Ludlow | |
| | | | Southwell | |
| 26 | Monday (Bank Hol) | Ayr | Hereford | Kempton Park |
| | | Sedgefield | Huntingdon | Newton Abbot |
| | | Wetherby | Market Rasen | Wincanton |
| | | | Wolverhampton | |
| 27 | Tuesday (Bank Hol) | Wetherby | SOUTHWELL (AWT) | Chepstow |
| | | | Wolverhampton | Kempton Park |
| 28 | Wednesday | Newcastle | Stratford-on-Avon | Plumpton |
| 29 | Thursday | Carlisle | Warwick | Fontwell Park |
| | | | | Taunton |
| 30 | Friday | | Leicester | Folkestone |
| | | | | Newbury |
| 31 | Saturday | Catterick Bridge | Nottingham | LINGFIELD PARK (AWT) |
| | | | *WOLVERHAMPTON (AWT) | Newbury |

# Racing Year
# Planner 1994

| | JANUARY | FEBRUARY | MARCH | APRIL | MAY | JUNE |
|-----|---------|----------|-------|-------|-----|------|
| Mon | | | | | | |
| Tue | | 1 | 1 | | | |
| Wed | | 2 | 2 | | | 1 |
| Thu | | 3 | 3 | | | 2 |
| Fri | | 4 | 4 | 1 | | 3 |
| Sat | 1 | 5 | 5 | 2 | | 4 |
| Sun | 2 | 6 | 6 | 3 | 1 | 5 |
| Mon | 3 | 7 | 7 | 4 | 2 | 6 |
| Tue | 4 | 8 | 8 | 5 | 3 | 7 |
| Wed | 5 | 9 | 9 | 6 | 4 | 8 |
| Thu | 6 | 10 | 10 | 7 | 5 | 9 |
| Fri | 7 | 11 | 11 | 8 | 6 | 10 |
| Sat | 8 | 12 | 12 | 9 | 7 | 11 |
| Sun | 9 | 13 | 13 | 10 | 8 | 12 |
| Mon | 10 | 14 | 14 | 11 | 9 | 13 |
| Tue | 11 | 15 | 15 | 12 | 10 | 14 |
| Wed | 12 | 16 | 16 | 13 | 11 | 15 |
| Thu | 13 | 17 | 17 | 14 | 12 | 16 |
| Fri | 14 | 18 | 18 | 15 | 13 | 17 |
| Sat | 15 | 19 | 19 | 16 | 14 | 18 |
| Sun | 16 | 20 | 20 | 17 | 15 | 19 |
| Mon | 17 | 21 | 21 | 18 | 16 | 20 |
| Tue | 18 | 22 | 22 | 19 | 17 | 21 |
| Wed | 19 | 23 | 23 | 20 | 18 | 22 |
| Thu | 20 | 24 | 24 | 21 | 19 | 23 |
| Fri | 21 | 25 | 25 | 22 | 20 | 24 |
| Sat | 22 | 26 | 26 | 23 | 21 | 25 |
| Sun | 23 | 27 | 27 | 24 | 22 | 26 |
| Mon | 24 | 28 | 28 | 25 | 23 | 27 |
| Tue | 25 | | 29 | 26 | 24 | 28 |
| Wed | 26 | | 30 | 27 | 25 | 29 |
| Thu | 27 | | 31 | 28 | 26 | 30 |
| Fri | 28 | | | 29 | 27 | |
| Sat | 29 | | | 30 | 28 | |
| Sun | 30 | | | | 29 | |
| Mon | 31 | | | | 30 | |
| Tue | | | | | 31 | |

242

| | JULY | AUGUST | SEPTEMBER | OCTOBER | NOVEMBER | DECEMBER |
|-----|------|--------|-----------|---------|----------|----------|
| Mon | | 1 | | | | |
| Tue | | 2 | | | 1 | |
| Wed | | 3 | | | 2 | |
| Thu | | 4 | 1 | | 3 | 1 |
| Fri | 1 | 5 | 2 | | 4 | 2 |
| Sat | 2 | 6 | 3 | 1 | 5 | 3 |
| Sun | 3 | 7 | 4 | 2 | 6 | 4 |
| Mon | 4 | 8 | 5 | 3 | 7 | 5 |
| Tue | 5 | 9 | 6 | 4 | 8 | 6 |
| Wed | 6 | 10 | 7 | 5 | 9 | 7 |
| Thu | 7 | 11 | 8 | 6 | 10 | 8 |
| Fri | 8 | 12 | 9 | 7 | 11 | 9 |
| Sat | 9 | 13 | 10 | 8 | 12 | 10 |
| Sun | 10 | 14 | 11 | 9 | 13 | 11 |
| Mon | 11 | 15 | 12 | 10 | 14 | 12 |
| Tue | 12 | 16 | 13 | 11 | 15 | 13 |
| Wed | 13 | 17 | 14 | 12 | 16 | 14 |
| Thu | 14 | 18 | 15 | 13 | 17 | 15 |
| Fri | 15 | 19 | 16 | 14 | 18 | 16 |
| Sat | 16 | 20 | 17 | 15 | 19 | 17 |
| Sun | 17 | 21 | 18 | 16 | 20 | 18 |
| Mon | 18 | 22 | 19 | 17 | 21 | 19 |
| Tue | 19 | 23 | 20 | 18 | 22 | 20 |
| Wed | 20 | 24 | 21 | 19 | 23 | 21 |
| Thu | 21 | 25 | 22 | 20 | 24 | 22 |
| Fri | 22 | 26 | 23 | 21 | 25 | 23 |
| Sat | 23 | 27 | 24 | 22 | 26 | 24 |
| Sun | 24 | 28 | 25 | 23 | 27 | 25 |
| Mon | 25 | 29 | 26 | 24 | 28 | 26 |
| Tue | 26 | 30 | 27 | 25 | 29 | 27 |
| Wed | 27 | 31 | 28 | 26 | 30 | 28 |
| Thu | 28 | | 29 | 27 | | 29 |
| Fri | 29 | | 30 | 28 | | 30 |
| Sat | 30 | | | 29 | | 31 |
| Sun | 31 | | | 30 | | |
| Mon | | | | 31 | | |
| Tue | | | | | | |

# Racing Year
# Planner 1995

| | JANUARY | FEBRUARY | MARCH | APRIL | MAY | JUNE |
|-----|---------|----------|-------|-------|-----|------|
| Mon | | | | | 1 | |
| Tue | | | | | 2 | |
| Wed | | 1 | 1 | | 3 | |
| Thu | | 2 | 2 | | 4 | 1 |
| Fri | | 3 | 3 | | 5 | 2 |
| Sat | | 4 | 4 | 1 | 6 | 3 |
| Sun | 1 | 5 | 5 | 2 | 7 | 4 |
| Mon | 2 | 6 | 6 | 3 | 8 | 5 |
| Tue | 3 | 7 | 7 | 4 | 9 | 6 |
| Wed | 4 | 8 | 8 | 5 | 10 | 7 |
| Thu | 5 | 9 | 9 | 6 | 11 | 8 |
| Fri | 6 | 10 | 10 | 7 | 12 | 9 |
| Sat | 7 | 11 | 11 | 8 | 13 | 10 |
| Sun | 8 | 12 | 12 | 9 | 14 | 11 |
| Mon | 9 | 13 | 13 | 10 | 15 | 12 |
| Tue | 10 | 14 | 14 | 11 | 16 | 13 |
| Wed | 11 | 15 | 15 | 12 | 17 | 14 |
| Thu | 12 | 16 | 16 | 13 | 18 | 15 |
| Fri | 13 | 17 | 17 | 14 | 19 | 16 |
| Sat | 14 | 18 | 18 | 15 | 20 | 17 |
| Sun | 15 | 19 | 19 | 16 | 21 | 18 |
| Mon | 16 | 20 | 20 | 17 | 22 | 19 |
| Tue | 17 | 21 | 21 | 18 | 23 | 20 |
| Wed | 18 | 22 | 22 | 19 | 24 | 21 |
| Thu | 19 | 23 | 23 | 20 | 25 | 22 |
| Fri | 20 | 24 | 24 | 21 | 26 | 23 |
| Sat | 21 | 25 | 25 | 22 | 27 | 24 |
| Sun | 22 | 26 | 26 | 23 | 28 | 25 |
| Mon | 23 | 27 | 27 | 24 | 29 | 26 |
| Tue | 24 | 28 | 28 | 25 | 30 | 27 |
| Wed | 25 | | 29 | 26 | 31 | 28 |
| Thu | 26 | | 30 | 27 | | 29 |
| Fri | 27 | | 31 | 28 | | 30 |
| Sat | 28 | | | 29 | | |
| Sun | 29 | | | 30 | | |
| Mon | 30 | | | | | |
| Tue | 31 | | | | | |

| | JULY | AUGUST | SEPTEMBER | OCTOBER | NOVEMBER | DECEMBER |
|---|---|---|---|---|---|---|
| Mon | | | | | | |
| Tue | | 1 | | | | |
| Wed | | 2 | | | 1 | |
| Thu | | 3 | | | 2 | |
| Fri | | 4 | 1 | | 3 | 1 |
| Sat | 1 | 5 | 2 | | 4 | 2 |
| Sun | 2 | 6 | 3 | 1 | 5 | 3 |
| Mon | 3 | 7 | 4 | 2 | 6 | 4 |
| Tue | 4 | 8 | 5 | 3 | 7 | 5 |
| Wed | 5 | 9 | 6 | 4 | 8 | 6 |
| Thu | 6 | 10 | 7 | 5 | 9 | 7 |
| Fri | 7 | 11 | 8 | 6 | 10 | 8 |
| Sat | 8 | 12 | 9 | 7 | 11 | 9 |
| Sun | 9 | 13 | 10 | 8 | 12 | 10 |
| Mon | 10 | 14 | 11 | 9 | 13 | 11 |
| Tue | 11 | 15 | 12 | 10 | 14 | 12 |
| Wed | 12 | 16 | 13 | 11 | 15 | 13 |
| Thu | 13 | 17 | 14 | 12 | 16 | 14 |
| Fri | 14 | 18 | 15 | 13 | 17 | 15 |
| Sat | 15 | 19 | 16 | 14 | 18 | 16 |
| Sun | 16 | 20 | 17 | 15 | 19 | 17 |
| Mon | 17 | 21 | 18 | 16 | 20 | 18 |
| Tue | 18 | 22 | 19 | 17 | 21 | 19 |
| Wed | 19 | 23 | 20 | 18 | 22 | 20 |
| Thu | 20 | 24 | 21 | 19 | 23 | 21 |
| Fri | 21 | 25 | 22 | 20 | 24 | 22 |
| Sat | 22 | 26 | 23 | 21 | 25 | 23 |
| Sun | 23 | 27 | 24 | 22 | 26 | 24 |
| Mon | 24 | 28 | 25 | 23 | 27 | 25 |
| Tue | 25 | 29 | 26 | 24 | 28 | 26 |
| Wed | 26 | 30 | 27 | 25 | 29 | 27 |
| Thu | 27 | 31 | 28 | 26 | 30 | 28 |
| Fri | 28 | | 29 | 27 | | 29 |
| Sat | 29 | | 30 | 28 | | 30 |
| Sun | 30 | | | 29 | | 31 |
| Mon | 31 | | | 30 | | |
| Tue | | | | 31 | | |

## COURSE

Date

## FIRST RACE

| Winner | Second | Third | Fourth |
|---|---|---|---|
| SP | | | |

## SECOND RACE

| Winner | Second | Third | Fourth |
|---|---|---|---|
| SP | | | |

## THIRD RACE

| Winner | Second | Third | Fourth |
|---|---|---|---|
| SP | | | |

## FOURTH RACE

| Winner | Second | Third | Fourth |
|---|---|---|---|
| SP | | | |

## FIFTH RACE

| Winner | Second | Third | Fourth |
|---|---|---|---|
| SP | | | |

## SIXTH RACE

| Winner | Second | Third | Fourth |
|---|---|---|---|
| SP | | | |

## SEVENTH RACE

| Winner | Second | Third | Fourth |
|---|---|---|---|
| SP | | | |

## EIGHTH RACE

| Winner | Second | Third | Fourth |
|---|---|---|---|
| SP | | | |

| COURSE | | | |
|---|---|---|---|
| | | | |
| Date | | | |

| FIRST RACE | | | |
|---|---|---|---|
| Winner | Second | Third | Fourth |
| SP | | | |

| SECOND RACE | | | |
|---|---|---|---|
| Winner | Second | Third | Fourth |
| SP | | | |

| THIRD RACE | | | |
|---|---|---|---|
| Winner | Second | Third | Fourth |
| SP | | | |

| FOURTH RACE | | | |
|---|---|---|---|
| Winner | Second | Third | Fourth |
| SP | | | |

| FIFTH RACE | | | |
|---|---|---|---|
| Winner | Second | Third | Fourth |
| SP | | | |

| SIXTH RACE | | | |
|---|---|---|---|
| Winner | Second | Third | Fourth |
| SP | | | |

| SEVENTH RACE | | | |
|---|---|---|---|
| Winner | Second | Third | Fourth |
| SP | | | |

| EIGHTH RACE | | | |
|---|---|---|---|
| Winner | Second | Third | Fourth |
| SP | | | |

## COURSE

| | |
|---|---|
| Date | |

## FIRST RACE

| Winner | Second | Third | Fourth |
|---|---|---|---|
| SP | | | |

## SECOND RACE

| Winner | Second | Third | Fourth |
|---|---|---|---|
| SP | | | |

## THIRD RACE

| Winner | Second | Third | Fourth |
|---|---|---|---|
| SP | | | |

## FOURTH RACE

| Winner | Second | Third | Fourth |
|---|---|---|---|
| SP | | | |

## FIFTH RACE

| Winner | Second | Third | Fourth |
|---|---|---|---|
| SP | | | |

## SIXTH RACE

| Winner | Second | Third | Fourth |
|---|---|---|---|
| SP | | | |

## SEVENTH RACE

| Winner | Second | Third | Fourth |
|---|---|---|---|
| SP | | | |

## EIGHTH RACE

| Winner | Second | Third | Fourth |
|---|---|---|---|
| SP | | | |